Unveiling Eve

Reading Gender in Medieval Hebrew Literature

Tova Rosen

PENN

UNIVERSITY OF PENNSYLVANIA PRESS

Philadelphia

10 9 8 7 6 5 4 3 2 1

Published by
University of Pennsylvania Press
Philadelphia, Pennsylvania 19104-4011

Library of Congress Cataloging-in-Publication Data
Rosen, Tova.
   Unveiling Eve : reading gender in medieval Hebrew literature / Tova Rosen.
     p. cm. — (Jewish culture and contexts)
   Includes bibliographical references and index.
   ISBN 0-8122-3710-2 (cloth : alk. paper)
   1. Hebrew literature, Medieval—History and criticism.   2. Women in literature.
I. Title.   II. Series.

PJ5016.R67 2003
892.4'09352042—dc21

                                        2002042988

To my beloved sons, Oran and Yonatan

Contents

Preface

MY IMPULSE TO SEARCH PARABLES of gender in texts from the past was derived, first and foremost, from the need to fill a critical lacuna in the scholarship of medieval Hebrew literature, a field that has so far ignored gender as a critical key for literary inquiry. This urge was fostered by several critical habitats, to all of which I am indebted and to some of which I hope to reciprocally contribute. To feminist medievalists studying other medieval literatures (who might perhaps wonder at the book's belated publication considering the plethora of studies in their respective fields), I offer here completely new materials, most of which have been hitherto closed to non-Hebrew readers. In the context of Jewish studies, my appropriation of feminism to medieval Hebrew texts joins the growing body of gender-and feminist-oriented scholarship in various fields (Bible studies, Talmud and Jewish law, Kabbala, history of Jewish sexuality, history of women and gender relations in Jewish societies, and related fields).[1] The impetus to reformulate Jewish studies in accordance with feminist scholarship verges on the quest of Jewish feminists, thinkers, and activists (especially in the United States, and to a lesser extent in Israel) for new and meaningful paradigms of reintegrating women into living Judaism. My hope is that my work will be of interest to their ongoing discussions.[2] For my feminist colleagues working in modern Hebrew/Israeli literature, my excursions into the past may offer a more distant historical vantage point from which a broader panorama of Hebrew literature and its gender trouble could be viewed.[3]

The urge for writing this book, however, was not solely or purely critical. It was equally fostered by the current Israeli context, which has enveloped my growth as a woman, as a critic, and as a feminist—a context in which women's situation (as well as other no less acute political issues) is intricately caught between binding commitments to the Jewish past and the will to change the present and the future. While I cannot delve here into a detailed exposé of gender relations in Israeli society, law, and politics today,[4] I would like nevertheless to illustrate how Israeli feminists, in their struggle for actual change, are bound to refer back to metaphors from the Jewish past which still govern the symbolic representation of women. The following two examples demonstrate the positioning of women as outsiders vis-à-vis—and within—Jewish textuality. Both revolve around the metaphor of the women's back gallery in the synagogue and stress the continuities between old and modern forms of women's exclusion.[5]

In a series of essays (1984–89) reflecting on the position of the modern Hebrew woman writer, Amalia Kahana-Carmon, a leading Israeli novelist, compared the realm of Hebrew literature, past and present, to the Jewish synagogue. By that she meant not only that modern secular Hebrew literature has assumed the spiritual and communal functions of the traditional synagogue but also that, much like the space of the synagogue, Hebrew literature has been divided by a gender partition. Even after the advent, a century ago, of women writers into the male sanctuary of Hebrew letters, women continued to be relegated to literature's back gallery. As in the orthodox synagogue (still the mainstream form of worship in modern Israel), a woman cannot take on the task of *sheli'ah tzibbur*, the leader of prayer and the representative of the congregation. She may pray privately from the margin; "She Writes Rather Pleasingly, but on Things Marginal" reads one of Kahana-Carmon's titles in this series. While women were accepted as lyrical "poetesses," expressing private "gentle" feelings, it was quite impossible for them to act as central figures, the mouthpieces of public and political concerns. The entry of women writers (especially novelists) to the center of the literary scene has been blocked "since men writers and their audience conceive of Hebrew prose fiction, even if it is entirely secular, as the national synagogue of the spirit."[6] That the decade that followed this indictment saw an unprecedented flourishing—and acceptance—of women's writing, with women topping each annual best-seller list since 1997, is by no means a proof to Kahana-Carmon's weakness of argument, but the contrary. During the mid-1980s, while her discontent was voiced and heard, a younger generation of women writers, already exposed to the nascent Israeli feminist movement, began to sharpen its pens.

The recent fate of Maurycy Gottlieb's oil painting of the Yom Kippur prayer (1878) provides an equally acute metaphor to the actual problematic state of women's representation. Gottlieb's depiction of the synagogue scene was realistic—men inhabit the front and center (with the young artist standing next to an elderly man embracing the Torah scrolls); the women (including the artist's mother and his fiancée) watch the ceremony from the back gallery, distanced from the Holy Text. In

1978 the Diaspora Museum in Tel Aviv ordered a replica of Gottlieb's painting, from which the women figures would be virtually erased, leaving the back gallery completely void. Myriad visitors failed to notice the difference between the copy and the famous original (which, by the way, is permanently exhibited in the Tel Aviv Museum of Art, just a couple of miles away). It was only in 1992–93, following a wave of public uproar from Israeli and Jewish-American feminists that the fiasco was exposed. According to an explanation disclosed to the press quite inadvertently, one of the museum's curators admitted that the women were made to disappear "in order to lay emphasis on the male figures at the front, and in order to focus on the men's devotion [*kavana*]." And as if to add insult to injury, another (woman) curator added: "Our Gottlieb is not an [ordinary] reproduction. . . . Our leading concept was to re-tell the story of Jewish creativity. . . . Aren't the main actors of the Yom Kippur worship men? This is a fact. . . . It is men who represent the archetypal Jew. . . . The women in this picture do not serve the concept."[7] Fearing the reaction of donors, the museum eventually decided to exile the copy to a side room, where it has been stored and shrouded to this day.

These two examples of marginalization and erasure capture the ways in which traditional patterns still reverberate in Israeli culture. They also demonstrate how Israeli feminists make use of the past in their will to change the present.

"We cannot change the actual past," writes Daniel Boyarin. "We can only change the present and the future, in part by changing our understanding of the past."[8] In appropriating the medieval texts to feminist criticism, I am aware of my use of a two-edged sword pointing simultaneously to the past and the present. This stance raises a host of questions. Does a feminist reader have the right to approach an old text with new questions? Can one critique a past culture for reflecting and disseminating social views deemed oppressive to the modern eye? How can a woman/ feminist reader partake in a heritage that had excluded her kind? Should such a textual tradition be discarded altogether, or can it be transformed into leverage for change? Can the past be usable for present concerns, and how?

Questions of this sort inevitably haunt writers who revisit the past. Medievalist Paul Zumthor states: "The ultimate term we aim for is really to bring the ancient text into the present, that is to integrate it into that historicity which is ours. The pitfall is that in doing so we may deny or obscure its own historicity; we may foreshorten the historical perspective and, by giving an achronic shape to the past, hide the specific traits of the present."[9] Understanding the past "other" and anchoring him/her in its historicity is also Boyarin's advice to readers of the talmudic texts that he explores. Partaking in a cultural heritage which is "ours and not ours" involves an intricate perspective. And if this culture does not offer positive figures for women's empowerment, then, says Boyarin, the reader has to search for loci of difference and dissent within the ancient male texts (rather than viewing them as monoliths) and to ally with past voices that undermined hegemony. His proposition for an "anthropological ethics" requires one "to avoid assuming a position of cultural superiority from which to judge or blame the [past] 'Other.' "[10] Yet a critique of this ancient culture is unavoidable where it is still influential in producing gender practices unacceptable to us.

In the case of medieval Hebrew literature, where the reader cannot avoid rejection of and resistance to misogynistic texts, studying it "as if business were usual became an embarrassment."[11] Such attitudes of opposition and resistance can become, paradoxically, ways of participating in and belonging to the past heritage. Moreover, as Elaine Tuttle Hansen asserts, feminist criticism of the medieval canon can serve as a paradigm for the feminist critic in general. It can do so since it "offers a place in which to examine the risks and benefits of critiquing hegemonic discourses and masterworks from a position of exclusion, and to analyze the limits and powers of being constructed, as feminisms are constructed, in opposition to (rather than outside or beyond) the structures they seek to modify."[12]

Furthermore, through a feminist reading of medieval texts, the canon can be reclaimed not only for the feminist critic but also for modern readers in general. An old text can thus be salvaged from its oblivious past and made meaningful to new readers who confront it with new questions. "The tradition of art," states Hans Robert Jauss, "presupposes a dialogue between the present and the past, according to which a past work cannot answer and speak to us until a present observer has posed the question which returns it from its retirement."[13] During my not-so-short classroom experience I have witnessed how gender issues have animated the discussion and rendered medieval texts accessible and relevant to otherwise disinterested students. Significant disputes over religious, ideological, and practical issues of gender in modern Judaism attain more depth and validity when posed against the historical perspective of the Jewish textual heritage. In deliberately appropriating a historical work to present-day critical discourse, an old text can be made "a field on which currently interesting battles can be waged (and where a number of live mines . . . can be expected to blow up)."[14]

The chapters of this book vary in scope. Some attend to a theme or a genre, others examine a single work. Though not initially meant to methodically cover any generic typology or historical evolution, my chapters do roughly follow a certain generic and historical order. The early chapters discuss Andalusian-Hebrew poetry (eleventh and twelfth centuries), while the latter treat the prose forms cultivated in Christian Spain, Italy, and Provence (thirteenth and fourteenth centuries).

Chapter 1 ("No-Woman's-Land") deals with exclusion of Jewish women from the Hebrew "republic of letters." It also maintains that the androcentric nature of medieval Hebrew literature was to be reproduced by modern scholarship. Hence, various critical feminist strategies are considered in this chapter, by which representations of women, their presence in or absence from medieval Hebrew literature, can be described and assessed. While viewing the gallery of feminine images appearing in the writings of medieval Hebrew authors, and while listing the literary genres in which these images feature, the chapter also furnishes a brief overview of medieval Hebrew poetry (especially in Spain).

In Chapter 2 ("Gazing at the Gazelle"), I attempt to deconstruct some of the androcentric assumptions which underlie the male love lyric and which are concealed under the guise of love and admiration for the lady. In these poems the lady speaks through her silence. Silencing her is controlling her dangerous attraction. On the other hand, it is her mutinous muteness, perceived as passive resistance, which provokes the lover/poet and engenders his amatory speech. In unmasking the mannerisms of the tireless poet-suitor; in exposing "love" as a linguistic affair, as a power game in which the lover endeavors to subjugate the lady-of-hearts, in calling the bluff of the "feminized" lover and the "masculinized" beloved, I propose to unearth the sexual politics embedded in the love lyric. Making use of Freud's and Lacan's analyses of romantic love, as well as of postmodern theories of the gaze, I offer to deconstruct the gendered aspects of "love" hidden in the literary conventions of the poets. And, in reading the love poems against the grain, I suggest that the mute lady, when rebuffing the poet's florid wooing, is herself a resistant reader of male texts. The defiant lady inscribes the space for the discourse of the future feminist reader. Additionally, I reflect on the woman reader's response to the aesthetics of these poems. Is she not tempted by their beauty and erotic appeal? Or, if she resists their politics—will she still be able to enjoy their elegance?

Chapter 3 ("Veils and Wiles: Poetry as Woman") investigates the gendered ars poetica that underlies the poets' art. The best of poetry, like the best of women, is said to be beautiful and deceitful. Poetic speech and female speech both abuse language and veil the truth. Poetry and rhetoric, both empty and superficial, are thus considered, like women, the opposite of truth and the foes of the male philosopher. Such antipoetry utterances, I argue, have to be seen against the historical influence of Maimonides' misogynist ideas. Maimonides' ideas on poetry and on women, which are intrinsically and mutually related, advanced greatly the aversion toward poetry, even among the poets themselves, from the thirteenth century onward. Misogyny and misopoiesis are shown to be twin fruits of the same branch.

While the equation of Poetry as Woman was essentially effected by Aristotelian-Maimonidean misogynist ideas, the association of Soul and Woman, investigated in Chapter 4 ("Poor Soul, Pure Soul"), is basically Neoplatonic. Here I examine the ideological assumptions of the allegory of the human Soul when she is figured as Woman. Her shifting ontological positioning (vis-à-vis God, the human self, the Intellect, and the body) is allegorically cast in a variety of human relationships. The ambiguous symbolism of the female soul—being inferior and subjugated on the one hand, and being an agent of free choice and liberation (salvation) on the other—becomes a critical locus where the feminist reader can enter and rework the traditional binarisms.

Chapter 5 ("Domesticating the Enemy") is dedicated to the analysis of a single work. This is "The Offering of Judah the Misogynist," a narrative which provoked a continued literary debate between Jewish women-haters and women-lovers in Christian Spain and Provence throughout the thirteenth century. Its story line follows the adventures of an avowed bachelor and professional antifeminist, who, in his fierce objection to marriage, practically spells out all the notorious and much-recycled misogamous and misogynist stuff. The misogynist accusation of woman's big mouth is thematized in the garrulous spouse who opens her bottomless mouth in endless complaint and reproach. The story's ideological ambivalence toward marriage, together with its narrative strategies of ambiguity and dramatic irony, render marriage as an unsolved existential predicament for men. I offer to read this bizarre Jewish misogamous work (and the literary debate that it incited) as concurrent with conflicting views about marriage among Jewish intellectuals, and against the background of the struggle between the Catholics and the Cathars in the early thirteenth century.

Common to my treatment of all *maqāmāt* by al-Ḥarizi and Immanuel of Rome studied in Chapter 6 ("Among Men: Homotextuality in the *Maqāma*") is the attention to the texts' own reflection upon the gendered conditions of their production. Male speech is shown to be a rhetorical sport in which woman is positioned as object—topic, prize, wager. In one *maqāma*, fashioned extraordinarily as a rhetorical debate between "a man" and "a woman," a woman's voice, clear and assertive, objects to its silencing, claims its right of speech, and refutes one by one men's assumptions of her inferiority. But even when woman is made to speak, she still occupies an ambivalent locus—that of a capable advocate of womankind and that of an object, an abstraction endowed with the right of speech. A harbinger of the feminist resisting reader inscribed into the text, this woman counterbalances her male partner in theology and in sophistry. Hence, she becomes an implied critic of patriarchy in a text devised by a man to make other men laugh. Why would the author who argues for man's superiority lend a mouth to a female voice? Why would a male text dispute itself and subvert its own privilege?

The cultural signification of cross-dressing is the topic of Chapter 7 ("Clothes Reading"). In the four stories studied here, cross-dressing plays a vital axis in the dramatic plot. Transvestism is read as a laboratory where questions of gender boundaries, sexual binarism, and the constructedness of gender are explored. The assumption that the transvestic theme, signifying gender anxiety, might also be read as a sign of other—ethnic, cultural, literary—anxieties is investigated throughout the chapter. It is suggested that the historical signification of the theme may relate to the changing intercultural situation of Spanish-Hebrew authors in the thirteenth century and to the anxieties these changes exerted.

Moving from transvestism to transsexuality, Chapter 8 ("Circumcised Cinderella") deals with a unique prayer to God by a male who wishes to be transsexed. What is actually transformed in the text, however, is the grammatical gender of the speaker. While he is complaining about the hardships of being a male, his voice suddenly transforms into that of a fantasized woman. This changing and merging of voices yields a specular perspective in which man and woman see themselves and each other. It also enables a most peculiar and subversive critique of the cultural construction of Jewish gender—of femininity as well as of masculinity. Written concurrently with the "invention" of the woman's blessing ("Blessed art Thou . . . who hast made me according to His will"), this piece by Qalonymos might be considered the first historical comment on that blessing.

It is my hope that this book will make a contribution to the fields of Jewish studies and Hebrew literature and, at the same time, also to scholars of medieval European literatures. In my translations[15] throughout the book, from Hebrew poetry and prose, I aimed at making medieval Hebrew writings accessible and helpful to other medievalists. I intended in particular to acquaint feminist medievalists with gender trouble in yet another classical literature of that era.

No-Woman's-Land: Medieval Hebrew Literature and Feminist Criticism

Lonely Female Voices in the Silence

A SINGLE POEM ATTRIBUTED TO a woman has reached us from the wide literary corpus of medieval Hebrew literature.[1] This lonely female voice, from the latter part of the tenth century, is a wife's intimate recollection of her husband's departure from Spain. Evoking the sad scene of parting with the exchange of farewell gifts, she conceals a subtle complaint for being deserted with a child:

> Will her love remember his graceful doe,
>   her only son in her arms as he parted?
> On her left hand he placed a ring from his right,
>   on his wrist she placed her bracelet.
> As a keepsake she took his mantle from him,
>   and he in turn took hers from her.
> He won't settle in the Land of Spain,
>   though its prince give him half his kingdom.[2]

This poem of the wife (whose name remains unknown) was saved from oblivion only thanks to the reputation of her husband, Dunash ben Labrat, the initiator of what will later be known as the poetic school of the Jewish Golden Age in Muslim Spain.[3] The wife manifests a complete mastery of both the Arabic form and the biblical language—these two distinctive marks of the nascent poetic school which her husband pioneered. Nevertheless, this poem reveals lyrical qualities that are hardly to be found in the whole oeuvre of her more famous husband or in those of other poets of his generation.

What is even more astounding about Dunash's wife is her utter solitude in the vast terrain of Hebrew poetry. Not only is she the first identifiable woman poet in the Hebrew language since the biblical poetesses Miriam and Deborah, she is also the only one for centuries to come. For the next name, Merecina of Gerona (Catalonia), from whom we have another single poem and about whom too nothing is known, we will have to wait another four and a half centuries.[4]

The singleness of Dunash's wife as a medieval Jewish woman writer is manifest compared to the relatively significant number of medieval non-Jewish women writers. In medieval Europe, "however much outnumbered by men and however much excluded from the literary canon, women did write perceptions of reality."[5] Especially nuns and women of aristocracy were readers of literature and occasionally acted also as patrons. The writings of the fourteen women troubadours of Provence, Marie de France, Héloïse, Hildegard of Bingen, and Christine de Pisan are just a few famous examples from Christian Europe. Other, less famous names have been rediscovered, reread, and reintegrated into the Western canon, thus somewhat correcting the historical imbalance.

Even more pertinent to our context are the Arabic women poets. Muslim sources have preserved the names, and sometimes also the texts, of several women poets from the East and about forty women poets from al-Andalus. Slave girls (mostly of Christian origin) were known to be musicians and singers—and to also invent their own lyrics—in the vibrant Andalusian courts. Others were princesses or courtesans. Known by name are, among others, the Cordoban princess Wallāda, Ḥafṣa of Granada, Ḥamda bint Ziyād, and the Granadan courtesan Nazhūn.[6] All of them were well-versed in the learned classical poetry of their time, and their own poetry was evaluated by Arabic contemporary critics by the same standards as male poetry. Their poetry, far from being prudish, is dedicated mostly but not solely to themes of love and flirtation and "show[s] surprising freedom in the expression and fulfillment of their feelings of love."[7]

Among the names of Andalusian poetesses listed by Arabic literary historians we find also a Jewish poetess by the name of Qasmūna. It was her father, Ismāʿīl the Jew, himself a poet, who taught her the art of poetry. It is told that the father would challenge Qasmūna with some Arabic verses, and she would respond then by completing them into a whole composition. It had been suggested that the father, Ismāʿīl ibn Baghdāla (as is the manuscripts' version), was none other than Samuel

Ibn Naghrela, better known as Samuel ha-Nagid, the eleventh-century major Hebrew poet and scholar, the vizier of Granada and apparently also the chief of its army.[8] It is known that this dedicated father also instructed his sons in the writing of Hebrew poetry. If indeed Qasmūna was the daughter of this famous father, it is doubly intriguing why Jewish sources keep silent about her existence. Was it because she composed in Arabic, not Hebrew, or because she was a woman?

The scarcity of medieval Jewish women writers is thus striking. The three single extant names over a span of five centuries (and not many more in the vast expanse of time between the Bible and the revival of modern Hebrew poetry)[9] only highlight the fact that Jewish women were excluded from the literary marketplace. The prospects of recovering more women-authored literary materials in this no-woman's-land of Hebrew literature are scant. This makes the feminist project termed by Elaine Showalter as "gynocritics" impracticable.[10] The path left for the Hebrew medievalist feminist is thus approaching the issues of women and gender via male-authored texts.

Seeking the Absent Historical Woman

Despite the irrevocable silence induced by their illiteracy,[11] we know that medieval Jewish "women were real in ways absent from the texts. . . . We know that [they] lived . . . endured, triumphed, suffered, and died in the silence we now hear when we listen for them. . . . The historical self of women is a compelling and yet elusive subject of study."[12]

Considerable progress has been made in recent years by historians, feminist and nonfeminist, working in the field of medieval Jewish studies, to reconstruct women's lives from what men wrote about them. Avraham Grossman's recent book *Pious and Rebellious* is a comprehensive study of the history of Jewish women in Europe (Ashkenaz as well as Spain) in the Middle Ages, based on halakhic sources, responsa, commentaries on the Bible and the Talmud, and on moralistic compositions. Juxtaposing these male-authored sources, claims Grossman, "may provide a picture, though partial, of the status of women. . . . It is harder to restore the voices of the silent women."[13]

Shelomo Dov Goitein's pioneering and monumental work on the documents of the Cairo Geniza is remarkable in its restoration, to minuscule details, of the lives of medieval Mediterranean Jews, men as well as women.[14] Goitein's work on the presence of women in the Geniza is outstanding in its methodology. Rather than residing on the ideological views of rabbis, philosophers and poets—who, by and large, forged abstract ideals about, and rules for, women—he listens to the utterances of the simple men who inadvertently voiced their mentalities in these documents. Aware of the androcentricity of his material, he enters the gap between the prescribed ideals for women, on the one hand, and the actual life stories of individual women (as inferred from male-authored "trivial" documents), on the other hand, to penetrate "a world within a world," "The World of Women" (as his chapter on women is titled). Even then Goitein is still aware of the scholar's difficulty in accessing women's subjectivities. The only indication, tangential as it is, to women's creative imagination and verbal artistry is, in Goitein's view, the names they gave to their daughters, some of which express women's strife and aspirations.

In the Geniza documents Jewish women are shown to be much freer than one might have thought. While they are normatively said to be confined to the house, many of them were involved in small-scale industry and commerce, selling and buying products and houses, bargaining, appearing in courts (even in gentile courts), traveling, going on pilgrimages, teaching children, contributing to synagogues, and even having illicit love affairs.

An even more penetrating glance into Jewish women's lives is availed by a corpus of nearly two hundred letters found in the Geniza written by women between the tenth and thirteenth centuries, a period parallel to the literary works discussed in this book. The letters, sent by women from and to Egypt and other Mediterranean (including Spanish and Italian) communities, were collected and commented upon by Joel Kraemer who pursued Goitein's project.[15] The women's letters, though probably mostly written by professional scribes or dictated by women to husbands, brothers, or sons, succeed in retaining the Arabic vernacular and are thus more direct, authentic, and emotional than the male documents. They are addressed by women to their parents, husbands, and grown-up children, or to rabbinical (and at times also gentile) courts. They include complaints about deserting husbands, accusations of beating and abuse, grudges about the unkindness of mothers-in-law and the cruelty of the husband's family, complaints about heavy house chores, expressions of love for spouses, longing to distant siblings and children, laments of young, especially orphaned women married to old and sick husbands, invitations for holiday stays, shopping lists sent by women to traveling husbands, and even a protest of a mother whose son sent her as a gift a ridiculous dress which made her the town's laughingstock.

This vibrant existence of women, this materiality and facticity of women's lives, which emerges from the nonliterary documents is to a large extent missing from the fictional literature. Paradoxically, the "dry" documents mirror women's lives in ways richer, more diverse, and unexpected than the more imaginative belletristic literature, which tended on the whole to be stylized and stereotyped.

Poets, Courtiers, Rabbis: Historical Background to Medieval Hebrew Literature

In medieval Hebrew literature it was only men who voiced their opinions and feelings through their texts. The textual institutions were men's sanctuaries from which women were banished. The study of Scriptures and rabbinical literature, mysticism, and philosophy and even the practicing of liturgy had all been the exclusive domains of male creativity. In medieval Judaism, even more than in its hosting cultures, writing was considered an exclusively male—and essentially virile—competence. "The poet's pen is in some sense (even more than figuratively) a penis."[16] The pen (and pen-*man*-ship)—metonymic of writing, and of the writer himself—often stands for men's productivity and prowess, authorship and authority.

From its very outset, in mid-tenth-century Cordoba, the Andalusian-Hebrew poetry of the Golden Age was distinguished by its dual—courtly and clerical—face. The poets came from the circles of the intellectual leadership of rabbis, community leaders, talmudic scholars, Bible exegetes, moralists, and philosophers. From these echelons came also the Jewish courtiers who served as financiers, physicians, and diplomats to the Andalusian rulers. Some poets were courtiers, others were patronized by them or were close to their circles. This unprecedented brand of courtier-rabbis managed to live in two worlds—that of Jewish tradition and learning, and that of Arabic culture. The Arabicization of the Jewish intelligentsia was manifest not only in their adoption of Arabic as both the vernacular and the language of writing (everything but poetry was written in Arabic), but also in embracing Arabic learning, customs, and ways of life. Notwithstanding their devotion to Jewish tradition, their admiration for Arabic letters and culture resulted in an eventual modification of Jewish culture—

even in its religious aspects—according to Arabic models. Jewish philosophers adopted doctrines of Arabic-Greek thinking, grammarians explored
the Hebrew according to Arabic linguistics, Jewish doctors practiced Arabic medicine, and poets modeled their poetry, secular as well as religious,
on Arabic ideas, themes, and forms. While adhering to pure biblical idiom
as the marker of their Hebrew/Jewish identity, the poets appropriated
Arabic prosody, poetic genres, and thematic.[17] Conceived in the Andalusian courts, the new brand of secular Hebrew poetry, intended for the milieu of the serving elite, introduced typical Arabic courtly themes (such as
the depiction of palaces and gardens, wine banquets, and romantic love)
as well as the concepts of courtly aestheticism.[18] The acculturation of the
Jewish poets and thinkers resulted also in their adopting a variety of attitudes toward women and sexuality prevailing in their non-Jewish circles.

Far-reaching historical events around and after 1150 (the Berber-
Almohad invasion of al-Andalus and the Christian Reconquista) resulted
in the shifting of most Jewish-Spanish communities to Christian domains.
The Jewish elite, which emerged around the Christian courts, readily
adapted to the new ambience. And though Arabic learning and Andalusian poetry remained the declared cultural ideals, the changing historical
circumstances (and to some extent also the encounter with the dominant
Romance culture) resulted in a "jumble of continuities and transformations of the Andalusian traditions."[19] The hybridity of old and new literary paradigms characterizes the writing of Jewish intellectuals in Castile
and Catalonia, Provence, and Italy. To these we must add two major inner developments which took place in Jewish spirituality from the thirteenth century on. One was the efflorescence of philosophy and sciences,
the other the advent of the mythical-mystical Kabbala. The heated controversies which arose between the "Averroistic" and pietist circles (cen-
tered mainly around the writings of Maimonides) exerted, in their turn,
considerable intellectual and social tensions and left their mark on Hebrew literature as well as on the Hebrew language.[20] Beginning in the
thirteenth century Hebrew expanded from a language for poetry and
liturgy alone into a language including also varieties of scientific, speculative, and artistic prose.

The major literary innovation in Hebrew after 1150 is no doubt the
introduction of rhymed prose and the emergence of the narrative mode.
The *maqāma* (pl. *maqāmāt*), an Arabic literary form written in rhymed
prose and dispersed with poems, was adopted by Jewish authors who took

to its narrative and rhetorical potentialities.[21] Though its provenance is the Muslim East, it is among the Jewish writers of Christian Spain that this Arabic genre reached its efflorescence in the Hebrew language. While investing the Arabic form with Jewish elements, some of the authors also permitted for Romance influences to enter in. Preceding and parallel to the literary Hebrew *maqāma* (and its various cognates in rhymed prose) is a long chain of Jewish popular storytelling, beginning with the narrative parts in the Talmud as well as the Midrashim and continuing through popular oral traditions preserved in medieval compositions and anthologies. Some of the narrative plots fashioned in literary rhymed prose include variations and adaptations of Jewish folkloristic storytelling (itself drawing occasionally upon non-Jewish sources).[22]

This busy crossroad, which medieval Hebrew literature practically is, encourages its student to explore for intra- and intercultural relations: contacts, conflicts, and correspondences. On the level of the texts discussed, all these translate into a rich intertextual web. Hence, throughout this book I have constantly endeavored to point to references, allusions, comparisons, and analogues, to biblical and talmudic sources, to Arabic literature, to medieval Jewish and Islamic philosophy, and to Latin and other European literatures.

The emergence and evolution of the artistic Hebrew narrative literature, from the later part of the twelfth century on, has to be considered also against the backdrop of the rising Western novel in the High Middle Ages. Its topics, plots, and atmosphere justify viewing it in the context of other classics of world literature, such as the earlier versions of *The Thousand and One Nights*, Petrus Alphonsi's *Disciplina Clericalis*, Boccaccio's *Decameron*, and Chaucer's *Canterbury Tales*.[23] Much as in these illustrious works, in the Hebrew rhymed stories the topics of women, sexuality, the body, marriage, and the like occupy a central place.

The Good, the Bad, and the Ugly: Representations of Women

Women "good" and "bad" inhabit the width and length of the medieval Hebrew corpus. Much like other medieval literatures, Hebrew literature too tended on the whole to follow predicted stereotypes, depending on the genre employed. Stereotyping women was well suited to the disposition

inherent in medieval writing itself toward fixed imagery, conventional thematic, rigid generic rules, and recurrent rhetorical topoi. Intertextuality—
the endless repetition of recycled clichés, the quotation and elaboration of
previous authorities—turned this literature into a vast echo chamber
which further reverberated the fixated views about women.

The pages that follow aim to furnish the reader with an introductory
overview to the various literary Hebrew genres and to the gallery of feminine images represented in them. Briefly touched upon here will be genres treated elsewhere throughout this book. Others will be outlined in
more detail. In employing here, if only by way of introduction, the "images of women" approach (tendentiously avoided in other parts of the
book), I am perfectly aware of its critical pitfalls. "To study 'images of
women,' " cautions Toril Moi, "is equivalent to studying false images
of women."[24] Based on a naive assumption of "realism," the listing of
stereotypic images of women does not advance women's presence in literature; rather, it induces their absence and occlusion. As Moi convincingly argues, this approach neither allowed access to the historical world
of women, nor did it account for the diverse literary functions of these
images.

The "ideal woman" in this literature is either a prescription, a
dream—or in short supply. In the male love lyric (treated in Chapter 2),
she is the exalted lady, the mute beloved, the tempting nymph, or the defiant amazon. She is aloof but lethal, tempting but unyielding. She is devoid of personality and speech: the perfection of her physique dominates
the poets' descriptions.

Contrary to the image of the silent lady in the male monologues in
the love lyric are the passionate voices of the singing maidens in the *kharja*s.[25] The young women play an active role in the love relationship. They
daringly suggest secret rendezvous, despite spies and slanderers. They
coquettishly offer their bodies to their sweethearts, instructing them in
lovemaking, or bashfully stop an admirer's too bold advances. They send
messengers, consult fortune-tellers, or confess their feelings to mothers
and girlfriends. Many of these small songs are complaints about departure
and desertion. For instance:

> Don't touch me, my love, I don't want him who hurts me
> My breast is sensitive, stop it, I refuse all [suitors].
> (Judah ha-Levi, *Dīwān*, 2:3)[26]

I won't put on the necklace, mother, my dress is enough,
My love will behold my fair white throat, and won't need a necklace.
(Judah ha-Levi, *Dīwān*, 2:114)

Some scholars hypothesized that these couplets (in vernacular Arabic
or in Romance, incorporated into the Hebrew poems) quote, and thus
represent and preserve, an oral poetic tradition of old Iberian women's
songs in a Romance dialect. Others suggested that the kharjas are counterfeits of popular female poetry, forged by male courtly poets, and used
as ornament and spice.

Another female image is that of the ideal bride featured in wedding
songs. The bride is as perfect as the poets' lady, but is not dangerous as
the lady is. The imagery of the wedding songs both draws upon and deconstructs that of the love lyric. While the love lyric exalts extramarital
love with its attractions and perils, the wedding poems depict a prelapsarian paradise, devoid of danger and sin. The groom is encouraged to ignore the serpents that surround the beloved and enjoy the fruit in the
bride's garden of delight:

The time for lovemaking has come!
Go down, why do you tarry
To pasture in her garden?

Her fresh pomegranates are out of sight,
But you, don't fear when she brings them out
From behind the veil of her vipers—
For her snakes have no venom!
(Judah ha-Levi, *Dīwān*, 2:29)

Not only does the bride yield herself to her betrothed groom, but it is she
who entices him with a promise for future harmony and joy: "I will call
you my lot and my portion . . . / To you alone I will give my love / And
you will lie between my breasts" (2:26); "Here I am my beloved, I will
stir your affection / And cleanse my love of disobedience" (2:320).

The wedding songs reflect patriarchal imagination at its most favorable position toward woman. Love is not a forbidden fruit. It is there to
be consummated. The bride embodies the best of all worlds—erotic yet
pure and obedient, virgin yet a promise of future procreation. Her sexuality

is legitimized in the eyes of God and men. While the unattainable lady is a fantasy fostered to kindle the poets' poetic imagination, the ideal bride serves to integrate Eros within the frame of family and society. The wedding poems advocate the rabbinical view of marriage as the locus of sanctioned sexuality.

Eros in medieval Hebrew literature fades away when the bride becomes a wife. In marriage she is required to repress her feelings, opinions, appetites, desires, likes, and dislikes. She will earn the title of "the princess of the house" only if she agrees to be her husband's servile maid. In the following catechistlike series of questions and answers, men are taught how to pinpoint the good wife:

> [Being asked] who is the wife who ignores her husband's folly?
>   I answered "the wise one."
> And the one who cheers up her husband when he returns home sad?
>   I answered "the amiable one."
> And who obeys in silence without strife and deceit?
>   My answer was "the pious one."
> And who tolerates the brutality of a wicked husband?
>   My answer was "the orphaned one."
> And where will one find decency, nobleness and piety?
>   I answered "in the princess within [the house]."
>   (Samuel ha-Nagid, *Ben Mishle*, 178)[27]

A wife is not born a wife, but is made into one. The final product, the Wife, is made of the crude material that is Woman. Hence, she must be disciplined and domesticated. Mothers, no less than fathers, were agents of the patriarchal construction of wifehood. The following voice is that of a mother guiding her daughter in the ins and outs of marriage:

Beware of whatever makes your husband angry. Do not express your own anger when he makes love to you, or when he relaxes. Speak softly to him to abate his anger. Cook for him whatever he desires, and pretend to like his favorite dishes even if you don't. Don't remind him, when he is sober, of the follies he committed while he was drunk. Drink when he orders you to do so, but never get drunk. Save his money, for it is fit for a man to be generous and for the woman to be thrifty. Don't expose his secrets. Don't dislike the servants he likes. Don't disobey his orders, even if your advice is better than his. Don't be jealous. Don't request him to do for you things that are hard for him to do.[28]

No parallel notion of the ideal husband exists. The ideal wife must be in full control of her words and actions and in total denial of her feelings. On the contrary, her husband is allowed any kind of excess; he can be angry and hungry, drunken and spendthrift. Elsewhere the perfect wife is described as wise and resourceful—her husband's shield and fortress against hunger, cold, and strife.

The winged fantasy of the ideal bride/wife shatters when it hits the solid ground of marriage. Woman's base nature is said to reveal itself fully blown in marriage. And if she does appear as good and obedient, it is only to mask her greed and treachery.[29] It is in the morning after the wedding that the groom will reveal that he has been deceived. The perfect bride will prove to have been a bait; someone has replaced her with an unbearable, ugly, complaining harridan.[30] The wife is not mute, as is the courtly lady, nor is her voice comely as is the bride's. The wife's mouth is ceaselessly open—gulping food; demanding money, maids, house utensils, clothes, and jewels; complaining, lying, rioting, gossiping, revealing secrets, and constantly scandalizing her poor husband:

> A woman's face is a semblance of a demon;
>   when looking at her my body tears apart.
> Her tongue makes my hair bristle on my head,
>   her voice loosens the bonds of my heart.
> She closes gates of peace and friendship
>   and opens doors of quarrel and strife.
> On top of Mount Complaint she builds her house,
>   there her tent is spread and stretched tight.[31]

Married life becomes then the arena for the taming of the shrew. Husbands are advised to behave as men and to exercise their authority. If woman is rebellion and chaos, the making of a wife out of the base material of woman is a result of disciplining. If womanhood is crude nature, wifehood is the result of a culturing process. If woman is a boundless abyss, she should be contained within walls. If woman is a vagina, she should be covered and hidden.

Samuel ha-Nagid who wrote some of the most exquisite courtly love poems in the Hebrew language, is explicit in his moral advice to husbands: "Women were created as helpmates, but some are indeed rebellious / They were not created to share secrets with, and most of their advice is fruitless" (*Ben Mishle*, 340); "A woman [needs] a husband, like a son [needs] a father / like fools [need] the whip, and like subjects [need] their kings" (284); "Beat your wife daily, lest she rules over you like a man, and raises her head up / Be not, my son, your wife's wife, and let her not be her husband's husband" (162);[32] "Arrange for your wives a chamber and a lock and never share your secret with a woman (395); "Walls and castles were erected for woman—her glory lies in bedspreads and spinning / Her face is pudendum displayed on the main road that has to be covered by shawls and veils" (283). The hoped-for result of this kind of socialization is an obedient, silent, passive, immobile, totally devoted and dependent wife. But the female beast always lurks underneath.

The following detailed account of a woman-monster comes from the mouth of a duped groom, upon unveiling whom he thought to be his pretty bride. This horrifying yet ludicrous description shares in every aspect of the definition of the grotesque. The lists of woman's ugliness and disfigurement are the sheer opposite of the beauty lists current in the lovelyric, employing similar techniques of dismemberment and exaggeration:[33]

[H]er face—a face of a fury; her voice—a thunder; her image—like Jerobaam's calf; her mouth—like that of Balaam's ass; her breath—putrid; her cheeks—dried up, as if Satan has plastered them with murk and painted them with coals; [so dark] that I thought she's of the daughters of Ham. But if her complexion was darker than blackness itself—her hair was white, and her days were waxed old, and her lips protruded, and her teeth were like the teeth of wolves or of bears, and her eyes the eyes of scorpions. Then I made a poem:

> Her teeth make her the like of bears, devouring all they can find,
> Her scalp is covered with sore boils, and her eyes cancel all joy,
> Her stature is like a townwall, her thighs like two treetrunks,
> Her cheeks like coals, her lips—twisted like those of a donkey,
> She is in the image of Death Angels—killing whoever draws near.
> . . . .
> Are you derived from devils and illspirits? Will God's curse be
>   upon you!
> It's as if your brothers are angels of fury and ruin—and you are their
>   older sister.
> You resemble the Scape-Demon—how did you escape punishment?
> It is as if when Time desired Lilith, he sent you to her as a love gift.
> Your maker made you as helper to Death Angels.

I wish your father had died when conceiving you, and your mother
was barren.
Your lips are like oxen lips, your mouth is a grave, your belly—a cave.
Your teeth are putrid like bears' teeth, full of slime and excrement.
Your eyes smoky like a stove, your face murky like a pot's bottom
. . . .
Your belly is inflated like a goatskin. Your form is black like your
fortune.
Your hands are hairy like monkeys', your fingers look like coals in the
stove.
Your speech is like turmoil at midnight, your breath like a whirlwind.
Your mouth—a grave to your food and drinks. I wish they were
poison.
Your teeth grind like a pestle and mortar, shipping everything to
your deep abyss.
May God turn you upside down in hell like He did to Sodom and
Gomorrah.
May lions' bellies become your shrouds and grave!
(Judah al-Ḥarizi, *Taḥkemoni*, sixth *maqāma*)[34]

The extent to which Woman is allied in patriarchal imagination with
base nature and its uncontrollable forces is manifest in this grotesque depiction of the female body. She is identified with formlessness (turmoil,
abyss, murk), with vacuity (cave), with putrid matter (excretion, slime,
menstruation, coals), with the corporeal (diseases, body discharges, the di-
gestive system),[35] the ugly, the beastly (donkey, ox, bear, wolf, scorpion),
the demonic and evil (Satan, demons, ill spirits, Death Angels, Lilith, and
the Scapegoat).[36] The female body is thus dismembered and fragmented,
with each limb hyperbolically compared to another scary object. When the
parts are reassembled the result is a disproportionate, mythical, surrealistic,
horrifying human monster.[37] It is also noteworthy that her mouth, lips,
teeth, and spittle, together with the breath and voice that come out of her
mouth, occupy much of the description. Her gargantuan mouth and, similarly, her belly are likened to a grave, a cave, or a deep abyss. Her mouth,
analogous to the insatiable vagina, is constantly occupied with indiscriminately shoveling all kinds of foodstuff, grinding, gulping, and shipping it
down to her belly. The horror induced by the female grotesque—in whom
ugliness, foulness, demonic evil, and raw sexuality are inextricably united—
is said to be reduced by the laughter it produces.[38]

Another appalling female representation is that of *Tevel* (World, Earth), the allegorical personification of the world's evil.[39] The belief that women are the cause as well as the embodiment of the world's evil went hand in hand with the perception that this corrupted world was essentially feminine. Hence, the material world and its temptations were imagined as a woman whose outward attractive appearance hides her true nature as an ugly crone, a rotten prostitute.[40]

Tevel hypnotizes her human victims with her material riches, beauty, scarlet skirts, gold, jewels, wine, nectar, fruits, and so on. She marries men and then divorces them; makes love—and slays her lovers. He who loves her loves his foe. Men who covet possessions, honor, and stature submit to her dark power:

> In vain does Earth don her jewels.
>   Only fools will covet her looks.
> She lures the boors with her riches;
>   she tempts them with fine silks,
> Then she upsets them with much grief and pain—
>   and so few are the drops of her cure!
> She feeds the fools with a touch
>   of nectar—and they turn her captives.
> Those who desire her deem her a garden
>   of delights—but then discover her fruit!
>   (Moses Ibn Ezra, *Secular Poems*, 1:86)[41]

Tevel is the cannibal mother of her philanderers. Her womb is their tomb. Earth's mouth, vagina, and belly equal hell and the underworld. She feeds her children and then feeds on their flesh. "She devours her children—though they have hardly savored her bread and flesh." (Ibn Gabirol, *Secular Poems*, 1:305).[42] The poets point to the semantic affinity between *tevél* = *world* and *tével* = *incest*,[43] insinuating Tevel's incestuous nature. "She is named after her deeds—she is called a whore" (Moses Ibn Ezra, 1:85). Her offspring, "Bnei (sons of) Tevel," are born in her image and bear "the Name of the Mother." "Tevel is her name, since she and they are just the same / Were Tevel's sons wiser, they would publish her blame" (1:85). Or: "Tevel's children will always betray you—as she will do at the day of doom / True, they are like their mother—let them return to her large, deep tomb" (Isaac Ibn Khalfun, *Poems*, 105).[44]

Having no father, Tevel's perverse children ignore the incest-prohibiting Law of the Father. They are reluctant to detach themselves from the Mother's body and wish to have sex with her.[45] "Men are lechers, the world—a whore . . . / They denounce her in public, but their heart goes after her splendor" (Samuel ha-Nagid, *Ben Qohelet*, 18, poem 30).[46] They marry her, but ambivalence is their curse: "Aren't you like a man married to two wives—when he pleases the one he enrages the other?" (188, poem 354); "Let him not declare: 'I have abandoned her!' whilst she seizes his secrets [or: secret parts] / Lest he be like the man who expels his wife, yet withholds the divorce-bill in his hand" (Ibn Khalfun, *Poems*, 106, lines 17–20). The virtuous man ought to call Tevel's bluff:

Tevel, pay heed, open your eyes and lend your ears.
. . . .
How long will you tempt the fools with your smooth speech?
. . . .
You allure them with your golden jewels, your make-up,
You put on embroideries for them; in vain do you wear your scarlet
    skirts.
. . . .
"A harlot," I called you to your face, witnessing your lechery and
    lewdness.
. . . .
You fornicate with all, except with your husband; you boast your evil
    and foulness.
You equalize all men in betraying them all—your lovers as well as
    your foes,
Rich and poor, all will quench their thirst drinking from your poison-
    goblet.
. . . .
You marry their sons, but woes are the gifts you send to your daugh-
    ters and in-laws,
With your butts you signal peace to your suitors, but then bite them
    with your teeth,[47]
Their blood is still smeared in your house—and you deny you've
    killed them.
. . . .
If you set your table for them—it is bread of deceit that you serve,
If you pour wine into silver cups—it is mingled with vipers' venom . . .

If you spread flowers—serpents lurk among your roses and myrtles,
Or if you lay luxurious carpets—they are strewn with thorns and
    thistles.[48]

(Moses Ibn Ezra, Secular Poems, 151)

This Mother should be dishonored and her shame dis-covered. The symbolic act of renouncing her—exposing her sex—is, itself, incestuous:

One should respect one's mother—except for your sons whose law is
    your disgrace.
They ought to expose your shame, and strip off the rims of your coat
    over your face.

The mythical female image of *al-dunyā* (the Arabic equivalent of
Tevel) entered medieval Arabic (and Hebrew) literature via translations
from Indian literature. In many of its respects this image corresponds to
the Jungian-Neumannian archetypes of the Great Adulteress and the Terrible Mother.[49] In the Middle Ages, maintains Erich Neumann (and this
is true also for the Arabic/Hebrew realm), the mythical archetype of
Mother Earth was enhanced by the conceptual binarisms (spirit/matter,
soul/body, and male/female) inherited from Greek philosophy. (The
common etymology in Latin of *matter* and *mater* preserves this conceptual link.) The terrestrial world, its matter, and the human body were
conceived as the female element in creation, while the Intellect, the Logos, was conceived as male.[50] Medieval asceticism translated these ideas
into praxis, demanding that men should distance themselves from the
body and its satisfactions, from the material world and its values, and
from women and their temptations. The hatred of everything worldly,
preached by religious and philosophical ascetic trends, was thus strongly
entangled with a deep aversion to women.

The mythological Mother Earth is almost the sole representation of
motherhood in Hebrew literature. (This rarity can only be compared to
the surprising absence of children figures.) Mother as mourner of her
dead child appears in a certain group of lamentations over the dead.[51]
Unlike the bulk of the lamentation genre, which is typically masculine—a
male voice praises the virtues and mourns the demise of another male—in
this subgenre the female voice predominates. Widowed wives mourn their
husbands, or bereaved mothers weep over young daughters abducted

from their homes to be wedded to the Son of Death. Some of these poems are arranged in balladlike dialogues between the living and the dead,
with the voice of the deceased woman herself arising out from the grave.
The song form, the simplified rhetoric, the folkloric elements, and the intense emotionality of these poems written in the woman's voice suggest
that the poets who put them to writing may have followed an oral female
tradition of lamentations. The woman's voice here might be representative of the women keeners who, in traditional societies, are burdened with
the task of expressing the grief of the community. It is this social task
which grants women the right of speech in lamentation poems.

Similarly laden with communal emotions is the speech of the allegorical representative of the Nation, the Synagogue (Kneset) of Israel.[52] In
countless liturgical pieces she speaks as a wife abandoned without divorce
who longs nostalgically to be reunited with her husband; as a disgraced
widow, a bereaved mother, a sinful wife, a stray daughter, a repentant—or
as the passionate paramour of the God of Israel. Following the traditions
of prophetic and midrashic allegory, the voice of exiled Kneset Israel, po-
litically oppressed and socially inferior, finds its figural embodiment in the
legal and social miserable state of a despised and disenfranchised divorcée,
a widow, or an outcast. The question arises (and this question arises
whenever a female figure is chosen as symbol for a concept, or property,
she is devoid of), why should the Jewish praying congregation—all men—
choose to address God through the agency of a female voice?[53] And if, as
endlessly repeated in medieval texts, *"qol ba'isha 'erva"* ("a woman's voice
is pudendum"); and if women are barred from public prayer—how can a
female voice represent the community? Read as a political discourse, medieval Hebrew liturgy is the expression of a powerless minority. In this
case it is her present powerlessness (and the hope for a future status of
power) which unites the signifier and the signified and enables the render-
ing of Nation as Woman. It is ultimately Kneset Israel's suffering which
rehabilitates her voice for public expression.

Another female allegorical abstraction is that of the human soul. Attracted to the body; polluted by evil and crude matter; divorced from the
intellect—the menstruating, sinful woman soul is called upon to purify
herself, to rid herself from her femaleness so that she can be reallied with
the elevated male elements of Creation. In liturgical poetry and moral allegories (treated in Chapter 4) she speaks as a beloved gazelle yearning
for union with her lover; a deserted plaintive wife enslaved to her enemy,

the body; a stray daughter entreating her father God to return her home; a pupil listening to Intellect's lectures, or as the intellectual soul, preaching to the stubborn body.

Like Tevel, Kneset Israel, and the soul—all gendered as feminine in Hebrew grammar—poetry too is allegorized as female. She is a decorated bride, veiled and perfumed; a lustful paramour or a whore; the poet's mother, daughter, or servant. The best of poetry, like the best of women, is said to be beautiful and deceitful. (This gendered ars poetica is discussed in Chapter 3).

Criticism: Past and Present

Medieval Hebrew literature was, even to a greater extent than its Arabic hosting literature and its European counterparts, an entirely male realm. This has been true for too long also with regard to the scholarship of the Hebrew field. Inasmuch as women were absent from the literary arena, inasmuch as the female voice was hardly heard in the medieval poems and stories, so has a woman's critical perspective been missing from their modern readings.

If eavesdropping—the surreptitious listening to men's private talk, of which, among other sins, women were accused in medieval texts—has long been the lot of the woman reader of medieval Hebrew texts, then, in a sense, the business of the medievalist feminist is to make eavesdropping a legitimate act.

The lack of a feminist approach has been increasingly felt during the last three decades when the feminist agenda became one of the leading perspectives in medievalist criticism.[54] While the bookshelves of medieval literary scholarship in European (and other) languages have become loaded with new feminist readings of the old texts, Hebrew literary medievalism remained miraculously untouched by the advent of feminist criticism.[55] I could have been luckier, perhaps, if, like my medievalist-feminist colleagues in other fields, I were able to pursue previous feminist works in my field—to rely on, to quote from, and to argue with or against them. My 1988 article "On Tongues Being Bound and Let Loose: Women in Medieval Hebrew Literature,"[56] in which I dwelt on the opposition of women's speech and silence as a deep semiotic, discursive, and generic structure, remains, as far as I know, the only theoretically informed feminist sortie in this direction.

The historical reasons (or excuses) for this belatedness of feminist critical work on medieval Hebrew literature are accountable considering the overall deferred agenda of the field. On the whole, the scholarship of medieval Hebrew literature is a relatively young field. Its early history is inextricably connected with the endeavors of the great scholars of the European *Wissenschaft des Judentums* in the nineteenth century, who first traced, edited, and published the scattered medieval texts. Much of twentieth-century scholarship has been, and still is, preoccupied with the tasks of editing and reestablishing the canon—tasks not entirely completed yet. Hence, much of the work done even to these days has been of philological, taxonomic, historical, and biographical nature. The entry of modern trends of literary criticism has roughly occurred not earlier than mid-twentieth century, when questions of rhetoric, stylistics, aesthetics, theory of genres, and so on only began to be asked. Various critical approaches (comparative, new critical close readings, formalist/structuralist) have been gradually appropriated, and usually a generation or two after their prime in Western criticism. Yet, as late as 1964, Jefim Schirmann, the leading scholar in the field at the time, cautioned in a lecture he gave in Jerusalem that "one cannot take an exhaustive and reliable investigation of any literature without a detailed list of all manuscripts . . ." He was aware that "for a number of years now" European scholarship had applied "new methods of examining the literary writings of old," but was not entirely convinced whether the time was ripe for such "risky" projects in medieval Hebrew literature.[57] It is noteworthy that in 1967, when this lecture appeared in print, feminist literary criticism in America had already launched its undertakings. My belated reading of gender in medieval Hebrew literature is then a consequence of the overall delayed scholarly agenda of the field.[58] Nevertheless, there were also, in my view, ideological impediments involved. Not the least of them was the trap of equating "hedonism" with profeminism. The images of women (and other gender issues) have been often cataloged (and thus obscured) under either the rubric of "love" (when a "positive" image was involved) or under that of "humor and entertainment" (when the images were negative).[59] In dealing with the love lyrics and wine poetry, as well as with the romantic and comic narratives, most critics were so enchanted with the very fact that these "universal" works of art, celebrating worldly pleasures, were written by revered rabbis and thinkers that they have been reluctant to expose the invisible and not-so-invisible androcentric and misogynistic politics embedded in them. Being so enthralled with the emergence of a new Jewish "hedonism" in the heart of the Middle Ages, critics generally failed to contextualize this truly innovative literature against other expressions of this culture. Hence, the ambivalences toward the erotic and the body, and other gender implications, tended to be underplayed. With Eros becoming conflated with "love and admiration for women," the prevailing atmosphere of antifeminism was overlooked.

Late nineteenth- and early twentieth-century scholarship, ideologically identified with the emancipatory movement of Haskala and later with secularized Zionism, readily harnessed these hedonistic utterances not only in order to contradict the puritanical "exilic" image of medieval Judaism, but also to positively anchor ideologies of Jewish modernity (emancipation, secularization, and Zionism) in these antecedents from the past. They viewed the "free" indulgence in matters of love, beauty, laughter, and other worldly sentiments as symptoms of a "new Jewish feel" and as early precedents of Jewish "normalcy," "secularism," "humanism," and "universalism." Superlative expressions like "the jubilation of eros," "return to nature," "authentic zest for life," "intimacy with the body," "a feeling for beauty," "unrestrained humor" were not uncommon. Hence, with all their claim for "universalism," and notwithstanding their unawareness of their own politics, extant readings of medieval Hebrew literature tended to be inadvertently political. They were political also in their obliviousness to questions of gendered reader's response.

Reading Medieval Hebrew Literature through the Lens of Gender

"We, men, women and Ph.D.'s have always read as men," wrote Carolyn Heilbrun.[60] Traditionally trained as I was in the field of medieval Hebrew literature, I too gradually found myself alienated from the materials I was reading and teaching. Like Judith Fetterley's reader, I had been for too long "intellectually male, sexually female, immasculated" (xxii); "coopted into participation in an experience from which she is explicitly excluded . . . asked to identify with a selfhood that defines itself in opposition to her; . . . required to identify against herself" (xii). It was my growing awareness of precisely this "endless division of self against self" (xiii) which turned, paradoxically, into a passionate impetus to reenter the texts and ask them, and myself, new questions.

How is the female "other" represented and positioned? How does

she relate to the hegemonic male "I"? In what ways do the definitions of
"woman" reflect back and redefine the definition of "men"? What artistic
strategies do the texts employ to signify gender difference and gender relations? How do men's articulations about women render their perceptions of love, sexuality, marriage, and the body? How is female speech
signified? In what ways does this literature relate to culture and society?
How can a feminist reader, experiencing herself as a reading subject, partake in a corpus which denied woman's subjectivity? How can I reclaim
those texts that excluded women as readers? How can a position of alterity and resistance become a critical vantage point? What are the gains of
reading "from the margins"?

Feminist criticism began answering these questions long before I
began asking them. Fetterley wrote: "While women obviously cannot
rewrite literary works so that they become ours by virtue of reflecting our
reality, we can . . . change literary criticism from a closed conversation to
an active dialogue."[61] And Adrienne Rich insisted on re-vision as an existential imperative: "Re-vision—the act of looking back, of seeing with
fresh eyes, of entering an old text from a new critical direction—is for us
more than a chapter in cultural history; it is an act of survival."[62]

In my excursions into the medieval Hebrew texts, I made use of various feminist theories and methodologies, depending on the issues considered, while at the same time paying special attention to the specific
conditions of medieval Jewish textuality. Hebrew fictional literature—
alongside prayer, Torah learning, exegetics of the Scriptures, linguistics,
philosophy, ethics—was one among other Jewish textual all-male institutions. By sharing their written products with other Jewish men,
male authors constituted their authority and enacted their privilege.
Intertextuality—quotations from, elaborations of, or references to established traditions of male textual activity—was a significant aspect of the
male corpus. Intertextual traffic did not remain confined to Hebrew or
Jewish texts (Bible, Talmud, Midrash, later rabbinic literature) only, but
extended also to relations with the hosting Arabic literature. Jewish authors allied with Islamic authors at the expense of women. Whether
serious or light, Hebrew literature was another gentlemen's club from
which Jewish women were entirely excluded, both as writers and readers.
Literature was an exchange market where men enlightened or entertained
other men by passing on poems, stories, jokes, and gnomes *about* women.
In these triangular transactions "woman" was the verbal commodity
delivered. This "homotextual" dimension of Hebrew literature has been

almost altogether elided by the mainstream literary scholarship of the field.[63]

In several chapters of this book I attempt to show how the homo-textual conditions underlying the different discourses are problematized within the texts themselves. The social framework of male talk together with its products—discourses of love and hatred, ideologies of gender hierarchy and sex difference, constructions of indoctrination and of humor—are all shown to be interwoven within the fictionalized texture. In the love lyric (Chapter 2), for instance, I argue that the male discourse of love is generated not so much by sheer love to the lady as by the poet's drive to please a courtly male audience which shares his own aesthetic values. Chapter 6 in particular dwells on homotextuality as the deep structure of the *maqāma*. (The *maqām*, which lent its name to the genre, was the tribal, and later the caliphal, assembly place.) Several examples of this genre are studied in which the male bond is shown to engender male speech. In one *maqāma*, a poetic contest is held between a lady's husband and her two suitors. The winner's prize is the lady herself. In another piece a man falls in love with a pretty and prudish woman described to him by another man. And it is ultimately male rhetoric which leads to the woman's death. A woman who speaks as woman but like a man is the antagonist of patriarchal discourse in yet another debate *maqāma*.

The issue of humor, handled in several chapters (5, 6, 7 ,8) is not to be separated from the homotextual frame. The humor engendered by the male social setup of the texts is almost unavoidably gendered: Jokes not to be told in mixed company are told; a man makes other men laugh at the expense of an absent woman; grotesque descriptions of women pass as entertainment; or fictional unlettered women are made to comically parrot biblical or talmudic (male) texts. Cataloged by critics as parodies, travesties, satires, grotesques, or just funny jokes, most extant treatments of these works offer to view them as light pastimes. And while relegating them to the realm of the comic, scholars and critics occasionally joined the hilarity of the implied audience, especially when the ridicule of women was at stake. Alternatively, critics suggested that the humoristic "intention" of the writers must necessarily dissolve, or altogether undercut, misogyny. Either way they dismissed themselves from handling the more serious implications of gender, and of sexual politics, shrouded in this literature under "humor" and failed to see how humor is not the opposite of misogyny but rather one of its most effective tools.

The inferiority of women based on metaphysical, biological, or ascetic grounds was rehearsed by Jewish philosophers, doctors, and moralists. Such opinions, which are, by and large, part and parcel of the vast Western misogyny, promulgate their presence also in the literary Hebrew works. Women were identified with matter, body, and defiled sexuality. Men were repeatedly warned against women's threat to their well-being and were urged to exclude and silence them. Women were relegated to the realm of the beastly, the evil, and the demonic and banished from the sphere of the intellect and the divine. They were considered an obstacle to man's peace in this world and to his redemption in the hereafter. Obviously infected by misogyny are the negative images of the wicked wife and Tevel, discussed earlier. Chapter 5 addresses a work whose protagonists extensively recycle misogynist wisdom, and whose author titles his namesake narrator as "Judah the Woman-Hater." Such straightforward ideas are also present in several works discussed in Chapter 6. Misogynistic ideas are also shown to underlie the gendered perceptions of poetry (Chapter 3) and of the human body (Chapter 4).

If feminists today call to avoid ruminating over misogyny, they do so in order to counterbalance the extensive preoccupation of early medievalist feminism. To list the sins of antifeminists, they insisted, is to replicate the latter's endless lists of women's sins. Tracing the misogyny in the Hebrew texts has by no means been my central engagement in this work. If I did so, it is to a great extent to make up for the reluctance of mainstream critics to acknowledge it altogether. In exposing the views of medieval Hebrew women-haters, I followed Daniel Boyarin's insistence that "when the ancient culture is powerfully (and painfully) effective in producing aspects of our current social practice, an important part of our descriptive work must be to criticize the culture. To pretend to an objectivity . . . is, in effect, to further bolster the effects that those practices still have."[64]

Another question entangled in the treatment of misogyny is that of the simultaneous poetics of women's adoration and condemnation. As against ascetic sentiments that tended to demonize women, a great deal of medieval Hebrew poetry and fiction is obsessed with the idolization of women, with romantic love and carnal desire, with corporeal beauty and the pleasures of the Eros. Are these extreme attitudes really contrasts? Is the "good" woman the counterpart of the "bad" one? Does the idealization of women or the preoccupation with love and desire balance or undercut misogyny?

This dialectic relationship toward women and the erotic has also been a persistent issue in the reflections of modern scholars on other medieval cultures. The ramifications of this controversial subject are far from being exhausted here. C. S. Lewis saw the "idealism and cynicism about women" as being "twin fruits of the same branch."[65] Ambivalence is also the key word in Jane Burns's feminist discussion of the poetics of explicit adoration and implicit condemnation in troubadour poetry. Psychologizing Lewis's contention, she suggests that it is the "male soul" which is divided against itself. The uncanny medusan woman that lurks behind the adored lady is the projection of male fantasies and phobias. In her view, "this paradoxical portrait of the 'lady' who is admired and the 'woman' who is feared betrays a fundamental [male] ambivalence about females."[66]

Following trends of French feminist psychoanalysis, Fatna Sabbah, a North African feminist, addressed a similar dialectic in Islam. Exploring medieval Islamic "discourses of desire" (in love lyric, fiction, pornography) and "discourses of power" (Islamic theology and law; marriage sex manuals written by religious authorities), she argued that the concept of Eros is not (as sometime perceived) the opposite of Islamic misogyny but rather its direct outcome. Although (as it is in Judaism) married intercourse is sanctified as a religious deed, sexuality (and especially woman's) is identified with chaos and heresy. The discourses of desire reduce woman to an insatiable vagina ("the devouring crack") that the Muslim male has both to satisfy and control. The obsession with virginity, on the one hand, and with the religious ideal of the mute and obedient wife both are male fantasies which stem from the attraction to the horror of the "omnisexual" vagina and at the same time are devised to mitigate them. In her view misogyny lies at the heart of the Islamic thinking on sexuality.[67]

Howard Bloch's definition of misogyny is the most far-reaching (and therefore also most controversial). Misogyny according to him is any speech act which categorizes "women." Two procedures take place in any sentence that begins with "Woman is": persons are reduced into abstract qualities, and qualities are reified into personifications. Hence, any utterance, in which "woman," whether good or bad, is reduced into a category is for him a misogynistic assault.[68] Against formulations of "symmetry" (Lewis's) or "ambivalence" (Burns's), he argues: "The simultaneous condemnation and idealization of woman and love are not contrasting manifestations of the same coin. They are not opposites at all. Rather antifeminism and courtliness stand in a dialectical rapport which . . . assumes a logical necessity according to which woman . . . [is] neither one nor the other but both at once, and thus trapped in an ideological entanglement whose ultimate effect is her abstraction from history."[69] Positive images of women remain, according to Bloch, under the ruling spirit of antifeminism.

Challenging the views of historians and literary critics that European courtly love served as an antidote for misogyny, Bloch contends that "the invention of Western romantic love," beginning in twelfth-century Europe, did not stand as opposition to misogyny but was rather a historical moment within the persistent presence of the all-embracing medieval Western misogyny.

The ambivalences in medieval Jewish-Spanish culture concerning sexuality, women, and marriage are discussed by David Biale:

Indeed two souls often beat within the breast of the elite itself, and sometimes within the breast of the same individual. On the one hand, Jewish culture shared with its surroundings an extraordinary openness to the erotic and a willingness to cast it in purely secular terms. Poets experimented with a range of hitherto unheard-of subjects, including unbridled sensuality and homosexuality. . . . On the other hand, Jewish philosophers, under the influence of Greek philosophy mediated through Arab sources, took the ascetic leanings of talmudic culture even further. The result was a much more negative stance on sexuality and the body than anything to be found in northern Europe. . . . This was an elite very much in conflict over its own sexuality, torn between the competing norms and practices of the Jewish and non-Jewish cultures in which they lived. . . . Also hotly debated by the elite in the twelfth and thirteenth centuries was the nature of women. . . . Some authors blamed women for the ruination of men, while others glorified women and the virtues of marital love. The very institution of marriage was troubling for elements of the Spanish Jewish intelligentsia, who projected their ambivalences onto women as either the source of the problem or its cure. Ambivalence over erotic behavior therefore plagued the Jewish elite. If the philosophers rejected sexual pleasure, they did so in the context of a culture that affirmed it.[70]

Can the poets' "extraordinary openness to the erotic" be used as a sign for the culture's affirmation of sexual pleasure? Were not the "secularity" and the hedonism of the Golden Age poets rather a historical moment, an exception, in a culture whose attitude toward sexuality was basically negative? Were not the poets' themselves divided between their "unbridled sensuality" and the culture's deep ascetic leanings? I would then rephrase Biale's conclusion and read: "If the poets affirmed sexual pleasure, they did so in the context of a culture that rejected it."

To what extent do the literary texts reflect not only perceptions about women but also the reality in which women (and men) lived? Early

feminist-medievalist criticism of European literatures attempted to read
literary texts as historical documents and to retrieve, through male- (and
occasionally also female-) authored texts, the lived experience of medieval
women. This "reflectionism" (together with the "images of women" approach)[71] has led to an impasse—and not only because medieval authors
had little stake in representing the living reality of women, but rather because it failed to acknowledge the complicated relations between literature and history. Reflectionism and its demand for "authenticity," argues
Toril Moi, undermined the autonomy of literature to create its own fictional universes, be they "according to oppressive and objectionable ideological assumptions." Such projects practically rule out the greater part of
world literature. Moi adds, "Extreme reflectionism simply cannot accom-
modate notions of formal and generic constraints on textual production."[72] No less than for any other literary critic, the business of the
feminist critic must be the "literariness" of literature: the workings of
genre and form, the interplay between fixed conventions and their versatile and often surprising variations. It does make a literary difference
whether an image, an idea, or a voice appears as a semblance of reality or
as a symbolized abstraction, as a topic for intellectual discussion, poetic
description, moral exempla, allegory, rhetorical exercise, comic anecdote,
or any other kind of manipulation.

The autonomy of literature to construct its own symbolical "possible
worlds"—rather than passively mirror reality—does not stop literature
from reflecting back its invented fictions onto the real world. Literature is
"one practice among many by which a culture organizes its production of
meaning and values and structures itself," says Daniel Boyarin.[73] And
Robert Hodge writes, "Literature [is] a process rather than a simple set of
products; a process which is intrinsically social, connected at every point
with mechanisms and institutions that mediate and control the flow of
knowledge and power in a community."[74]

With this double perspective in mind—of literature as both contex-
tualized and autonomous—I read medieval Hebrew literature as both
history-at-work *and* fiction. Although the works studied here rarely convey a sense of real time and place, individual persons or concrete events,
some of them do seem to encode, though in ways indirect and tangential,
historical moments and, hence, to invite an attempt at their historiciza-
tion (which I did in several chapters). These fictions of gender are not just
compelling embodiments of the social situation that engendered them,
but they are shown also to have actively participated in replicating the ex-

isting order. The literary strategies that they employ to objectify, distance, and silence women fictionalize the social practices held by other discursive and nondiscursive institutions.

Another problem involved in the intricate relationship between history and literature is the difficulty of dealing with the postulated presence of medieval women in history as against their absence from literature:

We need a literary method—or methods—that will respect the many forms of their presence in history, while developing ways of gauging or describing their absence from the literary record. We should not displace them again; but neither should we simplify their presence, create them in our image, or romanticize their occlusion by "restoring" them."[75]

And Roberta Krueger writes, "If we cannot hypostatize historical woman's presence, we must evaluate the implications of her absence."[76] If feminist criticism cannot restore women from their abstracted figurations, it can account for the ideological functions women served in literature. It can map the positions and positioning of female figures and female voices within the patterns of male discourse and procedures of signification.

There are ample ways by which women can be made to disappear from the texts, even though they seem to be present or represented. When women are positioned as abstractions without bodies, or else when they are reified as bodies without subjectivities and minds—they are absent either way. Feminist methodologies are helpful in thematizing and problematizing this absence and making it the focus of discussion. They furnish useful tools, many of which are employed throughout this book, for describing and assessing this absence, and for accounting for its textual manifestations. The various chapters of this book aim to follow the varied ways in which women and concepts of gender are fictionalized, fantasized, poeticized, metaphorized, narrativized, dramatized—in short, the modes by which they are textually manipulated in male literature. Woman's absence is shown to be effected by procedures of silencing (presenting women as either ideally mute or factually garrulous), stereotypization and abstraction (woman as "the good," "the bad," and "the ugly"), mythologization and dehumanizing (woman as nymph, Medusa, amazon, demon, beast); objectification (woman as matter, commodity, chattel, prize); allegorization and symbolization (woman as sign for material world, soul, temptation, wisdom, nation, or poetry), and the like.

Closely related to the question of women's presence/absence in medieval literature is the representation of women's speech/silence. The issue of the female voices captured within male texts has engaged much of feminist criticism and is also one of the axes around which several chapters in this book revolve. To what extent are these female voices "authentic" and unmediated? Why would a male author volunteer as a ventriloquist of a female voice? How does a female voice serve—or to what extent is it determined by—the author's androcentric position? Though often muffled by male transmission, such utterances of female protagonists arrested in these texts help to reveal the limits of the androcentric logic that produced them.

While many, though not all, of these voices aim to embody patriarchal "truths" about women's abuse of language (lying, quarreling, complaining, enticing, and so on), some of them may also indicate points from which the homotextual monolith can be dismantled. In listening to the choir of female voices inscribed in the pages of male texts, be they constructed as they are, I seek to read something other than the hegemonic discourse that they are designed to serve. If women are permitted to speak in a system threatened by female speech—moreover, in a culture where female silence is a virtue—then these "illegitimate" utterances of the "other" situated within the dominant discourse invite reading them as sites of empowerment and embedded resistance. When the women protagonists are made to speak, they lose their status as the still object (or subject matter) of male speech and come close to that of a speaking subject. Rather than dismissing female voices in male-authored texts as collaborating with the system, it is suggested here to consider them as possible niches of embedded critique; seeds of otherness which defy the male texts' own self-proclaimed and solid assumptions.

By seeking women's resisting voices inscribed in male texts, the modern "resisting reader" can undermine the positions and values of male writing. Woman's speech has thus been an issue in feminist theories focusing on readers' response. For Jane Burns, for instance, the inscribed female speaker, who defies the male speech from within the text, becomes the model for the feminist medievalist who provokes it from without.[77] And Roberta Krueger sees the modern feminist as the incarnation of the missing hypothetical medieval female reader. In reflecting on her own reading procedures from a position of alterity, the feminist reader both constitutes her stance vis-à-vis the texts and restores that empty locus of the missing subject of the medieval woman reader.[78]

Having a similar effect of destabilizing the texts from within are various constructions of gender which seem to undermine the firm assumptions of androcentric gender division. In reading the texts against the grain one finds that the problem of women's representation is inextricably entangled with that of the representation of masculinity. Any endeavor by the male text to define "woman" ultimately rebounds on the definer. The ideal lady in the love lyric reciprocally defines—as well as refines—her courtly admirer. And in embodying the lofty values of "courtliness" she redefines courtly manhood. Love is shown to subvert the proclaimed patriarchal dichotomies in yet another way. Men in love, admitting their total subjection to the lady, are figuratively rendered as feminized, while the ladies who fight and resist them are virilized. Experiments in fictions of transvestism and transsexuality are other textually based loci of undermining patriarchy from within. Gender borders are also crossed when poetry—an exclusively male vocation—is imaged as female. The poets' professional preoccupation with beauty, similitude, and vain rhetoric renders them feminine, and even effeminate—the fellow travellers of the enticing woman. While Poetry is the personification of the male aesthetic values, the Neoplatonic Soul, figured (in penitential poems) as feminine, personifies male moral conflicts. Having an "androgynous" potentiality, the Soul is required to abandon her corporeal "feminine" traits and reinforce her intellectual "masculine" powers. The dilemmas of manhood (how does one become a man—by devoting oneself to meditative life or to family life? by creating or by procreating?) are present in a series of misogynist *maqāmāt*. Apparently focusing on women, these works are clearly projections of men's concerns and anxieties onto women (and onto marriage).

2

Gazing at the Gazelle:
Woman in Male Love Lyric

The Absent Lady and the Present Woman Reader

ISSUES OF GENDER PERVADE ALMOST every aspect of medieval Hebrew love lyric: What is the gender of author and audience? What is the gender of lover and beloved? Is it heterosexual or homosexual love?[1] Which gender roles do the partners assume? What is the real/imaginary power balance between the sexes? Who speaks and who remains silent? What are the moral and aesthetic values on which the love discourse is grounded? And whose values are they? What sexual politics do they serve? Whose interests do they tend to?[2]

Alongside these gender-involved concerns, another question arises, and this is the gendered identity of the actual reader: "If the meaning of a work is the experience of a reader, what difference does it make if the reader is woman?"[3] And what difference will it make if this poetry, written and read exclusively by men, is intruded, nearly a millennium after its conception, by an unsolicited modern woman reader? Will this male discourse of love be understood differently today by male and female (or rather feminist and nonfeminist) readers? Will it appeal to them in different ways?

Until recently such questions have hardly occurred to scholars and critics of medieval Hebrew poetry. The "love relationship" was treated without problematizing the aspects of gender, as if love and gender could be separable. Much like their peers in other literatures, critics of medieval Hebrew poetry identified, consciously or unconsciously, with the male positioning of the love poems. Believing their attitude to be "objective" and "universal," leading (mostly male) critics faithfully followed in the footsteps of medieval writers and readers, all men, who denied woman's right to her own perspective of love. Woman's voice, virtually absent from the medieval poems, has also been absent from the critical modern discourse on medieval Hebrew love poetry.[4] This lack has become increasingly acute during the last three decades when the feminist agenda became a leading approach in American and European medievalist criticism.[5]

While focusing on the androcentricity of the love poems, this chapter will also lend an ear to the absent female voice. "If we cannot hypostatize historical woman's *presence*," writes Roberta Krueger, "we must evaluate the implications of her *absence*."[6] And following Nancy Miller's call "to imagine the lady's place . . . the place of a woman's body,"[7] we may ask what "place" should the modern feminist/woman reader of Samuel ha-Nagid or Judah ha-Levi imagine? Should she put herself in the place of the silent lady "on the pedestal" or in that of the absent medieval Jewish woman reader? Will she be able, while resisting the poems' androcentric bias and distrusting their alleged "disinterestedness," also to rediscover their appeal, emotional as well as aesthetic? Will she recognize a redeeming quality in their beauty? Rereading these texts as a woman involves a complex, rather sophisticated stance. It entails a constant conscious account of the reader's dialogue with the texts, insisting on retaining their aesthetic fascination, while, at the same time, being aware of their manipulative power.

The Courtier-Rabbis as Love Poets

Among other literary practices and social vogues that the acculturated Jewish Andalusian elite adopted from their Arab surroundings, around the turn of the eleventh century, was the composition of courtly love poems.[8] Notwithstanding their own ancient legacy of love poetry—the Song of Songs—it was chiefly from Arabic models that the Hebrew poets drew their poetic inspiration. The highly conventionalized forms of Arabic poetry were readily and successfully adjusted then to biblical Hebrew phraseology.

In Arabic literature love poetry was only one variety within a vast repertoire of other erotic and romantic modes (including epic romances, narratives and anecdotes, legends and biographies, pornographic manuals, religious guides, and theoretical compositions on the philosophy and psychology of love). Hebrew literature, for its part, adopted from the Arabic mainly the mode of the highly stylized love poetry.[9] Hence, whereas Arabic literature furnished modern critics with extensive materials

from which they could reconstruct the erotic mentalities of medieval
Muslims, Hebrew love poetry remains an insufficient source for the attitudes and the real practices of the Jews in the realm of love. If this poetry
bears any concrete evidence, it is mainly to the extent to which the Jews
of Muslim Spain actually absorbed the lifestyles, social mores, and aesthetic tastes of their neighbors.[10] A poem by Moses Ibn Ezra does not
just reflect the good life lived by the Andalusian Jewish elite, but using an
ironic, inverted moralistic tone, it unreservedly preaches for it:

> Caress a lovely woman's breast by night,
> And kiss some beauty's lips by morning light.
> . . . .
>
> Immerse your heart in pleasure and in joy,
> And by the bank a bottle drink of wine.
> Enjoy the swallow's chirp and viol's whine.
> Laugh, dance, and stamp your feet upon the floor!
> Get drunk, and knock at dawn on some girl's door.

And the poem ends with a Jewish version of the *carpe diem* creed. Employing a biblical allusion which grants to the priests the choice meat portions (Exodus 29:26–28), the speaker urges each man to enjoy the best
share of world's joys—woman's flesh, her breast and thigh:

> This is the joy of life, so take your due.
> You too deserve a portion of the Ram of
> Consecration, like your peoples chiefs.
> To suck the juice of lips do not be shy,
> But take what's rightly yours—the breast and thigh!
>   (Moses Ibn Ezra, *Dīwān*, 1:263)[11]

Do the love poems in both languages reveal the love lives of the individual poets? When a certain Arabic princess asked a poet which ladies he
had hinted at with this and that line, he replied: "To no particular one. I
am a poet who likes to make gallant songs and to praise female beauty."
Another poet, upon being asked whether the love affairs he had written
about bear any truth, answered to the opposite effect: "Yes, and I beg
God's forgiveness."[12] But while Arabic literature yields abundant stories—
fictitious as well as real—about the loves and flirtations of its poets,[13] vir-

tually nothing is known from sources outside the poems themselves about the private lives and the romantic adventures of the Jewish poets.[14] Exemplary love stories—like those of Majnun and Layla in Bedouin lore or Ibn Zaidūn and Wallāda in al-Andalus, as well as Abelard and Héloïse or Dante and Beatrice in the European tradition—are completely lacking from the Hebrew literature. "We would like to believe that the beautiful women described in the poems were real women, that the passions and heartbreaks really happened . . . but their purpose was to write poetry not autobiography."[15]

It is most likely that the sweethearts about whom the Jewish poets serenaded were similar to those admired and desired by their Arab peers. As the promiscuous practices of the Muslim court poets are well documented in chronicles and anecdotal literature, much is known about their flirtations with princesses, slave girls and young boys, Muslim as well as non-Muslim. Whether the Jewish poets who wrote poems about similar experiences actually flirted in the courts or just imitated the Arabic love poems, reflecting the air of their courtly milieu, remains a question for speculation. Even if they "were merely fantasizing," or "mere[ly] aping the literary conventions," says Raymond Scheindlin "we would still be left to account for the poets' devoting so much intellectual energy and creative power to these particular conventions, so removed from those of traditional Judaism."[16]

The idealization of the ladies and the stylization of the poems make it usually difficult to identify, in the Hebrew poems, the social type of the women described. The two following portraitures, one of a noblewoman, curtained in her luxurious mansion, and the other of an attractive court songstress, are quite rare.

> Take this word to a genteel princess,
>   bred on cinnamon and incense—
> Who sleeps till midday while her maids
>   carry home plentiful foods;
> Who does no work, labors not at the distaff;
>   who's neither too dun nor too pale;
> Who, since birth, has been tended
>   by fine damsels, pleasing and tender—
> Tell her: "My heart is redeemed in the day of your grace;
>   my doomsday lies in the day of your wrath!"
>   (Samuel ha-Nagid, *Dīwān*, 302)[17]

Another poem (in fact an introduction to a *qaṣīda* intended as a panegyric to a Jewish courtier), describes a court singer (*qayna* in Arabic), usually a slave girl of foreign, non-Arab origin. Continuing an Eastern trend, the *qiyān* (plural) served as entertainers in the opulent courts of al-Andalus. They were not only performers, but at times also composers of their own lyrics and melodies. "Their playful licentious verse . . . echoed the banter of literary and social gatherings."[18] Often they were the subject of description and praise by Arab male poets. A ninth-century treatise dedicated to these pretty and frivolous slave girls allows one to look at, talk to, joke and flirt with them as long as one does not touch them. If one owns a *qayna*, he can use her as a concubine, but she is prohibited to admirers and concert fans. It happens that a number of admirers attached to one girl (see lines 13–14 below) meet in her house hiding from one another. "She, on her part, weeps with one eye to one and laughs with the other to the other, twinkles at this one behind that one's back, bestows her love on one in secret and on the other in public, making him . . . believe that she belongs to him alone."[19] Judah ha-Levi describes her in a concert:

> What an enchantress! So long is her absence—
>   and short are the lives of her lovers.
> Her beauty compares with the sun's.
>   Nay, she outsuns it—she never sets down!
> Her cheek is a rosebed—
>   with roses that never wither!
> She's soft and tender, so thin, that
>   a bracelet girdles her waist!
> Peering through dark veils of hair,
>   she shades the moon with a cheek so fair.
> Even when stripped, she's never bare—
>   grace, splendor, and beauty clothe her.
> "Welcome, you daughter of beauty!" all lovers salute you;
>   I'm one of many servants who greet you!
> . . . .
> My life for just one night of delight
>   that will free me from the prison of lust!
> [I fancy] sipping from the cup of her mouth, her ruby-red lips,
>   the nectar she drank from the mouth of her cup

. . . .
She parts her scarlet lips, holding the
    lute like a mother hugging her babe,
She leans to it, as if lending speech to its mouth;
    like a mother teaching her baby to speak,
She parts her lips to sing of parting; and as she trills
    her voice—here pour out her tears.
Her eyes pour water, crystal tears—but mine expend
    their treasures; it's red pearls of blood that my eyes shed.
. . . .
                            (Judah ha-Levi, *Dīwān*, 1:14)[20]

Love as a Linguistic Affair

These quite concrete descriptions, of the elegant princess and the alluring slave-singer, are, however, uncommon. The bulk of medieval Hebrew love lyrics address a fictional, almost abstract lady. Most poems are cast in the mold of the dramatic monologue: a man in love appeals to an absent lady, praises her beauty, implores her to pity him and to respond to his advances. It is the male who supplicates, yet it is he who controls the speech situation. The beloved lady inspires poets to sing about her and for her, yet she remains silent:

All hearts admire you—yours is hard as stone.
    All mouths praise only you—but you return silence!
            (Samuel ha-Nagid, *Dīwān*, 1:308)

There is a basic imbalance between the lovers: Man speaks, woman is mute. Woman is the absent addressee of the love poem. She is the subject matter of poetry but never "a speaking subject."[21] It is her missing voice that is echoed throughout the male poetic texts. And it is the man's speech acts—his supplications, imperatives, questions, threats, vows—which replace all real action:

Why, O gazelle, do you withhold your couriers
    from a lover whose loins ache for you?
. . . .

If parting is to be our lot, then
    halt a while, let me see your face.
Did my heart stop in my breast
    or did it follow your trek?
In Love's name! Cherish the days of my passion, as
    I hold dear the nights of your desire.
Let my image enter your dreams
    as I let yours walk in mine.
An ocean of tears roars between us; its
    waves bar me from reaching you.
But if your feet approached [its shores]
    its waters would split at once!
. . . .

Two are my witnesses that you have shed
    my blood: your cheeks and lips are red.
How could you deny this [double] offense—
    that my blood was shed, and that it was your hand?
Why do you seek my death?—I wish
    to add to the count of your years.
You steal my sleep in nights of longing, yet
    I'm bidding my sleep to your eyes.
Your fire has licked the waters of [my] tears;
    [nay,] your water has ground stony hearts to dust.
I jumped into the fire of my desire and the water of my tears.
    Alas! My heart [has sunk] in tears and ashes.
My heart lies amidst bitter and sweet—
    the poison of parting and the honey of your kissing.
I have put you as a seal on my right hand, wishing
    you will put me as a seal on your arms.
I'll forget my right hand from my left, O gazelle,
    if I forget your betrothal love.
. . . .

Remember me on the day you command to revive
    the victims of the passion [you ignited].
Return my soul to my body; my soul that
    followed you on the day of departure.
. . . .

Wish well for your lover, and
    let Time fulfill your wish.

Come back, and let God return you to your
   native soil and to your soul's desire.
                        (Judah ha-Levi, *Dīwān* 2:7–10)

The love affair becomes a linguistic affair, a desire enacted through language for an absent woman. As Jane Burns puts it, it is precisely the lady's absence/silence which is desired to promote poetic production: "The song he composes tends to objectify and distance the desired woman. . . . Poetic creation is generally motivated by the lady's rebuke; the choice of the poet to be a composer of songs depends precisely on his not being loved. . . . Longing for the lady becomes more valuable to him . . . than the possession of her."[22] Or, using Jacques Lacan's paradoxical metaphor: "Love is a love of the obstacle which forever thwarts love."[23]

    The lover's self-esteem and his ardor for life depend entirely on the woman he loves. Without her he is valueless and wishes death, preferably by her. When this suicidal rhetoric does not seem to affect his beloved, the lover would resort (as he does right in line 6 below) to straightforward seduction:

Go on fighting [me], a victim of desire,
   [Go on] kindling love with the flame of departure!
You loathe me, you draw your sword toward me—
   Go on, draw it! I loathe my soul no less!
O gazelle, it's no good enslaving your lover.
   Draw near and lay off the chariots of separation.
Turn the sickbed into a love-couch,
   breast-feed your lover with milk and honey!
                  (Judah ha-Levi, *Dīwān*, 2:34)

In a melodramatic apostrophe, the lover plays up his powerlessness. Already slain (*ḥalal*, literally, a body hollowed by a weapon) by love, he urges his armored beloved to penetrate him once again, this time to death. But then, in a sudden change of mood, not untypical of these love poems, the initial posture of love's martyr turns into an empty rhetorical gesture. What the lover truly desires is not his own death but the joys of love granted by a compliant beloved. He wishes that the cruel amazon would be transformed into a passionate nymph. But the dream lady never succumbs; she is remote and unattainable, and love remains ever one-sided and unconsummated.

The distance between lovers, so essential to the relationship, is rendered in ample motifs. It is created by parting and desertion of lovers, but also by social restrictions. Women's seclusion; the lady's superior status; the keeping with chaste norms, or the fear of tedious moralists, jealous neighbors, evil spies, and slanderers are all impediments to love. But above all distance is blamed on the lady herself, on her cruelty and haughtiness. In the poem below she is admired by a legion of lovers, all of whom she rejects. She speaks—and kills—with eyes, not words. She is a gazelle and a hunter in one. She is a heartless slave-owner, beating to death her devoted slave:

> For whom, O gazelle, do you sharpen your glances, pointed like lances?
>   Deal gently with me, sustain my heart, pity me!
> All hearts admire you—yours is hard as stone;
>   All mouths praise only you—but you return silence!
> Should you stab your slave to death with gazelle's eyes?
>   You'll have to pay—By God!—for your slave's blood![24]
>   (Samuel ha-Nagid, *Dīwān*, 1:308)

Her aloofness renders her a celestial being, one with the elements of heaven. Like Noah's rainbow after the flood (Genesis 9:13), she promises eternal peace, but then reveals her belligerent nature. Narcissistic and self-sufficient, she quenches her thirst with the crystal raindrops of her own tears:

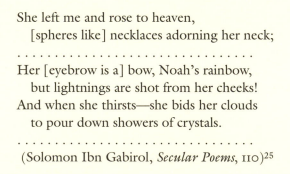

> She left me and rose to heaven,
>   [spheres like] necklaces adorning her neck;
> . . . .
> Her [eyebrow is a] bow, Noah's rainbow,
>   but lightnings are shot from her cheeks!
> And when she thirsts—she bids her clouds
>   to pour down showers of crystals.
> . . . .
>   (Solomon Ibn Gabirol, *Secular Poems*, 110)[25]

Messengers, real or metaphorical, bridge the distance between lovers:

> Would dawns chase me with the wind
>   that kissed her mouth and waved her frame;

Would clouds bring her my greetings—
    her heart would soften like her supple waist.
O gazelle, resting above stars,
    pity him who flies to his death.
                    (Judah ha-Levi, *Dīwān*, 2:45)

The lady is remote also as result of seclusion. She is immured within actual walls and, at the same time, enclosed within the loving heart. She is
paradoxically unapproachable yet most intimate:

Come out, pretty one, dweller-of-hearts,
    hurl flames from your radiant light!
Shine behind a veil, like the sun
    shines from behind clouds.
Enough hiding in innermost rooms—
    welcome a roused lover,
Let him carve pearls from between your lips
    like you've carved hearts out of his heart.
                    (Judah ha-Levi, *Dīwān*, 2:316)

Like the sun, the lady's beauty is radiant and healing. Her uniquenss is
such that even mighty Time (the personification of transience and fate)
desires her:

    O Sun, from behind a heaven of [dark] hair / reveal your bright
        cheek,
    A glimpse of your splendor / will save me, a slave, a hostage,
        lovesick.

    If Time schemed to kidnap you / and hid you like [Aaron hid the]
        manna,
    Have my heart / as your sound and a safe dwelling.
    If I bind you in my mind— / what will Time do?
        If I forget your image, O sun / I'll forget my Maker!
        You are my wish, my desire— / What's Time to me?

    Why rebuke a tortured heart / your encampment?
    An angel I deemed you / yet you set my thorn-bush aflame!
    If you wish my death—lo, / call me! here I am!

I'm not lying—I swear— / make a wish!
My days are few; and if you had mercy / I'd give them to you!

Why should I fear? Your face / is my light, my sun, my moon.
I seek sipping nectar and balm / from between your teeth, but soon
I'm halted by the weapons of your eyes— / your fury and ire.
  It's no weapon that kills me, O lady, / it's my desire.
  Hasn't your rosy cheek / promised to save me?
                              (Judah ha-Levi, *Dīwān*, 2:324)

Ferocious amazon or fierce hunter,[26] her lethal glances are contrasted
with her frail, harmless, gazelle-like beauty. She is a gazelle that devours
lions, or else a gazelle and a huntress in one:[27]

My love, will you free a gazelle that fell in a pit?
  Just send him the scent of your outfit.
Is it red paint that reddens your lips?
  Is it fawns' blood smeared on your cheeks?
Make love to your lover, reward him with love—
  Take my spirit and soul as your price.
My heart, pierced by both your eyes, will rise from the dead
  With your necklace—or even with one bead!
                              (Samuel ha-Nagid, *Dīwān*, 297)

This poem is an exquisite example of the sophisticated art of the Hebrew Andalusian poem. The huntress, the trapped male gazelle, the victim's blood, the prison of unrequited love, and the redeeming odor of the
beloved's clothes—all these are motifs imported from the repository of
Arabic poetry. However, the mesh of biblical echoes instills the stock
metaphors with freshness and playfulness.[28] Right in the middle of the
poem the victim offers a change of rules: no more hunting games, but fair
play. He will give her his soul if she gives him her body. He will readily die
for her because he believes in her power to bring about his resurrection.
Just a glimpse of her, or even the sight of just a single bead of her necklace, will suffice to revive him. But the poem's last verse lends itself to an
even more macabre insinuation: the dead bead is what was once the
lover's living heart! The cruel huntress steals hearts, perforates them with
her gaze, and then threads them into a necklace.[29] The lover sarcastically
consoles himself now—his dead heart, turned into an ornament, will

(as he had always desired) rest on his beloved's heart, enjoying thus a second life.

There is an established inventory of images and figures of speech put in the lover's mouth and aimed at gaining the lady's favors. The lady's face and body are dismembered into a catalog of limbs, each compared to another exquisite object. Her cheek is a lily or a rose-bed; her mouth a silken thread; her breasts ripe fruit; her waist a supple branch. She is often described as an artifact, with rocks and gems connoting her frigidity and cruelty: her heart is a rock; her breasts, stone-apples; her neck, an ivory tower; her cheek, red rubies; her teeth, pearls; her tears, solid crystals.

The lady is also a site of contrasts, with each of her parts contradicting another. Her "garden" is tempting, but the guarding serpents (her serpentine hair-locks) are terrifying. Her breasts seem like blameless rounded apples, but their pointed nipples stab like spears. Her nectar attracts but her arrows threaten:

> . . . She lures all hearts; she's bitter
>   yet so sweet she is!
> She sharpens lethal spears;
>   she draws swords from her sheaths,
> Yet she teases me with eager eyes
>   like a gazelle in thirst.
> . . . .

(Solomon Ibn Gabirol, *Secular Poems*, 110)

> The gazelle's locks surround her cheeks
>   like serpents guarding her fruit.
> Pause and watch that wonder!—
>   Both lie there, my heart's malady and its cure!
> It's my heart that her serpents bite.
>   So close to her cheeks—yet her they don't bite!
>   (Todros Abulafia, *Dīwān*, 1:40)

Color contrasts hyperbolize her beauty. Most common is her image in black and white: Her pale face is a sun hidden behind thick clouds of dark hair; she outshines the moon and the dawn; she is a miraculous midnight sun. Watching the marvel of her chiaroscuro portrait, the lover exclaims the liturgical morning benediction:

When I see the grace
Of morns and eves
Kiss your hair and face, I bless:
    "Blessed be He who made light and created darkness!"
                            (Judah ha-Levi, *Dīwān*, 2:50)

Redness of lips and cheeks is often added, with comparisons to roses, rubies, a crimson thread, and also blood. In the following poem the red is, exceptionally, the beloved's reddish hair:

The night the girl gazelle displayed to me
    her cheek—the sun—beneath its veil of hair
Red as a ruby, and beneath a brow
    of moistened marble (color wondrous fair!)—
I fancied her the sun, which when rising reddens the
    Clouds of morning with its crimson flare.
                            (Judah ha-Levi, *Dīwān*, 2:20)[30]

The lady's beauty and the lover's agony—expressively sketched in black, white, and red—are parallels and opposites at the same time. Moreover, they are mutually enhancing: He suffers because of her beauty; but the more he suffers, the more beautiful she becomes:

She painted her eyes with ashes from my heart;
    her teeth stole the luster of my pearly tears;
Her face—red and white—is dyed
    With my white hair and my liver's blood.
                            (Todros Abulafia, *Dīwān*, 1:38)

In a more radical reading, the poet may be shown to betray here, by inversion, his own manipulative art. While he blames her for stealing his features to construct her beauty, he exposes the technique by which he himself robs her pretty features to construct his own beautiful poem.

The conventionalized rhetoric of oppositions, paradoxes, and conceits, allegedly intended to highlight the lady's (and also the poem's) beauty, strongly implies the notion of woman's double face:

Balm [lies] in her face and on the thread of her lips—
    Death [lies] in her eyes and under her skirts.

I smile when she's glad—she smiles when I'm mad,
   I rejoice in her joy, she enjoys my rage.
               (Samuel ha-Nagid, *Dīwān*, 302)

Her true ("under her skirts") brutal nature contradicts her becoming appearance. The duplicitous female, whose exterior conceals her interior—a notion understated and implicit in love poetry—is central to the perception of woman in medieval misogynistic discourses.[31] What woman-haters say repeatedly and vehemently about women's dangerous beauty can ironically be redirected at their own love poetry. The elegant rhetorical finery of the love poems is sometimes deceiving apparel which conceals their antagonistic opinions about women.

Gazelle Gazing

Abdelwahab Bouhdiba's assertion that "Arabic poetry became a hymn to the eyes and a symphony of the gaze" can readily be appropriated to the Hebrew love lyric.[32] With love being ideally *un*consummated in this love poetry, it is the gaze which attains the utmost reality.

In a chapter titled "Of Hinting with the Eyes," the Andalusian author Ibn Ḥazm, extensively explored the semiotics of the eye. It is with eye language, he claimed, that lovers perform a wide range of speech acts: "By means of a glance the lover can be dismissed, admitted, promised, threatened, upbraided, cheered, commanded, forbidden. . . . A glance may convey laughter and sorrow, ask a question and make a response, refuse and give—in short, each one of these various moods and intentions . . . cannot be precisely realized except by ocular demonstration."[33]

The eye, he added, "is the most eloquent, the most expressive and the most efficient" of all senses. While pondering the projections, inversions, and displacements occurring in an ocular act, Ibn Ḥazm inadvertently formulates a theory of narcissistic gaze, foreshadowing Freud and Goldin (discussed below in this chapter). Based on Greek physiognomy, he compares a gaze into the mirror (resulting from the encounter between a ray issued from the eye and a ray issued from the mirror) to seeing oneself in the eyes of the other: "When the eye's rays encounter some clear, well-polished object . . . those rays . . . are reflected back, and the observer then beholds himself and obtains an ocular vision of his own person. This is what you see when you look into a mirror; in

that situation you are as it were looking at yourself through the eyes of
another."

But whose *eye* is it? And whose *I* does it serve? As the texts commonly have it (and as illustrations throughout this chapter show), the
eye—longing, teasing, penetrating, killing—is the female's eye. (Only in
crying is labor divided—the crying eye is usually the male's; the *falsely*
crying eye is the female's.) Using modern theories of "the gaze," I will attempt now to deconstruct this gendered phenomenology of the eye in
the Hebrew love lyric.

> Graceful gazelle, pity [my] heart / that is your cloister.
> Heed, the day you go away / is my day of disaster.
> My eyes, when breaking through / to watch your luster,
>   Met with the serpents circling your cheeks; / spitting venom,
>   They set fire in me / and scare me away from you.   5
>
> She robbed my heart with breasts / that lay on a heart;
> A stony heart that bears / a pair of apples,
> Jutting, left / and right, like spears,
>   Inflaming my heart / without even touching it;
>   They suckle my blood with their mouths, / unabashedly.   10
>
> The gazelle violates divine / law with her eyes.
> She kills me purposely / but pays not for my blood.
> Have you seen [in one] a lion's heart / and gazelle's *eye*lids?
>   Skilled in tearing prey like lions / and in sharpening arrows,
>   They suck and sip my heart's blood, / and seek for my life.   15
>
> . . . .
>   (Judah ha-Levi, *Dīwān*, 2:6)

The look—both looking at and being looked at—lies in the core of
this poem. The male speaker presents himself as traumatized by the female's devouring eyes, though the initial gaze, desiring "to watch her lus-
ter," is his own. It is by the expression "my eyes . . . breaking through"
(*yehersu ʿeinai*) that he betrays the violence of his own gaze. In using the
verb *h.r.s.* (connoting a violent transgression into a sacred space, as in Exodus 19:21–24), the male speaker characterizes his gaze as a violation of the
female's lustrous sanctuary.[34] Nevertheless, he sees himself as victim, and

the woman as aggressor. It is she, he says, who violates God's laws and gets away with murder (lines 11–12)! He finds his being looked at by the female intolerable, life threatening, annihilating.

Laura Mulvey's theory of the gaze may explain this kind of inversion: "According to the principles of the ruling ideology, the male figure cannot bear the burden of sexual objectification" caused by a female's gaze.[35] In her analysis of cinematic narrative and its gendered structures, Mulvey maintains:

In a world ordered by sexual imbalance, pleasure in looking has been split between active/male and passive/female. The determining male gaze projects its fantasy on to the female figure, which is styled accordingly. In their traditional exhibitionist role women are simultaneously looked-at and displayed, with their appearance coded for strong visual and erotic impact so they can be said to connote *to-be-looked-at-ness*. Woman displayed as sexual object is the *leitmotif* of erotic spectacle: . . . she holds the look and plays to and signifies male desire (p. 19).

For Mulvey, man's being the master of "the gaze" is correlative to his control of language. In the patriarchal symbolic order, "man can live out his fantasies and obsessions through linguistic command by imposing them on the silent image of woman still tied to her place as bearer, not maker of meaning" (p. 15).

Mulvey's insights about the gendered roles of viewers and characters, already embedded in the cinematic gaze, are most fruitful, so I find, to the reading of our medieval love poems, where the gaze is also signified by a gendered division. It is the male lover/poet/onlooker whose speech/gaze constitutes the female as an object of desire and horror, and it is he who presents himself as the object/victim of her glances. In other words, the signification of both gazes is all in his hands.

In the above poem, as is the genre's convention, the face of the graceful gazelle is encircled with venomous, scaring serpents, barring the lover from reaching her "fruit." However, here the implications of the clichéd imagery are extended to extremes. Her breasts, initially compared to a pair of inviting juicy apples, undergo a set of figurative metamorphoses. They turn "stony," and then are likened to erect spears, which, in turn are transformed into thirsty vampires. This mixed metaphor renders the life-giving suckling breast, the issuer of vital juices, into a blood sucking creature (lines 7–10).[36] Similarly, her innocent-but-cruel eyes, sending lethal arrows, turn into gulping vampires (lines 13–15). Establishing, through the vampire imagery, an analogy between her pair of breasts and her pair of eyes, her body becomes that of a monster, full of eyes/breasts/mouths.

An association, almost an unavoidable one, with Freud's "Medusa's Head" arises.[37] Relating to the image (common in art, as in our love poems) of the woman's hair as multiple snakes, Freud formulates the equation of Medusa's head with the female (the Mother's) castrated genitals, the sight of which provokes the terror of the castration of the onlooker himself. "To decapitate = to castrate. The terror of Medusa is thus a terror of castration that is linked to the sight of something." Furthermore, Freud equates the petrifying effect of looking at the Medusa with erection. In Freud's interpretation, the snakes both provoke and mitigate the horror; they replace the penis, and thus confirm its presence. Thus the same sight which enhances the fear of castration is also consoling the spectator, reassuring him of still having a penis. In the Greek myth, we are reminded, Perseus is able to finally decapitate, that is, castrate, Medusa only when he avoids looking directly at her face/genitals, and, instead, looks at her reflection in his shining shield.

Is not the love poem, through which the lover/poet looks at the sexual beloved, the equivalent of Perseus's shield? Is not the woman's artistic visage, poetically embellished, such an apotropaic shield which enables her castration, while, at the same time, reassures the male poet of his poetic phallus?

Rehearsing Freud's mutual link between scopophilia and castration anxiety, Mulvey makes clear how the horror turns into a pleasing fetish, a work of art:

Thus the woman as icon, displayed for the gaze . . . of men . . . always threatens to evoke the anxiety it originally signified. The male unconscious has two avenues of escape from this castration anxiety: pre-occupation with . . . the original trauma, . . . devaluation, . . . punishment, . . . or else complete disavowal of castration by the substitution of a fetish object or turning the represented figure itself into a fetish so that it becomes reassuring rather than dangerous. . . . This . . . fetishistic scopophilia builds up the physical beauty of the object, transforming it into something satisfying in itself.[38]

The first traumatic "avenue" is exemplified in the previous poem. The following poem, however, is a splendid illustration of the other avenue, that of fetishistic scopophilia, turning the fetish into an art object:

Pretty, tall as a flag, with curls like
   serpents—biting and curing her lovers—

She looks as if, at begetting her, her father was told:
"Make a [bronze] serpent and put it on a pole."
(Todros Abulafia, *Dīwān*, 1:40)

Phallic insignia (flag, serpent, pole) dominate this intricate miniature. While employing the conventional trope of the serpentine beauty that bites and cures, the poem also makes use of the biblical allusion to the "bronze serpent," the phallic fetish with which Moses cured the sick in the plague (Numbers 21:8). The looked-at woman, both castrated and phallic, turns, through this allusion, to be a phallic fetish. And it is her poetic "father" (line 3) who made her thus. Unlike in Freud, where the father is the castrator, the one who deprived the girl of the phallus she once had, here the father is the one who makes a fetish in fear of his own castration. He, the male onlooker, the maker of symbols, the creator of meanings, the male poet, disavows the threat of his castration by turning her into a work of art, an artifact, a gratifying object of worship. "The fetish in fact results from a real compromise and from a split between denial and affirmation of castration. . . . This compromise is sometimes visible in the construction of the fetish itself."[39]

This poem's imagery seems also to illustrate Lacan's identification of the object of desire with the phallus. By the power of language, the male constitutes the woman as the phallus, and thus has it:

[E]ven if [the woman] does not *have* the phallus, she may *become* the phallus, the object of desire for another. . . . Ironically, in this aim of becoming the object of the other's desire, she becomes the site of a rupture, phallic and castrated. . . . Paradoxically to be affirmed as the phallus is to be annihilated as woman. . . . The phallus functions only intersubjectively, for it is only by means of the other that one's possession of or identity with the phallus can be confirmed. . . . [T]hrough a man a woman can become the phallus (his object of desire); through sexual relations with a woman, a man be affirmed as having a phallus.[40]

If Mulvey, following Freud, speaks about the scopophilic drive as springing from a patriarchal unconscious which is "universal," Abdelwahab Bouhdiba, following Sartre, contextualizes the idea of looking at the other in Islamic society and culture.[41] He shows the exchange of looks to be but a deep social structure, immanent and vital in a society where walls and veils mark the spaces of gender:

The look, the last entrenchment of the frontier of the sexes, was to become the object of strict religious recommendations. . . . The confrontation of sexes as conceived by Islam, transforms each sexual partner into an "*être-regard*," being-as-a-look, to use Sartre's term. The "upsurge of the other's look" has been so clearly felt by Islam that one may speak quite literally of a subtle dialectic of the encounter of the sexes through the exchange of looks. . . . How to look and how to be looked-at are the object of a precise, meticulous apprenticeship that is an integral part of the socialization of the Muslim. To be a Muslim is to control one's gaze and to know how to protect one's own intimacy from that of others.[42]

The Fiction of Loverhood

A poet talks nothing but nonsense,
    setting his fiction in form of verse.
What is a poem but the tale of a liar,
    sung by a poet to the tune of the lyre?
A poem is garnished with tropes and lies,
    Like a tree is ornate with leaves.
Thus, it's the custom of bards
    to introduce untruths to their chants.
· ·
Many a poet would sing on passion alone,
    wasting their songs on lust;
One poet speaks always of love past,
· ·
Another swears he is drawn,
    heart and soul, not with ropes, to a fawn;
He would tell a gazelle stole his heart—
    but in fact he's inapt in the act.
· ·
(Todros Abulafia, *Dīwān*, 1:173–74)

In this disillusioned parody on poets Todros unreservedly divulges the secrets of his profession.[43] Poetic love is not a guileless gush but a literary fiction. Rather than a genuine expression of devotion and pain, the love poem is a sophisticated artifact. It is not personal confession but public entertainment. The love poem does not bear any actual referentiality to individual experience, and, at times, as Todros insinuates, it is quite the opposite which is true. Moses Ibn Ezra in his *poetics*, legitimizes erotic Hebrew poetry precisely on the basis of its conventionality and fictionality: "One can write love poems without having ever loved a woman."[44]

Dan Pagis, Ray Scheindlin, and others already pointed to the tendency of the Hebrew love poetry toward typical situations, ideal characters, recycled motifs, and stock imagery.[45] The conventionalized and stylized nature of the medieval love poem, together with the impersonal "I" of the male lover and the anonymity of the beloved, all enhance the poem's fictionality.

Much has been written about the fiction of love in other medieval love poetries.[46] Following Paul Zumthor, Jane Burns claims that the troubadour's *moi* is a generic feature, a grammatical convention of the love poem, and that the sentiment of love elaborated in poetry is "a product of social conditioning," a cultural construct articulated in the lyrical mold.[47] Writing on Persian court poetry, Julie Meisami asserts that the imagined love affair is intended to "provide the occasion for the poet's song and [is] the pretext for his presentation of the various states of love. . . . [The] experience itself is both an ideal and a fiction."[48] Frederick Goldin, whose approach both Burns and Meisami embrace, observes, in his study of the German minnesingers, a basic stereotyped fiction, "fragmented, analyzed into a fixed register of episodes, moods, postures, from which the poet draws in order to arrange a certain nonnarrative pattern. The courtly audience knew this fiction thoroughly . . . Every lyric finds its place in the fixed and universal fiction of courtly love."[49]

Central to this fiction is the feudal metaphor of the beloved as a queen-of-hearts who has dominion over a host of lovers. The lady stands above the law ("She kills me purposely / but pays not for my blood," Judah ha-Levi, *Dīwān*, 2:6). At times cruel, at times merciful, it is in her power to decree life and death to her vassals ("My heart is redeemed in the day of your grace; my doomsday lies in the day of your wrath!" Samuel ha-Nagid, *Dīwān*, 302). Her lovers, usually submitting to her tyranny, remind her, at times, that there is a high above high ("You'll have to pay—by God!—for your slave's blood!" Samuel ha-Nagid, *Dīwān*, 1:308).[50]

The lover's inferiority, submission, and devotion pertain also to the metaphor of love as religion. "My religion is the religion of love. I will never convert!" writes Judah ha-Levi (*Dīwān*, 2:322).[51] The lady's worshipers are the devotees of "the religion of love," an elaborate ideology of conviction and conduct.[52]

Here is the monologue of Love, personified as a feudal ruler demanding the total obedience of his/her (gender here is ambiguous) subjects:[53]

I am Love, ruling over / all living things.
I dwell in the hearts— / souls are my abode.

Noble minds are my lovers— / ignoble ones my foes.
Kings fight each other— / but all lie at my toes.
I have chased warriors / and triumphed over lords.
Gazelles are my troopers, / damsels draw my swords.
Lasses' breasts are my arrows, / gazelles' brows—my bows
· ·
My name is renowned on earth, / earls are my thralls!
                           (Todros Abulafia, *Dīwān*, 1:41)

Noblemen are both the slaves of love and its elite. He who is capable of love distinguishes himself both as a man and as a nobleman. Paradoxically, the more noble one is, the more is he capable of submitting himself to love, even to love of his inferiors.[54]

Kings [too] are prisoners of Love— / though they rule over rulers,
Oppress barons' hearts / and enslave their souls.
And so many lords, when in love, / become slaves to slaves.
                           (Todros Abulafia, *Dīwān*, 1:42)

Like the capacity for submission to love, the refined taste for exquisite love poetry is also considered a distinguishing mark of the courtly elite. In another poem Abulafia finds Love and Poetry mutually enhancing:

Earls raise their voices in our praise / while we laud damsels' beauty
· ·
We sing about damsels' love, while all poets/ turn their hymns to us.
[We are persons] never enslaved to anyone— / and now handmaids
    rule us.
Heaven is our footstool / while their feet tread on our hearts.
                           (Todros Abulafia, *Dīwān*, 43)

The dominance of the feudal metaphor in Todros Abulafia has in all likelihood to do with his biography and personal experience. As I have shown elsewhere, Todros, a Jewish courtier to two kings in Christian Toledo, assumed the garb of a Jewish cavalier and troubadour.[55] It has also been suggested that certain love poems by Abulafia might have been influenced by troubadour poetry.[56] However, the theme of submission to love, and especially love to inferiors, was present also in Arabic poetry and in Andalusian Hebrew poems.

In Muslim courtly circles "to be a devoted servant of love was . . . a defining quality of any man who claimed to possess *adab* [culture]."[57] The same holds true for the Jewish Andalusian courtier-rabbis whose poetry was a ritual manifestation of their class ideals. Much like their Arab comrades, "they used poetry to articulate their devotion to beauty as a cardinal value of the spiritual life . . . displaying a sensitivity so extreme . . . as to say: 'such is my capacity of submission to the power of beauty' "[58]

But must we accept these idealistic pretensions without any mistrust? Is the ethos of lovers and the aestheticism of poets above questioning? Is there not a hidden agenda, of individuals as well as of their social class, behind this "pure" idealism?

Sigmund Freud, in his exploration of the emotional foundation of chivalrous love, uncovered the egocentric gain of the romantic lover. When the lover elevates his beloved and abjects himself, it is *his* position as lover that is valorized rather than *her* unique qualities. Hence, in his devotion to a perfect love object the romantic lover seeks to prove his own value. In "producing" an ideal of a beloved woman he can love his love object as he loves himself and affirm his control over her. The ardent lover is in love with love itself as well as with his own position as lover. The repetitious style of love poetry is thus deeply connected to the nature of Freud's "serial lover" who repeats his commitments to endless women, all being replicas of the ideal one.[59]

Taking Freud's theories as his departure point, Jacques Lacan, relating specifically to courtly love, sees it as the deep structure of any love relation. Courtly love is not just an idealization, exaggeration, or aberration of "regular" love, but its very epitome. Hence, any human love is a love of the impossible, "a love of the obstacle which forever thwarts love." What lovers aspire to—the union of two in one—is an impossibility. The obstacle is not external, but is the internal condition of human subjectivity and sexuality. Courtly love is for Lacan a masculine self-deception, a way of refusing to recognize that the love for the woman is a quest for the ultimate Other. Thus, unlike Freud who emphasizes the narcissistic impetus of love, love for Lacan is always a quest for the other/Other.[60]

What Freud found in the individual lover Frederick Goldin relates to a social class. In his book on the minnesingers (the German troubadours), tellingly titled *The Mirror of Narcissus*,[61] he displays the love poet as being in love with himself. His mirror is the lady. Her "motionless and emotionless" (76) image personifies the perfection that he and his audience aspire to attain. She stands for all he "wants to become, what he can never be" (74). In loving the lady the love poet enhances his own social standing and is thus ennobled and empowered:

The unattainability of the lady and the suffering of the lover are ethical necessities in the fiction of courtly love. Courtly love . . . is the love of courtliness, of the refinement that distinguishes a class, of an ideal fulfilled. . . . This love-relation enables the courtly man to declare his commitment to the ideals of his class . . . and to exemplify the behavior in which those ideals are realized. . . . The [poet] describes for his audience how, in his devotion to this mirror of courtliness, he has known such suffering and joy as only a man of inherent nobility can experience. . . . This despair brings him great joy, for it proves beyond all doubt the steadfastness of his devotion . . . and his devotion proves his courtliness.[62]

But why should a female image be chosen to embody male values? How did the woman become the emblem of courtly manliness? Taking Goldin as a vantage point, Jane Burns develops a feminist critique of the troubadours. She argues that courtly love conceals not only class interests but also gender biases. The emphasis on the elevated male values (beauty, service, devotion, and so on) only screens covert misogynistic inclinations. The feudal metaphor, she says, is a "polished deceit," a manipulation employed for a sexual gain. The troubadour promises the lady everything if only she will make love to him—as do the Hebrew poets: "Make love to your lover, reward him with love— / Take my spirit and soul as your price" (Samuel ha-Nagid, *Dīwān*, 297); "Take my life as reward for just one night—that night in which your prisoner will be released" (Judah ha-Levi, *Dīwān*, 1:14). In Burns's view, courtly love is

an elaborate rhetoric of coercion disguised as service. . . . The poet's promise to serve his lady is a deft ploy designed to make her serve his ends. Whereas he stands to gain the much wished for *joi*, his dedicated service is not shown to produce any comparable reward for her. . . . [He is] subservient but dominant. Service is but a thinly veiled form of seduction leading ultimately to subjugation. [The] elevating of the lady to a position of dominance, is the very means towards taming and subjugating her."[63]

If the lady refuses she is denunciated as being cruel. Burns argues further that the admiration for the ideal lady conceals a profound ambivalence about female sexuality. Being a projection of male desire as well as of his phobias, "the ideal lady is thus rendered both powerful and sexual, a passionate Virgin and a compliant nymph. . . . [She] is not a woman at all. . . . [This] portrait of the Lady masks a fantasy of power which excludes the female" (268). Moreover, poetry becomes "the very tool which empowers the poet/lover against the object of his desire. . . . The purpose of his writing/singing is to attenuate the menace of female sexuality by codifying desire and seduction. . . . The end-product of this literary appropriation of sexual power is the portrait of the Lady" (266).

The Canon of Beauty and the Woman's "Thing"

Fatna Sabbah, a North African feminist, offers an even more extreme model than Burns's for the dual portrait of the female in Islamic writings, a model which, as I will later show, seems to work for the concept of woman also in medieval Hebrew poetry. Investigating the sexual semiology of various medieval discourses (poetic, philosophical, religious, legal, as well as pornographic), Sabbah points at two polar female images in the patriarchal Islamic imagination. One is the placid ideal of a lovely, silent, passive, and immobile woman, recommended by patriarchy as helpmate for the Muslim believer. The other is an "omnisexual woman," "a voracious crack." The latter is the raw material of which the first is forged. The domesticated, immured, and veiled woman is the end product. "[The] omnisexual woman [is] a creature whose most prominent attribute, which determines her whole personality and behavior, is her sexual organ, called in Arabic *al-farj* (slit . . . crack)."[64] While recommending the ideal of the placid, asexual wife, endless Arabic writings, according to Sabbah, are obsessed with fantasizing this "crack" enveloped by female flesh, and with the ways of either disciplining or satisfying it. This omnisexual woman is exclusively physical and lacks any spiritual or psychological dimension:

Her physical attributes (shoulders, arms, forearms, mouth, lips, cheeks, face, eyebrows, forehead, hair, neck, breast, waist, belly, hands, feet) are minutely captured in a rigid robot-like portrait to which whiteness of skin and blackness of hair take the lead. But the most important element in this portrait . . . is what she has between her legs. . . . Certain physical attributes, easily seen because exposed to view, like the mouth, lips, breasts . . . eyes, neck . . . provide precise information about the emotional capacity of this woman and the shape of the vagina, especially its narrowness. . . . A small red mouth, and hard, full breast indicate a narrow, hot vagina. . . . A large mouth reveals an enormous vagina."[65]

For Sabbah these are not simply "aesthetic" lists. "Beauty" is simultaneously the mask and the cipher of female crude sexuality. More than telling about women these beauty lists disclose the sexual imagination of Islamic patriarchy.

Hebrew poetry follows these images of the placid spouse and the sexual belle. In the epigram below the wife is portrayed as a picture of still life, a perfect apple. She stimulates all of her husband's senses but one. The missing sense of hearing highlights the absence of her voice; her silence is certainly no less of an attraction (and a requirement) than her other manifest assets. She is an Edenic fruit—forbidden to all other males—and allowed to her husband alone:

> Choose as your bed-mate a God-abiding wife,
>   one who resembles a perfect apple—
> Perfumed as is its scent, sweet as is its taste,
>   smooth as its skin, and pretty as its form.
> But unlike [a gold-cast][66] apple which none can touch or eat,
>   she is allowed to none—but to her husband's hand and mouth.
>   (Samuel ha-Nagid, *Dīwān*, 278)

The next Hebrew poem (by an anonymous, presumably twelfth-century Egyptian poet) is more explicit in treating woman's body as an assemblage of limbs:

> [. . .] A mouth as *round* as a signet-ring,
>   fit for a royal hand to seal with;
> Teeth that are like crystals,
>   or like the pellets of hail as they fall to earth;
> Also, a neck like the neck of a gazelle when
>   it thirsts and lifts up its eyes to heaven;
> Breasts like apples of henna,
>   studded at their tips with a bit of myrrh;
> A belly like white dough,
>   or like a heap of wheat;
> A navel at her belly like a cistern,
>   as though she were an *empty* well;
> Very *narrow* waist like the waist
>   of a bee as it flits through the vineyard;
> Legs like pillars, on which the thighs
>   can rest as well as ample buttocks;

> Hands and feet that are both *small*
>   and *fresh*, like those of a young girl;
> Wholly beautiful from head to foot,
>   flawless, perfect.
>
> . . . .
>
> And whoever falls in love with such a woman,
>   how can he ever fall asleep at night?[67]

The result of this meticulous fragmentation is flatness and superficiality, the lacking of an inner dimension.[68] Each limb is carefully measured, weighed, and compared through a precise simile to an accepted standard of perfection. Though somewhat reminiscent of the beloved's depictions in the Song of Songs, this catalog of female limbs is a reproduction of the Arabic beauty lists analyzed by Sabbah. The poem's indulgence on the features (italicized above) of roundness, emptiness, smallness, narrowness, and freshness of the female visible physique seem to implicate, as in Sabbah's formulation, "the shape of the vagina."

In a later poem,[69] this correspondence between the seeable and the unseen becomes even more explicit. Its blatant "mechanical" manner of description "lay[s] bare (so to speak) what many lyricists and romancers were already doing in better taste."[70] Significantly, woman's perfection is "scientifically" registered in this poem in "thirty-three conditions of beauty." These attributes are further categorized into triads: Length is commended in three features, the hair, hands, and legs; but ears, breasts, and teeth are preferred to be short. Three should be wide: forehead, chest, and hips. Thick should be her forelocks, arms, and buttocks; thin should be her hair, fingers, and lips; round—her neck, buttocks, and arms; small—her mouth, nose, and feet; white—her teeth, throat, and hands; red—cheeks, lips, and fingernails; black—eyebrows, eyes, and hair. The beholder is urged to choose the woman whose visible narrow organs disclose her hidden "thing":

> Look well, [o beholder], and choose the woman whose *thing* [*'inyan*]
>   is narrow, who has narrow thighs and waist.[71]

The vagina (like all other body parts) is beautiful *only* if it answers specific and narrow (so to speak) "conditions" of beauty, as prescribed by the tastes and needs of the male consumers. In this respect the "beauty lists" serve a similar function as today's "consumer's reports," helping man to choose the right product. Though perhaps sex-positive, the poem is clearly androcentric. And as if to prove Naomi Wolf's contention that " 'Beauty' is a currency system like the gold standard,"[72] our poet concludes his list announcing: "The woman who fulfills these conditions of beauty—not even the Gold of Parvaim [i.e., of the best quality] can measure her worth."

In her book tellingly titled *The Beauty Myth: How Images of Beauty Are Used against Women*, Naomi Wolf relates to such mandatory demands. Deconstructing the politics of "beauty," she forcefully argues:

The beauty myth tells a story: The quality called 'beauty' objectively and universally exists. Women must want to embody it and men must want to possess women who embody it. . . . Strong men battle for beautiful women. . . . None of this is true. . . . Like any economy [beauty] is determined by politics. . . . On what is it based? It claims to be . . . a celebration of women. It is actually composed on emotional distance, politics, finance, and sexual repression. The beauty myth is not about women at all. It is about men's institutions and institutional power.

Conventional Uniqueness

The beloved's ultimate beauty is claimed to be unique: her beauty is beyond description; the poet's praise of her is exclusive; none deserves to be lauded but her; her charms surpass words; they cannot effectively be listed or captured in poetic conceits, and so on and so forth. However, all these claims repeat well-worn rhetorical topoi. Contrary to their alleged uniqueness all poetic beloveds look alike. The superiority of one to all others is not expressed by completely newly coined imagery, but is rather a matter of degree. She is rendered unique either by a slight and sophisticated variation of a familiar motif or by the superlative mode. In the same vein, the lover's excessive suffering is also described by extreme imagery and by superlatives. His disaster is total; no suffering compares to his; words can hardly capture his unique state—yet all lovers are unhappy in quite a similar way.

Pointing to this paradox of clichéd uniqueness, Ray Scheindlin distinctly formulated that "the style of [the poets'] work is at odds with one of its dominant themes."[73] He resolves this paradox in stressing the ritual nature of the literary experience. Similar to Goldin's social observations about the minnesingers, Scheindlin maintains that "the courtier-rabbis of

the Golden Age used poetry as a ritual expression of an ideal shared by
their social class. . . . The poet's audience never tired of his celebration of
beauty and of himself as a uniquely sensitive man. . . . The poet's sensitivity was their own. . . . Hence the object of the love poet's adoration
is left . . . as unspecific as possible. She is not an individual but a shared
experience."[74]

The celebration of beauty as a class-shared experience pertains not
only to the poet's lady but also to the poet's art. While the lover is infatuated with female beauty, the poet strives to beautify his poem. While the
fictional lover (within the text) is busy with impressing a lady, the "real"
poet (acting in a social context) winks behind the lover's shoulder to a
real audience. It is the lover who declares "pure" ideals; the interests and
biases are the poet's. As a lover he is interested in consummating love, but
what nourishes his poetic muse is precisely the lady's absence! Commonly
it is the fictional lover who occupies the fore of the text, while the poet (as
person or persona) submerges to the rear. In the following pompous
monologue, the poet/lover presents himself in his double capacity, as the
master of love and the champion of song:

> I am a king—Love is my army,
>   Passion and Song are my servants.
> Song raised me over his sons,
>   Passion married me to his daughters.
> The audience of my love songs
>   draw pearls out of my words.
> For two things am I famous all over;
>   two are my titles: a Poet and a Lover!
> . . . .
>   (Todros Abulafia, *Dīwān*, 1:37)

The poem betrays the homosocial bond between the poet and his
male listeners/readers, a bond of which love poetry is a product. The
poet sings to an audience who enjoys his pearly words of love. While
singing about love and passion in the presence of other men, he gives
pleasure to other men and is himself pleased when they are pleased.

Another aspect of this male discourse is its intertextuality. While
acclaiming uniqueness, the poet also claims to surpass all other poets—
living and dead alike. While echoing his peers and predecessors, he
wishes, at the same time, to outdo them. A love poem, thus, does not

only desire for a (sexual) relationship with a woman, but seeks also to establish a textual relationship with other men's writings.[75] Thus, in the following poem, while exploiting conventional motifs, the poet also declares
his awareness of belonging to a long rhetorical tradition of male poets,
who, like him, have been singing about ideal female beauty:

> Like a rambler I roam by the hill of frankincense,
>   pressing my cheeks against your footprints.
> They mock me, I hear, their words plow furrows
>   on my back; I suffer because of you and for you!
> Poets have sung about you,[76] saying there's
>   no beauty like yours on God's earth.
> Why then do you paint your eyes with kohl?
>   Why do you redden your red lips with nut-oil?
>   (Samuel ha-Nagid, *Dīwān*, 299)

"Like a Woman": The Feminized Lover

There is another paradox pervading the love lyric: as lover the male is
powerless, yet, as speaker he controls the scene. The lover's servile position yields the petitionary rhetoric of the poem, yet, with his monologue
dominating the scene, it is the male speaker who manipulates the actual
speech situation.

It is to a similar misleading reversal of roles that Freud related when
he observed that the appearances of the romantic partners "belie the real
power relations invested in romantic myth." The woman *seems* to be powerful, superior, aloof, narcissistic, occupying a divine or royal position. The
man *seems* to be her obedient slave, desiring to fulfill her wishes. But, like
the phallic mother who both has the phallus and lacks it, says Freud, the
beloved is symbolically "superior" but realistically powerless.[77]

Phallic symbolism indeed abounds in the poetic descriptions of the
beloved woman in the Hebrew love lyric. Drawn out weapons, upright
branches, erect palm trees, towers, flags, and serpents are common images. The female is figuratively presented as bellicose and is thus masculinized. She is also masculinized, as Goldin's and Burns' argument goes
(see above), by becoming a symbol of courtly male values. The male, on
the other hand, is feminized; he features himself as penetrated (stabbed,
hollowed, perforated). While she is solid (like iron, stone, or crystal), he

uses for himself soft, liquid images. While she is ever an exterior, the male speaker projects himself, subjectively, from within. He is a receptacle of pain, blood, fire, and tears. His internal limbs disintegrate: his heart is broken, pierced, or torn, his ribs are burning and his liver and kidneys are melting. A whole physiology is devised to express his dismal state.

In the fragment below, the lover's interior, dissolved by the fire of passion, gushes out in rivers and showers of tears mixed with his blood. These floods are unable, however, to extinguish the painful fire; on the contrary, they rekindle it. Note how the hyperbolic metaphors of water and fire are fantastically manipulated as real nature forces:

> An ocean of tears roars between us; its
>   waves bar me from reaching you.
> But if your feet approached [its shores]
>   its waters would split at once!
> . . . .
> Your fire has licked the waters of [my] tears;
>   [nay,] your water has ground stony hearts to dust.
> I jumped into the fire of my desire and the water of my tears.
>   Alas! My heart [has sunk] in tears and ashes.
> . . . .
>   (Judah ha-Levi, *Dīwān*, 2: 8–9, lines 13–16, 29–32)

The lover's endless tear-shedding casts him as stereotypically "feminine." Unfulfilled love, maintains Roland Barthes, is of a "feminine nature." In his view, unlike in Freud's, no inversion of "real" power relations takes place in the romantic situation:

Historically the discourse of absence is carried on by the Woman: Woman is sedentary, Man hunts, journeys; Woman is faithful (she waits), man is fickle (he sails away, he cruises). It is Woman who gives shape to absence, elaborates its fiction, for she has time to do so; she weaves and she sings. . . . It follows that in any man who utters the other's absence *something feminine* is declared: this man who waits and who suffers from his waiting is miraculously feminized. A man is not feminized because he is inverted but because he is in love.[78]

Elaine Tuttle Hansen's feminist reading of feminized men in Chaucer is apparently quite similar. However, unlike Barthes, whose universalistic and essentialistic assertion seems itself to be tainted by stereotypical thinking, Hansen attributes essentialism to contemporary culture, not to the

"Woman." Describing Chaucer's male victims of love—emotionalized, vulnerable, submissive, subservient, self-sacrificing, suicidal, and in short "feminine"—she writes:

Men . . . cannot live with themselves in the emasculated state to which they have been reduced. . . . In fact, femininity, pervasively associated in medieval culture with passivity, weakness, irrationality, [and] self-indulgence . . . seems to be an almost inescapable condition for all the men in the world of the poem. [They] are caught up—like women—in the plots of other men, constrained by forces beyond their control and unable to rule their own destinies. . . . [M]en are always entrapped by heterosexual relations—if not in the lady's arms, then in a vicious circle of feminization.[79]

A man feminized by frustrated love and petrified by menacing forces is the protagonist in one of the earliest Andalusian Hebrew love poems:

Aroused by passion, I skip like a deer
    to peek at my [cloistered] beloved, so dear.
I come—she's there with her mother, encircled
    by father, and brother, and uncle.
I catch one glimpse—and then withdraw
    as if I'm not her friend, her beau.
Them I dread—but for her my heart mourns,
    like a woman mourning her only-born.
                (Isaac Ibn Khalfun, 63)[80]

An abrupt change takes place in this short poem. It begins with a young man, imaging himself as a potent, charging male animal, and ends with the man's self-image as a bereaved mother. The shift from Eros to Thanatos is enhanced by the symbolic gender reversal. It indicates not only the extent of the speaker's grief at love's labor lost, but above all his impotence, his unmanning. What causes this feminization is his alarming confrontation with the male relatives of his beloved. They are there to guard the girl's "honor."[81] Seeing them, he becomes aware of the gap between love (be it as chaste as it is here) and the patriarchal order. As illustrated by the spatial setup of the family—the girl and her mother are girdled by "father, and brother, and uncle"—romantic love has to stay outside the family circle. Knowing that the exposure of his desire might endanger the chasteness of his beloved, he chooses to pay the dire cost of giving up his love altogether. What makes this poem so outstanding is that the woman here is neither man's "other" nor his femme fatale but his true reflection. His "others" are other men. His escape does not liberate him; he is subjected to the law of the fathers as much as the woman who remains enclosed. Both, the female and the feminized man become equals here; both are victims of patriarchy. Hansen's observations are in order here:

Feminization in this world is hard to avoid because the rules of patriarchy are incompatible with the rules of courtly love. . . . Whereas patriarchy devalues the culturally feminine and insists on the difference between men and women as well as the power of the former over the latter, the heterosexual union, idealized by the laws of Cupid, values traits associated with femininity such as irrationality, self-sacrifice, submission, and service, and thus diminishes in theory both the difference and the power differential between male and female.[82]

In another poem, the lover manages to "cheat" and kiss the girl:

> Her cheek seems a shining star; her hair—a veiling cloud;
>   her breasts—ripe fruit; her figure—a tall bough;
> I cheated and kissed her—night spread its wings above;
>   we were the secret and night was the veil.
>   (Todros Abulafia, *Dīwān*, 1:107)

Their mutual secret, thickly veiled by cloud and night, suggests that it is not the girl that he cheated, but her guardians. Love is celebrated here despite the patriarchal prohibitions and constraints.

Divided against Her Self

Can a woman reader identify with the "universal" aesthetic and moral values of the male love poems? Experiencing herself as a reading subject, how can she enjoy poems into which women are inscribed as silent objects? It is indeed in the male love lyric, more than in any other body of poetry, that the feminist reader becomes acutely aware of the rupture in her consciousness between her attraction to the enticing beauty of many of these poems and, at the same time, her resistance to the ways women are objectified and misrepresented in them.

Judith Fetterley's answer to the question of how a woman encounters an androcentric text is unambiguous. Such a text, she claims, "immasculates" the female reader; it teaches her to accept a male system of values as normal, legitimate, universal. This "immasculation" weakens her since her self-as-a-woman is constantly being divided against her self-as-a-"universal" reader. Her goal should be to become a "resisting reader": to expose the androcentricity of the "universal" text and thus to disrupt the process of her immasculation.[83]

Roberta Krueger focuses on the specific position of the feminist medievalist and suggests that it would help to read medieval texts from the perspective of a hypothetical medieval female reader. The way this reader can be reconstructed is by listening to women's resisting voices built into male texts. Krueger thus suggests to look for Fetterley's "resisting reader" in women's responses as they are inscribed in medieval texts. "By identifying with these female reactions to the text's male values the feminist reader will be able to reflect . . . upon her own female role."[84] A rare occasion to meet such an "inscribed reader" in a Hebrew text is inadvertently furnished in a scene in a *maqāma* by Judah al-Ḥarizi. A poet, in love with his patron's beautiful daughter, serenades her with polished yet clichéd love poems, and pleads to her to "open her ear." Her response is not just a rejection of a tedious wooer, but a straightforward feminist assault on his poetic endeavor: "Your discourse is lacking in reason and wisdom. / Your poem is like all poetry of flattery and lechery."[85] She at once unmasks his romantic prattle as an attempted sexual harassment. And as Krueger observes: "The seeds of the reader's critical resistance, are sown within the text's ironic and self-reflective structure."[86]

Patrocinio P. Schweickart adds another dimension when she points to the irresistible power, even on feminist resistant readers, of some male texts. She urges feminist readers to ask further questions: "Where does the text get its power to draw us into its design? Why do some (not all) demonstrably sexist texts remain appealing even after they have been subjected to thorough feminist critique?"[87] Her answer is that the reading experience of the woman reader, especially in erotic texts, is emotionally bifurcated. She simultaneously identifies with the female figure *and* with the male protagonist. Identifying with the female object of desire alienates her; it puts her in the place of the "other." However, at the same time, she is captivated by the active male, the desiring subject, who strengthens, according to Schweickart, woman's own "desire for autonomous selfhood and for love." Considering this complex reading situation, Schweickart suggests that *"certain* (not all) texts merit dual hermeneutic: a negative hermeneutic that discloses their complicity with patriarchal ideology, and a positive hermeneutic that recuperates the . . . authentic kernel . . . of emotional power."[88]

Whereas Fetterley and Schweickart stress the emotional contradiction, Lea Dovev (in an essay about the female nude in painting) points at another breach embedded within the feminist response, that between the moralistic and the aesthetic. When encountering great masterpieces of nudes, often infected with misogyny, the woman viewer often becomes indignant with their values, but, nonetheless, she may, at the same time and against herself, enjoy these works *aesthetically*. It is as if one eye of hers is a woman's eye, says Dovev, and the other is neutral, innocent, genderless.[89] While realizing how problematic this assertion by Dovev is (assuming first, that a woman's eye is blind to beauty, and second, that there is such thing as an "innocent," disinterested position), I tend to accept hers, as well as Schweickart's, commendation of a "bifurcated" approach. In reading certain Hebrew male love poems, the feminist reader can mend the rupture. In certain outstanding poems, she can perhaps, even against her self, respond to their emotional impetus and aesthetic appeal.

3

Veils and Wiles:
Poetry as Woman

Woman as the Figure of the Text

WHEN TOUCHSTONE, SHAKESPEARE'S CLEVER fool in *As You Like It* (right in the middle of the play, act 3, scene 3), wishes to express his dissatisfaction with Audrey, his gullible and unsophisticated beloved, he says: "Truly, I would the Gods had made thee poetical." And when plain Audrey inquires: "I do not know what poetical is; is it honest in deed and word? Is it a true thing?" Touchstone answers: "No, truly; for the truest poetry is most feigning . . . if thou wert a poet, I might have some hope thou didst feign." The jester wishes his beloved to be "more poetical . . . most feigning," that is, to be his selfsame. While following the common late medieval trope (poets lie as do women), Shakespeare turns this comparison on its head in demanding that woman become the like of the poet—dishonest "in deed and word."

The jester's desire for a mate to match his skepticism, to undermine his poetic "truths," and to respond with poetical "truths" of her own is frustrated. In the absence of such a female mate, Shakespeare dialectically foreshadows the Nietzschean ideal of the female as skeptic; the female who, like the poet and the postmodern philosopher, is aware of the elusive nature of truth. The female's distrust of the truth, according to Nietzsche, derives from the fact that she does not ever consider truth; truth does not concern her. And so, for Nietzsche, woman paradoxically becomes the symbol of elusive truth, that same alluring but noncommittal entity, beguiling and seductive, that the male forever tries to attain—but in vain. Jacques Derrida, in his reading of Nietzsche, uses the metaphor of woman to describe Nietzsche's own skeptical standpoint.

The skepticism of the woman, for whom the only truth is the realization that there is no truth, coincides with the philosophical view that Nietzsche exemplifies and which underlies his thought. It is from this stance, "woman's stance," that the deconstructive project begins. Woman's skepticism becomes the model for a deconstructive reading that exposes the relativity of meaning. "The discourse of man," writes Gayatri Spivak about Derrida, "is in the metaphor of woman." This shift in modern thinking is seen by her as "a feminization in the practice of philosophy.[1]

What are the uses of "the metaphor of woman" in the discourse of medieval Jewish poets and poeticians? As I will attempt to show in this chapter, the act of positioning woman as the figure of the poetic text was not alien to medieval Jewish poets and philosophers, whose theories of poetry—much like those of their non-Jewish colleagues—implied genderized notions of poetry. What was conventionally perceived as the inherent problem of poetry—its beauty versus its untruth—was cast in the mold of contemporary stereotyped perceptions of "femininity." This association between the beautiful-but-untruthful poem and the attractive-but-deceitful female was exploited in a variety of modes and resulted in varying attitudes toward poetry and the poetic enterprise.

In my exploration of the trope of "poetry as woman," I dwell on the basic dualisms which underlie the medieval conceptualizations of "poetry" and "woman," showing how each of these terms became the embodiment of dualism and ambiguity, and, consequently, how these terms became synonyms and substitutes for each other. My line of argumentation will first contemplate the subtext (itself ambiguous) of poetic beauty—the notion of *poetry* as ornament and garment, and thus as a cover of or subsidiary to truth. Then, considering the convergence of *woman* with ornament and garment, I will follow to the implication of woman as being the concealer of her essential (un)truth (and hence the enemy of truth).

Surveying the equation of woman and poetry in a historical perspective, I was also able to trace a steady path in the conceptual genealogy of the trope. In the early poets (eleventh and twelfth centuries) the manipulation of the trope seems rather "innocent." Beauty is praised even at the expense of untruth ("The best of poetry—its lies."). In later poetics, however (from the thirteenth century on), poetry's falseness comes to the fore. My argument throughout this chapter is that the attitude to poetry and poets became increasingly adversely affected by attitudes typical of medieval misogyny. A strong analogy thus becomes manifest between the disdain for women in Aristotelian philosophy (and the female phobia in ascetic writings) on the one hand, and the rejection of poetry, up to the point of its total delegitimization, on the other.[2] *Misopoiesis* and misogyny will be shown to be mutually enhancing.

The Ornaments of Poetry

Like a woman, poetry is required to be beautifully decorated. What makes poetry beautiful is first and foremost its use of rhetorical ornaments. (The Arabic *maḥāsin al-shiʿr* or *badiʿ* are the equivalents of the Latin *ornatus*.) Comparisons to embroidery and jewelry are commonplace in Ibn Ezra, as they are in Latin and Arabic poetics of the time. Moses Ibn Ezra, the most prominent representative of Arabic poetics among Hebrew poets, stated in a poetic tract written in Arabic and modeled upon Arabic theories of poetry, that rhetorical devices adorn the literal utterance "as a fancy garment adorns the naked figure."[3] The naked, literal speech is truth (*ḥaqīqa*, or *muḥkam* in Arabic), but naked truth, unadorned by lies, is not what poetry is made of. Poetry's embellishments are its images and metaphors (*majāz*).[4] While expanding on metaphor, Ibn Ezra claims that: "Naked speech, when it is clad with the festive garments of metaphor, and wears the jewels of enigma and allusion, then its silken embroidery is enriched, and its enamel enhanced. For ornate speech relates to nakedness as eloquence relates to stammering."[5]

In the name of Aristotle, he urges poets to study the rules of eloquence and "ornaments" ("poetry's tools and devices"), whose presence beautifies the poem, and whose absence makes it unsightly and deficient.[6] No explicit link is made here between the beauty of the poem and its femininity. Similarly, in Arabic poetics the ornaments (or garments) of poetry are neither masculine nor feminine. However, the affinity between poetic ornamentation and femininity is made manifest in Hebrew poetry.[7] When a Hebrew poem relates to its own beauty (in self-referential or ars-poetical passages), it beholds a female face (or rather a veil) in the mirror.

In the following example the author of an epistolary panegyric likens his faultless poem (*shira*) to an elegant bride. She is sent by her father, the author, to her bridegroom, the poem's addressee—in this case, Samuel ha-Nagid:

Accept this perfect, well-proportioned poem,
    a present given out of pure, everlasting love.

She is enveloped in her attire as a bride,
    secured in her jewels as a maiden.
You are her fiancé—though she is to remain forever a virgin,
    I am her father—though she is an orphan.[8]

Not only is a poem ornamented, it is itself an ornament. Samuel ha-Nagid praises his own poem saying: "My discourse adorns my books like / exquisite jewels adorn a perfect bride" (*Dīwān*, 73:33). Or: "O brother, put on this ornate / jewel and let it adorn you! // It is a poem, perfumed / like a scented bride" (150:19–20). And admiring a poem sent to him by a colleague, he writes: "Your handwriting is splendid / like emeralds set in lines . . . // And their scent is like myrrh coming / from a perfumed bride" (34:1, 4).

But a different variant on the woman-poem analogy is also brought into play. The ungainly poem, that which does not meet the required aesthetic standards, is also likened to a woman. Samuel ha-Nagid expresses his disappointment to a poet who sent him an inadequate poem. Before he read the poem he assumed it to be "a revered princess" or a "royal paramour," perfumed in many scents, but after having read it he found it undeserving of mingling in the noble assembly of the poet's other poems: "I weighed this poem against your others, they are / bridegrooms, while she is like a menstruating woman" (*Dīwān*, 228:6). Poetic beauty here is masculine ("bridegrooms"), while its obverse is identified with the unclean female. This strange metaphor for an imperfect poem begins to make sense if we remember that the term for eloquent language in Hebrew was *lashon tzeḥa* (cleansed, clear, purified language), and that the art of rhetoric was called *Tzaḥot*. Hence, the poem is valued or rejected according to the same criteria of purity by which the woman is conventionally judged.

The use of feminine ornaments becomes quite bizarre in ha-Nagid's most virile poems of war. The poems are "bracelets" on his arms and "earrings" in his ears, and they exude "myrrh and aloe" (*Dīwān*, 14:143–44).[9] The same ornate imagery is used in war poems as in enthusiastic hymns to God, the Lord of Hosts:

To God whose deeds are magnificent, I'll magnify my poem.
    She will rule over all other daughters-of-poetry,
With utterances woven like sapphires
    and phrases sown like crystals . . .
               (Samuel ha-Nagid, *Dīwān*, 14:137–38)

The poet also boasts in his beautiful and forceful war-poem whose demeanor is that of a haughty lady-warrior: "A poem strides along, her head and neck raised over / other poems, like a military commander surveying his troops" (138:53).

The Veil and What Is Underneath

A good poem, then, is a beautiful one, and its beauty is exhibited as "feminine." This "feminine aesthetic" is far from being innocent. In medieval thought and poetry, beauty is the first and often the only attribute required of a woman, yet woman's beauty is charged with ambivalence. Beauty can easily turn into its opposite. The beautiful young lady turns out, when unveiled, to be a repulsive monster, an old hag,[10] or else—a male in disguise.[11] This phobia of unveiling reveals the male's anxiety about the transformation or deformation of female beauty. Whether it is ephemeral or dangerous, woman's beauty is never what it appears to be. And the lover praising the lady's beauty knows it:

> Balm [lies] over her face and on the thread of her lip—
> Death [lies] in her eyes and *beneath her skirts.*
> (Samuel ha-Nagid, *Dīwān*, 302:1)

This is not simply a statement about woman's dangerous allure. The sophisticated set of oppositions implied here—(sur)face/depth; red lips/(labia); (life)/death; balm/(reek)—suggests that each exterior sign should be read as its opposite. Beauty masks woman's "nature" (and *natura* in medieval Latin also means "genitalia.") Lacan (and Freud) would agree with our poets as to the signification of woman's artifice, "her thick veil": "[She] can only seduce when at least one veil remains. . . . [Woman] retains her position as the object of the other's desire only through artifice, appearance, or dissimulation. Illusion, travesty, make-up, the veil become the techniques she relies upon to both cover and make visible her 'essential assets.' They are her means of seducing or enticing the other."[12]

But woman, so maintains Freud in one of his most misogynist utterances, has a better reason to stick to the veil. "For wishing to remain enigmatic, she has to hide this 'cavity filled with pus,' she has to hide the fact that she has 'nothing' to hide. By seeking to make herself enigmatic, woman is only continuing the work begun by nature, which covered over her sex with pubic hair. Woman in inventing weaving was only imitating nature."[13] Freud remains ambiguous as to the source of woman's modesty/shame. Is it natural or cultural? Is modesty "a trick of nature" to cover woman's natural defectiveness? Or is it an artifice by which women "can excite and charm men, who would otherwise recoil in horror before that gaping wound that threatens to contaminate them"?[14]

The ambiguity of the veil is unveiled in Samuel ha-Nagid's following epigram:

> Walls and castles were erected for woman—
>   her glory lies in bedspreads and spinning.
> Her face is pudendum displayed on the main road
>   that has to be covered by shawls and veils
>   (Samuel ha-Nagid, *Ben Mishle*, 283)[15]

"Modesty," as the poem divulges, is not woman's own virtue, but a euphemism, a semantic veil on "shame" imposed by patriarchy. Textiles, veils, and skirts should neutralize woman's corrupting influence. But is the veil a barrier to sexuality or a manifestation of it? Is this investment in vestment effective? Chaucer's Wife of Bath ridicules this very dialectic of "chastitee and shame" in her rereading the Apostles' "text" regarding modest clothing, a text quoted to her by her husband.[16] As she shows, the garment itself is unreliable. It undermines its purpose. Instead of concealing shame, it becomes the extension of the female's seductive body. Clothes cover the contours of bodies, and, as they substitute anatomy, they symbolize it and publicize it.

In ascetic writings men are chided to flee the temptation of woman's beauty. The man who is wise is warned about the fire burning underneath the glowing (sur)face:

> Do not let woman's beauty to tempt you
>   and lust to entice you.
> Behold her cheek, glowing like a candle, but if,
>   my son, you approach, its heat would consume you.
>   (Abraham Ibn Ḥasday)[17]

To avoid marriage is to avoid the nexus of woman and garment. These are a dying father's last words: "Do not take a wife. She talks peace but means trouble. . . . You'll clothe her with silks and satins and she'll fornicate with strangers. . . . Do not let your heart desire her beauty. Banish evil from your midst." But sure enough the disobedient son does marry, and right away does his newly wed wife demand dresses, earrings, veils, wraps, shawls, gowns, mantles, nose rings, purses, and so on.[18]

The double-faced nature of the woman also makes her a convenient figurative vehicle for the representation of the terrestrial world.[19] This material world of vain appearances, as constructed in these texts, is seductive and hazardous. It assumes the freight of the femme fatale, or that of the Great Mother, and as its main intertext relies on the image of the whore from Proverbs 7 (which we will revisit later). She wears purple silks and velvet skirts under which she hides her daggers; she is embellished with fine perfumes, but her flesh stinks; venomous medusan vipers lurk among her locks. The world (*Tevel*) is a whore feeding her suitors with "bread of deception" and poisonous wine. The wise male, the philosopher or ascetic, has to reject *Tevel*'s worldly allurement and call the whore's bluff. (" 'A harlot,' I called you to your face, witnessing your lechery and lewdness," Moses Ibn Ezra.) He has to discover/uncover her real whorish face. And he will best do so by "raising the rim of her coat over her face, and exposing her genitals."[20]

Inasmuch as clothing is described as the female's perversion, the male is required to develop an aversion toward it. The revulsion toward the garment reflects the disgust with body and flesh. The ascetic is expected to shed his body and, indeed, the material world, as one takes off a shirt. The purity of the soul lies in its nakedness, in its freedom from the yoke of the body and corporeal passions. In this context, nakedness is signified as positive while clothing is signified as negative.

This ambivalent dualism of body and clothing plays a part in various medieval commentaries on Creation. In Midrash Bereshit Raba on Genesis 3:7, the sages wonder about Adam's and Eve's "eye opening"—were they blind before? Their answer is: "Even that one *mitzvah* which they had been given, they stripped off." The metaphor inverts the "facts" of the story: When the first couple were naked—they were actually "clad" (with the *mitzvah*), but when, after loosing innocence, God gave them clothes—then they were really "naked."[21]

"With words the garments entered," averred Tertulian,[22] thus linking, very much like Roland Barthes,[23] the dualism of signified and signifier in language with that of body and garment. For Tertulian, prelapsarian nakedness signifies the primal state of unity and innocence. The original sin, and its ensuing shame, introduced the dualism of essence and appearance, of surface and depth. No wonder, then, that in medieval semiotics and hermeneutics, the clothed body becomes the paradigm for metaphor and allegory. Language both cloaks true meaning and betrays it and is thus deceitful like a garment, or—like a woman. This nexus between "garment" and "betrayal" is splendidly exemplified in the Hebrew word *beged*, which carries both these designations. (Similarly, both *me'il* [mantle] and *ma'al* [betrayal] carry the same contradictory semantics.)[24]

The garment, then, is a grand metaphor in medieval thinking: It is the metaphor for figurative speech, and indeed for language at large. It is the trope of concealment and betrayal, ambivalence and dualism—and sure enough, it also becomes the synonym for woman herself.

Turn It Inside Out—Garment, Woman, Poetry

"One day as he [Socrates] was walking with his disciples in the cool of the day, there passed before him a woman of comely figure and beautiful appearance, and one of his disciples gazed at her. Socrates said to him, 'Woe is thee, wherefore dost thou gaze upon her? . . . Turn her inside out; then wilt thou understand her ugliness' "[25] To expose her vileness, woman has to be turned inside out. The spatial metaphor implied here is that of a garment; woman is like a fine coat with an ugly lining. Interestingly enough, Moses Ibn Ezra in his definition of poetry implies a very similar metaphor: "Poetry is an utterance whose back is unlike its belly." While, seemingly, "belly" and "back" use the image of a body's front and rear, the semantics of the Arabic word used by Ibn Ezra for "belly" (*baṭn*) alludes rather to the notion of "exterior" and "interior." Stemming from the same root are the Arabic words for "lining" (*biṭāna*) and for "interior" (*bātin*). As a literary term, *bātin* also indicates a figurative meaning, or "the hidden, abstract meaning of an allegory."[26] It is the implied metaphor of garment, then, which associates both utterances. Woman and poetry have to be turned inside out so that the inside (woman's true nature; poetry's truth) can be seen.

Poetry lies, says Ibn Ezra, as many Arabic critics had already stated before him. Nevertheless poets are the only liars, he opines, who are to be forgiven. Poetry lies with regard to its style, not with regard to its reference to reality. It seems that Ibn Ezra distinguishes between a poetic lie and a factual lie. A lie, in life as in poetry, is a deliberate distortion of the factual truth. The sophists are explicit liars, he says, and, like them "inferior" poets are lacking in morals. The poetic lie, however, is not a deviation from empirical truth, but a clash between the layers of language itself: between the literal meaning and the figurative "cover." The poetic lie occurs "when the poet leaves behind that which exists and embraces that which does not exist, and is interested in the figurative only." In other words, the ornate garment of the poems is not meant to represent reality, but only to allude to it. Moreover, this coupling of the literal and the figurative is precisely what distinguishes poetic language from other linguistic usage. "Poetic elegance is the aim of its practitioners." Indeed, the criteria for truth lie in its logical proof, but this precept does not apply to the poetic lie: "The poetic lie applies to the style of poets, not to their content." It is on this basis that Ibn Ezra draws his famous conclusion: " 'The best of the poem—its lie.' It has been said, 'the best of composition—its truth' and this is true; but it does not apply to poetry, since it has been said, 'the best of the poem—its lie.' A question regarding poets was answered: 'They are the only ones whose lies are forgiven' . . . and a poem devoid of lies, is not a poem."[27]

Moses Ibn Ezra forgives poets and defends poetry.[28] This liberal stance vis-à-vis poetry is exploited in poetry itself. Using it as a rhetorical device, poets warn their readers not to be entrapped in poetry's false speech:

> When a friend incites you with a dream-like, false speech;
>> when he recites poetry to deceive you—
> Lo, my son, not all dreams come true, and likewise
>> not all a poet says is truth.
>>> (Samuel ha-Nagid, *Ben Mishle*, 248)

> Enjoy my charming story, gentle friends,
>> But don't be taken in by what you've heard.
> A tale of lovers' folly this, no more,
>> A pack of lies—I made up every word!
>>> (Solomon Ibn Saqbel)[29]

> They asked me: "You smart one, who is it
>> who cannot tell good from bad?"
> . . . I told them: "It is I, my friends;
>> I myself am the lying poet!"
>>> (Meshulam da-Piera)[30]

A poet talks nothing but nonsense,
   setting his fiction in form of verse.
What is a poem but the tale of a liar,
   sung by a poet to the tune of the lyre?
A poem is garnished with tropes and lies,
   Like a tree is ornate with leaves.
Thus, it's the custom of bards
   to introduce untruths to their chants.
. . . .

        (Todros Abulafia, *Dīwān*, 1:173)[31]

"Poetry's Daughter"

From the thirteenth century onward the simile—the poem is *like* a woman—becomes a metaphor. This is especially true of the Hebrew poets in Christian Spain, in whose imagination poetry is personified and awarded a name: *bat ha-shir* ("the daughter of Poetry").[32] Instead of the emphasis on beauty, evident in the earlier poets, it is the sexuality of the woman-poem that comes to the fore, thus amplifying the link between Eros and poetic creativity. "Poetry's daughter" is an enchantress: "She hunts her lover's heart without a hook / but with the sweetness of her mouth" (Solomon da-Piera, *Dīwān*, 15);[33] she adorns herself with the poet's good reputation, she flirts with him, and dresses him with a mantle of respectability:

She always wears your name like a bracelet
   on her arm, an earring in her ear.
She hugs and kisses you; she garbs you
   with a gown of glory and grandeur.[34]

In some instances, Poetry's daughter is the poet's intimate lover, in others, she is a young beauty put off by her elderly lover: "At old age, poetry's daughters are sick of me, as are all gazelles and pretty girls" (Todros Abulafia, *Dīwān*, 2:390). At times she is the poet's faithful maid: "Poetry's daughters are at his disposal, / cooking for him and serving his soup" (Solomon da-Piera, *Dīwān*, 46). The metaphor evolves into a dark family plot insinuating possible incest: Using his pen/penis, the poet fornicates with Poetry's daughter, who is his minor wife as well as his adopted daughter:

> Poetry's daughter [is] betrothed to my pen.
> Since I first desired her, I adopted her as my daughter,
>   and included her among my inheritors.
> At my hands she gathers strength as she gets
>   older, and keeps renewing herself.
>   (Solomon da-Piera, *Dīwān*, 16)

She is old (in her wisdom), but in the hands of the poet who cultivates her, she keeps her youthful appearance. And similarly in Abulafia: "In [carnal] matters she is young and virgin / but in her verbal skills, she's old and not-at-all-virgin" (*Dīwān*, 2:390).

In a series of invective polemical poems between Abulafia and a poet called Pinḥas, the sexual imagery becomes much more blatant, rather obscene. Poetry has not only daughters but also sons. Pinḥas claims that his own poetry is a male who will not go to bed with his rival's menstruating daughter until she purifies herself in a ritual bath. Abulafia retorts that his poetic daughter is a pure virgin, while his rival's son is an impotent who is unable to penetrate her even if she were a married woman.[35]

The femininity of poetry is intensified in metaphors of motherhood and childbearing. She is indeed the "daughter of poetry," but she is also the mother of poets!

> Poetry's daughter is the mother of armies of musicians.
> She keeps breast-feeding them until they are weaned.
>   (Joseph Ben Lavi)[36]

The poet impregnates the "mother of the poem" who gives birth to a "completely mature daughter" (Solomon da-Piera, 15:38). And: "Poetry's daughter is pregnant with eloquence; since my ideas / penetrated her—she who'd been barren" (Solomon Bonafed).[37]

The Portrait of the Poet as Liar

Beginning with the thirteenth century another shift takes place. Parallel to the emergence, in poetry, of the sexualized metaphor of poetry, a new, philosophical, quite abstract discourse evolves. This tendency, resulting in the wholesale rejection of poetry (which I would coin as *misopoiesis*), occurs mainly (but not solely) in speculative prose writing and essentially ignores the difference between figurative and factual lie. This attitude, as will be shown, is not to be divorced from the alleged "femaleness" of poetry and is indeed deeply embedded in it.

Two poets who draw extreme conclusions regarding their problematic occupation are Shem Tov Falaqera (Navarre, thirteenth century) and Qalonymos ben Qalonymos (Provence, fourteenth century).[38] In both instances, the authors do not hesitate to divulge their contempt for the poet's profession. Qalonymos scolds the poets for not "delving in the depth of the Halakha" (as real men should), engaging instead with the "feminine" indulgence of poetry. Qalonymos charges the poet with being haughty, having an enticing tongue and effeminate body language: "He sashays down the street, taking small, dainty steps, in a slow pace, like a pigeon." His audience is uncooperative, and the dandy poet chides them: "You fail to understand the art of my drums and my holes (*neqavai*) [of my flute]"—a remark which might be read as a vulgar insinuation concerning the "femaleness" of poetic art.[39]

These two authors identify the poet by his "saccharine" rhetoric and shallow aestheticism. "His palate is full of sweets," says Qalonymos, and Falaqera compares the sweetness of poetry to honey, butter, and nectar dripping from the poet's tongue and from his songs. In the preface to his *Sefer ha-mevaqqesh* (The Seeker),[40] Falaqera confesses his resolution "to give up the love poetry of the knights, to reject the songs of the troubadours and minstrels who wander about in the wilderness of desire, for all this is mere vanity and derision."[41] As a protest against the aesthetic/erotic appeal of poetry, both, Qalonymos and Falaqera, decide—midway through their books, as a matter of fact—to suspend rhyme. Both resort to writing in simple, unrhymed prose.[42]

In Falaqera, this decision takes place after his protagonist, called "The Seeker," meets a poet and is filled with disgust at his profession. The Seeker is an adventurous young intellectual in search of the truth. On his quest, he meets representatives of all social strata and occupations, proponents of the sciences and arts,[43] and stays with each of them for a period of time. His spiritual quest ends, of course, when he encounters the philosopher, with whom he will stay happily ever after.[44] But meanwhile, alas, he meets a poet, whose sleek way with words and feminine seductive charm he immediately detests. "His poems are [drenched with] rivers of honey and streams of butter; his lips drip honey and nectar runs from his songs; . . . rivers of oil pour out when he issues his words . . . with the grace of his lips he entraps the souls."[45] Poetry is too sweet, too oily. It's kitsch. In a long speech, using every possible Hebrew synonym and biblical allusion for lie, flattery, betrayal, and deception, the Seeker blames the poet for neglecting the real sciences and for wasting his time and brains on vanities. Poetry, according to the Seeker, is not only vain and futile, it is also blatantly fallacious:

Homo poeticus . . . I've been observing your poems . . . and have listened to your songs . . . and found your discourse sweeter than honey. . . . However, since God endowed you with intellect, it is your duty to investigate the *real sciences* and explore their secrets that deal with Man and his image. . . . It is improper for you to devote your time to the *vanities* of the poets "with *lies* upon their lips, and whose tongues speak *falsehoods*" (Ps. 144:8); "who call evil good and good evil" (Is. 5:20); who fashion their poems on the foundation of *deceit*, "while truth is never to be seen" (Is. 59: 15) . . . ; who maintain *lies* bred by the imagination and attract worthless fellows to their circles. How right were those who claimed that wisdom is like fruit and poetry like leaves. . . . I have now beheld that the words of the poets follow a *crooked* course, which is *alien to the wise of heart and foreign to the truth*. . . . *Wickedness* is inherent to it, and *nonsense* and *wiles*. On a *false* foundation he builds a dark house, coats it with plaster and covers it with *dross* inside and out. . . . What is expected of him is that his words include *fabrications*.[46]

As he continues, the Seeker explains the philosophical foundation for his aversion to poetry:

Poetry belongs to the fifth syllogism, *inferior* and dark. . . . Inasmuch as the craft of poetry is *far from the truth*, there is a *lying* spirit in the mouth of all its "prophets," and it is *empty* and *devoid of truth*. Those who practice it use only figurative and metaphorical terms which are *far removed from the truth*. And they do not employ conventional [i.e., literal] terms which wise men [i.e., philosophers] employ.[47]

Poets (like women) are the embodiment of rhetoric, the art of deception. A Latin medieval poet known for his virulent misogyny wrote: "Woman brings man to his end by five kinds of sophism."[48] And Howard Bloch comments that "If the reproach against woman is that she is a bundle of verbal abuses . . . such annoyances make her at least the fellow traveler of the trouvère." Both are "conceived as that which escapes logic. Rather she is portrayed as a kind of false logic. . . . Woman . . . is posited as the opposite of the truth . . . she becomes, in the misogynistic thinking of the high Middle Ages . . . associated with rhetoric, the art of persuasion that . . . was synonymous with poetics. Woman is figured as the sophist . . . the seducer with false arguments. . . . She is also the very figure of ambiguity." Bloch concludes, "indeed any writer can only be defined as a woman; and the discourse of misogyny then becomes a plaint against the self."[49]

Maimonides against Poetry

The animosity to poetry and poets on the part of Shem Tov's Falaquera is evidently influenced by his great mentor, Maimonides. Ezra Fleischer clearly relates Falaqera's and others' views on poetry to the sway of Maimonidean thinking: "The status [of poetry] was far from being strong in Christian Spain and other Jewish literary centers during this period. . . . Unlike in al-Andalus, in Christian Spain poetry was not in any case prestigious. . . . In the eyes of philosophers . . . it represented a world of 'deception,' and was, thus, contemptible and disqualified. . . . Maimonides' determined negation of poetry heightened this hostility . . . and adorned it with ideological validity and authority."[50] In relating poetry to the fifth syllogism, Falaqera discloses his authoritative source.[51] In his distinction between valid and invalid syllogisms in his book *Words of Logic*, Maimonides is explicit concerning his stand on poetry. The fifth syllogism, he says, is used by sophists, jesters, and poets alike and

is therefore called the art of deception, or the art of poetry. Sophists adorn their speech with analogies and imitations. Hence, any syllogism which includes a figurative premise is called poetic syllogism. *The making of these syllogisms, and the knowledge of methods by which they lie and deceive*, is called the art of deception [sophistry]. [The sophists] adorn what they speak about by using analogies and imitations. And so, any syllogism which includes a figurative premise is called a poetic syllogism. *And the practice which produces these syllogisms and makes use of imitations and analogies is called the art of poetry.*[52]

Maimonides and Falaqera clearly follow the Platonic reasoning against art, namely, art is a twice-removed imitation. Art imitates sensual reality, which is itself but a faded imitation of the real world of abstract ideas. "Poetry is a discourse composed of things which imitate other things, namely, things which resemble other things." And metaphor is a misleading substitution, "for a man might be inclined to conclude that the thing similar to the object is the object itself" (*The Seeker*, 82–83).

For Falaqera, as well as for Maimonides, poetry is also faulted because it originates in the imagination, which, in turn, has its own dubious origin in the inferior, desirous soul. When asked by the Seeker why poetry is favored by the ignorant and brutish masses, the poet responds: "The reason for it is that the poem is built on imagery, and the masses are attracted to images. . . . And so imagination takes over reason. . . . And so, the words of the poets seem more perfect and elegant in the eyes of the imagining soul that desires to behold elegance and beauty, like the artist [who] draws an image of the compass and makes it beautiful with colors and gold" (83).

The imagination is faulted not only for its illusory products, but also for its dubious origins in the Aristotelian corporeal, desirous, animal soul.[53] This part of the soul is identified by Maimonides, as it is in classical Greek thinking, with the female element, while the intellectual part of the soul is identified with the male element, in the macrocosm as well as in the individual.[54] This explains why, for Falaqera, women and the uneducated masses show an affinity for poetry: they are close to it in their element. This might also explain why in Maimonidean hermeneutics, it is women (as well as ignorant males) who tend toward the fictions of biblical narratives.

This stratification of the soul also affects the social thinking of these scholars. The ignorant masses, carnal and brutish, are akin to the animal/female soul, while the intellectual elite parallels the cerebral/masculine soul. The wise, therefore, incline toward abstract study. They ignore the figurative element in allegory and seek the hidden truth. In several places, Maimonides links women's narrow cerebral capacity with that of the illiterate masses.[55]

On the basis of such theoretical and psychological orientations, Maimonides also developed some practical stances regarding poetry and music.[56] In a list of forbidden heretical texts "that have no wisdom and no use, but waste your time in vanities," Maimonides includes the Arabic collection of songs and tunes known as *Kitāb al-aghani*.[57] Similarly he warns against the singing of songs whose "purpose it is to evoke an atmosphere of lust and fornication."[58] And when he is asked by a man from Aleppo, "Is it permitted to listen to the singing of the Ishmaelites?" he replies in very definite terms:

It is known that songs and music are essentialy forbidden. . . . And the Talmud has already explained that there is no differentiation between listening to the flute,

string instruments, or singing without instruments. All that causes the soul to ex-
pand and be excited is forbidden. . . . And the reason is quite clear, since it is the
power of lust which has to be submitted and harnessed. . . . Foolishness is forbidden to listen to even if it is not sung, so much more so if it is sung. And if it is accompanied by an instrument, it breaches three prohibitions: the listening to
stupidity, to obscenity, and to singing and playing. And if it occurs while drinking
wine, there is a forth prohibition. *And if the singer is a woman*, there exists a fifth
prohibition, based on the saying of the Sages: *"Woman's voice—pudendum," and
particularly when she sings.*[59]

That his extreme objection is to poetry as such, and not just to light or
secular poetry, can be evinced from his dislike to liturgical poetry, which
in his view, undermines the solemnity of prayer by adding to it an air of
frivolity.[60] Although in one case he does indeed point to the therapeutic
value of poetry and music ("And so if melancholy is upon him, poetry
and music will soothe him,"),[61] such aesthetic-sensual pleasure is not an
end in itself. Rather it is only a means to heal the body and so to release
the soul from captivity within the senses, enabling it to attain the abstract
sphere. However, on the whole, poetry and song, in instigating lust, lead
to the degenerate "disease of the imagination." Hence, Abraham Ibn
Ḥasday, another disciple of Maimonides, voices the following remonstra-
tion: "For a lusting man will listen to the songs and feel cheerful. He feels
cheerful, and he feels generous. He feels generous and so he . . . volunteers. He volunteers and squanders. He squanders and goes bankrupt. He
goes bankrupt and sighs. He sighs and worries. He worries and falls sick.
He falls sick and dies."[62]

Given that, according to Maimonides, the dominant streaks in the
female psychology are fickleness, excitability, irritability, and a leaning
toward the imagination,[63] poetry and music are seen as especially hazardous for men. In evoking excitement and emotionality, they serve as
agents of the male's feminization.

Ontological Whoredom

Maimonides, then, opposes poetry on logical grounds (it is contrary to
truth) and on psychological grounds (it derives from animal soul and ex-
cites it). But for him the refutation of poetry is also moored in his system-
atically gendered ontology. The devaluation of poetry is a function of a
total metaphysical hierarchy within which poetry is associated, one way or

another, with all the inferior aspects of the system, with negativity, with
absence—and with the female.

Maimonides' attitude to poetry can be shown as ultimately effected
by his systematic ontological separation between Form and Matter. The
story of Adam and Eve's creation is for Maimonides an Aristotelian allegory of the creation of Form and Matter.[64] For him the male element of
creation is Form, while the female element is Matter. While Form/Male is
always primary and self-sufficient, Matter/Female is secondary and is in
permanent need of Form. The dependence of Matter on Form is illustrated by the harlot parable in Proverbs 7.[65] Like the harlot, Matter also
hunts Forms seeking copulation.[66] Elsewhere (*The Guide*, 1:6), the word
woman is explained by Maimonides as a metaphor for that which forever
needs to be joined to something else. Full of admiration for Solomon's
metaphysical wisdom, Maimonides reads Proverbs 7 as an allegory on
Aristotelian ontology:[67]

How extraordinary is what Solomon said in his wisdom when likening matter to a
married harlot, for matter in no way is found without form and is consequently always like a married woman who is never separated from a man and is never free.
However, notwithstanding her being a married woman, she never ceases to seek
another man to substitute for her husband, and she deceives and draws him on in
every way until he obtains from her what her husband used to obtain. And this is
the condition of matter.[68]

Maimonides' allegorization attains two things at the same time: it identifies woman with matter in a most essentialist fashion, and it reifies woman
as matter. Daniel Boyarin names this status of Matter/Female in Maimonides "ontological whoredom," and adds: "What is astounding here is
how quickly Maimonides' ontology and its connected hermeneutic practice bring him to expressions of virulent misogyny."[69]

Similarly, the unity of body and soul in the individual is a kind of
"psycho-physical whoredom" between the male soul and the female body.
It is the male soul to which religion, intellectual faculties, and emotional
control are attributed. Conversely, it is the female-corporeal element in
the male from which passions, instincts, emotions, imagination, and even
criminal impulses derive. "Man's apprehension of his creator, his mental representation of every intelligible, his control of his desire and his
anger . . . are all of them consequent upon his form. On the other hand,
his eating and drinking and copulation and his passionate desire for these
things, as well as his anger and all bad habits found in him, are all of them

consequent on his matter . . . which calls upon man every imperfection and corruption" (*The Guide*, 3:8).

Allegory and Metap(w)hor(e)

Maimonides, the enemy of metaphor, consciously uses in his hermeneutics another figurative mode—allegory. On what grounds, we may ask, does he prefer allegory to metaphor? It seems that Maimonides makes an implicit rather than explicit distinction between allegory and metaphor. Allegory, in his opinion, is similarly subordinated to the concept of matter and form.[70] Allegory's "matter" consists in its imagery, which is exoteric, sensual, and concrete, while its "form" consists of esoteric, abstract, spiritual meanings. Hence, in accordance with the Maimonidean system of thought, allegory, too, combines (female) matter with (male) form. While the ignorant masses, enslaved by passion, require the figurative, exoteric layer of the allegory, the proficient reader—the philosopher—can easily dissociate the two. During the process of decoding allegory, its figurative signifiers become superfluous and one may discard them. Not so the with metaphor that depends simultaneously on the figurative-perceptual and the abstract-conceptual. In metaphor, so it seems, unlike in allegory in the Maimonidean view, tenor and vehicle, form and matter are closely linked. For Maimonides, then, allegory represents the divorce of matter and form, while metaphor and poetry at large embody an inseparable union of signifiers and signifieds. This "semiotic whoredom" parallels the "ontological whoredom" on the metaphysical plane.[71]

Mutual Discrediting

While Ibn Ezra is tolerant vis-à-vis the poetic lie and the artistic fiction and criticizes both on an *aesthetic* basis, Maimonides totally repudiates poetry and does so on an *ascetic* basis. For Maimonides, the discussion of poetic language is meshed in a total system of binary oppositions, which involve his ontology, semiotics, and concepts of gender. Sexual discourse and poetic-semiotic discourse cross paths in the mutual discrediting of poetry and woman. The woman is repudiated because of her identification with the characteristics of poetry (with the signifier, the esoteric, the figurative, the derivative), and poetry is repudiated for its identification with the feminine (the garment, the secondary, the carnal, the material). This juncture between the hatred of women and the assault on poetry is typical of the thirteenth century, the Aristotelian Century, not only in Jewish culture, but in Islam and in Christian Europe as well.

The allegorist who prefers the abstract over the sensual, the ascetic who subordinates body to soul, the misogynist philosopher who detests the female and exalts the male are all of a similar intellectual variety. The banishment of the artistic and the aesthetic, from the thirteenth century on, can be understood then as a facet of the repression of sexuality and the exclusion of the feminine.

Poor Soul, Pure Soul: The Soul as Woman

The Femaleness of the Soul

"THE MALENESS OF THE MAN of Reason," claims Genevieve Lloyd, "is no superficial linguistic bias. It lies deep in our philosophical tradition. . . . Reason is taken to express the real nature of the mind, in which, as Augustine put it, there is no sex." However, the implicit maleness of our ideals of Reason can be easily brought to the fore, says Lloyd, even when they appear to be sexless. "Our ideals of Reason have historically incorporated an exclusion of the feminine, and that femininity itself has been partly constituted through such processes of exclusion." Similarly, maintains Elizabeth Grosz: "As a discipline, philosophy has . . . excluded femininity, and ultimately women, from its practices through its usually implicit coding of femininity with the unreason associated with the body."[1]

In the same manner as their Islamic contemporaries (who, in their turn, followed the great Greek schools of thought), the Hebrew Andalusian poets viewed the human subject as a dichotomous being made up of mind and body, reason and biology.[2] Such "dichotomous thinking," says Grosz, "necessarily hierarchizes . . . the two polarized terms, so that one becomes the privileged term and the other its suppressed, subordinated, negative counterpart. . . . Body is thus what is not mind. . . . It is what the mind must expel in order to retain its integrity."[3]

If intellect has traditionally been identified as male, the human soul has stereotypically been conceived of as female. The Greek *psyche*, the Latin *anima*, the Hebrew *nefesh* (as well as *neshamah*, *ḥayah*, *yeḥidah*, and so on), and the Arabic *nafs* are all gendered in the feminine. Following Lloyd, we might add that the femaleness of the soul "is no superficial linguistic bias" either. Both in poetry and in philosophy, in ancient times as well as in the Middle Ages, writers widely exploited this grammatical disposition, using it to demonstrate what they thought to be the female *nature* of the human soul. Joan M. Ferrante writes: "To a great extent, the gender of an abstract noun determines the gender of the personification. . . . [In] the early and high Middle Ages, ideas were believed to have an existence of their own. . . . The fact that a human quality . . . was represented as a woman meant that it must have female characteristics."[4] Conceived as feminine, the soul takes on biological and behavioral qualities believed to be essentially female. She is desirous, lusting, sinning, menstruating, in need of being cleansed and corrected; she is either servile or disobedient; she is emotionally feeble; but she is also capable of love and devotion. She is thus portrayed as a disloyal wife, a straying daughter, a penitent pilgrim, a toiling maid, a captive princess, a prostitute, or—a loving companion.

The implications of the gendered appearances of the soul-as-female in the religious poetry (*piyyut*)[5] of the Golden Age will culminate, at the end of the chapter, in the examination of a full-fledged thirteenth-century allegorical *maqāma*.

When the Andalusians cast the soul in a shape of a woman they had two main sources to draw upon: the first was the Bible, which they used as a repository of diction and imagery; the second was the tradition of Greek-Islamic philosophy, which served as a source of philosophical ideas. As far back as the biblical Psalms, the soul is portrayed as a woman in love, thirsty for affection and intimacy. She passionately yearns for her Lord; she bows down to dust with sadness; she cries to her Lord to save her from turbulence. It is her task to praise and bless His name, and the psalmist encourages her to do so.[6] According to this variant of biblical psychology, the femaleness of the soul rests in her weakness, dependence, intense emotionality, and, above all, in her being perceived as a receptacle of emotions—agony, bliss, and elation.

This portrayal of the soul as an emotional female, capable of directly addressing God, inspired greatly the lyrics and the rhetoric of the Andalusian *piyyut*. However, it was Neoplatonic philosophy, shared by most religious Jewish poets of the Golden Age, from which the poets derived their conceptual framework regarding the soul. In the Neoplatonic hierarchic ontology, the soul is located "between" the immortal, abstract realm of reason and the mortal, material body.[7] And it is her duty to bridge the chasm between the two. Her task as an intermediary is described in various and rather contrasting ways. On the positive side, and as an emanation of the cosmic intellect, she is the representative of reason in the body; she illuminates the body with the light of the Logos; she is the body's moral guide; she is its form; she is derived from the Source of Life and is sent to the body to enliven it. The body is a dead corpse before she enters it and after she deserts it. Hers is a regulatory task: in regulating the body's biological, sensory, and emotional functions, the soul rules it according to the laws of reason. The soul is superior to the body, but is subordinate to intellect.

But there are also other—negative—images for the soul's agency. The soul is in constant threat of being infected by the body's criminal nature. The body is the soul's prison: she resides in it as a punishment and will be released from it only after atoning for her sins. The soul is the maidservant of the body, compelled to perform its dirty chores.

The relations between intellect and soul are not only hierarchized but are often also explicitly gendered. The female soul relates to the male intellect as subject to king, maid to master. In her relation to the body, however, it is the rational soul who must rule the body. While it is indeed her task to serve the body, she is at the same time exhorted to be permanently aware of her otherness to the body; to transcend its materiality and mortality through the cultivation of rational thought.

This ambiguous status of the soul, her being in contact with the realm of intellect and, simultaneously, with the realm of nature, led the Neoplatonists to devise a binary hierarchical model of the soul, according to which the soul itself is divided into two levels: higher and lower. The higher part, "the rational soul," is connected with the universal intellect, and the lower part, "the animal soul," is responsible for the less noble functions: the control of emotions and desires and the maintenance of life through nutrition and reproduction. This hierarchization also implies genderization: the animal soul is identified with the female principle of nature, while the higher soul is advised to rid herself of her feminine aspects and to adopt rational (that is, masculine) conduct.[8] A most negative attitude to the lower soul, the one which is immersed with the corporeal and the material, developed among the Muslim ascetics. Basing themselves on the Qurānic verse, claiming that it is "the lower self [*nafs*] that incites to evil" (Sura 12:59), they thus equated the *nafs* and woman.[9]

How does the soul fit into the basic binarisms of intellect/body, male/female? Is she intrinsically male (as the intellect from which she emanates), or female (as the body in which she resides)? Is she superior (as she is to matter), or inferior (as she is to intellect and God)? What are the feminist interpretative options suggested by the soul's intermediary position?

The poetic material explored in this chapter seems to work in several directions. Some poems, especially penitential ones, exploit ascetic notions of sin and pollution, thus enhancing female inferiority. Others, of more philosophical nature, emphasize the soul's purity, nobility, and superiority, as well as her intellectual faculties. In the latter, though the soul is feminine by gender, she is capable of restoring the masculine values of the source from which she emanated. In this sense the soul may be perceived as having an "androgynous" potentiality.[10] In many poems the soul, in her bodily existence, is figured as suffering a constant identity crisis. She is urged to end this confusion and make up her mind as to her true "nature." She may either reinforce her masculine identity by desiring to identify, and ultimately unite, with the intellect, or else she will succumb to and identify with the body. Her ideal existence is in transcending her femininity and elevating herself to the male ideal of the intellect. The right of choice given to the (higher) soul renders her a thinking subject, a decision-maker, and hence capable of self-liberation and salvation. (It is this concept of the soul that makes itself visible in the narrative allegory scrutinized at the end of this chapter.) Seen this way, the female soul defeats the conventional dichotomies of intellect/body, male/female and emerges indeed as a woman-empowering figure.

The Soul's Round-Trip

The soul's intermediary status in Neoplatonic thought dictates her fate as a ceaseless voyager. She is either on her way "down" to the world or "up" to her divine source. Her residence in the earthly body is a temporary sojourn, a station in her journey.

Numerous liturgical poems outline this round-trip of the soul: her "fall" from her pure, lofty source down to the earth, her embroilment in the ephemeral, her involvement in worldly follies, her subordination to the indulgent body, and, then, her ascent back to God. The turn-off occurs when the soul, instead of desiring earth's delights, uses introspection to find inside herself that image of glory which is the reflection of the glory of her divine source:

Flowing from the fount of life, ennobled, full of light,
    derived of a holy, pure site—
. . . Lo! What is your mission in this world low?
    Why are you locked in this dark corpse?
Will you forever chase childhood and youth,
    and those cursed follies of earth?
Sleep was sweet to you at first
    but rough and bitter is its end!
Leave Time's delights behind—
    exile yourself [from this world].
Bethink that when exploring your own glory
    you will better know your source;
. . . Be advised, while you are still in this world, so
    that in the next you will stay next to God.
      (Abraham Ibn Ezra, *Liturgical Poems*, 1:54–55)[11]

The didacticism of this poem, so typical of many penitential *piyyutim*, is enhanced by the recurrent imperatives (whose feminine gender is lost in the English translation).[12] The soul is portrayed here as an ignorant young female in need of correction, while the male speaker—the liturgist qua the voice of reason—assumes the role of father-teacher-preacher who chides, advises, reminds, intimidates the soul and makes promises to her. While Plotinus insisted that "the soul *is* the self" (*Ennead* 4:7.1),[13] the rhetoric of the poets introduces a split between the male speaker and his addressee, the female soul:

My Soul, mind your deeds / before ascending to your Rock,
Repent your misdeeds, / reveal your crimes and guilt,
Be shut in your inner rooms, / lock the doors-of-sin,
Hide under your Rock's wings, / tremble until His rage declines,
. . . Rise when it is still night, / do not sleep, do not idle,
Chant and make songs, / praise and hymn Him,
Bow to your Lord, / bend, kneel,
Watch, make ready, / sing, plead,
Arise, wake up, / storm, whirl around . . .
Pray, fall in front of Him, / play for Him your drums and flute . . .
Make a pilgrimage to God's House / where you'll [again] wear your
    precious jewels.
      (Ibn Gabirol, *Liturgical Poetry*, 1:291)[14]

The accumulation of feminine imperatives, the mention of the "drums and flute" (musical instruments typically associated with women),[15] and, finally, the promise of jewels as a reward for virtuous feminine conduct, all add to the stereotypical portrayal of the soul as female. This figurative tenor is intensified in a group of allegorical poems which render the Neo-platonic "return" of the soul to her divine source in terms of a matrimo-nial reunion.[16] Here, the soul is represented as having been a sinning wife. Only after having been punished and banished from her home, and after having repented her wrongdoings, will the soul be ready to return to her forgiving husband:

> My soul craves for her rest place,
> She longs for her source,
> And yearns for her holy abode—
> To go there day and *night*
>
> . . . .
>
> So dismal is she in exile,
> Her jewels stripped off,
> She wanders, tears on her cheeks,
> Bitterly she weeps at *night*
>
> . . . .
>
> Good tidings, daughter! I'll pardon you
> And lead you gently to my abode.
> You have no kinsman closer than I—
> Stay, wait out the *night*!
>   (Moses Ibn Ezra, *Liturgical Poetry*, 68–70)[17]

The nocturnal atmosphere (evoked by the biblical phrases in the fourth lines of each stanza) serves as a backdrop for the lonely female figure, whose untiring journey back home takes place against the darkness of ex-ile. The feminine nature of her anguish is stressed by an allusion to the lonely lamenting woman ("tears on her cheeks") in the Book of Lamen-tations (1:2). The poem ends happily with the allusion to the romantic denouement of the Book of Ruth (3:13). Boaz, Ruth's next of kin, "re-deems" the widow by marrying her. Their kinship here signifies the Neo-platonic idea of the soul's emanation from a divine origin, while their marriage symbolizes the soul's reunion with God.

Similar tones of intimacy also resonate through the following poem by Judah ha-Levi, where the poet informs the soul that her Lord has already pardoned her. She is reminded that her way back home is long, that she has to take provisions (that is, good deeds) on her journey, and that she must be sure to cleanse herself. Finally, he encourages her to return from her exile:

Return, my soul, to your rest,
   For the Lord has been good to you!
. . . .

Don't you thirst to behold his beauty
And forever serve him?
Return, Return, O Shulammite,
   To your Father's house, as in your youth![18]
(Judah ha-Levi, *Liturgical Poetry*, 2:372–73)[19]

The ending apostrophe "Return, return, O Shulammite" (Songs of Songs 7:1) echoes the one with which the poem began (Psalm 116:7), and thus identifies the Shulammite, God's female spouse in the midrash of the Songs, with the psalmist's soul. In reading the dialogue of the lovers in Canticles as an allegory of God and the individual soul, the poet offered here an exegetical innovation, unprecedented yet by Jewish Bible exegetes.[20] The familiar stages of the national narrative (love, union, sin, exile, and redemption), as read by the rabbis into the Songs, were read now by the poets as representing the Neoplatonic trajectory of the individual soul: her fall or exile, her repentance and return, and her final salvation.

Intellectual bliss, rather than erotic or material gratification, is the reward of the soul in the following poem:

How long will you nap in babyhood's lap?
   Don't you know that childhood wastes like chaff?
Will black-haired youth forever stay? Rise, step out,
   watch those envoys of white hair, your moral guides,
And shake off Time, like birds
   shake off the dew of night.
Soar, like a sparrow fleeing [the traps of] Sin,
   above the storming Sea of Time,

Follow your King to Divine bliss, among a flight
    of souls flowing like a tide of light.[21]
                    (Judah ha-Levi, *Liturgical Poetry*, 1:25)

The soul's transition from ignorance to knowledge is illustrated here as a
rite of passage from infancy to maturity, from the realm ("lap") of the
pre-oedipal mother to the abstract sphere of the Logos, the divine king-
father. The topos of awakening from the "slumber of foolishness" entered
the tradition of penitential Hebrew poetry from the Arabic.[22] Here is a
passage from an Arabic religious philosophical composition:

When the soul awakens from the sleep of negligence . . . and throws off the shell
and veil of the body, i.e., natural habits, beastly dispositions, and foolish opinions,
and is cleansed of material appetites, she escapes and experiences her resurrection.
She will become luminous, and her . . . gaze will be sharpened. She will then behold . . . eternal substances of light; . . . she will cling to them, even as the lover
clings to the beloved. She will become one with them.[23]

The image of the soul as a sleeping beauty significantly aligns the infantile
with the feminine as both being disposed to inertia, laziness, and sleep.
"In associating woman with sleep," writes Genevieve Lloyd, "Nietzsche
only pushed to its limits a long-standing antipathy between femaleness
and active, 'male' Culture. . . . From the beginning of philosophical
thought, femaleness was symbolically associated with what reason suppos-
edly left behind—the dark powers of the earth goddesses . . . associated
with mysterious female powers."[24] These dark female powers are figuratively implied in our poem in the image of the (mother's) lap. In order to
relinquish her infancy and femininity, the soul has to separate herself from
the Great Mother (mater), the goddess of matter (of earth and sea and
time).

Spatial vectors are also explicitly gendered in this poem. The down-
ward trajectory spirals toward engulfment in the dark mother, whereas
the upward trajectory soars in pursuit of the male King of Reason. The
maturing baby bird,[25] which shakes the dewdrops, the leftovers of (motherly) night, from its wings, is a powerful symbol for the individuation of
child from mother. With the avian metaphor of passage from the mate-
rial/maternal world to the metaphysical world of the Divine, blackness is
changed into light, and multiplicity becomes Oneness.[26]

The Soul Slaved and Saved

One of the most elaborate renderings of "the biography of the soul" is found in the following allegorical poem, which depicts the soul as a pure maiden enslaved by a brutish body:

> Comely is that charming damsel who's hidden from every eye.
> It is for you, O philosophers, to know her "where," her "how" and
> her "why"!
>
> Down she went to live in a mud house—Form then met with
> Flesh—
> There was she hid, against her will, imprisoned.
> Captive—but not by man's arm: sold—but not for gold.
> [There she stayed] to toil the body's soil, to form it and make it
> Fear [the Lord's] law, and, by Reason, to distinguish it from beast.
> . . . .
>
> The singular one, she called to be of labor freed, [she yearned]
> For the day of rest, the end of heavy chore. For, unlike Matter
> Which, in death, is lost—*her* element will live forever.
> If Matter is of old—she, the Soul, was there before he even showed.
> It's she, who for her deeds, will get [God's] punishment or reward.
>   (Yosef Ibn Zaddiq)[27]

The protagonist here is a "hidden maiden" (*'alma*). On the overt figural level she is a secluded, veiled lady, "hidden" (*na'alama*) from the eyes of lascivious males (who are unable to "know" her in the carnal sense). On the covert, conceptual level, as soul, she is "hidden," that is, abstract, imperceptible to the senses, having neither body nor substance.[28] Both levels of the allegory become completely conflated with the apostrophe to "men of wisdom" to intellectually "know" the *'alma/* soul.[29] The philosophers are urged to interrogate the "hidden maiden" about her realm (*where*), about her mode, or cause, of existence (*how*), and about her purpose (*why*).[30] Here the aspect of the soul as an intelligible, passive object, contemplated by the philosophers' minds, is stressed far beyond her capacity as a knowing, intelligent being.

The noble lady who went down in stature resides now in a mud house (the body) and has been made responsible for its maintenance. After years of toil in subservience to its needs, she yearns for liberation and for her return to her fatherland (the realm of intellect and the divine). Her true father and lord, unlike her earthly owner, will reward her justly, according to her deeds. Despite the patronizing tone of the male-poet, some empathy for the anguish of the captive woman is discernible. The body (and the material world) indeed constitutes the confines of the soul's imprisonment with hard labor, but the soul is nevertheless also perceived to be on a mission in the body. The soul is the body's form and its lawgiver. She represents, in the body, intellect and religion. It is the soul which "distinguishes man from beast"; it is she who epitomizes the human essence.

Several biblical allusions come to the fore here. One is the biblical law regarding "the pretty captive woman." The victor in war who takes her into his house is instructed—should he no longer find her pleasing—to "let her *go free*, you must *not sell her for money*" (Deutronomy 21:10–14, and compare to line 5 in our poem). Another allusion is to the tilling of the soil, which is here much as in the Genesis story, a consequence of the "fall." Unlike in the biblical story, however, tilling the soil here is the woman's, not the man's, job.[31]

Beyond the biblical allusions, a far more important intertext for this poem is Plato's "Phaedo," where, based on an earlier Greek myth, he recounts the "fall" of the immortal soul from her celestial abode of souls down into the material world. The soul, conceived as a fallen "daimon," is entrapped in a defiled body and must, according to these early ascetic doctrines, to purify herself before she can escape back into her original godlike immortality.[32] In the "Phaedo," the rational soul has to purge herself from the follies of the body, her prison-house, from which she will be released at death. Through reason she will resume her kinship with that which is pure, eternal, immortal, and unchangeable. The senses, in contrast, drag the soul back to the realm of the changeable, where she wanders about blindly and becomes confused and dizzy like a drunken man:

But the soul which has been polluted, and is impure at the time of her departure, and is the companion and servant of the body always, and is in love with and fascinated by the body . . . —do you suppose that such a soul will depart pure and unalloyed? . . . She is held fast by the corporeal . . . and this corporeal element is heavy . . . and [by it the] soul is dragged down again into the visible world . . . prowling about tombs and sepulchres, near which, as they tell us, are seen certain ghostly apparitions of souls which have not departed pure. . . . And these must be the souls . . . of the evil which are compelled to wander about such places in payment of the penalty of their former evil way of life. . . . No one who has not studied philosophy and who is not entirely pure at the time of his departure is allowed to enter the company of the Gods, but the lover of knowledge only. ("Phaedo," 466–67)[33]

It is only the rational soul that has the option of purification; the animal soul dies with the body's death. In Ibn Gabirol the fate of the Platonic "wise" soul is cast in the mold of two biblical female models: The pure soul, like the woman of valor, has no worries and is not afraid of her fate (she can afford to "laugh at the last day," Proverbs 31:25), while the impure soul is like a menstruating woman who should be banished: "The wise soul does not see death, but receives for her sin a punishment more bitter than death. And if she be pure she shall obtain grace, and smile on the last day. And if she be polluted, she shall stray to and fro full of anger and wrath. All the days of her uncleanliness she shall sit alone, outcast and isolated. 'She shall touch no hallowed thing nor come into the temple, until the days of her purifying be fulfilled.' "[34]

No wonder, then, that the rhetoric of penitential poetry is often obsessed with cleanliness: "My soul, bless your Lord . . . clean and distill yourself, hurry, shining in your cleanliness, rid yourself of impurity, change your clothes. Then, perhaps, will the King, your Lord be again attracted to your beauty. . . . Cleanse, purify yourself from your pollution" (Judah ha-Levi, *Liturgical Poetry*, 1:142, 144).

The Body as Female and the Politics of Pollution

The soul's "pollution" is signified as both typically "feminine" and essentially corporeal. This unholy nexus between corporeality, femininity, and uncleanliness is, as Elizabeth Grosz's survey shows, a commonplace in Western thinking. In Western thought, ancient and medieval, and persisting into modern times, the body is identified with feminine matter and is subjected to patriarchal conceptualizations of femininity.

Like woman, the body has been perceived as "unruly, disruptive, in need of direction and judgment; . . . a brute givenness which requires overcoming, a connection with animality and nature that needs transcendence. . . . Most relevant here is the correlation of and association of the mind/body opposition with the opposition between male and female, where man and mind, woman and body, become representationally aligned."[35]

Such an equation is explicit in Maimonides, for whom the human body (man's, no less than woman's) is categorically signified as female. Interpreting the Creation story as an Aristotelian allegory, Maimonides understands the creation of Adam and Eve to stand first for the inception of cosmic form and matter. The human individual (man as well as woman), being a microcosm, is respectively constituted of "Adam" (namely, form, including intellect and higher soul) and of "Eve" (namely, material body and animal soul).[36] Though it might seem that Maimonides' Aristotelian philosophy is impertinent to our poetic materials, which are mainly of Neoplatonic provenance, Ibn Gabirol, the Neoplatonist,[37] elaborates this very same association of the body and Eve in his following poem. The soul accuses the body of yielding to temptation (line 3).

> My holy God has disfavored me. He has locked me in darkness.
> I am busy with cleaning the body's filth. I wish to escape from this
>   stinking cadaver.
> I can no longer bear it. *The scoundrel body tempted me [to eat], and I*
>   *have eaten . . .*
> He is bound to every lust, never stops eating and drinking,
> His belly, like the belly of the wicked, is ever insatiable . . .
> He may hunt me all of a sudden, open his jaws and swallow me.
>   (Ibn Gabirol, *Liturgical Poetry*, 1:32–33)

Moreover, the body's pollution, its insatiability, and especially its voracious jaws are reminiscent of the archetypal *vagina dentata*, which, in misogynistic thought, epitomizes the corporeal essence of the female.[38]

This nexus between dirt, the viscosity of body fluids, the voracious and indeterminate vagina, and the "horror of the feminine" as expounded by the anthropologist Mary Douglas,[39] is lucidly present in the ascetic attitude of the Hebrew liturgists toward the body. Their detailed indices of material/corporeal substances and many fluids depict the body as ephemeral, low, repelling, disintegrating, formless and contourless: "Is the body not a *dissolving* thing, a trodden corpse, derived from a *muddy fountain* and a *polluted source*, created from a *fetid drop* [i.e., the seminal fluid], . . . a worm-like cocoon, a horror, arrested in a *filthy* womb, locked in a *dirty* belly? (Ibn Paqūda);[40] "[The body is] a *muddy* and trodden corpse, a flower that withers and fades out in heat, dry like grass, ephemeral like smoke, worn away like an old garment, shattered like straw, *dissolves* like a snail and *melted like wax* (Ibn Gabirol, *Liturgical Po-*

etry, 1:223–25); "I am a lump [of clay] and larva, the dust of the earth . . . a passing shadow, a mute stone, a blowing wind, a spider's poison" (Ibn Gabirol, "The Kingly Crown," *Liturgical Poetry*, 58); "Will [God] forgive . . . a man conceived with *blood of sin* and *water of guilt*? . . . Can he endure who was composed of a *watery drop* [i.e., semen] and *blood of menstruation* (Judah ha-Levi, *Liturgical Poetry*, 1:606–7).

In italics above are phrases "positing the body in a synecdochal relation to the fluids it contains."[41] The body's fluids, claims Mary Douglas, especially those of the "Other," represent a threat. "What is disturbing about the viscous or the fluid is its refusal to conform to the laws governing the clean and proper, . . . [and] its otherness to the notion of entity" (195). Julia Kristeva radicalizes this line of thought, saying that the body's fluids embody "a horror of the unknown . . . that permeates, lurks, lingers . . . leaks out of the body . . . flow[s] . . . seep[s], infiltrate[s]. . . . They betray a certain irreducible materiality. They assert the priority of body over subjectivity" (194). Douglas, and even more so Luce Irigaray, associates this clinging viscosity with the horror of femininity and maternity, the voracity and indeterminacy of the vagina dentata, the dread of being entrapped and absorbed. Thus, the female body—construed "as a leaking, uncontrollable, seeping liquid; as formless flow, . . . entrapping, . . . a formlessness that engulfs all forms, a disorder that threatens all order" (201)—becomes metonymic for the human body in general. When the liturgists speak in first person of men's bodies as objects of disgust, it is because they conceptualize their ideal self as identical with the mind, and the body, their own bodies indeed, as absolute alterity, as female in essence.

The Melodrama of the Soul

The problematic relationship between soul and body, and between soul and intellect (as well as between self and soul), found one dramatic expression in an allegorical *maqāma* by Jacob ben Eleazar, written in Toledo around 1233.[42] The soul's efforts to transcend the body and to unite with the intellect take the form of a psychological melodrama. It is "psychological" not only in that the psyche is its central character, but also because a great part of the drama is staged, as will be shown, *within* the inner space of the human self. The fervent emotions—of longing, lust, hostility, contempt, and envy—with which the plot is imbued add to it a melodramatic flavor.

This *maqāma* is one of the first instances in Hebrew of an amatory allegory. C. S. Lewis describes this moment in literary history when secular romance (in which the plot takes place in the outer world) turns into an amatory allegory (in which the events are staged within the self or the mind) as "man's gaze turned inward." And he says: "[A] gaze so turned sees . . . the contending forces which cannot be described at all except by allegory. Hence the development of allegory, to supply the subjective element in literature, to paint the inner world, followed inevitably."[43] The famous allegorical love poem the *Roman de la Rose* by Guillaume de Lorris (the first part of the thirteenth century) is for Lewis the epitome of this historical moment. Guillaume's *Roman* shares ample similarities with Ben Eleazar's contemporary *maqāma*, not the least of which is the fashioning of the mental plot as a courtly romance—a love story between a lady and a knight. Could Ben Eleazar have been inspired by this contemporary illustrious model? A no less significant affinity between the two works is the employment of dream as the inner speculum of the outward world; as a space in which the human mind and psyche live and act.[44] Another organizing theme in Ben Eleazar, namely the battle within the psyche of the various aspects of the self, entertained a long history in European literature since Prudentius's *Psychomachia*.[45]

The dramatis personae in our *maqāma* are the narrator (using both a fictive appellation, Lem'uel Ben Ithi'el, and the author's real name Jacob ben Eleazar)[46] and the different parts of his self. These comprise his heart of flesh (a synecdoche for the whole body); his rational soul (not identical with the self) who is portrayed as a passionate and quite temperamental woman of nobility; her desired beloved, the intellect, embodied as a handsome army general; and the general's paramour, a feminine personification of wisdom.

The first scene takes place outdoors, in a street bustling with heavy traffic. The "chariots of love" drive noisily to and fro, and troops, led by a handsome knight, the "general of the armies of love,"[47] march back and forth waving their colorful banners. They all hurry towards the narrator, hugging and kissing him. As this occurs, the soul (that is Jacob's soul) is asleep, deep in a dream where she envisions a symbolic love scene between the (male) sun and the (female) moon. Taking the dream as foretelling the imminent approaching of her beloved, the general, she urges herself to awaken. The lines between "reality," dream and fiction are entirely blurred, with the narrator too becoming a character in the dream dreamt by his own soul. The "realistic" street scene that opens the plot is colored with dreamlike qualities, while the fictional episodes, within the dream, attain utmost reality. The inner life of the active soul turns out to be occurrences taking place in the real world, that world in which the human individual lives and strives.

The soul's erotic dream makes the heart "rage in his chamber." Intent on stopping the soul from meeting her lover, "the general of love," the heart kidnaps both the narrator, Jacob, and the soul and hides them "within his inner chambers." (Note that the heart has its own heart, with chambers inside it, within which he dwells and within which he hides the soul). This triple conceptualization of the heart—as organ, as persona and as space—together with the fuzzy definitions of inner and outer space, add to the surreal and paradoxical quality of the scene.

When it becomes known to the "troops of love" that Jacob and his soul have been captured, they besiege the heart, "sitting on their chairs around it," as if for a spectacle or show.[48] Jacob and his soul are now doubly enclosed: they are entrapped inside the jealous heart and, at the same time, are encircled on the outside by "the army of love."

In the next scene, the awakened soul first peeps out through a latticed window (of the heart's chamber) to steal a glance at her General of Love; but, being unable to see him, she puts on her best clothes and perfumes and climbs to an upper chamber. While she is dazzled by the light of her beloved's face, he is angry at her keeping indoors, at her not coming out to welcome him after he drove his chariots from afar to watch her. She apologizes and blames her conduct on the heart. The general departs, still angry, and the soul is left "wrapped in the bitterness of parting."

Incited by the devious heart, the desolate soul is made, in the third scene, to believe that it was the narrator who caused the lovers' separation, and she refuses to talk to him.

At this point, Jacob wakes up from *his* dream. Now we realize that the whole plot, including the soul's dream and awakening, was but part of the narrator's own dream. Let us reiterate here the immensely complex ontological status of the plot. The first three scenes are the narrator's (Jacob's) dream,[49] in which he himself, his body and soul, and the personification of love appear as characters. But within his dream, his soul dreams a dream (about the sun and the moon). Later she awakens and acts, while the narrator goes on dreaming. Her romantic dream comes "true" when she awakens and meets her beloved—within Jacob's dream. The medieval theme of "awakening from a dream" is fraught with moral signification. "Awakening" is the turning point in one's life from illusion to disillusionment, from cherishing life in this false world to the awareness of the life of the soul in the hereafter. Hence the fourth and fifth scenes are the dramatization of Jacob's moral conversion. In the fourth he is still caught in a struggle between body and soul, between man's mortal and eternal aspects, but later he will wholeheartedly follow the path of the soul. His dream, man's dream of moral perfection, will come true when he joins the soul in her excursion to the Garden of Intellect and Wisdom.

Awakened, Jacob is even more determined to settle the misunderstanding between him and his soul—which provides the context for the fourth scene. Jacob implores the soul to be reconciled to him "as is customary among human beings." This offends the soul even more, since, as she says, she is of a noble extraction, while he, the narrator, is just an ordinary mortal.

In turn, this arrogance of the soul infuriates the heart (metonymic of the body), who volunteers now to become the narrator's advocate. The narrator, however, sides with the soul.[50] The heart = body admits the soul's class superiority, her beauty and purity, but ridicules her pomp. Using Neoplatonic phraseology, he reminds her of her intermediary place in the social ladder (i.e., the metaphysical chain of being): "Your element is indeed pure . . . and lofty . . . and fair is your form . . . but do you not remember that all your glory and splendor have been stolen . . . [from] high [i.e., from the Logos] . . . and from higher above high?" Indignant of her ingratitude, the body continues to chide the soul in a style that parodies moralistic discourse. True, he admits, this earth body is not the ideal residence for a fine lady like her. But still, how can she be so loathing of that temporary clay house in which she dwells? Did the body not worship her? Did he not consider her his god and himself her anointed prophet? Why does she insult and disgrace him?

At hearing the speech, sarcastic and full of intellectual pretense, of his unsolicited advocate, Jacob silences the body by reducing him to lowly matter: How dare the body, he asks, use such spiritual discourse? How has he, "a sickly body, a trodden corpse," become a talking creature? "How can clay and mud compete with the soul?" Ironically, after assigning the mute body a speaking role in his allegorical play, the allegorist himself deprives the body of the right to speech. In silencing the body, the self, Jacob, declares its unequivocal identity with the soul. Nonetheless, and however denied, the speech of the body is not erased from the text. It remains represented—partly as a comic gesture, partly as an immanent feature of allegory (which, commonly, makes the mute speak). By granting speech to the speechless, despicable and despeakable, the discourse of the body becomes a voice of resistance, contesting the patriarchal moralistic efforts to delegitimize it by silencing and objectification.[51]

Having now become convinced that Jacob has finally dissociated himself from the body, the soul urges him to escort her in search of her beloved, "the general of love" (i.e., Intellect). He resides, so she has heard, in the Garden of Delight owned by the general's mistress, Lady Wisdom (Hokhma), and is, in fact, her gardener. It is he who has planted this garden and "sown it with the seeds of reason." The soul is eager to learn everything about Wisdom: "her name and shape, her habits and form."[52] But Jacob is reluctant to leave, and humbly excuses himself for being an ignoble mortal, unworthy of mixing with spiritual beings. After chiding him for always having been mentally lazy, the soul reassures him that "he who pursues intellect will achieve it. Intellect is indeed lofty, but the wise have their ways to bring it down." The soul also throws in erotic temptation, for good measure, fantasizing how they—she and Jacob—will make love to Wisdom, quenching their thirst with her kisses, and fondling her breasts. This Garden of Delight replicates at once the garden of the Song of Songs and the courtly garden of Andalusian poetry, where lovemaking is consummated. As I will later point out, this is also the mythical garden of Platonic and Neoplatonic eternal intellectual bliss.

Jacob finally joins the soul, and the story ends with the soul giving Jacob, at his own request, a long poetic lecture on Neoplatonic philosophy, the great chain of emanation, the hypostases, the four elements, and the order of Creation.

Who does the feminine "wisdom" represent? And how does she conceptually relate to the masculine "intellect"? The intellect here has to be understood as the Cosmic Intellect (Logos), God's first creation in Neoplatonic terms, and man's target in his philosophical enterprise. Wisdom is the Hebrew equivalent of Sophia, the allegorical embodiment of philosophy,[53] the medium through which the human intellect can elevate itself to the impersonal level of the cosmic intellect. The first initiative, however, for man's upward trajectory must come from the soul. She first introspects, and then contemplates with love at the intellect. Experiencing the delights of wisdom is the philosopher's path to the utmost bliss of the intellect.

Jacob Ben Eleazar's story is Neoplatonic not only in its explicit philosophical teaching, but also in its mythical imagery. The Garden of Delight, where the soul unites in love with the intellect, is reminiscent of Zeus's garden in Plato's "Symposium." In this garden was Eros conceived "in beauty" on Aphrodite's birthday, after his mother, the goddess of poverty, slept there with the god of plenty who was then drunk with nectar.[54] Plotinus interpreted this myth as a parable for his own philosophy: "plenty" is the intelligible world of ideas, and "poverty" is the boundless thirst of the soul for the intellect. In Plato's "Phaedrus," Zeus is clearly identified with the intellect and Aphrodite with the soul. And in Plotinus's exposition: "If the male gods are the Intellect, and the female gods are their souls, than Aphrodite is the soul of Zeus. . . . The soul, that was created with and from the Intellect . . . and is herself beautiful, gracefully adorned and plentiful, strewn with sparkles and reflections of all things beautiful—is in its entirety Aphrodite, and the rational elements in it are all of abundance and plenty, like nectar pouring out from above. And its sparkles . . . are called Zeus' Garden, and it is said that 'plenty' resides there."[55]

The various images for the intellect in Ben Eleazar also seem to have a Neoplatonic provenance. In Plato's "Phaedrus," the intellect is presented as a high commander and a "charioteer."[56] Likewise, the image of the intellect as gardener, planter, and sower, is a personification of Plato's notion in the "Symposium" regarding the procreative powers of the intellect. "The pursuit of wisdom is a spiritual procreation. . . . [It] shares a common structure with physical procreation; but its aim is a superior power of immortality."[57] As Genevieve Lloyd sees it, in the treatment of intellect as itself passionate and generative, the old conflicts between fertility and reason—that is, between the ancient cults of the fertility goddesses and the newer rites of the rational gods and goddesses that replaced them—are subsumed.

In Plato, and especially in the "Phaedrus," images of physical beauty and passion play an important role in the philosopher's road to enlightenment. The attraction to the beauty of the flesh together with the energy which invigorates bodily love are the models on which the soul draws in her pursuit of knowledge. These "low" models are said to remind the soul of the beauty of the nonbodily, changeless forms that she should be contemplating. Reason itself draws on the energizing psychic force of love. Furthermore, Plato "saw passionate love . . . as the beginning of the soul's process of liberation through knowledge."[58]

As the last point of my reading of Jacob Ben Eleazar's *maqāma*, I would like to maintain that the author is aware of the task of aesthetic experience (in this case the enjoyment of literature) as an exercise preparing for the higher joy of philosophy. Two metapoetic declarations envelop this *maqāma*, in which the allegorist furnishes the reader with reading instructions. Both disclose his awareness of the implications of the allegorical praxis. The first couplet (right before the *maqāma*, at the end Ben Eleazar's introduction) reads:

> I have devised the allegory of intellect / as an amusing love tale,
> Read it and enjoy / its tremendous pleasures.

The other is the postscript to our *maqāma*:

> Here ends intellect's allegory / devised as a love tale.
> Ponder [its] positive [aspect], my friend, / and shun its frailty.

Such overt reading instructions are not uncommon in this literary mode.[59] While evidence indeed of the overdidacticism of allegory, they also seem to disclose the allegorist's attentiveness to the ambiguous nature of his art: Should allegory teach or amuse or do both? The two couplets quoted above seem to represent two different attitudes. In the first couplet the emphasis is on "delight": the reader is encouraged to enjoy the romance, the beauty, and the sensuousness of the figural envelope of allegory. In the second couplet, the allegorist assumes the moralist's pose for the purpose of delegitimizing and suppressing the alluring effects of his own story. To this extent, his warning resembles Maimonides' stance on allegory. In his theorization of allegory, Maimonides makes a sweeping analogy between allegory and ontology: allegory's figural level ("the parable") is analogous to (female) matter, while its abstract level ("the moral") is analogous to (male) form. His ideal reader, the philosopher, has to extract form ("moral") from matter ("parable")—before completely discarding the latter.[60]

If in the second couplet, Jacob Ben Eleazar paid tribute to the religio-philosophical hermeneutics of his day, his more genuine position, so it seems, is expressed in the first couplet, where he points to the beauty of his love tale and stresses the joy of reading. For Ben Eleazar, the figural side of his text is not merely the cloak for an edifying idea, but it is intrinsic to his Neoplatonic aesthetics. Inasmuch as enjoying corporeal models of beauty and love is, according to Plotinus, a necessary stage in the philosopher's training toward experiencing divine beauty and love, so, in allegory, the pleasure the reader takes from the charm of the romantic tale is indispensable to his full realization of the text.

Domesticating the Enemy:
Misogamy in a Jewish Marriage Debate

"Never Take a Wife"

One of the great men built him a new house and wrote over the lintel: "Let no evil enter here." Diogenes, the philosopher, passed and saw the inscription, and then wrote underneath, "And how will thy wife enter?"

BASED ON A FALSE SYLLOGISM, this witty anecdote aims to show how evil, that is, woman, is unavoidably built into the familial-social system.[1] The contradiction in terms inherent in the concept of "a house without evil" encapsulates two of the main concerns of medieval misogynist discourse: one is the discord between the negativity of woman and the positive postulate of marriage; the other is the contrariety between the philosopher's spiritual path and the indulgence in matter which is caused by family life. In the male philosopher's view, these were practical and indeed most excruciating problems.

In medieval ascetic thought (Christian and Islamic alike) the male/female difference was made to fit into a series of other Manichaean dichotomies (good/evil, spirit/flesh, intellect/instinct, order/chaos).[2] Hence, marriage, the place where male and female legitimately (though not unproblematically) meet, became a powerful metaphor for the paradoxical encounters of the two opposing metaphysical orders. Asceticism, in its extreme manifestations, preached the absolute dissociation of the male/spiritual from the female/material not only in the mind but also in the life of the true believer. Thus, "divorcing" matter entailed also avoiding matrimony. However, society and its religious institutions continued to advocate and sanction marriage and family life.

To what extent did medieval Jewish thinkers and writers participate in this contemporary discourse on women and marriage? And if they did, was there any Jewish cultural specificity to their rendition of the conflict between married and meditative life? The texts of medieval Jewish authors from al-Andalus, and later from Christian Spain, show that they shared the discourse of their contemporaries, including also views on gender and sexuality. However, despite expressions of virulent misogyny occurring in many speculative and literary Jewish texts, marriage, together with the injunction to be fruitful and procreate, remained sanctioned cornerstones of the Jewish way of life and thought.

Given this unquestionable attitude toward marriage, the existence of a Jewish literary controversy over marriage is indeed surprising. This controversy, held in a series of Hebrew novellas written in Spain and Provence during the thirteenth and fourteenth centuries, is the topic of this chapter.

The earliest and most important in this series is an early thirteenth-century work titled *Minhat Yehuda sone ha-nashim* (The Offering of Judah the Misogynist), written by Judah Ibn Shabbetai in Toledo in 1208.[3] The twenty-seven extant manuscripts of this work attest to its popularity in the Middle Ages.[4] The story is saturated in misogyny and does explicitly declare its hostility to marriage. However, as its plot thickens, the story begins to display a growing ambivalence regarding the institution of marriage. The author, as I intend to show, speaks from both sides of his mouth, for and against marriage, transforming thus his ideological qualms into narrative devices.

On the other side of the controversy stand three other works reacting to *Minhat Yehuda*'s apparent misogamy. Two of them, *'Ezrat ha-nashim* (In Defense of Women) and *'Ein mishpat* (The Fount of Law), were written in 1210 as immediate responses to Ibn Shabbetai by a younger contemporary by the name Isaac.[5] The third work, *Ohev nashim* (The Lover [Defender] of Women) was written toward the end of the century by the Provençal Hebrew poet Yeda'aya ha-Penini. All the works are written in eloquent rhymed prose, a form adopted from the Arabic by Hebrew poets beginning in late twelfth century. *Minhat Yehuda* is in fact among the earliest examples of rhymed narratives in Hebrew.[6]

After expanding upon the literary interpretation of *Minhat Yehuda* and exploring its ambiguities I will examine the responses of readers, medieval as well as modern. Finally I will suggest some conclusions about the social context of this controversy. But before that a brief synopsis of *Minhat Yehuda* is in order:

After being asked by friends, in the prologue, how he was lured into marriage and upon confessing his sin, the first person author, Judah, tells the story of Taḥkemoni and his son Zeraḥ, two victims of marriage as well as devotees of antimarriage propaganda. Taḥkemoni, a dying old sage, adjures his son Zeraḥ never to marry. After taking an oath of abstinence Zeraḥ with three noble friends establish a fraternity and proselytize men to celibacy. Their success among both bachelors and husbands brings about a women's rebellion. The women, led by an old crafty hag, plot to undermine Zeraḥ. They will introduce him to a perfect lady whose charms he will be unable to resist, and then will replace her, at the wedding, with an ugly shrew. Once married, Zeraḥ reveals his bride's real face (and voice!). He regrets his error and sues for divorce. The shrew, aided by a host of women, persuades the judge to decree for Zeraḥ a death sentence. He is finally rescued thanks only to the author/narrator's direct interference in court, and with the latter's declaration that the whole plot was nothing but the figment of his own imagination.

Is this work misogynistic or not? Is it misogamic, or does it reaffirm marriage? How does it employ humor? In my opinion any attempt to reduce the work to a single message or an ultimate end misses the significance of its complexity. Combining a historical approach with an analysis of the narrative from a feminist perspective, my reading will focus on points of instability and ambivalence in the text, both narrative and ideological. The ambivalence felt in the author's cultural ambiance toward women and sexuality (and expressed at the time in literary as well as nonliterary works) is in my view a key to understanding its structure and thematics. The fact that it evoked a heated controversy (as well as the polemical materials interwoven in the work itself) attests to an atmosphere of a public debate. Rather than identifying with either side, the work, in fact, thematizes the debate itself and dramatizes its different voices.

"How did the ocean of marriage overwhelm [an intelligent man like] you?" This question, addressed in the prologue to the narrator Judah, the author's namesake, by his good friends, determines the rhetorical as well as the ideological boundaries of the story: intellect and marriage are considered to be diametrically opposed. The author, who is both enlightened and married, embodies a logically impossible state, an oxymoron. His friends beseech him to explain his erroneous deed and to write down—as a moral lesson for others—the story of his calamity. He is also encouraged by a divine spirit (who "came into me and stood me on my feet," as did the spirit to the prophet Ezekiel in Ezekiel 2:2) to perform this literary task. Hence, Judah writes this work as an offering (*minḥah*) to his friends and to man-kind in general. "Here is the life story of a man whose soul was ensnared by a woman," he writes in the poem heading the work. The author expresses a hope that the history of his calamities ("his grief and gloom"), eloquently related, will be used as reproach to and "exemplum" for all "men of wisdom and piety." Ibn Shabbetai's manifesto brings to mind the Latin subgenre known as the *dissuasio de non ducenda uxore*, dissuasion from taking a wife, advice given by a philosopher to a friend. This mode enjoyed a considerable popularity in Europe around the period when *Minḥat Yehuda* was written.[7]

The story of Zeraḥ and his father, Taḥkemoni,[8] takes place in a pseudobiblical space, against a background of an allegorical apocalypse. Folly and Evil (who are the supporters of marriage) have won the upper hand in their battle against Wisdom (who opposes it), and the world is about to collapse. Two survivors only, old Taḥkemoni and his son Zeraḥ, manage to flee to the mountains. Taḥkemoni is visited by an angel,[9] who reveals the cause for the world's imminent upheaval: It is women who will soon turn the cosmos back into chaos. The angel's mastery of antifeminist lore is quite impressive:

Who can undo the knots woven by women? They avert common sense and distort all truth. Their friendship and love are ephemeral. They cause all quarrel and trouble. Many a man has been put to shame on account of them.[10]

These commonplaces are followed by a list of wicked women in the Bible.[11] Eve is blamed not only for Adam's but also for the snake's downfall; Rachel's theft of the idols caused the oppression of the children of Jacob; Dinah and the concubine of Gibea (both rape victims) are held responsible for inciting bloody feuds; Delilah caused Samson's mishap; women's lust for gold motivated the making of the Golden Calf; Abraham was lucky not to have any daughters; and how clever was Pharaoh's ploy to persecute the children of Israel by killing the males and sparing the females (lines 124–35). Is the reader supposed to yield to the serious pathos of the visionary scene or catch on to the double entendres in the angel's misreading of the Bible?

Taḥkemoni initiates his son Zeraḥ into misogyny. In a lengthy admonishment (of which only a small part is quoted here), he preaches to him the divine imperative:

Never take a wife. She talks peace and means trouble. Whoever touches her is destroyed. You will clothe her with fine satins and silks, and feed her with delicacies, then another man will come and sleep with her. . . . Do not covet her beauty in your heart, and let not her delights allure you. For she has cast down many wounded; all her slain are a mighty host. . . . Do not share the fruit of your toil and all your precious possessions with others. Do not let yourself become a pimp and do not give birth to any offspring. . . . My dear son, do not invest your wealth [and strength] in women, and let not evil inhabit your house. Better to keep company with wild wolves and bears than with a woman in her chambers. Ancient sages have already said their word: "The storm will come from the [women's] ward!" Better to sit among thorns and thistles and not with a woman in her suite; between oven and furnace—not her breasts; among bramble and brier—not her curled hair; among nettles—not her necklets! . . . Do not let a woman's word fool you. . . . They are all erring at heart. . . . My son, lend your ear and listen to the words of the wise. . . . He who talks much with a woman paves his path to hell. She will be close to you when you are young and abandon you when you lose your strength. . . . Who can seize upon women's wiles and ruse? How many heroes have they let down? How many agonies have they caused? . . . (141–233)[12]

With whom is the medieval audience of this work expected to side? Would they side with the fictional representatives of Wisdom (the angel and Taḥkemoni) in totally rejecting marriage, or rather support marriage as do the fictional followers of Folly? How can the reader reconcile the fact that the advocating of marriage, which in the real social world is identified with rabbinical-communal norms, is here attributed to the vile and the foolish? This perplexing reversal of norms built into the structure of the narrative throughout undermines any possibility of a univocal reading of the story.

It is noteworthy that Taḥkemoni's message, whose implementation is said to revolutionize the existing "order of things," is cast in a discourse devoid of any originality. Saturated with traditional misogynist clichés, his text is a pastiche of recycled fragments and tatters originating from "ancient wisdom." The sources of his "wisdom" are biblical phrases, rabbinic quotations, citations from Arabic misogynist literature, and sayings attributed to anonymous sages.[13] The effect of this "citational discourse" here tends to adorn the message with an aura of legitimacy. Taḥkemoni utters no capricious newfangled ideology, but voices a sanctioned and authoritative tradition. The technique resembles that of Chaucer, of whose Wife of Bath Jill Mann writes: "In this vast echo-chamber of antifeminist commonplace the voices blur into each other, endlessly repeating the same message."[14] One example will suffice here to illustrate the vastness of this "echo chamber" in Ibn Shabbetai's *maqāma*. A large part of Tahkemoni's address is built on the rhetorical formula "It is better to . . . than to . . ." This echoes the Solomonic dictum from Proverbs 21:9: "It is better to dwell in a corner of a housetop, than with a brawling woman in a wide house." This biblical formula, mediated by St. Jerome and other Latin sources, found its way also to Jankyn's Book of Wykked Wyves, which the Wife of Bath parodies.[15]

The Marriage of a Women-Hater

Tahkemoni concludes his speech, and just before he dies Zerah takes an oath of celibacy (235–39) and hurries to preach his doctrines to three noble friends (250 ff.). Together they establish a celibate brotherhood and search for a remote uninhabited refuge. After a long journey they find the perfect site for their utopia in the Valley of Besor ("Good Tidings"). There they rest, study, and play. Theirs is an ideal world without women, an "ascetic paradise" where the masculine philosophic soul can finally find rest (257). Their refuge from sensual human nature takes place, ironically, amidst nature itself. Moreover, while the absence of women is celebrated, this prelapsarian asexual Eden swarms with symbols of femininity, fertility, and sexuality. Fedwa Malti-Douglas makes an observation that can hold true also for our story. Discussing an Islamic male utopia, she maintains that though the author "was able . . . to cast aside the female, it would seem that woman's body was a permanent fixture of the world in which he set his tale. . . . The choice [of a far off and fecund island] manifests a tension between a philosophical ideal of a society devoid of sexuality and a geographical locus imbued with that very sexuality the philosophical ideal is fleeing. Sexual geography and a-sexual philosophy are two poles [brought together]."[16]

Similarly in our *maqāma* the valley is lush with flowing streams, "planted with the trees of Eden," every kind of fruit tree with branches spreading in all directions, "and in their branches nested birds of every wing . . . every kind of fawn and deer took shelter there under every verdant tree" (258–73). A description of the garden's heavy fruitage as a sexy bosomy bride highlights this incongruity.[17] Also, ironically enough, Zerah's fantasy of an ascetic haven is a replica of the Andalusian palace garden, the conventional setting for lovemaking and flirtation in courtly poetry.[18]

As it turns out, Zeraḥ's utopia is not located in an entirely isolated valley, but alas, amidst the country of the fools who are committed to the business of marriage and reproduction. Despite their ascetic convictions, Zeraḥ and his company have no choice but to cope with the real world around them. So, for one month each year they leave their haven and wander around the neighboring towns proselytizing their misogamic "religion" (284)—dissuading the young from marriage and persuading husbands to divorce their wives. Crossing the geographical—and symbolical—boundaries of Utopia will, however, prove fateful. What seems to be a successful mission—many men do "convert" (283) and abandon their wives—will turn upside down when Zeraḥ, the enlightened prophet of abstinence, blindly falls into the dark pit of marriage.

In every town where Zeraḥ comes to preach, the abandoned wives and young desperate maidens are filled with rage. They responded to Zeraḥ's propaganda with (stereotypically "female") symptoms of mass hysteria: they trembled like women in labor, "they tore at their skin in their fashion. Their cry and their wail waxed; great was their groaning, terrible their turmoil, and loud their lament" (286–88). Bodily reaction, accompanied by a series of uncontrollable animal sounds, comes first. "Hysteria is inchoate feminism," writes Daniel Boyarin, and rather than viewing "feminism as hysteria," he considers "hysteria as feminism."[19] In our story too, the rebellion of the body is but an overture to political militancy. The speech that follows the bodily spasms by which the women's sexual anxiety is artlessly spoken heightens the nexus of female voice and lust:[20]

Not a man in the land will lie with us. Who indeed has a heart that would embolden him to touch us after this man has put us to scorn? The lasses languish, their wombs are waste, their fruit fails, all are virgins not known by man! Zeraḥ has turned us into objects of fear. And now one man has to be shared by seven women. See how great is our trouble! Every virgin is shut up and sealed off; no one enters, and none departs. Why should we lie here in our shame, covered by disgrace? Rouse yourselves, think what to do that the ladies may find lovers![21]

The effect of the women's language in this passage is double edged. Since in real life Hebrew was the language of a male literate elite, the representation of a female and vernacular register of speech in a literary Hebrew text would have been thought of as an impossibility. Hence, Ibn

Shabbetai has to let his women characters speak like men, using high Hebrew impregnated with biblical (often decontextualized) allusions. Such
grotesque parroting was probably entertaining for a male audience, but at
the same time it touches upon men's fears of women's intrusion into their
discourse. For medieval men the division was quite clear: sex is synonymous with woman's nature, but the discourse of sexuality and the control
of sexuality are man's monopoly. These women's speech about their un-
satisfied sexuality is not only funny; it exposes men's anxiety about a reversed world where women both usurp male language and employ it to
express psychological and physical needs.

Women here become political agents too. They gain an independent
voice and they act in the public domain, which, in real social terms, is exclusively men's territory. A political public assembly of women is thus a
contradiction in terms; it can be a farce or a nightmare—or both. Men's
derision of women's power is one way of dealing with the dread it
arouses.

The panicky women's mob that is about to lynch Zerah is finally
hushed by an old "shrewd woman . . . a woman expert in sorcery and deceit" (303) named Kozbi bat Yeresha, the wife of Sheker. Her typological
name denotes her hereditary deceitful nature.²² Kozbi is thus the opposite
of old Taḥkemoni: he represents patriarchal logic and intellect, she stands
for matriarchal manipulation and conspiracy. Kozbi's plot—to tempt
Zerah into a marriage with a perfect irresistible bride—places Zerah in
precisely the situation against which he was warned by his father. His soul
now becomes a battleground for two opposing powers: that of the righteous fathers and that of the dangerous tricky women.

While Kozbi urges the crowd of women to search everywhere for the
perfect bride, Zerah has two devastating premonitory dreams. In one he
falls into a deep abyss; in the other he is surrounded by wild beasts, one of
which mutilates his sex and is about to swallow him alive. His companions
easily decipher the dreams: The abyss is marriage and the beast is a
woman.

Kozbi furnishes the women with a detailed description of the ideal
woman, which parodies men's common fantasies: She should be a girl of
matchless beauty, an immaculate virgin, elegant and perfumed, a generous hostess, clever and resourceful (310–13). She must also be "a girl of
culture and counsel, knowing poetry and rhetoric, speaking eloquently
and composing verse, her speech sweet as honey and firm as a cast-metal
mirror; a girl who can call on wisdom both esoteric and exotic . . . ; who

can play the harp and lyre so as to provoke the listener to laughter or lament" (313–16).

In short, the ideal woman must also qualify for the title of ideal poet! This last requirement, strange as it is, will prove to be an important part of Kozbi's machination.

Kozbi's delegation has found the right match for Zeraḥ—a girl by the name of Ayala Sheluḥa ("a fleet-footed doe")—and Kozbi now prays to God, "who chose man and rejected woman; who made flourish in men the beard and member for his fame and glory, and who gave the daughters of Eve the burning womb of desire" to blind Zeraḥ to the truth (374–79). Kozbi recognizes the reality of sexual politics: It is the difference in genitalia, she says, that determines the hierarchy of value and power. Later, though, when Kozbi and her husband Sheker try to talk Zeraḥ into marriage, they assume the role of mouthpieces of family values. Sheker's arguments are ideological in kind; he advocates tradition, the norms of the "generations of old" (412–14). Kozbi, on the other hand, lectures to Zeraḥ in the language of Genesis that "it is not good that the man should be alone; I will make a helpmate for him." She enumerates the material benefits and comforts of a man's married life: "A woman of valor is her husband's crown. On a rainy day she is his shield and breastplate, and on a cold day—his cover. She is a fort for the poor and the weak. Her eyes will guard you when you lie down to sleep, and she will greet you when you open your eyes. With her you shall know no fear."[23]

Zeraḥ insists in his refusal: "My youthful sins will never be wiped out if I let a woman enter my bed. I'd rather spend my nights on top of a dung heap and my days in the street. I'd rather eat my bread solitary than look at delicacies" (420–22). Finally he succumbs, but not before securing an attractive dowry, and beholding the girl's beauty with his own eyes: the "rose garden" of her body and her "untouched pomegranates" (478–81), imagery derived from the Song of Songs. Zeraḥ's fall, like Adam's, begins with this fruit, which is "pleasant to the eyes" (Genesis 3:6). Zeraḥ is caught in a confusing opposition of seeing and blindness. The moment he sees his future wife he stops seeing Kozbi's and Sheker's ploy. "For if a look engenders desire, desire, in turn, forecloses all future possibility of seeing."[24]

Hearing joins sight, and after hearing the girl, Ayala, play the harp and improvise songs, Zeraḥ exclaims, "This enlightened [*maskeleth*] woman was sent by God" (483). A poetical tournament now occurs with

thirteen miniature love poems sung alternately by the couple. All poetic
conventions of courtly love are followed here except for one—instead of
the usual monologues addressed by a man to a woman, here the poetic
dialogue is symmetrical. The prospective bride has mastered the male art
of serenading. Her stylized epigrams describe Zerah's beauty in superlative terms, similar to those employed in descriptions of women in male
love lyric:[25]

> Why are your lips as red as blood?
>   Ask the midwives at your birth—
> Did they tie a crimson ribbon
>   round your wrist or on your lips?
>   (508–9)

And Zerah, like an echo, responds to her *motif*:

> You chose your lovers' hearts
>   as targets for your darts;
> Their blood cries from betwixt
>   your lips and scares my heart.[26]
>   (513–14)

It is poetry—male love poetry sung by a woman—that leads Zerah
into the snare. Had Zerah not been already blinded by the girl's looks,
the fact that her speech equals (or even outdoes) his own—in elegance, in
daring, and in quantity—might have alerted him. Ayala's poems serve for
him as a mirror in which he sees an erotic image of himself. Like Narcissus
he falls in love with his own reflection. As the poems become more and
more erotically daring, Zerah forgets all his reservations and invites Ayala
to share his bed.

Zerah is now consumed by lust and urges Kozbi to conduct the wedding instantly. In his eagerness he gives up the dowry and is even ready to
pay a bride-price. The fact that the ceremony takes place on the thirteenth
of the month of Adar, Purim Eve, heightens the carnivalesque features of
the work.[27] A ridiculous *ketuba* (parodying the formal style of the Jewish
marriage contract) is signed and Zerah, the fallen saint, becomes the
laughingstock of the event (562–80). Only upon unveiling the bride, Zerah
finds out that an ugly crone with an ugly name (Ritzpa bat Aya, "Coal,
daughter of Vulture") has replaced the perfect bride:

Kozbi took the girl and exchanged her for a quarrelsome hag, black as a crow, with lips like two inflated bladders—anyone who saw would gasp. The hair on her skin was like stubby brambles, and her face was covered with nettles—something to make infants and babes recoil (583–85). Her days were waxed old and her tits shriveled. Her face was dark and her eyes dismal, her teeth long and her forehead harder than rock. She farted. She was plaintive, shrewish, and contemptible.[28]

Seeing that "no gold and no beauty" remain, Zeraḥ cries, "A plot! Deceit! A pack of lies!" but to no avail.

Besides its comic effect, the "replacement device" betrays one of the deepest of men's fears, namely that the beloved maiden they marry may turn overnight into an unbearable spouse.[29] A popular medieval anecdote spells out this fear of transformation/deformation in a slightly different metaphor: When one of Socrates' disciples gazed at a beautiful woman, the master said, "Turn her inside out, then wilt thou understand her ugliness."[30]

The Wife Speaks

While Zeraḥ weeps, regretting his stupidity in "giving his soul into the power of its foes" (596), his wife makes the following shopping list:[31]

Go and fetch me vessels of silver and vessels of gold, dresses and chains, bracelets and mufflers; a house and a flat, a chair and a lamp, a table and spoons, a pestle and groats, a blanket and spindle-weight, a mat and a tub, basket and spindle, a cauldron and bottle, a basin and clothespress, a broom and a kerchief; a pan, furnace, barrel, and shovel; a pot, vessels, goblets and charms; gowns, veils, turbans and robes; linen, nose rings, purses, and lace; crescents, amulets and sashes, embroidery, headdresses, rings, checkered cloth, armlets and anklets and anklebands—and besides these: special clothes to wear on Sabbaths and festivals. . . . This is by no means all you shall have to provide. (609–16)

Ritzpa's first act thus attests to two of woman's cardinal sins: her excessive speech and her greed for material possessions. A symmetrical dialogue between the sexes (as in Zeraḥ's and Ayala's courtship) is possible only as an erotic fantasy; marriage is presented as a semiotic battle over the domination of language and signification. When Zeraḥ begins an agonized monologue, his wife stops him right away: "Stop taking up your rhyme! Do not even raise your voice! I have no interest in wisdom or culture, only in bread and meat. Your poems and your lyrics mean nothing to me—A poem does not buy a glass of wine" (787–88).

In voicing her opinion of her husband's "literature" this wife anticipates the more overt and articulate Wife of Bath, who expresses her criticism by tearing three pages out of her husband's misogynistic book.
Moreover, when Ritzpa opposes man's "wisdom and culture" to woman's
"bread and meat," does she simply reiterate hegemonic views about
woman's crude nature, or does she mock them? Her text, like that of
Chaucer's Wife, lends itself to more than one reading. According to one
reading, misogyny, when voiced by a woman, is far more comical and thus
more effective than when voiced by a man. According to another reading,
the tension here between speech and speaker relativizes the message, and
consequently subverts the male point of view.[32]

Garrulousness (the wife's verbose monologues) and gluttony (her
desire for bread and meat) are two female sins performed by the mouth;
they become interchangeable as displacements of woman's excessive sexuality. Zeraḥ's nightmare had similarly equated woman's "upper" and
"lower" mouths: for the mouth of the female beast that mutilated him is
clearly a realization of the *vagina dentata* whose "lips are the gates of
hell, and jaws—slaughter knives."[33] Ritzpa now pushes Zeraḥ to criminal-
ity, telling him what real manhood is:

Get up, take your plow and your plowshare, your quiver and bow, and go about
the town from dusk to dawn, stealing and murdering and swearing falsely. As your
household grows you will have to provide their daily bread. And you shall not appear empty-handed before me. Wasn't woman given to you to till her and to care
for her? If you fail to bring me every single thing I desire—you will stay outside![34]
(633–36)

Having won the upper hand in language, she now also gets the upper
hand in sex, controlling not only the household's economic affairs but
also the ins and outs of copulation. Abstinence, Zeraḥ's abandoned ideology, becomes Ritzpa's strategy in controlling Zeraḥ's body; his phallus
and its metaphoric replacements (his "plow and bow") are now, so to
speak, in her hands. Using the phrase "to till her and care for her" (borrowed from Genesis 2:15 where it is Adam's task "to till" the soil of Eden),
this woman reverses the sanctioned order of things. She is no man's helpmate but her husband's sovereign. And if he fails to care for her, she
threatens to expel him from her (sexual) paradise ("stay outside!").

We may note that Ritzpa's ultimatum consists of three clauses: food
(bread, meat, and wine), covering (veils, gowns, and so on), and intercourse. These three are, in Jewish marital law, the husband's obligations

toward his wife and thus the woman's rights (*she'erah, kesutah ve-'onatah*: "her food, her raiment and her conjugal rights," Exodus 21:10). Ritzpa actually threatens to stop her husband from fulfilling his third duty (*'onah*) in case her first two demands are not fully met. However, worse is still to come: "But all this is nothing compared with the day I give birth! Then you will really work! My brothers and my relations will be in your presence around your table, and you will provide a whole sheep for their daily delicacies. Nor will the midwife do without wine bread, or meat. You will have to call a wet nurse for the children . . . and buy slave women and maids to tend for them to eat their dung and drink their urine, for I will not touch them!" (636–40).

As in the grotesque, the funny and the threatening meet here, in Ritzpa's rejection of all motherly functions. But did Taḥkemoni not warn Zeraḥ against "becoming a pimp" and having to support prostitutes and their children (166–67)? This picture of the tribulations of the paterfamilias has hardly any parallels in Jewish literature, but is matched in Latin literature in the theme of the poor husband who has to resort to crime to fill his family's insatiable bellies.[35]

Marriage Saved

While listening to his wife, Zeraḥ's hair turns white. Like Job he sits, bemoaning his fate, with three companions alternately rebuking and consoling him. His decision to eventually dissolve the marriage starts a heated debate among his townsmen. The townswomen, however, unite in support of Ritzpa. Everybody goes to trial in the court of "King Abraham."

Here historical reality trespasses on the confines of fiction. "King Abraham" is Abraham Ibn al-Fakhkhar, Ibn Shabbetai's patron. A Hebrew writer himself, Ibn al-Fakhkhar served as a courtier to Alfonso VII and was a communal leader in Toledo.[36] As the guardian of societal norms, he is expected to elicit the truth. Upon listening to the accusations of the townswomen's advocate—Zeraḥ ruined families and disgraced women—the judge decrees a death penalty for Zeraḥ. Ambiguity dominates even this crucial point of the narrative: For the supporters of marriage the death sentence proves that Zeraḥ was the villain of the piece, but for those who oppose marriage Zeraḥ is convicted for betraying his own misogynist creed.[37]

Rescue comes unexpectedly. The author, Judah himself, appears in

court like a deus ex machina and puts himself, instead of Zeraḥ, to the
judge's trial (777). The author's defense is poetic license. Zeraḥ, he says, is
only a fictitious literary creation. Unlike Zeraḥ and the misogynist narrator, he, the author, is a loving husband and father. Moreover, this piece is
but an entertaining farce intended to please his patron, Abraham. It is a
comic purpose, he says, which caused him "to reverse things" (785). What
is now put on trial is Ibn Shabbetai's artistic achievement, not the moral
of his tale. Hence Abraham, to whom everyone looked as the *arbiter mo-
rum*, becomes an *arbiter elegantiae*. His laughter is proof of the author's
literary success. With the piece being dedicated to Abraham, and with Judah being generously rewarded, the contract between author and patron
is fully completed and the story is happily brought to an end.

Misogyny Remains Intact

How did modern critics interpret this complex and sophisticated work? How
did medieval readers read it? Among modern critics only Norman Roth
reads *Minḥat Yehuda* as unequivocally misogynistic and misogamic: "The
satire . . . is clearly directed against woman in general and *any* kind of
marriage."[38] Most other critics, however, have seen the misogyny as di-
luted or canceled out by other aspects of the text: "The satire is directed
against those who go to extremes. It is both a warning to the misogynist
and a protest against hasty marriage. . . . This evidently is not only a satire
on women, but also a reproach to those who despise them";[39] "Ibn Shabbetai did not mean in fact to preach women-hatred, but put it in the
mouth of his protagonist. . . . All he intended was to please, entertain and
divert his patron and audience";[40] "Its chief aim is indeed to divert, not
to denigrate";[41] "It is hard to view 'The Misogynist' as a seriously misogynistic work . . . [although] the author knows and enjoys the conventions
and stereotypes of misogynistic literature";[42] "The ending alters the
meaning of the central story line. . . . The author's ultimate exposure of
the entire tale as illusory undercuts the work's misogynist content at the
level of broad structure, just as his assertion that he loves his wife and
children plays that role on a narrative level."[43]

By focusing on the author's intention, these critics limit themselves
to reading the work through the author's eyes, and thus fail to consider
its diverse meanings for diverse readers. Adopting the author's perspective, critics fail to see humor as an ideological instrument by which mi-

sogyny is—inadvertently or purposely, but always efficiently—disseminated. They see humor rather as a way of diluting or even disarming its virulence. My argument is that Ibn Shabbetai's disclaimer of seriousness at the end of his work does not itself have to be taken seriously, and his entertaining purpose does not necessarily mitigate antifeminism. Nor does the defense of fictitiousness. Some critics argue that the ending (where Ibn Shabbetai admits that he concocted "the thing in order to turn it upside down") reverses the apparent meaning of the piece. This argument overlooks a structural pattern quite common in endings of *maqāmāt*: the self-referential exposure of the fictional nature of the tale.[44] Does the recognition of fictionality as such necessarily contradict the values of a discourse? Similarly, on the level of narration, does the narrator's avowal of loving his wife and children vindicate his expressed misogyny? Is the proclamation of loving one's wife not the last refuge of the male chauvinist?

Another position holds that the work is "egalitarian," that is, as critical and satirical of men as it is of women. This ignores the double standard in this maqāma. Men are censured here for acting stupidly (Zeraḥ) or falsely (Sheker), but women are deprecated simply for being what they are; men are judged for deeds, woman are incriminated on an essentialist basis. In addition, while men in the fiction are divided into two camps, the good and the bad, women are all bad; and if there is a good one, like Ayala, one finds that she was a fantasy, a bait, too good to be true. Lastly, some critics admit misogyny but assert extenuating circumstances: Jewish misogyny was the product of the "bad influence" exerted by Islamic or Christian sources.[45]

In my view, Judah's misogamic message is contradicted in the story's conclusion, but its misogyny remains intact. The restitution of marriage as a societal norm does not logically alter the negative view of woman. An absurd, even tragic, aspect of the mentality of medieval men is thus disclosed: marriage is good, though it entails a union with an essentially evil partner.

While agreeing with Matti Huss on many points of his comprehensive discussion, including his conclusion that no univocal conclusion can be drawn from this self-contradicting complex work,[46] I differ with him on the question of humor. Indifferent to the gendered aspects of humor, Huss writes: "Ibn Shabbetai makes it clear to us, as he did to his historical readers, that the sheer representation of absurd 'reversed worlds,' in which unexpected and illogical occurrences take place, is indeed very funny."[47] Who is Huss's "us"? Does the reader response as analyzed by Huss apply equally to the medieval reader and to the modern reader? Does it apply equally to readers of both sexes? Is the humor of these "reversed worlds" funny also from a woman's perspective? There is no reason to believe that Ibn Shabbetai's audience, a literary circle at Abraham Ibn al-Fakhkhar's "court," was not exclusively male. Its ambience must have resembled those sessions in gentlemen's clubs where piquant jokes, not intended for a lady's ear, were told. Freud's definition of "smut" is relevant in this context:

> Where a joke is not an aim in itself—that is, when it is not an innocent one . . . —it is either a hostile joke (serving for the purpose of aggressiveness, satire, or defense) or an obscene joke (serving the purpose of exposure). . . . We know what is meant by "smut": the intentional bringing into prominence of sexual facts and relations by speech. . . . A person who laughs at smut that he hears is laughing as though he were the spectator of an act of sexual aggression. . . . Smut is like the exposure of the sexually different person to whom it is directed. . . . It cannot be doubted that the desire to see what is sexually exposed is the original motive of smut. . . . Generally speaking, a tendentious joke calls for three people: in addition to the one who makes the joke, there must be a second who is taken as the object of the hostile or sexual aggressiveness, and a third in whom the joke's aim of producing pleasure is fulfilled. . . . Through the first person's smutty speech the woman is exposed before the third who, as listener, has now been bribed by the effortless satisfaction of his own libido.[48]

Shoshana Felman, in discussing this passage, calls attention to the essentially male structure of the sexual joke: "Although originally seeking an exposure of the female body, [it] is in turn motivated in an exclusively male structure of address. . . . The act . . . of joking is rhetorically addressed to male accomplices. . . . Women do not occupy the place from which the joke is funny. If the joke is an exchange of laughter or of pleasure between two men at the expense of women, women are completely justified to put themselves in a position to miss the joke."[49]

Not all medieval readers of *Minhat Yehuda* thought it to be funny. At least three literary responses written during the thirteenth century attack its misogyny. Two of them were written in 1210, just two years after Ibn Shabbetai's first version of 1208, by an author known only by his first name, Isaac, probably of a Provençal origin. *Ezrat ha-nashim* (In Defense of Women) closely follows *Minhat Yehuda*, but is a reverse mirror of its model.[50] Here too the prologue is a revelation scene: an angel orders Isaac to listen to the complaints of Jewish women about Ibn Shabbetai's disastrous influence on their husbands. The desperate women urge Isaac to take vengeance on their abuser, whereupon he undertakes to write a story in praise of conjugal love. Hence, the characters in Isaac's story are antithetic to those of Ibn Shabbetai's. A dying patriarch encourages his son to marry, and a young wife is a perfect lady, an ideal helpmate and her husband's lifesaver.[51] In the prologue to his second work, 'Ein mishpat (The Fount of Law), Isaac foretells the end of the world, which will be caused by husbands who followed Ibn Shabbetai's teaching and abandoned their wives. Isaac sees it as his mission to persuade men to rejoin their families.[52]

This literary marriage debate was still current in 1295 when the eighteen-year-old Yeda'aya ha-Penini of Provence wrote Ohev nashim (The Lover [Defender] of Women) as another pro-woman response to Minhat Yehuda. One of ha-Penini's characters is Ibn Shabbetai himself, who is defeated in a literary contest, in which the winner is the author, the defender of women and marriage.[53] In the heat of these rhetorical battles between woman-defenders and woman-haters one should not be deluded as to the nature of the "defense." The defending voices spring from the heart of patriarchy. The case for women is made by male voices. It is men who retaliate against other men for their misogyny. The admiration of "feminine virtue" is in fact a commendation of patriarchal feminine stereotypes. Rachel in Ezrat ha-nashim is "good" because she is good for her husband: she is long-suffering, loyal and resourceful. The women in the other two "defenses" win male sympathy because they are abandoned and needy. As Alcuin Blamires observes in a book wholly dedicated to the medieval literary advocacy of women, this "profeminine discourse" has an "unfeminist quality."[54] R. Howard Bloch extends the definition of misogyny to include any "speech act in which woman is the subject of the sentence and the predicate a more general term [negative or positive]."[55]

Ambivalence over Women and Marriage in Jewish Circles

In what way do Minhat Yehuda and the works that responded to it reflect the culture that produced and consumed them? Is the debate between Judah and Isaac to be seen as a sheer literary tournament or does it indicate some real social tension? Is a debate over marriage plausible in a Jewish community guided by halakha? Prima facie the answer is negative: "Marriage is the positively marked term in rabbinic culture, while virginity is marked as negative."[56] Where can a Jewish travesty of marriage, then, originate?

The possibility that Ibn Shabbetai may have been inspired by Christian culture is not implausible for an author whose patron was an important official at the Castilian court. Whether Ibn Shabbetai was acquainted with Latin language and literature is unknown. However, despite the difficulty in tracing the precise route of literary transmission, motifs and topoi culled from Latin literature may be readily recognized in Ibn Shabbetai's work (as indicated above). Moreover, it is likely that controversies around marriage which plagued Catholicism at this period were known to Ibn Shabbetai and other Jewish intellectuals.[57] David Biale refers to this sociocultural unrest in southern France and Spain, and to its resonance in Jewish circles:

Jewish intellectuals were undoubtedly aware of developments in canon law and scholastic theology. . . . Christian theologians of the High Middle Ages were deeply concerned with problems of sexuality and marriage. In precisely this period, southern France, Spain and Italy were gripped by the Catharist (or Albigensian) dualistic heresy, which preached renunciation of the material world. As medieval heirs of Gnosticism and Manichaeanism, the Cathars vehemently rejected marriage and procreation. It is not unlikely that the challenge of these heretics prompted a renewed Catholic affirmation of marriage; at the same time . . . church lawyers developed the medieval doctrine of marriage as a sacrament and of procreation as divinely decreed. During the twelfth century, though, the church also experienced a movement of reform that dissolved clerical marriages and unequivocally established clerical celibacy. As opposed to the Catharist desire to equalize clergy and laity under a common doctrine of celibacy, the church drew a sharp distinction between a celibate clergy and a married laity. The rabbinic class, which no doubt saw itself as the counterpart of the Christian clergy, must have felt the need to defend its own continuing marriages against the ideal of a celibate clergy.[58]

And later he suggests: "We know not of Jewish 'Cathars,' although the sect's gnostic doctrines may well have been familiar to . . . Jews."[59]

The assumption that Ibn Shabbetai concocted this story as a satire on actual events in the Christian surrounding is, thus, not entirely inconceivable.[60] However, the adaptation of the theme in a Jewish context raises the question whether the internal Christian polemic over marriage could have touched a sensitive nerve in Jewish culture. Whether or not *Minhat Yehuda* reflects the Christian polemic, it might very well reflect a dormant discontent among Jews. In *Eros and the Jews*, David Biale writes:

"The very institution of marriage was troubling for elements of the Spanish-Jewish intelligentsia, who projected their ambivalences onto women as either the source of the problem or its cure."[61] I would like to argue that works like *Minḥat Yehuda* and its rejoinders could not have been written were there not some ambivalence toward marriage in the Jewish tradition as well as in the medieval Jewish milieu in and for which they were written. Although halakha is unequivocal in its positive valuation of marriage and procreation,[62] this does not necessarily annul the possibility of other voices, of discontent and tension, within Jewish culture. Following Daniel Boyarin's advice to read talmudic culture "not as a monologic language but as a heteroglossic collection of dialects,"[63] I would apply the same perspective to medieval Judaism. In other words, the prevalence of halakha did not prevent the expression of nonhalakhic tendencies, nor did it prevent the permeation of ideas and controversies from the ambient cultures.

A fascination with celibacy, created by the contradictory commitments to marriage and to the study of Torah, was already present in talmudic culture. Despite the sacred obligation to marry and procreate the rabbis had still "to combat the attractiveness of celibate life . . . [which] was the ideal of much of the ambient culture, both Jewish and non-Jewish."[64] Following are several explicit ascetic pronouncements, made by medieval eminent authors, legal authorities, and religious figures, which are not compatible with the spirit of halakha. Saadia Gaon, the tenth-century leader of Babylonian Jewry, expresses repulsion toward sexuality but advocates it for procreation. Nevertheless, he is ambivalent in regard to raising children and lists the tribulations in providing for them, in health and in sickness, as well as in suffering heartache caused by their improper behavior.[65] Even more astounding are warnings against procreation itself, voiced in Hebrew poems of eleventh-century al-Andalus. Samuel ha-Nagid, a halakha authority, a communal leader, vizier of Granada, a master of love poetry, and a dedicated father of four, writes:

> Men in their folly beget children
>   in vain, and celebrate their birth.
> Had they known the world's end
>   they would not rear children nor procreate.[66]

In a similar vein the celibate Solomon Ibn Gabirol (eleventh-century Zaragoza), poet and philosopher, writes:

> If you wish to inherit Paradise
>   and if you fear hellfire,
> Loathe this world's values; be not tempted
>   by riches, honor or offspring.[67]

Even if these epigrams are rhetorical exercises on an ascetic theme and not sincere utterances, still, the very fact that they were voiced in a Jewish milieu speaks for itself. The eleventh-century philosopher and moralist Baḥya Ibn Paqūda, although intellectually attracted to extreme Islamic ascetic celibacy, eventually yielded to halakha in matters of marriage and procreation.[68] More daring was Abraham Maimuni (Egypt), Maimonides' son and Ibn Shabbetai's younger contemporary, who, influenced by Sufi mysticism, referred to the tribulations of family life, and praised the prophets for their abstinence from sex.[69] In their apologetic style both reveal their fascination with Muslim celibate ascetics, but ultimately align themselves with the Jewish consensus.

Most ambivalent on sexual issues was Maimonides. For him physical pleasure is an animal drive, adverse to meditative life, yet he admitted it as beneficial to health. Sex and the body are shameful, but marriage and children are primary postulates. The advantage of marriage, he added, is in that it dulls sexual desire. Like Islamic ascetics he recommended abstinence within the framework of family life. During intercourse it is commendable for a scholar to be restrained so that procreation is separated from desire. The commandment of ʿonah, that is the husband's obligation (according to the rabbis) to ensure the woman's sexual pleasure, goes unmentioned by Maimonides.[70]

Rabbi Abraham ben David of Posquières (a rabbinical authority, circa. 1120–1198, usually referred to as Rabad) was Maimonides' vehement opponent. Criticizing Maimonides' opinions on intercourse, Rabad "restored the commandment of ʿonah as equally legitimate. The sexual rights of women now found a defender against the misogynist philosophers!"[71] In a "marriage manual" composed circa 1180, Rabad maintains that though a husband should not indulge in his own sexual pleasure he owes his wife not just the minimum of ʿonah as is required by the law but as much as she desires.[72] The protest of women in *Minḥat Yehuda* (repeated also in *ʿEzrat ha-nashim*) and their insistence on fulfillment of their sexual pleasure may thus be a comical and exaggerated expression of this debate over the issue of ʿonah.[73]

To conclude, though ultimately guided by the consensus of official halakha, eminent Jewish leaders and thinkers did voice varied opinions on matters of marital life. Thus Ibn Shabbetai's *Minḥat Yehuda* is in all likelihood informed by the author's knowledge of contemporary Christian controversies. Yet there was enough of dissent in Jewish literature at the time to make the debate theme effective in a Jewish context. Hence the perplexity of the reader transcends the realm of literary response to become a symptom of the qualms and ambivalence of the contemporary intellectual Jewish milieu.

6

Among Men:
Homotextuality in the *Maqāma*

Triangular Transactions

A FAMOUS SAYING IN Mishna Avot (81) warns: "Do not talk much with the woman. . . . He who talks much with the woman brings evil upon himself, and is idle from learning the Torah, and will end in hell." In his commentary to Avot, Maimonides added: "It is well known that conversations with woman are mostly on matters of copulation. This is why it was forbidden to talk with them much. And the 'evil that one brings upon oneself' is the increase of passion. And by 'end' the sages meant that this talk will incite him to rebellion, and justify his punishment."[1]

The ideal is that the speech worlds of men and women be separated. An Arabic anecdote tells about a caliphal crown prince who, after being served dinner and wine by his newly wed wife, hinted to her that "something" was missing. "What is it?" "Someone to talk to." She brought in her two brothers, who became his boon companions. S. D. Goitein recounts this anecdote as an illustration of what he observes as "the male's incapacity of 'talking' to a woman." The medieval civilization that emerges from the pages of the Geniza, which Goitein so masterfully succeeded in reconstructing, was, as he phrases it, one "characterized by its strong and compact groups of males. . . . [Men] were brothers to one another. . . . A man's company consisted of men."[2] However, as he comments, men did talk—much too much, and among themselves—about women and about sex. "The opulent and mighty . . . loosened their tongues and secluded their wives. The littérateurs . . . provided us with abundant and unrestrained reports about sex as it was discussed and practiced in those circles. [The poor] had had little power to seclude their wives, and no cause to restrain their tongues."[3]

Men's talk pervades the *maqāmāt* and other varieties of the rhymed

Hebrew story: wayfarers meet at inns, crossroads, and graveyards, telling each other their whereabouts; gentlemen conduct elegant after-dinner discussions about serious as well as idle matters; and poets convene at city gates where they exchange rhymed couplets, moral proverbs, and coarse anecdotes. However, men talking to other men is not merely the content of an overriding number of *maqāmāt*, but, as I intend to suggest, an essential generic structure. Deriving from the Arabic *maqām* ("standing place," originally the assembly place of the Arabian tribes), the word *maqāma* was borrowed in later periods for the all-male assemblies of intellectuals, scholars, and poets in the caliphs' courts. Subsequently, the meaning shifted to designate also the products of these meetings: eloquent lectures or alternately, the tales told by vagabond beggars at the city's gates.[4]

In the classical model of the genre, which is best represented in Hebrew by the fifty *maqāmāt* of Judah al-Ḥarizi,[5] the narrative content is conventionally "enveloped" by men's talk. The occasion is always the same: the narrator Heman ha-Ezrahi meets his friend Ḥever ha-Qeni and listens to his tale (or his lecture).[6]

Typical is the exposition of al-Ḥarizi's forty-fifth *maqāma*, where Heman invites Ḥever to wine and dine. Then, "after giving rest to tongue and tooth," penniless Ḥever offers to pay for his meal with proverbial currency:[7]

[Ḥever] said: I am obliged to pay you . . . so I will tell you the choice of proverbs that I have heard from wise men. . . . Our forefathers told us about a great sage . . . who gathered one day twenty-four famous wise men and asked each of them to tell a parable of wisdom. . . . One said: A man was asked to praise his beloved's beauty, and said: Her belly is the full moon, her face—a garden, her lips—manna, her cheeks—roses. . . . And another said: A man was asked to praise his beloved's beauty, and said: . . . Standing she's a golden rod, sitting she's a gazelle, walking she's a haughty dove, talking she kindles fire in the heart. . . . And another one said: A wise man saw his son watching a pretty woman, and told him: O my son, what is it that you love in women? Their bellies are hollows, their breasts—goatskins, their beauty—nudity, and they [themselves] are caverns filled with craving.

Interestingly, though not unexpectedly, a great deal of this discourse revolves around the topic of women. Noteworthy is also the intertextual dimension of this male talk. While reenacting that renowned symposium, Ḥever recycles second- and thirdhand citations of male wisdom. This characteristically discloses a much wider paradigm common to the medieval literary canon. Literature is the marketplace where "triangular transactions" between men take place, in which women (or writings about them) feature

as objects for exchange. Inasmuch as it is the author's concern to please
other men, so do the protagonists wish to please each other and, at the same
time, to be pleased *as men*. This economy of pleasure tightens the male
bond, and enhances gender identity through literature. Hence, the *maqāma* identifies itself as being a homo(inter)textual activity, "one in which
male writings [are] referred to, responded to, manipulated, and project desire upon other men and other's men writings as much, if not more, than
they claim . . . to represent the extraliterary world and woman in it."[8]

The present chapter deals with several such *maqāmāt* where this
"homotextuality" is central. Four *maqāmāt* by Immanuel of Rome,[9] in
which the "triangular transactions" involve not merely the amusing exchange of words about women, but, furthermore, a thematization of that
exchange and a concretization of the status of woman as object are discussed here. As I will show, women figure here as objects that change
male hands, as pawn and prize in men's literary games. I also include in
this chapter Judah Al-Ḥarizi's "Debate between the Man and the Woman,"
where a woman is apparently given a speaking role equal to that of a
man's. However, entering a male playground, playing to the eyes of male
spectators, and exchanging typical male "wisdom," she is yet a player in
another homotextual game.

To Describe Her Is to Control Her

Description is a serious business. It may prove fatal, especially for the perfect woman who happens to be the subject (or rather the object) described. Shakespeare's Lucrece died because of having been described by
a man, in her case her husband, to other men. She committed suicide after one of the listeners, so infatuated by the perfection of her verbal icon,
raped her.[10] Similar is the fate of Immanuel's "nun," in his third *maqāma*
discussed below. Her starving herself to death is, too, ultimately a result
of a male description.

In both stories descriptive art is a tool used by men to boast to other
men of the beauty and virtue of "their" women. Lucrece's husband, like
the nun's half-brother, both brag about a rare and exclusive possession of
theirs, which is a taboo for others. However, in publicizing the dignity
and inaccessibility of their women, both describers, paradoxically, expose
their private assets to the "thievish ears" of other, lascivious males.

The celebration of female beauty has always been a central topos in male rhetoric. But, in a way, the stories of Lucrece and of Immanuel's (Jewish?) "nun" manifest the risky limits of this seemingly innocent tradition. In a discussion of Shakespeare's *Lucrece*, Nancy Vickers comments: "[Rhetorical] tradition was, in large part, the product of men talking to other men about women. The canonical legacy of description is a legacy shared predominantly by the male imagination. . . . [M]en praise beautiful women among men . . . a battle between men that is figuratively fought out on the fields of woman's 'celebrated body.' " Hence, as Vickers explains, description becomes a means of control: "Description within a like context clearly serves the describer, not the described . . . for to describe, is in a sense, to control, to possess, and ultimately to use to one's own hands." And, she adds, the result of Shakespeare's rewriting of Lucrece's classical story "is a heightened insistence on the power of description, on the dangers inherent in descriptive occasions."[11]

The nun's, like Lucrece's, tragedy begins with men's games and with the careless mention of her to too-eager ears. The rhetorical occasion is similar. Immanuel and his patron have just returned from the town's gate, that meeting place of idle gentlemen, where they were entertaining themselves and others with the poetic sport of women's description.[12] While they were sitting there, two women passed by: one was most dazzling, the other most repulsive. So extreme was her ugliness, such a danger to the world's order was it, that the men at the city gate where about to lynch her. She was saved only thanks to Immanuel's patron's proposal to embark on a poetic contest: "one of us will praise the beautiful one, the other will condemn the ugly, and we will so overplay it in both praise and abuse, until all springs of poetry will gush forth, and all clouds of rhetoric will pour out, and until all muses will bow down [to us]" (28–31). Adoration and violence readily translate into rhetorical energy. In a swift exchange of short verses, and in escalating hyperboles, Immanuel praises the pretty one, Tamar, while the patron denounces the ugly. The first mounts the peaks of pathos while the latter descends to the bottom of bathos. Both women, angelic Tamar and demonic Bri'ah, are excuses for oratorical bravura, triggers of men's tongues, reifications of abstract ideas rather then representations of flesh and blood women:

SAID I: Tamar—when she looks up to the sky—all stars rise, and when she looks down to earth—the dead arise.
SAID THE PATRON: Bri'ah would kill a viper with her eyes, and if the devil saw her—he would flee.

SAID I: Tamar exhausts all eulogy; if the angels met her they would cry
out: "Let's climb up!"

SAID THE PATRON: Bri'ah is useful at vintage season—to scare away the
wolves.

SAID I: Tamar—if angels knew her they would use her as fetish to revive
the plague-stricken.

SAID THE PATRON: Bri'ah—I wonder why don't the rich tie her to the
doorjamb, to play with her as with a monkey.

SAID I: Tamar challenges the rising sun, saying: "Come up, you bald
one!"

SAID THE PATRON: Bri'ah—I wish I could recall her at my father's death,
to stir my grief.

SAID I: Tamar looks out from the window and bids: "Stand still O Sun
in Gibeon; stand moon in the Vale of Ayalon."

SAID THE PATRON: Bri'ah—if she's on my mind when I make love, I'll
have no erection all night long.

SAID I: Tamar took from Beauty its best, and from Virtue its finest.

SAID THE PATRON: Bri'ah—if all women were her like, incest would not
have to be forbidden.

SAID I: Tamar—at midnight I went out, not once but twice, to check if
the stars can replace her eyes.

SAID THE PATRON: Bri'ah's shame exceeds all shame, no curse is adequate
for her, and no blame.

SAID I: Tamar—if we saw her just once a month, to our Lord we would
bow in awe.

SAID THE PATRON: Bri'ah consists of all defects and faults; her mouth is
like a pig's, and like excretion.

SAID I: Tamar would be Moses's—if she lived in his time.

SAID THE PATRON: Bri'ah was conceived by her mother on a day of darkness and gloom, dusk, and smog.

SAID I: Tamar—if Betzalel knew her, he would cast the Cherubim in her
image.

SAID THE PATRON: Bri'ah was not born from woman and man, but from
stench, stink, and reek.

SAID I: Tamar—if the artist's apprentice needed one unit of time to create the entire universe, the master himself would have needed double
the time to create her.

SAID THE PATRON: Bri'ah—if not for her coat, I would not be able to tell
her from a bat.

SAID I: Tamar—if Amnon only dreamt of her he would not pretend to
be sick to Tamar, Absalom's sister.

SAID THE PATRON: Bri'ah—I wonder how she mixes with ladies and not
with rats, mice, and tortoises.

SAID I: Tamar—I wonder whether men can die while she lives, or
whether men could live after she dies.

SAID THE PATRON: If Time had genitals, Bri'ah is its genitals, and if Time
stinks she is its stench and reek.

SAID I: If Joseph saw Tamar he would chase her, rather than leaving his
shirt in her hands and flee.

SAID THE PATRON: Bri'ah—if she dwelt in clefts of rocks and cliffs—all
bats would tremble in fear.

(35–157, with omissions)

The male crowd who audited this exchange applauds with amusement—
and with the unmistakable imagery of rape: "You have breached the limits
of eloquence! . . . Rhetoric is yours alone . . . and that of other rhetoricians is an unwalled city" (159–62).

While the patron's grotesque description of the ugly gives vent to
male aggression, Immanuel's proclamation of the pretty one becomes his
own trap. He falls in love with the subject of his own verbose description.
The rhetorician was captivated by the power of his own verbal creation.
He goes into raptures over a stranger, a woman he has just met. Trying to
capture her uniqueness, he exhausts all conventional treasures of the
descriptive art.[13]

Immanuel, however, will soon forget all about Tamar and will immediately fall in love with her sister, or rather with the sister's irresistible description as imparted to him by his patron. The sister is a recluse,
"recoiling from the joys of Eros and love, fencing herself within the
[thorny] roses of abstinence and solitude . . . intent on reining her drives.
She strives to navigate from the ocean of passions to the continent of
continence" (9–14). Surpassing Tamar in beauty as well as in virtue, she
will make, according to the patron, a better match for a gentleman like
Immanuel:

I will impair today your desire for Tamar. . . . The lady that you have seen is not
deserving of your rank. Her sister is prettier; smart and chaste, extremely good
looking, a virgin not known by a man, nice to look at and pleasure to the eyes—
she surpasses all ladies in morality and humility. Beautiful like the moon, radiant
like the sun. She is skilled in poetry, able in rhetoric. Gold cannot buy her, silver

will not weigh her price. . . . Her wisdom won her fame, name, and glory. She is
the capital of poetry's pillars. A golden tongue lies in her mouth. . . . Those who
serenade or panegyrize her are thieves in hiding. Their eloquence is vulgar
tongue, foreign to her ear. . . . Noblemen proposed to her and were refused. If
you only saw her light, you would be maddened by the sight. (9–19)

Itself an exercise in rhetoric, the patron's presentation of the lady is,
ironically, also a comment on the shortcomings of rhetoric. The most glit-
tering gold and silver coins forged by the rhetoricians cannot weigh the
lady's value. Her praise is unutterable; it remains beyond their words.
When describing her uniqueness, poets boast of their originality of language but are, in fact, thieves stealing clichés from each other. The patron's
distrust of poetic language does not, however, stop him from praising the
lady's own poetical skill. She is deft in poetry but deaf to poets!

Rhetoric is short in capturing the lady's worth, but, alas, it is powerful enough to captivate a tried rhetorician like Immanuel himself. But
even more than by her beauty Immanuel is aroused by her being so hard
to get; so hard to be captured *in* words—and *by* words. The text seems to
deconstruct itself. Being an elaboration of the power of rhetoric, and at
the same time a comment on its limitations, the idea seems to cut three
ways: it demonstrates the manipulative sway of poetry; it shows the weakness of men enamored with their own words; and it serves the feminist
critique of male language as being a vain exercise that has little to do with
the woman in question.

The lady's inaccessibility to language and her immaculate virginity
become mutual metaphors. The poet desires to have that which no poet
can describe; he desires to own what no man can own—because owning
virginity is the same as ruining it. Moreover, the lady's resistance to male
poetry, and to malekind, only challenges Immanuel's poetic impulse as
well as arousing his sexual drives. His growing lust will become a threat to
that pure virginity which has ignited this very lust.

The patron's intention in presenting the lady to Immanuel is ambiguous in the first place. Does he really encourage Immanuel to fall in
love with Tamar's sister, who, as he will reveal to him later on (and, indeed, much too late), is also the patron's own half-sister? Or does he just
wish to boast of being acquainted with such a virtuous and pretty
woman? Does he wish to provoke Immanuel's desire as well as his poetic
skills in love lyrics, knowing that the nun will never succumb? Or is it the
nun's chastity that he is eager to test? As we shall see, toward the end, the

patron indeed instructs Immanuel: "Tell the lady your poems were devised just to put her to the test." If this was what he intended, is his obsession with his half-sister's chastity so great as to risk her honor—and his own? And what is the woman's role? "The heroines' role is that of an object of exchange between two knights who use her as a testing ground for their own honor," writes Roberta Krueger in her discussion of the subgenre of the wager romance. "The wager romance is a 'test' of the chivalric system ability to contain and control the threat of female sexuality."[14] Though the two gentlemen in our story do not openly negotiate a bet, betting seems to be their hidden motive. What Immanuel puts at stake is his reputation as poet and as lover; the patron's stake is his family's honor embodied in the nun's body.

Despite the patron's dissuasion ("Are you as stupid as to desire the queen of heaven?"), the poet, confident of his own potency, is determined to win her. In a tirade (full of hackneyed phrases) the poet boasts to the patron his own unsurpassable genius. Bragging his potency in the art of persuasion, he insinuates the language of rape: "My poems are as swift as lightning and as burnished as brass. My forceful idioms make breaches in damsels' hearts, and rip into their locked hearts" (29–30). His is not just a seductive art of heart penetrating. It is a violent act of breaching and tearing. Ravishing the ravishing virgin is what his "forceful idioms" aim at. Kathryn Gravdal points to the semantic shift in thirteenth-century French of the verb "ravish": "The shift reveals the assumption that whatever is attractive begs to be ravished: carried off, seized or raped. The ideas of woman's attractiveness and a man's desire to rape are conflated in *ravissant* . . . and the literal meaning of sexual violence is erased behind the romantic troping of ravishment."[15]

The patron, weighed down by the poet's bravado (and apparently deaf to his sexual insinuations), agrees to let him peek at the lady while she strolls to her morning prayers. The poet who already fell in love by the ear is now infatuated by the eye. The lady, so he tells her to her face, transcends all descriptions of her. Her immediate rebuke only encourages him to translate his oral flattery into writing.

In an embellished letter sent to her he praises not only her great beauty, but also the ingenuous artist who made her, Nature itself. Tellingly, Nature's job is very similar to that of the describing poet. Nature imitates the poet (who, in his turn, imitates nature) and competes with him. Both are artisans, experts in the technique of *collage*, the assembling of ready-made parts:

It is in you that Nature desired to demonstrate all his marvels. . . . Thus, he assembled them all in your design. He took the sun's glare and the moon's dazzle, the snow's white and the rose's red, a pomegranate slice, a palm's stature, doves' eyes, purple, honey, and the sweetness of manna—from which he made your eyes to look like those of the valley-doves, and your neck erect like David's tower, and your cheek like a pomegranate's slice, your lips like roses, your radiance like the rising sun, your dazzle like the moon's, your flavor like manna, your braids purplish red, . . . and your stature like a palm's. (96–103)

Woman's celebrated body is a masterpiece combining beauty with utility. It is an artifact; the sum of its parts glued together. Yet, each of the parts may function separately to satisfy man's fantasies: "And now beloved, what good is there in your arms, these golden rods, if you do not embrace your lover? And what good is there in your doves' eyes if they do not allure fawns? And your purplish red braids if they do not entangle a lover? . . . And why do your lips drip nectar if there is no kisser? And what are your breasts for if no sweetheart lies betwixt them? (104–14)."

But the nun refuses to identify herself in this male mirror. Her body, transformed into male art, "has turned," as Hélène Cixous puts it, "into an uncanny stranger on display."[16] She would rather contemplate, so she replies, in the "mirror of the mind" (146). She denounces desire. Asceticism is her path. In her unequivocal reply she upsets the common equation of male/spirit, female/body. She lets the male indulge in the corporeal, while she chooses the spiritual. In her bellicose imagery ("I will brandish my solid sword . . . to deter your love," 281), as well as in her sententious ascetic discourse, she discloses her intimacy with male knowledge and language. She speaks as a woman but like a man.

Interestingly, Immanuel is devastated not only by her rejection, but also by her great poetic talent, which, as he himself admits, surpasses his own ("and I despised my own proverbs and verse," 189). Her characteristically male eloquence sharpens his pen. Now she is not only a female object of seduction, but also a competitor, a co-poet whom he is eager to exceed. To master her as poet would mean to win her as woman. She is a competitor and a prize in one. Hence, his letters become exceedingly pompous, full of rhetorical verbiage to the point of sheer parody. Fueled by both her excellence and her obstinacy, he continues: "You despised my letter, but I was not baffled. You disdained my love, but I was not shattered. How did I enjoy this refusal, and the way you formulated it!" (242–45). The poet likes her retorts because they are a masterpiece of male oration.

"Poems are ladders on which lovers climb" (222), he believes. This so typically Italian metaphor of a serenading suitor climbing to his sweetheart's balcony and sneaking to her suite, responds to the woman's imagery of infiltration, or rather harassment:

Here is your hand, Sir, suddenly stretched out at me, pressuring me. And your poems, handwoven, arouse storms [in me], blowing me away, inciting me to follow lovers. . . . Your poems tell me: "We are messengers sent to you from the Master of all Lovers!" I was reading them and they felt bitter in my mouth, and set in me the fire of rage. And now tell me, you Captain of Lovers! . . . What will your poems do to me? Will they besiege me? Will they yell at me? My heart, like Mount Zion, will never tumble! (147–52)

This testimony of a woman reader's response is elucidating. While ridiculing his poetic trivia, she is also aware of the erotic allure of his text. Acting ultimately like Judith Fetterley's "resisting reader" ("Stop bringing me your false offerings," 282), the reading "nun" also recognizes, with Patrocinio Schweickart, the irresistible power of some male texts to draw women (even feminists) into their androcentric design.[17]

It will be Immanuel's third letter, with even more flattery and more desperate pleas for mercy, that will cancel her resistance and kindle in her the flames of love. Eager to experience all the joys she has hitherto only read about, she urges him now in a lengthy letter: "Who will escort me to the gazelles' abode? Who was it who led me to live among hermits, ignorant in love? It is twenty years that I have lived in their house . . . and never have I known any joy. Will my beloved come to my garden and eat my sweet fruit. There will I offer you my love. . . . Do with me as you please" (426–28, 440–41).

Having conquered the woman/poet, Immanuel hurries now to his patron. He wishes to break to him the news of his poetic victory and, even more so, to divulge to him that this woman is not as unattainable and as chaste as he, the patron, had thought. The physical sign, the letter (in the wager romance it is a ring or a flower), is in his hand. The patron, enraged and full of misgivings, reveals to him that this woman is his half-sister and that the continuation of this romance will damage her chastity and the family's honor. Forcing the poet to back off, he makes known his own hitherto obscured motives: "Tell the lady your poems were devised just to put her to the test. And do reinforce her belief in abstinence" (475–76). Anxious about maintaining the male bond, the poet now overdoes the task:

Did we not always wish to expose the secrets of the gazelles? . . . But only today have I succeeded to uncover their shame . . . Who would believe that this [lady], pure and holy, proudly wearing her nun's attire, . . . would fall in that trap? Why did you not resist when, like a devil, I came to tempt you? How did you not see that I was testing you? Do you lack reason? Have you abandoned your advisor? How did you divest the coat of spirituality and vest yourself with the attire of Eros? . . . Where is your diadem of divine abstinence? Where is your laurel of lofty existence? . . . "She is our . . . most precious treasure. . . . She is filled with the love of perfection. . . . She embodies the idea of humbleness and asceticism." Such and such did women use to say about you, not once and not twice . . . and what will you say now when the word of your shame is spread? . . . Will the women not lynch you for letting them down? (478–527)

Reading this last letter, she is overcome by melancholy and disgrace, and she starves herself to death. The arrogant patron was wrong twice: his sister could withstand neither temptation nor rejection. And the poet, realizing the tragic consequences of his cynical game—and of his devotion to his male comrade rather than to his female darling—is now, more than ever, enraptured with the dead, eternally unattainable beloved. Like Lucrece, Immanuel's heroine had to die, not as punishment for her actual deeds, but because she has become a pawn in men's rhetorical games.[18]

Her Body Is the Prize

Another battle between poets fought over a woman's body takes place in Immanuel's sixteenth and seventeenth *maqāmāt*.[19] Here, too, the woman is to be the competitors' prize. While in the nun's story male rhetoric is a threat to woman's most cherished virginity, here it is the loss of virginity that will be the woman's gain. She will be relieved from the burden of virginity if she is won as a prize. This is, indeed, if the winner is *not* her husband.

A paragon of beauty and wisdom, she is married to a vile person, "reek and stench among people," and, worse than that, an impotent. When she was eighteen her parents married her to this good-for-nothing, and she, afraid of dying a virgin, agreed. But, alas, a virgin she has remained, "a target to [her husband's] squishy-squashy arrow" (195). She envies her lucky neighbor who buried three husbands within thirty months.

The patron fell for her after seeing her just once, and when he hears that she is also inclined to poetry,[20] he urges the poet to pay her a visit. In a lengthy poem (160–211) she laments her lost youth, the suitors that she foolishly rejected, and her thoughtless parents. Though longish, the wife's lament is written in short and rhythmic verses, suggestive of women's folksongs.[21] She also begs her listeners not to despise her if, in her desolation, she yields to some of her many suitors. However, as soon as Immanuel grants the woman a voice—sentimental, expressive, and at times also sarcastic—the patron, his alter-ego, hastens to silence it. Inasmuch as he is delighted with her talent, he is indifferent to her plight: "This lament, I swear, is most fit for the occasion of your husband's death! But we did not come here to cry. We intended to cheer ourselves with your verses" (214–15).

It is on the second visit (in the seventeenth *maqāma*) that the patron and the poet find the amusement they sought. The whole scene is reminiscent of a commedia dell'arte. The wife leans out the window, the husband is down in the street hurling insults at her, and the two visitors, pretending that the husband is just another flatterer, make sexual hints at the lady, who waits to see her husband's response. The patron offers a deal: the three suitors will compete in improvising poems. The winner will gain the lady. The lady's husband refuses to join the merry tournament, nor is he willing to disclose to them that he, the third "suitor," is her husband. Love lyric, he says, is not his expertise. Instead, the wretched man surprises them in issuing a long series of philosophic quotations, moral maxims, and poems—most of which are extremely misogynistic. By citing the commonplace stock sayings about women's wiles and allure and by renouncing passion and sex, he intends both to impress and instruct the two gentlemen. However, unable to deter the intruders with epigrams, he advises them that the lady's husband is a sturdy thug who will readily use "his spear" against any male rival. The patron, aroused by the challenge, implores the lady to arrange for a duel between himself and that mighty husband. At that point, the wife betrays her still-incognito husband, calling out: "This leper, this despicable and filthy man, *he* is my husband," whereupon he retorts in turn with "unruly cow, a woman of folly and riot." Having now nothing to lose, the wife joins the noisy street row. Here is the overt and graphic report of her husband's destitution—and of her own physical affluence—that she passes on to her visitors: "Listen to me O sweet suitors . . . ! My husband is old and obsolete. He has dissolved into the darkness he emerged from. His limbs are all shadowy, fleeting like rafts. Lust he refuses; he won't listen to it. And as for me—I have pretty and stimulating merchandise to sell, world-known for its beauty. I have upper fountains and lower fountains, treasures my husband is too foolish to value" (290–93).

Rather than an expression of sexual liberty, it seems that the lady collaborates here with the male game. Her body is merchandise which she offers for sale. And since there are two eager clients, she proposes a deal; this time not a competition over her body, but the sharing of it. Who will get which part remains the men's business to decide: "Here you are, two lovers, knocking on my door! [And] here is my figure like a palm in stature! . . . I'll part my body into two. My belt will be the divide. You, sir, will have the right to choose first, and your friend last" (293–95). The belt, instead of girdling the woman's chastity, is here a sign for looseness; instead of delineating her forbidden zone, it duplicates the zones of accessible desire. The patron, reviewing her hair, lips, teeth, neck, and breast, chooses her upper part.[22]

The husband, mad at her volunteering her body, offers now to renew the poetic contest he previously was so reluctant to join. The prize, he agrees, will be the lady's body. The irony is not only that he hopes to win that which is legally his own, but, moreover, he hopes to win that which he practically will never be capable of having. The two friends ignore the wife's warning that her husband, despite his crippled physique, is poetically most potent. The husband leaves it to them to choose the genre of competition—they choose bawdy rhymes—implying that, being superior to them in rhetoric and poetry, he will be the one to win in any genre. And, indeed, after several exchanges of smutty verses (set of course in beautiful literary language), they have to admit that he excels them in that genre. At this point they propose a riddling contest, which he wins as well. The patron's riddle goes as follows:

Who is the woman born first, begotten with heaven and earth? Who is she who since her birth has doggedly called upon the houses of her adulterers? She is unfaithful to all those she has fornicated with. [With] gods and angels she has never kept company. Though married, she desires every leper and villain, [but then] betrays her philanderers. She is passive but receptive; desires strangers but despises her husband. She [is married but] will never become a widow. She has lived long but old she is not. (387–92)

The riddle seems to metonymically stem from the context which generated it, comically insinuating the lady's loose conduct. Though she is still a virgin, the riddle's metaphoric vehicle intimates she is a whore. This riddle/joke is probably meant as an ad hominem blow below the husband's belt. The patron's intention to knock down his rival in this verbal wrestling outweighs, so it seems, his love for the lady. But the husband is not so easily embarrassed, and immediately deciphers the riddle. He rightly locates it in the realm of philosophical allegory, rather than in the context of his own dismal life story. The adulterous wife, he pronounces, is "First Matter." Promptly and triumphantly he performs an intertextual act— improvising the prose riddle into a formal verse form, a sonnet (396–409).

Why would the First Matter be compared to an adulterous wife? The easiness with which the patron devises the riddle, as well as the readiness with which the husband delivers the answer, immediately distinguishes them (and, of course, their author, Immanuel) as students of philosophy, and, to be more exact, as followers of Maimonidean metaphysics.[23] The riddle is, in fact, a close elaboration of a pivotal paragraph in Maimonides. The homo(inter)textual dimension of the discourse is of great significance here. In *The Guide of the Perplexed* (3:8) the philosopher relates to the parable of the married harlot in Proverbs,[24] interpreting it as an allegory on Aristotelian form and matter:

How extraordinary is what Solomon said in his wisdom when likening matter to a married harlot, for matter in no way is found without form and is consequently always like a married woman who is never separated from a man and is never free. However, notwithstanding her being a married woman, she never ceases to seek another man to substitute for her husband, and she deceives and draws him on in every way until he obtains from her what her husband used to obtain. And this is the condition of matter.[25]

Underlying this allegorization is Maimonides' exegesis to the story of the creation of Adam and Eve as an ontological enigma: "For they concealed what they said about the first principles and presented it in enigmas. Thus Plato and his predecessors designated Matter as the female and Form as the Male."[26] Hence, Eve = Woman = Matter is never detached (widowed) from Form. Matter is incapable of independent action or reproduction, but is receptive to forms. Matter is thus ever in search of new forms/philanderers. This fickleness of matter Maimonides sees as inherently female. And if matter were essentially female, only a small step would lead to the easy but dangerous syllogism, that femaleness is essential whoredom.

What began as hilarious burlesque ends apparently with elegiac tones. The rivals admit the husband's victory and sadly leave the battlefield. The weeping lady is left to rot with the impotent who won a prize he will never enjoy. The irony is even more pungent, since the wife he won back is eternally a virgin and, at the same time, essentially a whore.

With the riddle's solution delivered, and the woman returning to her husband's hands, the exchange is completed.

The lady who was granted an active part in the comedy—even if merely as a conductor for male rhetorical energy—disappears from the riddling session. There is no need for her voice or presence in the purely intellectual transaction, where the male rivals become colleagues, partakers in a homotextual culture which is not hers. When her husband solves the riddle and collects his prize, as it were, she leaves the window and recedes to the background, back to the domestic sphere. The narrator comments: "She abruptly disappeared, like a swift whirlwind in the wilderness, her eyes pouring showers, ruining her vines and her figs [i.e., her beauty] and we have not seen her for a whole year" (412–14). Rather than dwelling upon the woman's plight, the ending focuses on the patron's devastation, his mourning and loss of appetite. His sons and daughters (yes, he is a married man) come to comfort him, but to no avail. Immanuel, failing to relieve the patron's pain, disappears for a long period. The male couple, presented in the prologue as based on friendship, solidarity, shared interests—and especially on shared *textual* pleasures— disintegrates. Marriage, however destitute and absurd, prevails.

When the Object Speaks

"But what if the object started to speak?" asks Luce Irigaray.[27] What if woman, the subject matter of abundant misogynist writings in the Middle Ages, stops being the silent ally of the dominant discourse that objectifies her and starts talking back? Will speech turn her into a subject? There is more than one possible answer to this question. Jane Burns, in her discussion of the French *fabliaux* claims that "the paradox of the female speaking subject [is that] even as she speaks, [she] cannot, it seems, escape primary identification as an object."[28] On the other hand stand the two famous women in the European tradition who did assert their subjectivity by talking back and challenging male literature. The two, Chaucer's fictional Wife of Bath and the real Christine de Pisan, showed a keen knowledge of what men wrote about them and offered a critique of male writing—be the critique parodic as in the case of the Wife of Bath, or profound and erudite as in Christine's case.[29]

Christine and Chaucer's Wife represent two modes through which medieval women could become acquainted with male patriarchal writings. Learned Christine read and studied them. The Wife—in all likelihood illiterate—heard them. Using Susan Schibanoff's term, she was an "aural reader, . . . an ear-reader, not an eye-reader. Her texts are read to her by her priests, her husbands, and others. Her choice of texts is largely controlled by the men who read to her, and . . . she is probably well versed in anti-feminist traditions."[30]

Were medieval Jewish women similarly familiar with the patriarchal literature of their time? Were they able to challenge the written opinions of their fathers, husbands, and brothers about their sex? Very little historical evidence exists (in Hebrew or in other Jewish languages) concerning women who read, responded to, or even just listened to male literature, not to mention Jewish women who defended themselves in writing against their defamers.[31]

Some rare illustrations of such female "aural readers," listening and responding to their husbands' wisdom, occur in Hebrew literature. One, the wife of a pious Muslim, requests her husband to recount to her some "legends" after the Friday dinner. Interestingly enough, the author chooses to cast her request in Aramaic—the male language of Jewish learning. The husband responds willingly, "*Listen*, my daughter, watch and lend your *ear* to the words of your Lord, your husband, and I will inform you with explicit morals construed by elders and patriarchs about women." But, instead of the "legends" she expects, he cites to her a sermon enumerating the virtues of the ideal, obedient, and modest wife.[32] No wonder then that when this woman implores her young lover to keep his promise and pay her a visit, she extensively quotes matters of halakha, regarding the keeping of vows, from several mishnaic and talmudic sources. In another case a newly wed wife, already weary of her husband's complaints, cast in the form of antifeminist gnomes, yells at him, revealing her critical opinions of male "literature": "Stop taking up your rhyme! Do not even raise your voice! I have no interest in wisdom or culture, only in bread and meat. Your poems and your lyrics mean nothing to me—A poem does not buy a glass of wine."[33]

How would a woman read—if she could read—the misogynist writings of men in Hebrew-Jewish culture? Or, how might she respond to male oral discourse were she given the right to respond? Inevitably, the reconstruction of such female voices must derive from traces of female expression captured in male literature. Given that such traces reach us already muffled by filters of male thinking and male wording; given that they are forged to fit the male author's ends, it becomes necessary to ask whether they are still able to represent possible women's responses to male misogyny? Or do they constitute what men imagine to be women's conceivable response? Is not the "ventriloquistic imitation of someone else's voice . . . a usurpation of that person's power"?[34]

Sheila Fisher and Janet Halley assert unequivocally that "the female speaker invented by a male author is the mark of female absence, because the male author is speaking not through, but across the female in order to address other men. . . . The appropriation of female voices underwrites female absence."[35]

Contesting this view, Jane Burns offers that instead of a wholesale dismissal of woman's voice in male texts, instead of exclusively handling them as appropriation or undermining of woman's power, the feminist reader will do better by attempting to deconstruct these expressions and see how they are divided against themselves: "If her voice is contained within the dominant voice of male culture, it can also speak to us in registers generally foreign to that dominant voice." And later, listening to female voices in the French fabliaux she adds: "As diverse as these female voices may be, when taken together they provide a kind of collective choral response to the dominant antifeminist stance of the texts they inhabit. . . . The remarks of female protagonists consistently help to reveal the limits of the misogynist logic that reduces woman to an irrational unknowing body."[36]

The voice of a woman, unyielding and protesting, is contained within the forty-first *maqāma* in the *Tahkemoni* by Judah Al-Ḥarizi, entitled "The Debate between the Man and the Woman as to Who Is More Essential for the World's Existence."[37] Critics did not find this *maqāma* deserving of a detailed discussion. Norman Roth dismisses it, saying that "this dispute has little literary merit, consisting merely of exchanges of insults."[38] Ezra Fleischer, listing this *maqāma* among other of al-Ḥarizi's debate *maqāmāt*, maintains that in speaking for and against a certain topic, they all boil down to a kind of "ludicrous 'opportunism'; . . . solid truths do not exist anymore . . . rhetoric is more important than meaning."[39] However, he adds, the speakers are at times in agreement with the literary convention (when they speak for "wine" or against "separation") and at times contrary to it (against "wine" and for "separation"). What is the convention when "woman" is the debated topic? And what would be the effect when it is a woman disputant who makes the case for "woman"? In my treatment of this piece I offer to read it as a text divided against itself, as an inadvertent self-contestation of its own premises.

Although it appears to be an adaptation of the fortieth *maqāma* by al-Ḥarīrī, the Arabic master of the genre, the Hebrew piece differs from the Arabic in several respects.[40] Whereas al-Ḥarīrī's story reads like a domestic scandal dragged into court, al-Ḥarizi's counterpart is modeled upon, or rather seems to parody, a public disputation held between scholars or poets.[41] Unlike the Arabic, the Hebrew elaboration is far from being a mirror of real life or a saucy folk anecdote. Staging a public *disputatio* between an "Old Man" and a "Harsh Woman," the text is a rhetorical construct, a confrontation between universalized abstract essences of femininity and masculinity, "talking heads" devoid of "story," biography or psychology.[42] The dialogue between *the* Man and *the* Woman brings to mind the allegorical debates, common in certain medieval genres, between inanimate objects, or between abstract binary oppositions.[43]

In al-Ḥarizi's *maqāma* a crowd is gathered in the town's square to listen to a debate between a Man and a Woman. We are led to believe at the outset that the Old Man is a prestigious patriarch ("old" also meaning honorable and wise),[44] while the female disputant is, before she even opens her mouth, delegitimized as being "a woman harsh and brash, robed in evil, brazen faced." It is not only her obnoxious appearance that does it, but the very effrontery of her preparing to speak in public. Speaking in public is "natural" for a man, but for a woman, it is manly, namely, "unnatural." In the public square—male territory—the Woman is an intruder. And intruder she is, too, in male philosophy and rhetoric, the tools with which she would so masterfully challenge the Man's monopoly over speech. As for the author of this text, he equips the Woman with the right tools, and allots fairly balanced chunks of text to both speakers, yet he nevertheless allows the Man to control significant segments of the text and gives him the privilege of the first and last words.[45]

The dialogue revolves around two central axes. One is self-referential and has to do with the conditions, indeed the very legitimacy, of female speech. The other involves a scholastic-sophistic disputation over the place of Man and Woman in the Order of Creation—as well as the social implications of their relative "natural" positioning.

The battle over speech reaches its violent crescendo immediately after the first round of dialogue, as the Woman first dares to expose the Man's faulty reasoning. The "respectable" Old Man berates the Woman with invective, lowering the level of the argument from the pseudoscholastic to that of a marketplace brawl: "Put your hand to your mouth, you vile and despised [creature], trodden like filth in a dung heap, loaded with shame.

How dare you compare yourself to males, and ignore your own defect?"
The Woman's defect (*mum*),[46] it transpires, the cause of her considerable
difference from men, is her genital cavity, which corresponds to her big
filthy mouth. In terms of this logic, "her voice is condemned typically as
suffering from bodily—and specifically vaginal—contamination. . . . An
unclean body [has] contaminated the female mouth."[47]

The Man's attempt to silence the Woman through the mention of
her anatomy results in an even more violent assault on her part. She does
not deny the accusation that her mouth is polluted; on the contrary, as if
to prove it, and as if to outdo his smut, her speech becomes even dirtier
than his. She constructs a further analogy between male and female orifices: namely, that if women's facial and vaginal mouths are, as the Man
claims, identical, then men's facial and anal holes must also be one and
the same. If woman talks from a facial vagina, man talks from a facial anus;
if she is reduced to a vagina, as the Man maintains—since "women are
pudendum"—and her speech is nothing but vaginal secretion, then his
speech, in her words, is best compared to excrement: "Aren't you
ashamed of yourself, you blockhead, you idiot, that you open your big
mouth at me! You are full of filth, a fount of foulness, a root of shit.
When you have spoken . . . filth has poured out of your mouth. Come on
now and cover your stools!"

The foul speech that al-Ḥarizi puts in the Woman's mouth sounds
outrageous to a gentle ear, until one is reminded that she is only made to
repeat here what respectable talmudic sages said about "woman":
"Woman is a jar full of shit; her mouth is filled with blood—and [despite
that] all run after her" (BT Shabbat 141:1). If anus equals vagina, it follows that man and his speech may also be defined in terms of an anatomical hole, an absence. Furthermore, the Man is feminized here in yet
another respect—the Woman's words reduce him to the lowest rank of
corporeality and materiality to no lesser extent than she is reduced by
him. There is no attempt on the Woman's part to refute the patriarchal
identification of woman and matter. Woman is indeed matter—but so is
man, too. And if man has a mind, so too has woman! Where the Man silences the Woman by advising her to shove her hand into her mouth, she
prays for God to cut off, to castrate, the Man's erect tongue. "It is
haughty and libelous; longer than the ocean and drawn out like a sword."
Man's tongue/phallus is a graphic symbol for his purported linguistic/in-
tellectual ability.

The battle over speech also involves the appropriation, by the

Woman, of typical registers of male discourse. Everything he can do, she can do better. Like him, she excels in fouling her mouth as well as in exploiting sophistic arguments. Her mastery of scatological speech only matches her command of prophetic rhetoric; at one point, the furious Woman addresses the Old Man, and through him the whole of malekind, with the enraged words of the prophet Isaiah "O sinful nation" (1:4).

Bound up with the issue of the legitimacy of women's speech is the contention over the gender of prophecy. The Man argues that the fact that the prophets—the select of humankind—were all male goes to prove men's superiority. The Woman will later argue that prophecy was not exclusively a male practice: "Has He not spoken with us as well? Some of us too were prophets." In her rhetorical question the Woman invokes the angry words of Miriam and Aaron rebelling against Moses' exclusive authority.[48] Much like a modern feminist, this Woman seeks to ground her own speech in a legitimate literary chain of women's creativity. She is eager to show that her discourse, though daring and novel, stems from the prestigious tradition of Miriam, Deborah, and Huldah. The Man, of course, spurns the very idea of women's share in the prophecy. In his history, women's prophecy is not an indication of gender equality, but rather of the immensity of Israel's sinfulness! Women's prophecy, he says, was punishment, not achievement, since women were sent to the nation only when it erred excessively.

In putting these pros and cons into the mouth of his debaters al-Harizi might have alluded, somewhat parodically perhaps, to references in Maimonides to the issue of women's prophecy. As against his own, and more well-known, solid identification of the male with the spiritual and the female with the corporeal, Maimonides surprisingly considered positively the possibility of woman's prophecy.[49] Miriam, who is harshly criticized by the talmudic sages, is listed by him, alongside Moses and Aaron, as one who attained utmost spiritual perfection.[50] It is to the debating Woman, then, that al-Harizi ascribes Maimonides' outstanding view in favor of women's prophecy, while he lets the Man follow the more traditional and demeaning attitude of the sages toward women prophets.[51]

The exclusion of women from prophecy is entangled in the Man's attempt to prove male supremacy, and hence man's rightful domination over *all* creatures. This is, in fact, the theme of the first round of the debate. That women are located low in the evolutionary hierarchy is for the debating Man not only a matter of ontology, but a rhetorical tactic meant to put his female partner in "the right place." Unlike men who are closest to God, he preaches, women are exiled from the sphere of holiness. The rule of men is not perceived by him as culturally constructed by men themselves, but as the teleological end of divine design, part of a natural order. The fact that the Jewish man has to adhere to religious duties, while the Jewish woman is exempt from them,[52] is demagogically exploited as still more evidence of man's closeness to God. Women are remote from God "because they are *pudendum*"; their sexuality is an obstacle to holiness. This entails that the closest a woman can get to God is by serving God's servant, her husband. Inasmuch as the wide world was created to publicize man's reputation, to be the stage for his honorable deeds, the home, so says the Man, was built to hide woman's shame. In so saying the Man inadvertently betrays the false logic of the famous patriarchal saying that "the honor of the princess is to be kept inside the house." As this saying was and is still being used in orthodox circles, the "princess" is recommended to stay indoors in order to increase *her* "honor." But the man here reveals the true spirit of the dictum: The house is designed to hide woman's shameful sexuality, and man's "honor" depends on, and is indeed the correlate of, his wife's/wives' "shame." Later on in the dialogue, the Woman will go on ridiculing her partner by further exposing man's faulty thinking: "Don't you know that men's honor depends on us women?" And what is male honor worth if it is wholly dependent on fickle women? If it is "locate[d] . . . between the legs of a woman"?[53] How can it be kept if it is easily damaged by woman's "bad" conduct?

Only toward the end of his first speech does the Man reveal the theological grounds of his tenets: "If not for man, woman would not have been created, and she was not given a name." Hence, man is woman's cause—both ontologically (since woman was created from man's rib), and semantically (since the word *woman* is derived from the word *man*).[54] Woman appeared second, hence she is secondary, derivative, subjugated by nature. The biblical "rib version" is again called up to account for and to legitimize women's oppression.

Elizabeth Grosz relates this logic to the conflation of the male/female opposition with the mind/body one:

Misogynist thought has commonly found a convenient self-justification for women's secondary social positions by containing them within bodies that are represented, even construed, as . . . imperfect, unruly, and unreliable. . . . Woman's corporeal specificity is used to explain and justify the different (read: unequal) social positions and cognitive abilities of the two sexes. By implication, women's bodies are presumed to be incapable of men's achievements.[55]

In her turn the Woman will not totally deny her "corporeal specificity," but rather she will exploit it sophistically. How, asks the debating Woman, does the patriarchal truism that man is the cause and woman his result—that is, that Adam begot Eve—measure up to the more mundane and visible evidence of biology that it is woman who gives birth to man? Woman is not secondary to man, she argues, not his "result" but his cause—"We are the root and you are the branches." But men are "brash and brazen," she says (repeating those epithets attributed by al-Ḥarizi earlier to the Woman herself). Not only do they stubbornly reject obvious truths, but they also cowardly hide in the "shelter of lies" and the "fortress of deceit."

Unlike the Man who conceives of his truth as absolute and exclusive, the Woman's is a relative truth that can embrace, dialectically, the opinions of both sexes. She says: "As you are superior to us, we, too, are superior to you. For your need for us is no less than our need for you." In this acknowledgment the Woman disputant actually does what Elizabeth Grosz attributes to Irigaray: "She refuses the 'either/or' logic of dichotomous models by presenting the feminine as a mode of occupying both alternatives, asserting 'both/and' logic of difference in its place. To speak *as woman* is already to defy the monologism of discursive domination under phallocentrism."[56]

The Old Man can scarcely deal with this idea of symmetry, complementarity, and the mutual dependence of the two sexes. That the corresponding needs of the two sexes, their two "lacks," are mutually fulfilled in human sexuality is unacceptable for him. His way of reestablishing the distance as well as the difference between man and woman is by referring to the female's biology and the social inferiority it entails. Woman was taken from man's rib so that she knows that she is dependent on him, a slave, a part of a whole.

The Man accentuates woman's corporeality so that he can disassociate himself from his own. "Misogynist thought confines women to the biological requirements of reproduction on the assumption that . . . women are somehow *more* biological, *more* corporeal, and *more* natural than men."[57] But the Woman refuses to "take on the burden of the other's corporeality."[58] In reminding her disputant that she has an active mind no less than he has a craving body, she dismantles the representational alignment of the mind/body and male/female oppositions. In so doing she anticipates modern feminists who, in Grosz's words, claim that "Women can no longer take on the function of being *the* body for men while men are left free to soar to the heights of theoretical reflection and cultural production."[59]

For the man the very mention of *his* "lack"—his sexual craving for woman—is, as already shown, sufficient cause for losing his temper. This demonstrates another claim made by the Woman, namely, that men's behavior is irrational and idiosyncratic: "When you need us you kneel before our feet, but upon obtaining fulfillment of your wishes, you become arrogant and all you want then is to humiliate us." In their ingratitude, she says, men resemble religious hypocrites, "those villains who delight in the Lord's favors, without even thanking Him . . . but in bad times cry to Him 'Rise and save us!' " This is the Woman's riposte to the Man's idolization of himself. In her analogy, instead, it is the woman who is positioned in the place of the Divine.

While the Woman adheres to mundane facts of life, the Man tries to shift back to sophistic arguments. Her metaphor of "root and branches" upsets him, not because it does not agree with biology and Aristotelian logic (according to which, as a rule, cause is superior to and more substantial than its effect). On the contrary, it upsets him precisely because it does so too perfectly. In his inability to cope with it, the Man again uses invectives: "If female is the source of male, then it is, indeed, a source full of shame and stench." In his eagerness to refute her, he twists accepted logic as well as empirical proof. The effect, he says, can, in fact, be superior to its cause. As examples he cites the deepest abyss from which the finest pearls are taken, or the dust from which all creatures—including prophets—were formed. But does it follow from here, he asks, that dust is superior to man?

The Woman ignores this ad absurdum argument and forces the man to confront her previous point, namely: "Despite your arrogance, lust makes you subservient to us." Now the man has to admit that "Male's lust for the female is bad . . . like the craving of a sick person for meat in which his sickness grows worse, not better. The sick person knows that in eating it his sickness will worsen, but he cannot stop himself from doing it. . . . So is the female the cause for man's harm."[60]

From here he goes on to enumerate all negative outcomes of lust. Lust causes marriage and its ensuing responsibilities (the wife's food, raiment, and sexual needs). However misogynistic this tirade is—especially in reducing woman to flesh and even to meat[61]—the man does partially admit the Woman's claims at this point. A man in need is a man indeed. Man does need woman to relieve his lust, but it is the woman who is to blame for the sexuality of both sexes. This is Elizabeth Grosz's analysis of man's fallacious thinking: "The coding of femininity with corporeality in effect leaves men free to inhabit what they (falsely) believe is a purely conceptual order while at the same time enabling them to satisfy their (sometimes disavowed) need for corporeal contact through their access to women's bodies and services."[62]

What the Woman achieves in this debate is an incipient erosion of the mind/body dichotomy that philosophers, ascetics, and comic authors alike worked so hard to assert. Woman, says our debating female, has a share in spirituality (prophecy) just as man has a part in corporeality (lust). The Woman is the winner in this contest not because she has defeated man—male dominance in sophistry and in Creation is not substituted for with female dominance—but by virtue of undermining his notions of hierarchy and difference.

Granting the last word to the Man (in a rhymed epilogue recelebrating male superiority), the author structurally reconfirms the male speaker's privileged position. However, with the presence of such a competent female voice, the text generates a contestation of its own ideology. "This raises the compelling question of why such texts interrogate their own privilege."[63] What could have been al-Ḥarizi's intention in incorporating such an efficient advocate of womankind? The question is all the more intriguing if we remember that al-Ḥarizi was a genuine Maimonidean, likely to be deeply invested in the great teacher's misogynistic views.[64] What was his interest in balancing his protagonist's, or for that matter, his own misogyny?[65]

Rather than aiming at a sincere female critique of male discourse, it is more conceivable that he consciously intended his *maqāma* as a diverting satire, creating in the text an absurd imaginary world in which women, illiterate as they are, parrot male learning. This *mundus inversus* in which women can speak and behave just like men, could also have been intended as a warning against this very possibility.

But regardless of what al-Ḥarizi thought he was doing, the voice of female resistance is irrevocably there. The text does speak to us with two voices: a man's and a woman's. The choice of the dialogic genre of disputation turned out to be the author's self-installed trap, in which he had to

implant a voice practically deconstructing his own, and his male protagonist's, "phallocentric monologism" (to use Irigaray's term). Furthermore,
in adhering to the inner dynamic of the genre, he necessarily had to employ two counterbalanced rivals, capable of responding to each other's
challenges. For the duel to be successful, that is, pleasing to the audience,
the Woman had to own a voice no less loud, an intellect no less sharp, and
an acquaintance with the logic of misogyny no less extensive than that of
her male rival. Thus, the woman's presence, even if as a "speaking object," a mere rhetorical construct, infiltrates the homotextual scene and
assaults it from within. And once the woman is given a voice she can
speak up.

Al-Ḥarizi's disputing woman is capable of resisting her male contes-
tant's views on the issues of sex difference, domination, and desire, because she is so much "drenched" in misogynistic texts. She enters the
debate already well-versed in traditions of patriarchal writings (scriptural,
philosophical, poetic, rhetorical). An "aural reader" (in Schibanoff's sense),
she also qualifies as a "resisting reader" in Judith Fetterley's sense. In its
critique of the male text the female voice becomes the inscribed embodiment of the feminist reader. For a woman "to read the [male] canon" un-
critically, argues Fetterley "is to identify as male, [to be] co-opted into
participation in an experience from which she is explicitly excluded; she is
asked to identify with a selfhood that defines itself in opposition to her;
she is required to identify against herself." Fetterley describes the female
reader of male texts as "intellectually male, sexually female, one [who] is
in effect no one, nowhere, immasculated." In order to overcome this
"powerlessness . . . which results from the endless division of self against
self" the reading woman must "become a resisting rather than a consent-
ing reader and, by this refusal to assent, to begin the process of exorcizing
the male mind that has been implanted in us." This resistance is for Fetterley the very condition, and the first act, of feminist criticism.[66] In this
sense al-Ḥarizi's Woman delineates the textual locus of the future feminist
critic. In fact, she prefigures her.

7

Clothes Reading:
Cross-Dressing in the *Maqāma*

Transvestism as Disruption

MEN DISGUISED AS WOMEN and women in men's attire make their appearance in the four Hebrew *maqāmāt* discussed in this chapter. As a motif, cross-dressing (along with masking, veiling, disguising, and imposing) belongs in the typology of hide-and-seek games prevalent in the *maqāma*.[1] These motifs serve as most vital narrative devices. They thicken the plot, provide dramatic turning points, create tension, and produce humor and relief. However, in being a gendered form of disguise, cross-dressing thematizes gender issues and is, thus, an effective clue to cultural interpretations of sexuality.

In her conclusion to *Vested Interests*, Marjorie Garber stresses both the multivalence and the relativism of the transvestite metaphor:

Cross-dressing is about gender confusion. Cross-dressing is about the phallus as constitutively veiled. Cross-dressing is about the power of women. Cross-dressing is about the emergence of gay identity. Cross-dressing is about the anxiety of economic or cultural dislocation, the anticipation or recognition of "otherness" as loss. All true, all partial truths, all-powerful metaphors.[2]

If clothing is a language, then cross-dressing poses a gender riddle. Clothes are intended both to cover and to reveal; they hide the body's sexual signs and, at the same time, signify the binarism of the sexes. The concealed anatomical differences are replaced by a culturally determined gendered symbolism of clothing. Thus, in texts, as well as in life, clothing functions as a code for sexual (and other) differences. Moreover, the language of clothing does not only encode "masculinity" or "femininity," but rather points to the very constructedness of gender categories.

Cross-dressing, on the other hand, manifests the discontinuity between the sexual body and the cultural gender and, thus, offers a challenge to easy notions of binarism. If "femininity" need not necessarily be read as a sign of biological "femaleness," nor "masculinity" need be read as sign of biological "maleness," then there is a rupture in the correspondence between body/sex and dress/gender. Cross-dressing brings to the fore the questions of essentiality or constructedness of "female" and "male." Garber writes: "This interruption, this disruptive act of putting in question, is . . . precisely the place, and the role, of the transvestite. . . . The transvestite is both the signifier and that which signifies the undecidability of signification. It points toward itself—or, rather, toward the place where it is not" (13, 36–37).

The Jewish attitude toward transvestism leaves no place for ambiguity: "The woman shall not wear that which pertaineth unto a man, neither shall a man put on a woman's garment; for all that do so are abomination unto the lord God" (Deuteronomy 22:5). This deuteronomic warning had persisted as an axiom in all medieval religions. Nevertheless, there is ample historical documentation and literary evidence in medieval Islam and Christianity for diverse forms of transvestism.[3] In both cultures transvestism was ideologically repudiated while practically exercised.

To Hebrew literature the transvestite theme was introduced through the agency of Arabic literature.[4] Hence, the gendered symbolism of clothes in Arabo-Islamic culture is of relevance to our discussion. Abdelwahab Bouhdiba, in his comprehensive survey of Islamic sexuality, sees what he calls the Islamic "fetishism of clothing" as theologically rooted. The harmony of Creation is said to rest on the bipolarity of the two sexes. Clothing, the symbolical signification of this binarism, "reflect(s) the sexual dichotomy of the world." At the same time, contends Bouhdiba, it transcends its biological and the utilitarian functions "towards the theological." Within the theological system, obedience to vestimentary regulations is a form of religious observance. Thus, the best way of realizing the divine intention "is for the man to realize his masculinity and for a woman to assume her femininity." This is done by wearing the "right" clothes for each sex. Wearing the clothes of the other sex is "a grave 'disorder,' a source of evil and anarchy."[5]

Opening before us the wardrobes of the Geniza Jews, S. D. Goitein remarks about their gendered clothing:

Male and female fashions did not differ very much in their make. . . . Precisely because the main words for clothing [includes a list omitted here] were used for
both male and female apparel, it was necessary to qualify a piece by gender. . . . By
contrast, the purpose of, and, consequently, the means lavished on, the outerwear
of men and women were entirely opposed to each other. While a woman should
show her respect to her fellow men by making herself inconspicuous, if not invisible, a man should demonstrate by his clothing what he was. As one may expect,
and as the Geniza shows, this principle was not always adhered to, especially on
the female side.[6]

The occasional, and almost neutral, mentions in the Geniza of husband and wife using, probably due to poverty, the same outerwear, cannot
be considered as instances of cross-dressing. Though I was not able to trace
evidences for transvestism in medieval Jewish societies, it could be assumed
that Jews living among Muslims and Christians must have been aware of
transvestite modes in their neighboring environments and literatures.

The occurrences of transvestism in the Hebrew *maqāmāt* are, indeed, adaptations of a gentile literary motif. However, the tension between keeping with clothing norms and disrupting them pertains to an
even deeper structure pervading the *maqāma* genre. Having much in
common with other "carnivalesque" genres, the *maqāma* is deeply concerned with the binarism of order and anarchy. Usually, in the narrative
maqāmāt there emerges some kind of threat to the accepted order, but,
after a series of complications and disentanglements, the good old order
of things is reconstituted. The transvestite theme fits into this overall
pattern—cross-dressing disrupts the order of sexual binarism, but that
same order is finally reinstated with the falling of masks and the removal
of clothes. However, I argue that the restoration of the sexual order does
not entirely erase the anxiety raised by transvestism. Transvestism will
continue to stand as a "powerful metaphor" for ambiguity, as a constant
reminder of the cultural constructedness of gender.

The signification of cross-dressing as a narrative device in the *maqāma*
will concern me in the following discussion. Concluding the chapter I will
contemplate the idea that the transvestite theme problematizes some inherent generic aspects of the Hebrew *maqāma* itself. Regarding the historical
and geographical circumstances of the Jewish authors, living and writing in
a liminal realm of intersection of three cultures,[7] I will also attempt to read
the theme of cross-dressing as a sign of a concurrent cultural ambiguity.

The Phallus Veiled

The earliest of the four Hebrew *maqāmāt* discussed here is Solomon Ibn Ṣaqbel's mid-twelfth-century *Neum Asher ben Yehuda* (Address of Asher ben Yehuda).[8] Asher, its protagonist, is tricked twice; at first he is scared to death by a warrior, who turns out to be a woman in disguise, and then he is enraptured by a lady who, as he discovers later, is a man. This comedy of errors which opens with Asher's coming of age, goes on to follow the stages of his sexual socialization, and culminates in his marriage, which, as in all good comedies, restores the sense of social order.

Asher, the first-person narrator of the story, is an adventurous wanderer who now returns to settle down in his hometown. Walking by a palace, an apple is suddenly thrown at him from a latticed window. On the apple two love poems are inscribed. At first he arrogantly ignores the apple and its message, but later he realizes that he has desperately fallen in love with the mysterious thrower of the apple. Time and again he serenades under the lady's balcony, but no answer comes. Lovesick, he roams the streets until he faints. Next he is awakened by a delegation of comely palace girls who deliver to him another love letter from the lady and lead him into the recesses of the women's palace. While he is waiting for the lady, the girls entertain him with song and dance. Asher is horrified when, instead of the lady, there enters a fierce warrior. Taking the warrior to be the lord of the palace, Asher realizes the danger he got himself into in breaking into a harem, a zone forbidden for male strangers:[9]

Heading toward me was a man dressed in full armor, drunk with rage, not wine. On his head he wore a white turban. . . . Like a Berber he wore a *veil*, and held a drawn sword. I . . . threw myself on the floor . . . greeting him "Peace, peace!" But he said: "Have done with your 'Peace'! Who brought you here? Is it how privacy is made public and the secrets of the harem room *exposed*?" I was shocked dumb . . . while he went on: ". . . You have breached the bond of nobles and rent the *veil* of kings. By my life, you are going to die!" My heart melted like wax. . . . But when he saw me trembling in dread . . . he *unveiled* and cried: "Son of man, open your eyes and behold the visage before thee." I looked up and saw there a shining light and a cheek radiant as the sky in its splendor. . . . I asked: "What is this, my lord?" He replied, "My master! I am but a girl of the chamber, a gazelle of the court."

Note the dominance of the symbolism of veiling and exposure (my italicization) in this passage. Rather than a transparent cipher for unambiguous femininity that one expects it to be in Islam,[10] the veil is set here as an opaque barrier to the correct reading of gender. It is the Andalusian specificity of the veil that accounts here for the veil's ambivalence. It has to be remembered that in the culture of al-Andalus, the veil was both the emblem of the feminine and, paradoxically, also part of the ethnic costume of the Berber male warriors.[11] In its double signification (signifying the modest female as well as the masked male fighter), the veil here becomes also the sign for an impasse of signification. It designates the opacity and illegibility of gender. It becomes indeed an index for the cultural constructedness of gender.

Even after the frightful Berber turns into a woman, Asher does not yet grasp his perplexing situation. As he has before misread gender, now he misreads class,[12] mistaking a slave girl for a princess: "I said: . . . 'It must have been you who hailed me from the chamber, then assailed me; who seduced me with the apple, then traduced me.' She replied, 'No, my lord. She is the lady of ladies, who puts the stars to shame. . . . I am but a slave of her slaves . . . for your amusement sent.' "

As in a true comedy, the duped character does not fall in a pit once, but twice and thrice. Still trusting his eyes, he again misreads gender:

Hardly has she finished her speech when I . . . beheld a parade of lovely, choice maidens, one of whom was taller by head and shoulder than the others, and so brilliant she made their shadows flee at her advance. . . . The veil of nobility covered her brow . . . but I could not see her eyes because of the veil. The [slave girls] left her presence, and I remained alone with the lady. . . . Turning to face her, I cried, "You have set me on fire, my sister, my bride; . . . reveal your light, my dear; spread over me your hair; remove from your face the veil; let your charms appear." But when I took off the headdress and the veil I beheld a long beard, a face like death and a mouth open wide as a steaming cauldron. . . . In terror I collapsed full length upon the floor.

Together with Asher, we face here another gendered symbol—the beard. According to Abdelwahab Bouhdiba, the beard in Islamic culture "enjoys a privileged position. It is the symbol of virility, just as the veil is the symbol of femininity. But whereas the veil, as is normal, must conceal femininity, the beard is intended on the contrary to draw attention to itself and in some sense exhibit virility." The measure of the beard is believed to correspond to authority, wisdom, power, and judgment. It may also indicate the size and potency of the male genitalia.[13] Hence, the sight of the awesome beard, and its implications of superior virility, terrorize Asher. He is calmed down only when the bearer of the beard "unbeards," and acknowledges himself as Asher's old pal: "But he laughed heartily enough . . . as he took hold and comforted me, saying, 'Don't take fright! It's all right! I'm your friend the Adullamite.' " After entertaining Asher and feeding him, the Adullamite, the lord of the palace, finally gives him his own daughter in marriage

The only one who does not take part in this travesty is the daughter, and it is not even clear whether she was the one who threw the inscribed apple at him. The whole story is now uncurtained. What seemed to be a perilous adventure of an unsolicited penetration into a harem is revealed to be a theatrical scene—and a transvestite theater at that. The stage director of this scene is the Adullamite, and the palace girls play as his complying actresses. But why should Asher, the misguided lover, be made a laughingstock twice? Is it how the Adullamite entertains his guest? Does he punish Asher? Does he teach him a lesson?

In my reading this is a story of the protagonist's growth, including his socialization, domestication, and sexual instruction. Asher's breaking into the harem betrays his ignorance of patriarchal rules. He breaches the boundaries of the public/male and private/female space, and thus is taught a lesson by being confronted with two gender riddles—the two transvestite figures—which he repeatedly misinterprets. His being successfully wed, at the end, heralds Asher's consummation of maturity and acceptance of the social order.[14]

Unlike Asher's story which takes place in the palace's innermost rooms, Judah al-Ḥarizi's twentieth and thirty-first *maqāmāt* are located in the outskirts of the desert. Their geographical locus, on the borderline of nature and culture, can be seen as itself a displacement and substitution of gender ambiguity.

Al-Ḥarizi's twentieth *maqāma*, "On the Seven Virgins and Their Ruses,"[15] finds his narrator, Heman ha-Ezrahi, rambling on the margin of a Middle Eastern desert where he encounters seven outstandingly beautiful maidens. Heman is attracted to the tallest and most stunning of them. As she is all veiled, he can only fantasize the loveliness of her hidden parts. Nevertheless, as is the convention in love poetry, he pleads to her to save him from the lethal "arrows of her beauty" which are aimed at him. Another veiled maiden reminds him that he is the aggressor who trespassed to a female private zone: "It is you who entered the battlefield. . . . Have you come to expose the ladies' secrets, to knock on the sealed doors of desire? How dare you penetrate the royal palace and enter the inner courtyard? Did you not fear that the arrows of eyes and swords of eyelids will cut your liver into two?"

Heman's answer is bold: as a nobleman by birth he has no fear; he is experienced in love and passion, but never has he met, in all his journeys from Spain to the East, with such dazzling beauty. The ladies are ready now to hand over to him the gentle lady whom he desires. Heman almost dies of fear, when, upon his request, the lady unveils and a bearded male, with his sword drawn, is revealed.[16] He is further surprised to find out that the man is no other than his old pal, "the father of great tricks," the master of masks, Ḥever ha-Qeni. Ḥever, who on this occasion assumes the role of a playboy traveling with a splendid female retinue and confesses that the hoax is a collaboration between him and the women. In his role as a woman, Ḥever enhances his (dis)position as the eternal trickster, the double of the notoriously wily woman.

In acting the transvestite in this *maqāma*, Ḥever is true to his celebrated position as the ceaseless role-player. Ḥever's transvestitism epitomizes the generic fascination of the *maqāma* with shifting identities. Ḥever seems to fit perfectly into Mikhail Bakhtin's type of the homeless, wandering rogue who is a "life masker." To be a "masker" is to be, at the same time, an "unmasker"; it is to expose the conventional masks of life. The Bakhtinian trio, the clown, the fool, and the rogue have the "privilege—the right to be 'other' in this world. . . . None of [life's] categories quite suits them, they see [and show] the underside and falseness of every situation."[17]

While in the other *maqāmāt* treated here cross-dressing serves as a narrative device, forwarding other narrative objectives, here the theatrical pleasure of transvestism is the core of the story. Transvestic fetishism in its purely theatrical function is what the story is all about. Woman's clothes act here "as transferrential objects, kindling a metonymic spark of desire. . . . [T]his mechanism of substitution, which is the trigger of transvestic fetishism, is also the very essence of theater: role playing, improvisation, costume, and disguise."[18]

The Grammar of Clothing

Whereas in the two stories treated above, transvestism acts as entertainment, as the essence of theatrical role-playing, in "The Bandit," al-Ḥarizi's thirty-first *maqāma*, cross-dressing highlights the juncture between gender and power. The bandit, like a Chinese box, hides several layers of identity. A masked highwayman to begin with, he then turns out to be a veiled woman, who, in turn, is exposed as a man in female disguise. The grammar of clothing is deconstructed in order to dismantle the stereotypical nexes between gender, beauty, sexuality, and violence.

While in the previous *maqāma* Hever ha-Qeni is a playful cross-dresser, the director of a transvestite scenario, in "The Bandit" he becomes a victim of a criminal cross-dresser. The bandit, this crafty impersonator, is, in a way, the double of Hever, the man of many masks. An ambiguous geographical locus—the vague borderline of civilization and wilderness—is chosen as the setting for this scene of ambiguous gender. More than alluding to specific locations in the Orient, the biblical place names invoke an exotic distance, an "orientalist" landscape, an air of an outlandish twilight zone.[19]

Hever ha-Qeni, so he tells Heman, was riding in the desert with other fine gentlemen, fully armed, when they suddenly noticed a distant horseman, swift as lightning. The lonely rider, veiled in the manner of the desert fighters, stops at the edge of a cliff, and an exchange of glances takes place, with the men of the caravan and the bandit mutually examining and defining each other. The standstill ends as they befall him, directing their lances at him. His surrender is fast. Falling to the ground he kisses the wheels of their wagons and implores them to listen to his story. When they encourage him ("Speak your words and reveal your secrets"), he literally unveils and reveals himself to be a young pretty lady.

As in the previous stories, the veil constitutes here a site of gender ambiguity, a barrier (or veil) to true reading of gender. But, whereas in the other stories the default assumption is that the veil stands for the female, here the false assumption, based on the desert situation, is that the veil signifies a male desert fighter. This way or the other, it is the optionality of the veil which problematizes the notion that gender is a language, a construct.

When the gentlemen realize their error, they readily interpret the female beauty that has been exposed to them as powerlessness. Deeming now that they have the upper hand, their suspicions vanish at once. Relaxed, they can now listen patiently to the "woman's" story. Her storytelling, like Shahrazad's, turns into a life-saving device.

Recalling her protected childhood—she had been raised as a genteel princess, sequestered and hidden from even the sun and the moon—and lamenting her lost virginity, she tells them about the violent thug who abducted her. "He penetrated the walls of my home and dragged me out of my mother's rooms. He brought me to this desert, lay me in a cave, in darkness, abused and oppressed me, and stood me as a target to his arrow." To escape her gloomy destiny she was ready to endanger her young life. At midnight, when her husband was drunk, she stabbed his heart with his own sword, until it came out his back, then, seizing his beard, she pulled the sword out and cut his throat. Note that the symbolism of piercing and penetrating marks her husband's, as well as her own, deeds. She manages to overcome him by using his own phallus (sword, beard) against him. Now, riding his horse (another phallic symbol) and looking for help in the wilderness, she has met with this fine company.

Her total submissiveness ("I am in your hands, do with me as you please") numbs their vigilance. Even her violent deeds do not seem to alarm them at all. On the contrary, it seems that the men are doubly impressed—her virility appeals to them no less than her servility, her brutality no less than her beauty, her savageness no less than her suffering. Blinded by her feminine traits, those that they see with their own eyes, and others which they only hear about, they fail to realize the danger of her atrocious masculinity, though she candidly discloses it to them. They sympathize with her plight, cursing the expired villain and promising not to hurt her. It is noteworthy how the "woman" makes use of the men's own patriarchal prejudices and values. She shrewdly exploits their collapsing of beauty and helplessness, their macho urge to defend a needy woman, their indignation at the violation of her virginity, and their admiration for her virile activism and sagacity. In other words, she kills them softly, using their phallus against them, just as she killed her husband using his own sword. She reaches the edge of irony in stupefying their senses by telling them the story of how she slew her narcotized husband.

At this point she volunteers to be their desert guide and loyal slave. She will lead them, so she says, to an idyllic oasis where they can quench their thirst with "honey-sweet water," promising to satisfy *all* their needs. The sense of utmost serenity—and illusion—is ironically highlighted by the allusion to Psalms (23:2: "she made us lie down in green pastures"). Her language connotes sensual, almost sexual, delight. She tempts them to relax around a pool, commanding them to tie up their horses (another sign for their emasculation). Against the virile roughness of the desert, the oasis constitutes a feminine, almost vaginal, locus—moist, fertile and satisfying. Resting by the springs ('*ayanot*; sing., '*ayin*), they "give rest to their eyes" ('*eynayin*; sing., '*ayin*), that is, they bring about their own blindness.[20]

Even when she takes off her feminine insignia (coats, turbans, and earrings) and performs men's jobs, they still go on praising her "rare" feminine virtues—elegance, innocence, gentleness, and resourcefulness. "You have praised my gentleness," she boasts, "but haven't yet seen all my skills!" She then shoots an arrow "right into the heart of heaven," and forthwith another, hitting the first one and splitting it into two. And while the company is still breathless with admiration, she shoots a third arrow, this time straight to the heart of one of them. Upon being asked to explain her deed she responds with the following tirade: "Shut up, you son of a whore! You have been charmed by the fare countenance and pretty lips and comely looks and lovely cheeks and perfect breasts and thin waist and round thighs and white arms and legs! You fancied embracing and kissing, laying breast on breast and thigh on thigh. How wrong were you!"

Her blaming them of abusive intentions (and notwithstanding "her" own abusive language) is for them a further confirmation for "her" sex. It is only when she commands: "And now, if you don't fetter each other, I'll tear out your hearts and feed them to the birds of the air," that they realize that "*she is a male.*"

These gentlemen, cheated by a woman who turned into a man, turn themselves now into stereotypically powerless women. Impotently they obey the bandit's commands. The narrator, Ḥever ha-Qeni, the last one to remain unfettered, is hit by the bandit and is ordered to take his shoes off. Luckily Ḥever manages to regain his manhood as he symbolically draws a (phallic) knife out of his (vaginal) shoe. In stabbing the bandit's belly and severing his head, he, in fact, replicates the murder of the husband fabricated earlier by the "woman." After untying the company Ḥever and his friends bury their dead colleague and praise God for their delivery.

Al-Ḥarizi's "Bandit" is based on an Arabic *maqāma* by al-Hamadhānī, the Iranian tenth-century inventor of the genre. Surprisingly, the transvestite scene is entirely lacking from the Arabic model. In the Arabic story, the fearsome bandit, when unmasked, is revealed as a ravishing young man whose rare beauty is distinctly feminine, alluring, and evoking a strong homosexual insinuation. It is his assumed effeminacy, and hence his presumed lack of power, which blinds the desert travelers from realizing his brutality and halts them from acting violently against it. However, unlike in the Hebrew story, he keeps his male identity throughout. The gender switching is thus al-Ḥarizi's original contribution to the plot.[21]

In a comparative analysis of the two stories, Yehudit Dishon suggests that the replacement of the male for a female figure in al-Ḥarizi "adds color to the monotony of desert landscape . . . and endows the piece with elements of elegance, humor and drama." To this she adds a further explanation, namely, that al-Ḥarizi's story was purposefully intended to facilitate a moral—the author's warning to men against men's dangerous attraction to female beauty.[22] Her interpretation seems to completely evade the gender implications of the Hebrew story.

Overlooking the fact that danger, in both stories, comes from violent men, not from beautiful women (and that, in fact, there are no women figures at all in these stories), Dishon falls into the same conceptual trap laid by the bandit himself. The bandit succeeds in deceiving the male travelers because they are captives of a too dogmatic notion of gender. For them sex and gender are one. They view feminine surface (clothes, voice, beauty) as female essence (helplessness), stereotypically identifying "the fair" sex with "the weaker" one. The bandit is here to expose the shaky basis of these patriarchal gender concepts. He both devises and deconstructs the rules of the game, manifesting the inessentiality of gender. The cunning bandit stands here, thus, as a reminder for the arbitrariness and cultural constructedness of gender.

From Martial to Marital

Two women disguised as men warriors feature in Jacob ben Eleazar's seventh *maqāma*, "The Story of Yoshfe and His Two Beloveds."[23] The implied threat of a "world upside down," which in other transvestite plots might be understood as "merely" comical, is underscored here by the explicit and even bolder vision of the warrior woman who usurps not only man's attire, but also his most distinctive gender role—fighting. The unique scene of a female duel, unmatched in Hebrew literature, raises questions as to Ben Eleazar's creative imagination, as well as to the possible literary sources he might have drawn on.

The male protagonist, Yoshfe, is a young gentleman on the run. He leaves his homeland, which is presently torn by political upheaval, and,

joining bandits and derelicts, he wanders in various exotic countries in the
Orient. Finally he reaches Egypt and is led by comrades to the slave
market. As he surveys the line of the girls for sale, all of them gorgeous,
his eye rests upon one who "makes his heart tremble." He buys her—
Yefefiah, "Beauty," is her name—and takes her to the luxurious mansion
where he resides. A detailed scene of gentle lovemaking takes place where
the couple are "drinking love's wine and eating love's fruit."

Now the story line regresses back to the market. While Yoshfe was
closing the deal on Yefefiah, another pretty girl, Yemimah, fell for him.
Jealous for being left behind, she sold her favorite necklace and, adding
the rest of her savings, bought a horse, warrior's apparel, a headdress, and
arms. In her knight's disguise she sneaked into Yoshfe's house and kid-
napped him while he was still asleep after a long night of lovemaking. The
"abduction from the seraglio" theme is turned upside down here with the
man, not the woman, being abducted. Yoshfe is still asleep when Yemimah fetters him and loads him upon her horse. When he suddenly awakes
and realizes his captive situation, he challenges his captor to have a fair
gentlemanly fight. The "knight" refuses and beats him harshly.

The next morning Yoshfe and his kidnapper see "a horseman approaching, stormy and noisy like a billowy ocean; relentless like a bereaved lion; his horse guzzling the earth and devouring it. . . . He speeds
like a flooding river, with his lance ablaze. Flames emit when he grinds his
teeth."[24] While the readers see Yefefiah in male costume riding into mid
stage, Yoshfe and Yemimah (herself clothed as a man . . .) see a male monster, an extravagant grotesque of brutal masculinity. (This overstatement
will, however, yield maximum surprise when, before long, Yefefiah's femininity will be disclosed.) The effort of the narrator to converge the two
perspectives (his and the readers' on the one hand, together with Yoshfe's
and Yemimah's on the other) into one is visible in the inconsistent use of
the gendered pronouns (he/she):

Descending from the mountain, *he* rushed toward Yoshfe and Yemimah like lightning, *his* horse underneath *him* like a dart shot in air. Then, *she* fell on them like
dew falling on the earth. *And here was she, Yefefiah, his beloved! But, in his anxiety,
he did not recognize her, while she did recognize him.* As she [Yefefiah] unfettered
him, Yemimah aimed at her with her spear, but Yefefiah ran toward her like a
gazelle, and a fierce fight started between them. (Emphasis added)

What Yoshfe witnesses is a showdown between two male warriors, but the
omniscient narrator, using the feminine pronoun (*zot*), describes fighting

women. Note also the change in tenses: while the story is narrated in the past tense, the descriptive digression is in the present, following in real time each and every detail of the combat:

This one [*zot*] is up while the other one [*zot*] is down; this one screams while the other one yells; this one chases while the other one escapes; this one bends in pain while the other one aims at her with her spear; this one goes right while the other one goes left; this one curses and the other one fouls her mouth. *Yet Yoshfe kept thinking these are men, but they were women!* [A cloud of] dust stood between them, and dirt covered their faces, until from so much dirt their faces blackened, and they could not see one another. . . . So they both left the battlefield, dragging their spears on the ground.[25]

The narrator's interpolation ("Yoshfe kept thinking") betrays his (and his readers') voyeuristic position.

The duel as spectacle and its erotic (and gendered) pleasures are aspects treated by Helen Solterer in an article about the medieval subgenre known as the "Ladies' Tournament."[26] The female duels, like the male ones, she claims, have an obvious homoerotic implication, with the presence of spectators from the other sex sharpening it further. The female homoeroticism hinted by the martial contact in our story, will become even more explicit toward the end, where Yoshfe and the two women "play together as do lovers." The erotic effect of the tournament, Solterer suggests, may also be shown in heterosexual terms, with men's (or women's) fighting accentuating an erotic charge between men and women. To the theatrical effect of the female joust, Solterer also adds that "the text caters to an audience who would regard women warriors as nearly clownish figures" (524). This seems even more true for the Jewish audience.

The travesty culminates when the two tired women fighters exchange invective poems, addressing each other in the masculine gender. Then the second round begins:

Then furious Yemimah hit Yefefiah with her spear under the armor, and she fell down, breathless, from her horse. Her [Yefefiah's] headdress slipped down and her veil was removed, revealing serpentine hairlocks around a radiant face. [Only then] Yoshfe recognizes her, *and it was not clear whether he was strong or weak.* Hastily he mounted her [Yefefiah's] horse, took her weapons, flags, and insignia, and smote her [Yemimah] at the belly, paying her back for the blows she dealt him the day before. She fell down from the horse, uncovering her hair and head, and here she was, a pretty girl, haloed with sunshine, face like dawn surrounded by raven-black serpents. Falling on her, he was hurt by her breasts which stuck out like firm apples, but he mistook them for spears. *When he saw that she was a woman*, he was ashamed and angry, fearing that people will now say: "She cheated him; it was a woman who stole him."

Yoshfe is tantalized between weakness and strength. One erotic gaze—when recognizing his beloved's body—empowers him, while another erotic gaze—at Yemimah's body—emasculates him again. In the two scenes of the women's exposure the narrator's erotic gaze conflates with that of Yoshfe's. But while the narrator and the reader take pleasure in the description of the exposed bodies, Yoshfe realizes his own feminized position and is ashamed.[27]

It is Yefefiah who relieves Yoshfe from his embarrassment, stepping forward to him, kneeling, and crying. The two hug and kiss while jealous Yemimah watches them and breaks into tears. Yemimah pleads for Yoshfe's pardon, confessing to him her desperate love. The man is spellbound by her, and since Yefefiah shows no objection to sharing her mate with the other woman, the scene ends with the three of them merrily making love. Yoshfe returns to his homeland where the trio is warmly welcomed by family and community. The *maqāma* ends with an idyllic picture of the ménage a trois. Marital harmony replaces martial violence, and the two women go on "as friends, not rivals . . . inspiring love, arousing their lover, without brawl or envy, hostility and hate."[28]

Cross-Dressing and Cultural Border-Crossing

The most outlandish and intriguing feature of this story is, no doubt, the fighting scene between the two women. Is it just an entertaining jest, or does it bear any deeper signification? How does this theme function within the story? What sources does this theme draw on?

The uniqueness of the theme in Hebrew literature is closely related to the question of the author's sources.[29] As I will show, the motif has its parallels in Arabic as well as in contemporary European writing. Ben Eleazar, a resident of Christian Toledo and, at the same time, an admirer and translator of Arabic literature, could have taken his models from both.

The exposure of the woman warrior's body, the men's embarrassment upon revealing her sex, and the single combat between two cross-dressed women warriors—all these motifs have their parallels in Arabic popular literature, in which the gallant female warrior was one of the stock characters.[30] The example par excellence of an Arabic epic featuring warrior women is, as shown by Remke Kruk, the seven-volume collection of the *Sirat al-amira Dhāt al-Himma*. Its envelope narrative focuses on the adventures of the fearsome Dhāt al-Himma, a legendary warrior princess of Bedouin descent who showed combative skills from an early age and was involved in endless fighting sessions. Embedded in her story are numerous stories of other heroines, most of them Christian princesses, who fought bravely against the Muslim forces during the Crusades. The ideological message of the Arabic stories is clear: they celebrate the Islamic superiority in warfare, as well as in religion and sexuality. The defeated Christian princesses are finally either killed, or they defect to the Muslim side, convert to Islam, and marry the Muslim fighters.[31] The courage of the Christian women warriors is singled out by, for instance, William of Tyre, a Christian chronicler of the Third Crusade. These legendary tales are also corroborated by the evidence of Imād ad-Dīn, an Islamic chronicler of the Third Crusade: "Among the Franks, there were indeed women who rode into battle with cuirasses and helmets, dressed in men's clothes; who rode into the thick of the fray and acted like brave men although they were but tender women. . . . [They] showed [masculine] endurance. . . . Clothed only in a coat of mail, they were not recognized as women until they had been stripped of their arms."[32]

Contemporary with these historiographical references are several little known French narratives describing furious jousts between female combatants "who ride into view, booted and spurred . . . show[ing] every intention of wielding their weapons expertly."[33] These narratives form "The Ladies' Tournament" subgenre within the wider genre of the *tournoiement*, the literary detailed descriptions of the jousts between knights. The male ideal of militancy, channeled into a refined form of a ritual sport, was the core of the male tournament. As shown by Helen Solterer, in the "Ladies" subgenre, the portrayal of the tourneying women as matching male warriors in courage and physical strength, can be seen either as parody or as breaking with the norms of the male genre. Lengthy digressions are also dedicated, in the "Ladies" genre, to the women's great beauty.

Unlike the Arabic narratives discussed above, the French narratives do not seem to have any explicit "serious" political purport. Their audience might have even viewed the fighting women as clownish figures. However, Solterer suggests that the register of female martial violence prevailing in these descriptions has to be read against the likely "realistic" referent of female militancy brought about by the Crusades. Notwithstanding its comical effect, as well as its dubious historical validity (did such ladies' sport really exist?), Solterer sees this literature as an indication of a con-current discussion about the participation of women in the Crusades. In her hypothesis, the genre testifies that "both writer and society [were] grappling with the problem of female militancy."[34]

With all differences between the contemporaneous Arabic and the French materials (military clash versus sport; explicit versus concealed ideological messages, and so on) taken into account, there is no question as to the common soil on which the topos of female militancy thrived in both cultures. In both, this topos is indeed the product of the historical and military encounters between Christianity and Islam. As a contempo-rary of the Third, Fourth and Fifth Crusades, could Jacob Ben Eleazar have been familiar with either of these literary bodies? Did he grasp this outlandish topic from Arabic literary sources, or was it "in the air" in his mixed Christian-Muslim ambience in Toledo? While no definitive answer can be given, it seems likely at least to surmise that the appropriation of this unique topos in Ben Eleazar is the fruit of the fecund climate of clashes and contacts between cultures.

There seems to be no Jewish specification to the transvestite theme in Ben Eleazar. A universal air pervades Yoshfe's story as well as the other stories treated here. Their ambiguous locations (Yoshfe's unidentifiable birthplace; Egypt, where the main part of his story is staged, or the deserts, where the two stories by al-Ḥarizi are located) seem all to signify not a distinct geography, but fictional, vague, "oriental" domains, loci for the exotic and the bizarre. The only story that does mention ethnicity or religion is Ibn Ṣaqbel's. His protagonist Asher is implied (by his father's name Yehuda) as Jewish, and the Adullamite is clearly identified as Berber.[35] Does Asher's marriage to the Adullamite's daughter indicate a fascination with, or alternatively, an alertness regarding mixed marriages? Yoshfe, in Ben Eleazar's story, is marked neither as explicitly Jewish nor as non-Jewish. However, his bigamous marriage to the two (probably Mus-lim) slave girls he met in the Cairo market may remotely reflect a state of affairs quite common among Jews in Christian Spain, who took their Muslim slaves as concubines. Ben Eleazar, while transporting his hero and plot to the Orient, may be dealing here with a sensitive (and polemical) issue in his actual environment.[36] Yoshfe's bigamy might be thus read as an index to the fascination of Spanish Jews with alliances with gentile women, or else as an index to the anxiety it induces. Seen in this light, cross-dressing in Asher's and Yoshfe's stories may function as displacement of border-crossing between ethnicities or cultures.

In her book *Vested Interests: Cross-Dressing and Cultural Anxiety*, Marjorie Garber strongly suggests:

One of the most consistent and effective functions of the transvestite in culture is to indicate the place of . . . 'category crisis' . . . by [which] I mean a failure of definitional distinction, a borderline that becomes permeable, that permits of border-crossing from one (apparently distinct) category to another: black/white, Jew/Christian, noble/bourgeois, master/servant. . . . [A] transvestite figure, or a transvestite mode, will always function as a sign of overdetermination—a mechanism of displacement from one blurred boundary to another. . . . The . . . presence of a transvestite figure in a text . . . indicates *a category crisis elsewhere*, an irresolvable conflict . . . that destabilizes comfortable binarity, and displaces the resulting discomfort onto a figure that already inhabits, indeed incarnates, the margin. . . . One of the cultural functions of the transvestite is precisely to mark this kind of displacement, substitution, or slippage; from class to gender, gender to class, or, equally plausibly, from gender to race or religion."[37]

The four stories discussed in this chapter are the only Hebrew works in which the transvestite theme appears. The theme is not to be found in works of later Hebrew authors. It is also altogether lacking from the Arabic corpus of *maqāmāt*, which, by and large, furnished the models for the Hebrew writers. Noteworthy is also the fact that all four were written by early practitioners of the Hebrew genre, around the late twelfth and early thirteenth centuries. The occurrence of all four in this specific location in time—a period of significant transitions and transformations in the history of Spanish Jewry—leads me to venture the hypothesis that in these works transvestism is a figure of cultural change, displacing or substituting other types of ambiguity. Hence, I offer to read cross-dressing as a symptom of cultural border-crossing and as an index of the dynamic historical and sociolinguistic circumstances in which the *maqāma* itself (and Hebrew prose at large) was engendered.[38]

From the mid-twelfth century on, following the Almohad invasions and the Christian conquests, most Andalusian Jews either emigrated to, or found themselves in, the newly occupied Christian domains where they reestablished their literary centers. And though the intellectual elite of Arabicized Jews continued to admire Arabic learning, the use of Arabic as a language for Jewish learning had gradually dwindled. The "ecological" balance between the literary functions of Hebrew, Arabic, and Judeo-Arabic began to change. The Hebrew, which was formerly exclusively devoted to poetic-aesthetic and liturgical functions, began now to assume other prosaic functions catered for before by Judeo-Arabic. As shown by Rina Drory, this change of linguistic balance between Hebrew and Arabic and the expansion of Hebrew as a literary language were affected by the new hosting culture—Romance.[39] Spanish and Provençal Jews reinvented Hebrew as a versatile and multifunctional (though not as a vernacular) language, fit for narrative, exegesis, science, and philosophy. This was accompanied by an extensive industry of prose translations from Arabic and Judeo-Arabic into Hebrew. That this occurred in Romance linguistic environments where vernaculars then began to emerge, and where Arabic works were widely translated to Latin and Castilian, cannot be overlooked.

This was also the climate where the Hebrew *maqāma* (and cognate types of rhymed prose) emerged.[40] Both al-Ḥarizi and Ben Eleazar reflect at length, in the respective introductions to their collections of *maqāmāt*, on the necessity of their renditions of the Arabic genre into Hebrew.[41] They refer to the historical relations between Arabic and Hebrew languages and literatures, to the legitimacy of adapting the new Arabic genre, and to the adequacy of the Hebrew to serve as a language for narrative. Their introductions clearly reflect the new complex linguistic situation of Jewish literature at the turn of the century.

Al-Ḥarizi—himself a figure of a border-crosser who voyaged from West to East—was also a prolific translator. Before writing his original *maqāmāt*, he translated to Hebrew al-Ḥarīrī's Arabic *maqāmāt*. He also translated Jewish philosophy (Maimonides) from Judeo-Arabic. Explaining the exigency of his endeavors, he symptomatically employed vestimentary (or rather cross-dressing) imagery. In one of his dedications to *Taḥkemoni* he described the writing of Hebrew *maqāmāt* as the cladding of the Arabic form with a Hebrew embellished garment.[42] Similarly, in his apologetic introduction to his translation of Maimonides' *Introduction to the Mishna*, he deplored the linguistic syncretism of the Jews, and referred to his own translation as the stripping off of gentile clothes and the donning on of Hebrew attire.[43]

To the cross-cultural circumstances of the birth of the *maqāma* we may also add the generic perspective. The *maqāma* par excellence (of which al-Ḥarīrī and al-Ḥarizi are the most characteristic models) is only one variety within a plethora of other rhetorical, and especially narrative, cognate rhymed modes in medieval Hebrew literature. However, the definitional borders between the *maqāma* and the other variants are loose and quite blurred.[44] Moreover, the genre allows for border-crossings within its own confines: It alternates (rhymed) prose and poetry; its tone fluctuates from the serious to the comic; it varies from the rhetorical to the narrative; it merges Eastern and Western elements; it reflects the lifestyle of the elite as well as scenes of lowlifes; it trespasses from the real to fictional and, at times, also to the allegorical.

Transvestism in the Hebrew *maqāma*, I suggest, might be a clue to its all-inclusive nature, its changing apparels, its stylistic variety, and its emergence in a climate of historical transitions.

8

Circumcised Cinderella:
Jewish Gender Trouble

A Transsexual Wish

AN UNUSUAL WISH OF A male to become female appears in a well-known medieval composition, *Even boḥan* (lit. touchstone), written around 1322 by the Hebrew author and translator Qalonymos ben Qalonymos.[1]

Our Father in Heaven! You who did miracles to our fathers by fire and water; you who turned [the furnace] in Ur of the Chaldees [cold] to stop it from burning [Abraham]; you who turned Dinah in her mother's womb [into a girl]; you who turned the rod [of Moses] into a serpent in front of tens of thousands; you who turned [Moses'] pure arm into a [leper's] white arm; you who turned the Red Sea into land, and the sea floor into solid and dried-up earth; you who turned the rock into a lake, the cliff into a fountain—*if only you would turn me from male to female*! If only I were worthy of this grace of yours, I could have now been the lady of the house; I could lounge at home exempted from military service![2]
 Why cry and be bitter if my Father in Heaven so decreed and crippled me with this immutable, irremovable defect? Worrying about the impossible is [indeed] an incurable pain for which no empty consolation will help. I keep telling myself "I shall bear and suffer until I die." But since I have learned from oral tradition that "one should bless [God] for the good as well as for the bad," I bless Him meekly, with a faint voice: *Blessed art Thou who did not make me a woman*!

Such an overt expression of a transsexual desire—especially when it takes the form of a prayer to God—is unique in Jewish literature and, to my knowledge, also in European and Islamic writings of the time. An ancient parallel (though by no means a likely one for Qalonymos) can be found in Ovid's *Metamorphoses* (4:380–86), where Hermaphroditus requests his godly parents to turn him from *vir* (man) to *semivir* (half-man): "Hermaphroditus stretched out his hands in prayer and with a voice no longer manly said: 'Father [Hermes] and mother [Aphrodite] grant this gift to your son." His request, unlike that of Qalonymos, was granted.[3]

An even more striking parallel—unnoticed hitherto—comes from the pen of the famous medieval woman author Christine de Pisan (1364–1430). Her grievance to God for not being born male—an inverted mirror-image of Qalonymos's—is included in the introduction to her *Book of the City of Ladies*:

Oh, God, how can this be? For unless I stray from my faith, I must never doubt that Your infinite wisdom and most perfect goodness ever created anything which was not good. Did You Yourself not create woman in a very special way and since that time did You not give her all those inclinations which it pleased You for her to have? And how could it be that You could go wrong in anything? Yet look at all those accusations which have been judged, decided, and concluded against women. . . . Why shall I not doubt that this is true? Alas, God, why did You not let me be born in the world as a male, so that all my inclinations would be to serve You better, and so that I would not stray in anything and would be as perfect as a male is said to be? But since Your kindness has not been extended to me, then forgive my negligence in Your service, most fair Lord God, and may it not displease You, for the servant who receives fewer gifts from his Lord is less obliged in his service." I spoke these words to God in my lament and a great deal more . . . and in my folly I considered myself most unfortunate because God has made me inhabit a female body in this world.[4]

Notwithstanding differences in their line of argumentation, both monologues are similarly seasoned with a great deal of ironic rhetoric. Both discontented speakers end their addresses in a similar tone of resignation. Both blame their Creator for their poor performance as, respectively, male and female. Being born each to his or her wrong sex, they could not but err to God. However, both pious speakers have no other choice but to accept, with reluctance, the facts of their biology as well as to repent the sins caused by their imposed genders. Despite similarities there seems to be no direct link between the two passages. Written in circa 1405, nearly one century later than Qalomymos's, Christine's passage could not have served as Qalomymos's model. Nor could Christine possibly be familiar with his Hebrew piece.

The singularity of Qalonymos's prayer in the realm of Hebrew literature has been a source of puzzlement for the few scholars who have dealt with his text. Most critics have labeled it as "satire," "parody," "amusing piece," and so on, thus relieving themselves of the task of engaging in a serious analysis of the cultural implications, especially the treatment of gender, in this text.

As I will propose, it is precisely under this comic guise that the text ventures to explore the boundaries of Jewish masculinity and to cross them over to the terra incognita of femininity. Through this transsexual travesty, Qalonymos investigates the assumptions of Jewish gender and produces a subversive critique of fundamental issues in Jewish life, the life of the man as well as the life of the woman. His inquiry touches upon social practices and religious rituals (such as prayer, circumcision, education, and marriage) that are vital to the cultural construction of Jewish gender.

A Man—According to God's Will?

In medieval Jewish thought—and this is not much different in Christianity and Islam—for a man fulfilling his masculinity and a woman assuming her femininity are ways of realizing the divine harmony in Creation. The wish to cross over to the other sex is already a grave violation of divine order. The impudence of the speaker in our text lies not only, or not so much, in his wish to become a woman, but in requesting that God Himself will perform this sex change. It is God who designed the order of things as it is, and it is He who can invert it. To support his unusual request, the speaker supplies numerous precedents of miracles and supernatural transformations engendered by God in biblical history. God saved Abraham in Ur by turning the fire cold, and all His miracles to Moses have to do as well with supernatural changes and transformations.[5]

The most relevant precedent on this list, and perhaps the one for which the whole list was created, is inserted in an apparently incidental manner. This is not among the miracles done "for our Fathers" but rather for the mothers. According to a talmudic legend, the expectant Leah prayed to God to transform the fetus in her womb to female. God paid heed to her prayer, and the fruit of this prenatal sex change was Dinah.[6] The speaker, however, entirely ignores the heavy toll Dinah had to pay for being a woman. Not only was she deflowered (Genesis 34), but she was also to become the victim of patriarchal readings that put the blame on her shoulders.[7]

How can one plead to God to make him a woman and at the same time thank God daily for *not* making him a woman? I refer, of course, to the words "Blessed art Thou God, our King of the universe . . . who did not make me a woman," which every Jewish male has to pronounce upon entering the synagogue for the morning prayers. This blessing is the third in a series of three, the other two being: "Blessed art Thou . . . who did not make me a Gentile" and "Blessed art Thou . . . who did not make me a slave." This cluster of three mandatory blessings, reiterated daily, forms the declaration of identity of the Jewish male. Two speech acts constitute his identity: one of differentiation and one of hierarchization. As in other cultures in antiquity, the religious-ethnic other, the other by class (slave), and the sexual other (female) are all perceived as both different and inferior.[8]

By the use of verbal acrobatics, our ambivalent speaker tries to reconcile his unorthodox wish with the content of the obligatory blessing. Since "I have learned from oral tradition that 'one should bless God for the good as well as for the bad,' "[9] he says, "I bless Him meekly, with a faint voice: 'Blessed art Thou . . . who did not make me a woman.' " The blessing is now charged with a new meaning: God is not to be blessed for the good, that is, for saving the man from being born a woman, but rather for the evil of creating the man as He pleased. It was indeed God's wish to make the male spiritually sinful and biologically incomplete: hence man has no other choice but to accept his ill fate.

In what would seem one of Qalomymos's many ironies of gender, he makes his speaker utter the male formula *as* a man—but *like* a woman. While maleness is reasserted, the tone is that of submissive acceptance, similar to that intoned in the woman's blessing when she abides with her unwanted predestined sex, saying: "Blessed art Thou . . . who hast made me according to His will." Is this a consciously calculated irony? Did the author purposely allude to the formula of the woman's blessing? Had this blessing already been in use in Qalonymos's time and place?

As far back as it can be traced, there is no direct documentation regarding the earliest origins of the woman's blessing, nor is there a mention of it prior to the first decades of the fourteenth century. Surprisingly enough, it is first attested to around the same time of *Even bohan* (1322). The first report comes from the Toledan authority Rabbi Jacob ben Asher (1270?–1340). In his commentary on liturgy, he writes: "It is the custom of women to bless 'who made me according to His will,' and they do so as someone who advocates an evil done to him by God."[10] (Note how Qalonymos employs this explanation but inverts it: for him, it is the man, not the woman, who upholds ill fate.) By the time Jacob ben Asher reported about it, the "woman's custom" was probably relatively widespread.

The proximity of dates, hitherto unnoticed, between his report and our piece supports the conclusion that Qalonymos responded to the spreading phenomenon of the woman's blessing. The nature of his reaction—whether sincere or satirical—is yet to be discussed. Moreover, if our text is a response to the blessing, it is one of the first historical evidences to it.

Maleness as Deformity

The evil and disadvantage of being a male are indicated in more than one way in the course of the passage. Maleness and, more precisely, the penis are marked as imperfection, defect, deformity, loss, and lack.

At the beginning of the section, the speaker exclaims, "Woe to me, my mother, that you ever gave birth to a male child! It is a great *loss* and no gain." His complaint is amplified by three allusions: one is Jeremiah's cursing the day of his birth;[11] the two others are mishnaic. In one, a male is protesting to the rabbis, "Just because I am male, should I *lose* out?"[12] The other one is Rabbi's assertion, "Lucky is he whose children are males, and woe to him whose children are females," which Qalonymos turns upside down.[13] Typical of his style is this manipulation and decontextualization of texts through which the male as loser and maleness as loss become one of the central axes of his text.

Qalonymos's protagonist goes on grumbling, "How badly was he stricken by finger [*kamah* laqah *be'etzba*], how much shame must he put up with, he who was coined in the coin of males!" The allusion to the Passover Haggadah insinuates that maleness is to be seen as a kind of plague or blow.[14] The Sages engage there in intricate calculations about the exact numbers of plagues that God dealt the Egyptians. How many blows did He strike with His hand and how many with His finger? Yet Qalonymos's witty use of language does not end here. In talmudic jargon the word "finger" also stands for "penis." Hence, the finger is of double signification: it stands both for God's phallic finger and for the penile "finger" of mortal males—it is the punishing organ as well as the punished one.

Following on another talmudic metaphor, all human beings are said to be minted like coins.[15] But alas, according to the speaker, the "male coin" is flawed! (Does it follow that the "female coin" is perfect?) No complaints and protests will do now after the wrong was done and God "crippled me with this immutable, *irremovable defect.*"[16]

Qalonymos makes a surprising and bold step here; a step that inverts and subverts accepted images and established concepts of patriarchal thought. According to Aristotle the female (including the human female) is a "deformation of nature," or a "distorted male." His argumentation is based on the assumption that each being aspires to realize its potentiality and to reproduce beings identical to itself. And since it is the male who is the active and formative force in the process of generation (in which women supply the passive matter only), it should logically follow that males will give birth to males only. Hence, the generation of females is an accident in the natural process, a result of a disruption in the active male force.[17] If in Aristotle maleness is the standard and femaleness is its deformity, Qalonymos's speaker turns this "natural" hierarchy upside down. For him deformity is the sign of the male! The male is a crippled creature. His defect is immutable, irremovable. In the dialectic that governs the following passage, it is the penis that is the male's defect: the penis is a surplus that is a loss; the foreskin is a surplus that is a lack (*mum*).[18] Hence, the male organ, and not the female's, is identified here as lack.[19]

Woe to me, my mother, that you ever gave birth to a male child! It is a great loss and no gain. . . . I was created closed-eyed and hardhearted. Uncircumcised of heart and flesh was I born. At three days, they cut my umbilical cord, and at eight days—my foreskin. However, my ears, heart, and mind [remained uncircumcised and] were not ready to join God's covenant. . . . Their foreskin is indeed their inherent lack.

Circumcision interests Qalonymos in two ways: as the first initiation ceremony of the Jewish male; and as an act of signification. The uncircumcised flesh is the tabula rasa upon which the covenant is to be written. The incision transforms the unmarked, unidentified flesh into a body having a particular identity—the body of a Jewish male. Circumcision is an inscription. The inscribed body becomes a collective, cultural text, a social category, a mode of inclusion of some and exclusion of others. As shown by Elizabeth Grosz, the body is coded by affiliations that not only make real the subject's social, sexual, and familial position or identity within a social hierarchy, but also engender it. Grosz leans on Alphonso Lingis's distinction between "the savage mode of body inscriptions" (tattoos, scarifications) and "the civilized production of the body, not as surface pattern but as depth, latency. . . . What differentiates savage from civilized systems of inscription is the sign-ladenness of the latter, the creation of bodies as sign systems, texts, narratives, rendered meaningful and integrated into forms capable of being read in terms of personality, psychology, or submerged subjectivity.[20]

Lingis's distinction is of relevance to Qalonymos's position. In agreement with the confessional-penitential parts of *Even boḥan*, the author presents himself here as a moral and spiritual failure. Following Deuteronomy 10:16: "Cut away, therefore, the thickening about your hearts," he confesses that it was merely his flesh that had been circumcised, yet his "ears, heart, and mind," namely, his subjectivity, remained unmarked, unaltered. Circumcision, then, is not just another mode of body scarification, similar to a savage tattoo that marks belonging to the collective. It must also have a dimension of depth; it must be read as a sign on the surface of a change in one's personality or psychology. Qalonymos does not go as far as the Christian attitude in altogether abolishing the circumcision of the flesh and replacing it with the circumcision of the heart. Yet he strongly emphasizes that the "conversion of the flesh" alone is of no significance if it does not symbolize the "conversion of the heart." The making of the Jewish male is not to be done with just by an operation on his sex. A Jewish male becomes one through a whole cultural operation having to do with texts.

Maleness as an Ordeal

From his birth, the Jewish male is trapped in a web of cultural expectations and obligations. Biology is destiny. The messenger who carries to a father the good tidings of the birth of a male baby is, in fact, a harbinger of doom. His happy message to the father enfolds a curse to the newborn. Hence, the harbinger himself, this symbol of the cultural predestination of the Jewish male, should be damned:

Cursed be the man who informed my father: "A male son was born to you! He will be intelligent and superior to a prophet. He will perform the holy rites of the Temple like the [High Priest] Ishmael ben Pavei. . . . He will erect the hall of science on its mound. A candle will shine from his head and those who walk in darkness will follow his radiant halo."

The spiritual leader that the male baby is expected to become is said to illuminate the dark world of ignorance. The image of the candle shining from his head alludes to the talmudic description of the fetus having a candle burning on his head to light for him the darkness when emerging from his mother's womb (Niddah 30b). Interestingly enough, in the same talmudic context, the yet unborn male embryo is said to be a diligent student of the Torah. Already in the womb "it is taught all the Torah, from beginning to end," only to forget it all, when an angel slaps its mouth at the moment of birth. The phallic candle of knowledge and enlightenment captures the notion that the Logos and the phallus are one.[21] It emblematically epitomizes the Derridian concept of phallogocentrism.

A male child is expected to be a sage, a prophet, a high priest, a spiritual leader—all in one. Qalonymos's speaker, who failed to stand to this standard, accuses the harbinger who foresaw for him such a brilliant intellectual future: "This messenger shall be held guilty of bloodshed; cursed be he. How could he twist the course of the stars so much? How could he have erred so in his astrology?" That his bitterness is not just a result of seeing himself an intellectual flop, an unfulfilled promise, but a wholesale critique of Jewish gender roles, becomes evident from the passage immediately following ours (*Even bohan*, p. 20). The author engages there in a stinging social criticism of the exaggerated importance parents relate to the birth of a son and their grief over the birth of a daughter. His revolt against the conflation of biology and destiny, sex and gender, involves not only the fates of men but also those of women:

Woe to them who, following gentile views, rejoice the birth of every male baby and bemoan the birth of female babies. It is as if every newborn boy is a Rabbi Yehuda . . . or a Rabbi Elazar . . . and every girl is source of grief and fury. . . . We have often found the opposite. Many a dishonest son, whose day of birth was a day of good tidings, was later to blaspheme the holy and violate the Torah. Their birth was celebrated in feast, offerings, and music. The house was filled with light. [And conversely] many a virtuous woman, when they emerged out of womb to this world of havoc, met with parents' faces thundered with rage, [as if that day was] a day of calamity. The family moaned and groaned as if they were plague-stricken, and the house was filled with smoke from cellar to ceiling. When a stubborn and rebellious son is born . . . his father and mother rejoice in him, singing and chanting: "A son was born to us! He will reach a high position! This son of ours will exceed Abraham and Moses. . . ." And many a pious woman when born were slighted by father and mother who shook their heads sadly hither and thither saying: "It is because of our sins that God sent us this disease."

The seriousness and striking realism with which Qalonymos depicts these rites of birth might be a clue to his intention in our passage too. His assault on gender prejudices and his sympathy with the female sex is unequivocal. This attitude should, in my view, guide also our reading of other parts of this text, which were hitherto read as parody or satire (see below).

In an earlier passage (*Even bohan*, 17) Qalonymos goes on lamenting the fate of the males:

Woe to them whose offspring are male! What a heavy burden of restrictions and prohibitions lies on them! Some are to be kept in private, other in public; . . . severe laws and awesome injunctions, six hundred and thirteen of them.

This heavy list of duties casts severe dread on the speaker, and, on the brink of collapse, he exclaims:

And who is the man who is capable of fulfilling them all to the letter? How will he escape—be he diligent or lazy—failure and fear? How will he not stumble? And even if he observed all these, he is not yet done with his list of duties.

In addition to the observing of the Law, the Jewish man has to engage himself in the study of the Torah and its commentaries, in the Mishna and its supplements, and in talmudic *pilpul*. The logocentric project of the Jewish student demands expertise in every book found on the Jewish bookshelf. But if he also aspires to acquire universal knowledge, he must immerse himself in yet another curriculum. Qalonymos lists here seven subjects of study that overlap in part with the seven liberal arts constituting the medieval *paideia*.[22] The study of Kabbala, ending the list, is the peak:

Seven are the pillars of wisdom. Up they soar from the top of mountain and hill. Here is logic; [here are] the valley of philosophy and the vale of vision and the secrets of arithmetic . . . and geometry . . . by which the seeker can measure the heights of heaven and the depth of abyss . . . and astronomy and natural science. [Those are] the seven steps of the ladder. And who will praise the prowess [needed for] the study of the divine and the pure Forms, which are ten, namely the Ten Sefirot [of the Kabbala].

Jewish maleness is thus not a matter of birth, nor is it the consequence of ritual circumcision. One is compelled to reverse the equation "biology is destiny." A man is not born a man but becomes one. It is his gendered life course which ultimately constitutes his sex. Maleness is shown to be a competitive life track, an unwearied race after summits of intellectual fulfillment, a phallic arrow launched into the expanse of knowledge, an enormous intellectual odyssey. The vertical dimension of the topography of the intellect is emphasized. The mental adventurer goes up mountains and down valleys, and aspires to reach the heights and depths of the universe. The images of the "steps of the ladder" and the "pillars of wisdom" depict knowledge as an edifice of monumental proportions and hierarchical structure.

That the biographical Qalonymos was closely acquainted with this loaded and arduous trail of the Jewish student might be learned from what is known about his own life. Jefim Schirmann writes: "He succeeded in the path he chose without digressing from it. He was one of the most prolific Hebrew translators of all times and contributed much to the dissemination of sciences among Hebrew audiences. His Hebrew erudition—and especially his expertise in the language of the Sages—was extensive and profound. He translated non-Jewish books in philosophy, natural sciences, astronomy, mathematics, and medicine. We currently know of more than thirty of his translations from Hebrew to Arabic . . . and one from Arabic to Latin."[23] Jewish and non-Jewish patrons invited him to Catalonia (where *Even boḥan* was written). Around 1324, he was invited to Naples by Robert d'Anjou, earl of Provence and king of Naples, to join a group of translators to translate a (now lost) book from Arabic to Latin. In Rome, he met his famous contemporary Immanuel of Rome. Among the Christians, he earned the name Maestro Calo.

The Female Sphere

That the journey ends with coming back home is of no wonder. And coming back home is coming back to femininity. Exhausted by the male project, the intellectual voyager iterates now his wish to become a woman:

If only the craftsman who created me would have made me a decent woman! I might today have been a woman, wise hearted and skillful, spinning with her hands. I and my woman friends [would sit together], holding the spindle, spinning in the moonlight, chatting with one another, in light and in darkness, talking of the daily events and gossiping some, too. And perhaps when I would be skilled enough in spinning I would say, "How lucky am I" to know how to make linen, how to comb [wool], and weave lace; [to design] cup-like buds, open flowers, cherubim, palm trees, and all sorts of other fine things, colorful embroideries and furrow-like stitches. And frequently, as is the custom of women, I would lie on the cinders, by the hearth, among the pots, between furnace and stove, chopping wood, stirring the coals, and tasting from this or that dish.

Female existence and female space invoke the male speaker's envy. In contrast to the infinite and threatening male universe, the female space is delimited and warm, kind, and protected. The woman is situated here "by the hearth,"[24] which is the heart, or rather the uterus, of the house, and she is encircled by items metonymic and metaphoric of the female anatomy: stove and cooking pots. Among the many archetypal images of the Great Mother, Erich Neumann records stoves and cooking vessels (which he calls "belly-vessels"). In the male's mind, woman is identified with "the fireplace, the seat of warmth and food preparation," and her duty is "the guarding and tending of the fire."[25]

The female sphere is also characterized here by material plasticity and concrete sensuality: the tastes of cooked foods, the warmth of fire, the many colors of embroideries and jewels, the hubbub of kitchen sounds, the abundance of utensils, foods, fabrics, and designs. This sensual-material dimension contrasts to the universalness, abstractness, and monotone of the male's universe. The vertical-phallic quest for the Logos takes place in an arid landscape, whereas woman's material sphere is horizontal and plentiful.

Women, according to this passage, do their work in an uncompetitive atmosphere. Their pretensions are humble, and thus a sense of fulfillment is readily attainable. ("And perhaps when I would be skilled enough in spinning I would say, 'How lucky am I!' ") Women are restful, but not inactive. Textile work is most often placed, as it is in our text, in a communal setting. The women's sisterhood stands in contrast to male individualism. This is picturesquely depicted in the romantic scene of young women weaving and chatting in the moonlight. The female bond is not constructed around lofty pursuits, but around the trivial matters of day-to-day domestic life.

The centrality of textile work in our text reflects its significance to the construction of femininity in patriarchal societies. Miriam Peskowitz in her study of spinning in talmudic culture shows how wool work, associated with sexuality and femininity, "becomes an icon of matronly domesticity."[26] And Helen Solterer writes: "Because it is a time-consuming labor associated increasingly with the domestic sphere, sewing comes to be recognized as woman's work. To embroider is to be identified as a discreet and obedient woman, occupied without being independently active.

This activity is most often placed in a communal setting. Women are depicted sewing together, thereby amplifying the image of serene feminine harmony."[27] Freud, in one of his most misogynistic utterances, associates textiles with woman's "natural" shame in her "genital deficiency" and views it as woman's most significant contribution to human culture.[28]

Textile is for femininity what *text*s are for masculinity. The index of textile work (linen making, wool combing, lace weaving, floral embroideries, and so on) sums up the proper feminine knowledge and parallels it to the male catalog of canonical texts. The allusions to the art of the Tabernacle (to which it is said that women donated their weavings, Exodus 35:25), as well as to the elegance of design ("cup-like buds, open flowers, cherubim, palm trees") in Solomon's Temple (1 Kings 6:29, 7:26), elevates the feminine crafts.[29] The aesthetization and idealization of the feminine reaches a peak in the analogy between the "craft" of the Creator and the craft of woman ("If only the craftsman who created me would have made me a decent woman . . . spinning . . .").

Whose Daydream Is It?

Let us return to the point in the text where the feminine voice is heard for the first time. How does the transition from the male to the female monologue occur? Where exactly does the change from the frustrated male to the satisfied female—a change in both grammatical gender and in sexual identity—take place?

The transformation occurs in the iteration of the conditional, "If only the craftsman who created me would have made me a decent woman! I might today have been a woman, wise hearted and skillful, spinning with her hands. I and my woman friends [would sit together], holding the spindle." Within a single sentence, and by the use of "indirect free style,"[30] the male's voice gives way to a female's in a nearly seamless manner.[31]

The fantasy of the man who dreams of being a woman grows into another fantasy, that of a woman who, like Cinderella, "lies on the cinders" in the kitchen and dreams of the coming of the appointed prince. "And at the end of days, when I'm ready, fortune will bring me a good man," she says. Carried on the wings of her dream, she imagines her elaborate wedding, the elegance of clothes, and splendor of jewelry that her husband will purchase for her. After marriage, her husband will sit her upon a *kathedra* ("a chair of leisure"), which, alluding to the Mishna, means that she will be free from household chores.[32] She is carried even further to the day of her first son's circumcision and the ideal life waiting for her and her husband forever after. Married life is depicted here as reciprocal and harmonious. The "righteous" husband would feed and clothe his wife, as well as satisfy her sexual needs (according to Exodus 21:10), while the dutiful wife will observe her three duties, "blood, fire, and bread."[33]

Whose dream is this, the man's or the woman's? Who is describing whom here? From whose perspective are we viewing the ideal marriage? Is this the voice of a Jewish woman describing the ideal husband, or the voice of a Jewish male describing the ideal woman? A consideration of the intertexts with which our text is intermeshed may lead to a better understanding of the questions of voice and perspective.

Whose Intertexts Are These?

Our Cinderella also adds a list of foods that the husband will "feed" her with. She says: "When I hunger he'll feed me with well-kneaded bread, and when I thirst he'll give me white wine [*gurdali*] or dark colored wine [*ḥardali*]." What are these exotic foods? Unknowingly, the woman's words here allude to the Talmud (Shabbat 62:2), where the rabbis had in mind to illustrate the sexual impudence of the people of Jerusalem: "The Jerusalemites were quite obscene. One would ask another: What have you feasted on today? On well-kneaded bread or unkneaded bread? On dark wine or on white? On a bed narrow or wide? . . . And Rav Ḥisda interpreted all these as pornography." What these Jerusalemites were curious to know was whether one slept with a sexually experienced woman ("well-kneaded bread") or a virgin, a brunette or a blonde? Thin or fat? Women are dealt with in this anecdote as goods for consumption, as objects to satisfy men's cravings, tastes, comforts—and as subject matter for their juicy jokes.

But what does this vulgar joke have to do with the modest and virtuous wife who is so proud of her ideal marriage? Does she say it tongue in cheek? Can she be aware of the talmudic intertext she invokes? The sexist humor betrays the identity of the real speaker and the nature of the speech situation. We are reminded that it is a man's voice imitating a woman's voice; and it is a man's voice speaking to (or rather, joking with) an exclusively male audience. Elsewhere in this book I have expanded on Freud's observations about the dirty joke, and why do men find it funny, and on Shoshana Felman's explanation why women "do not occupy the place from which the joke is funny" and "are completely justified to put themselves in a position to miss the joke."[34]

The contract between author and audience depends not only on common humor but also on common erudition. The community of educated males communicates over the head of the probably illiterate woman who parrots male texts. The saucy allusions are meant to be sevenfold funnier when they are hinted at by the object/victim of the joke.

Dramatic irony continues when the woman "stumbles" time and again on talmudic texts, of whose implications she is not supposed to be aware. This is the case, for example, when she speaks of matrimonial harmony and illustrates it with numerical symmetry: husband and wife, each has to observe three duties. The husband is obliged to provide for her food, clothing, and sexual rights (according to Exodus 21:10). And she proclaims her loyalty by observing her three:

Parallel to [his] three [conjugal duties], I, too, will keep three [commandments . . .]: blood and fire and dough. Sweeter than honey are these three, and one is not allowed to add to their number, or to inquire about them: "Whereby do women earn merit?"

Several intertexts are brought into play in this innocent and complacent proclamation. The prophetic triad "blood and fire and pillars of smoke" (Joel 3:3) is playfully used here as the pattern for "blood, fire, and dough," the three commandments women have to observe. These three commandments are the separation during the menstrual period, the lighting of the Sabbath candles, and the setting aside of the first portion of the dough when baking, as an offering to the priests. Women who are not careful in observing them are prone to die at labor. The Mishna (Shabbat 2:6) that specifies them is not an esoteric text; it is recited on Sabbath eve at candle lighting and is probably aimed at disciplining women. But this does not deter the woman speaker here from seeing these lethal three as "sweet" gifts for which she is grateful. Additionally, the woman exploits the Aramaic expression "Whereby do women earn merit?" for which the answer in the Talmud is: "By making

their children . . . and their husbands study" (Berakhot 17:1). Women,
however ignorant they themselves are, are promised reward for enabling
males to study.

Another intertext evoked here by the woman speaker, but one with
which she would certainly not be familiar, is Rabbi Yehoshua's incriminating midrash on these commandments:

Why was she given the commandment of menstrual separation? Because she
spilled the blood of the First Adam, therefore she was given the commandment of
menstrual separation. And why was she given the commandment to sacrifice the
first portion of the dough? Because she spoiled the First Adam, who was the first
portion of the world, therefore she was given the commandment to sacrifice the
first portion of the dough. And why was she given the commandment of lighting
the Sabbath candle? Because she extinguished the soul of the First Adam, therefore she was given the commandment of lighting the Sabbath candle."[35]

Daniel Boyarin views it as one of the most extreme (and, in his opinion,
quite rare) pinnacles of misogyny in the whole of talmudic literature.[36]
The naive woman speaker hints at this source lightheartedly and is unaware of the heavy weight of blame this text casts upon women.

According to Rabbi Yehoshua's explanation, these commandments
are collective punishments by which the daughters of Eve expiate for their
mother's crime. Hence, "blood, fire, and dough" stand for Adam's blood,
soul, and body, which were spoiled by Eve. Eve, then, is the mother of
humanity and its murderess; she is the mother of all living and the mother
of death! Each of the three "sweet" commandments that constitute
woman's religious life is, as a matter of fact, a constant reminder of Eve's
original sin. This implies that timeless feelings of sinfulness and guilt are
basic to the constitution of Jewish femininity. And this implication stands
in sharp dissonance to the explicit idealization of woman's life on the surface of the text. Beneath the surface of ideal marriage lurks a destructive
innuendo—to the first coupling that was spoiled.

Of special interest here is the way Qalonymos manipulates the gendered symbolism of blood in Judaism. In contrast to male blood, especially that which is ritually spilled in circumcision, which is signified as
sacred and saving, woman's menstrual blood is signified as polluting. Circumcision blood is a symbol of the covenant (*brith*), of inclusion into the
group of male members, while menses necessarily induces exclusion.
Furthermore, "Circumcision is a man's birth into his cultural state
whereas actual childbirth is 'merely' birth into the state of nature, meaning

that the signs of this birth—first and foremost the mother's blood connected with it—had to be devaluated."[37] Qalonymos's ambiguous speaker is thus playing on both sides of this gendered dichotomy. His speaker is a circumcised male dissatisfied with bodily circumcision that does not involve spirituality. He wishes to become a menstruating woman happily observing the duty of *niddah*. And she, in her turn, is eager to be the mother of a circumcised Jewish infant—from whose ceremony of circumcision she will probably be excluded because of her postnatal bleeding.[38]

Between the Sexes: Gender Trouble

The few and quite meager extant comments on this text revolve mostly around the questions of how sincere the protagonist's wish is, and how comic the passage is. One critic opines that "it is the author's humorous grievance at being born male and not female."[39] Another critic sees it as merely a rhetorical trick of sophistry. The author's statement (that the fate of the Jewish man is much worse than that of the Jewish woman) appears to be sincere, but in rejoicing the supremacy of the male it discloses its intention to ridicule women.[40] The envy of femininity is said to be fake and to be satirically exploited in order to reaffirm Jewish masculinity. Since the text is expected to be either "sincere" or "funny," other possibilities are not even taken into account.

For the critics who probed this text, only femininity was perceived as problematic, while masculinity was seen as nonproblematic, that is, genderless. My suggestion is to read this text as an indication of *male's* "gender trouble."[41] The man who desires to be a woman illustrates, in my view, the instability of gender division and social order. The text shows masculinity and femininity to be not dichotomous poles but a range between opposites. It explores the space between the sexes and shows them in their mutual specular relations. This perspective widens the range of possible readings of the text.

That the idea of marriage is viewed from a male perspective is quite obvious. Yet there is more than one mirror here and more than two reflections. There is the man who dreams about the woman he wants to become: happily married, sexually satisfied, fecund, and pious. Unlike the discontented man that he is, she is self-assured of her gender roles as the lady of the house and as a mother. In turn, this imagined woman dreams about the man that she wants to marry—and about the male child that she will give birth to. (What the unhappy protagonist wishes for, after all, is the birth of a male baby!) Femininity serves for the protagonist as an idealizing mirror. In the eyes of the dreaming Jewish Cinderella, the man meets an improved version of himself. Instead of his self-image as the harassed and incompetent man, he sees himself now as the perfect prince and the potent husband who feeds and satisfies his wife. But can we not also read this double fantasy as a homoerotic wish? By imagining himself to be a woman who is loved by another man, the male speaker can fantasize about this other man and be loved by him.

This, however, is not a symmetrical play in reflections. It is the male, tired of his maleness and desiring some rest, that has the privilege to encroach upon the realm of femininity and situate himself there. If only as an imaginary exercise, the man chooses here to abandon his central hegemonic position and to *pass*, as it were, to the female margins. Whether seen as a passion to become a woman or as a fascination with the feminine sphere, there is no escape from the text's androcentricity. The notions of feminine passivity and safety, serenity and beauty, are all stereotypes of male conceptualization and idealization of femininity. The dominant male allows himself the desire to retreat to the margin. Masculinity is not loathed or rejected, but momentarily deserted. The active male wishes to respite for a while from his demanding pursuits and dissolve into woman's coziness and inertia.

The longing for the feminine can also be explained as the yearning of the exhausted male "to return home." In patriarchal thinking, woman and home are one; woman is the womb, the lap, the shelter, the nest, the provider of food, warmth, and cover. This androcentric position sees woman/home as an imperative condition for man's independent existence. A man's life outside the house is made possible by the option of a later homecoming.

This homecoming can further be explained as man's return to his own repressed femininity. In "The Uncanny" ("Die Unheimlichkeit"), Freud "attributes the uncanny to the return of the repressed, to the reappearance of what was once *heimlich*, of that place where everyone began, dwelling in complete peace and *heimlichkeit*. It often happens that neurotic men declare that they feel there is something uncanny about the female genital organs. This *unheimlich* place, however, is the entrance to the former *Heim* [home] of all human beings, to the place where each one of us lived once upon a time and in the beginning. . . . The prefix '*un*' is the token of repression."[42]

In the process of constituting himself as male, of individuation from the mother, the male must not only distance himself from the feminine extraneous to him, but exclude or repress his own recollections of primeval maternal femininity. Hence, the longing for the feminine is not for something dichotomous or extraneous, but for an expelled or repressed aspect of the self. He wants to be the man that he is and, at the same time, the woman, the feminine/maternal, which was part of him before he excluded it from his constitution.[43] The wish of Qalonymos's protagonist to become a woman is the desire to reconquer a territory that was once his. The invasion of the female's body and into the woman's sphere enables the invader to see his male self with the eyes of the occupied female and through her knowledge. Being there, he discovers the sources of woman's power. The male body, threatened by symbolical castration (i.e., circumcision, impotence, intellectual inadequacy), is jealous of the already castrated woman, who is free of that anxiety. Paradoxically, woman's passivity and dependence appear to the speaker as inviting and enticing. They are experienced as potentially empowering and liberating from anxieties of impotence and failure.

The male's constitution is maximized to include the man that he is and the woman that he once was and still wants to be. The excursion taken by Qalonymos to femininity and back to masculinity is a widening of the scope of the male subjectivity, so that it can embrace some feminine aspects. The circumcised prince has finally found the Jewish Cinderella inside himself.[44]

Transsexuality and Transtextuality

The puzzlement of scholars in the face of the transsexual theme matches only their confusion over the generic problem—the genre of our passage, in particular, and the generic definition of *Even boḥan* as a whole. It is the instability and hybridity of genres that seem to be so problematic for extant criticism. The book is described as "not [being] cut of one cloth."[45] For the most part, it is obsessed with sin and punishment, death, rotting corpses, and the Last Judgment. "It mixes laughter and tears, . . . 'jumps' from . . . penitential and confessional pieces to witty satires and even jokes";[46] "a jumble of dismal and droll sections";[47] "a strange mélange of wild humor, caustic satire and despairing resignation."[48] Our passage is seen as "comic relief" amid a "gloomy sequence" of "caustic exhortations."

Ezra Fleischer explained this "unapt" insertion by the author's eagerness to retain what was in his eyes "a most successful passage in its own right," even at the cost of breaching the "continuity of the composition."[49] The thematic hybridity is accompanied also by shifts from a quasi-personal tone to sociohistorical descriptions; the language is a blend of biblical and talmudic Hebrew; the rhymed prose in the first part of the book changes into unrhymed prose in the second.[50]

Instead of seeing *Even bohan* as a disordered mess, an aesthetic failure, I suggest considering it as a legitimate offspring of medieval literature. As shown by Mikhail Bakhtin, medieval literature was rife with "seriocomic" genres that have "intensified comic elements, scandal scenes," and "inserted or mixed genres."[51] Unlike some of Bakhtin's examples, *Even bohan* is, admittedly, not a full-fledged carnivalesque work; nevertheless, it surely includes near-carnivalesque elements. Such are Qalonymos's picturesque, at times grotesque, descriptions of the Jewish festivals and the series of caricatures of Jewish social types. The customs of the Jewish communities in Provence at the time are depicted and criticized.[52] The narrator combines the detached view of an anthropologist, the angry preacher's tone admonishing against gluttony, debauchery, gambling, and fascination with clothes,[53] and the satirist's joy in the human body, its needs, and laughter.

Gender trouble, which is the subject of our piece, seems to be analogous to the genre trouble of the book as a whole. Both genre and gender are crossed here. Transtextuality becomes the sign of transsexuality.[54]

Afterword

THE SYMBOLISM OF THE "VEIL" seems to envelop significant parts of this book. Whether (and where and when) historical Jewish women were veiled is a question for historians to explore. My interest lies in the symbolical purport of "the veil" as a central trope in medieval Hebrew literature (and in its surrounding culture). In terms of the social reality, veiling, silencing, and immuring women were patriarchal acts of exclusion, for which "modesty" was often used as explanation and justification. If each member of a woman's body (including her face, hair, and voice) manifests female sexuality (and is thus metonymic to her genitalia), then women ought to be covered behind veils and walls. Hence, the veil, designed to conceal the female sex, became dialectically the emblem of women's sexuality. This synonymy of corporeality, sexuality, femininity, and the veil, especially in the ascetic mind, yielded the metaphor of the body as the soul's veil, which the ascetic had to despise and strip off.

The signification of the veil varies according to its positioning in various genres, modes and moods. Its ambiguity is visible in the erotic imagery of the male love lyric: The pretty face of the beloved is said to shine from behind her veils like the sun does behind clouds; or her thick dark hair is compared to a veil of vipers. In another vein, the dark night is itself a huge veil covering the lovers' secret. The beloved lady is a veiled enigma. The veil enhances the notions of her absence (or aloofness). For the male lover, the veil is both a frustrating impediment and a fetish provoking desire. The veil is the frontier in the battle of male and female gazes. The lover either implores the beloved to unveil or attempts to penetrate the veil with his desirous gaze and passionate rhetoric.

In epithalamia the obstacle of the veil (as a sign of social prohibitions) is removed. The legitimate act of unveiling the bride and seeing her face foreshadows the imminent act of sanctified marital sex. In rhymed stories this unveiling of the bride often ends disastrously, when behind the veil the groom finds a female monster in place of the woman he desired. In this context the veil symbolizes the dialectics of surface/interior, untruth/truth.

Masks and veils are common paraphernalia in rhymed stories revolving around impostors and crooks. In stories of cross-dressing, veiling and exposure attain special significance. The default assumption that the veil is an unambiguous cipher for the feminine gender fails when a male's face peeps from behind the veil. Rather than serving as a transparent sign for *woman*, the veil is set here as an opaque barrier to the correct reading of gender. In signifying an impasse of signification, it becomes indeed an index for the cultural constructedness of gender.

"Her thick veil" is also a mechanism of explanation in modern psychoanalysis. In a misogynous vein, not dissimilar to that of our medieval poets, Lacan (and Freud) identify woman with artifice, appearance, dissimulation, illusion, travesty, make-up, *the veil*—all of which cover the female's horrendous cavity, her lack. Woman "can only seduce when at least one veil remains." She retains her position as the object of the other's desire only through enticing the other. This she does with "her thick veil" which both covers and makes visible her "essential assets."

Enticing beauty, concealed truth, and veiled meanings are considered also the essential traits of poetry. In medieval Hebrew literature, the poetic description of Woman and that of Poetry share in the ambivalent dualism of face and veil, body and clothing, essence and appearance, depth and surface. In Hebrew ars-poetical poems, Poetry is thus rendered feminine. Poetry is beautiful, artificially ornamented, veiled, seducing, and deceiving. Poetry's veils or garments indicate its florid-but-deceitful figurative language. In poetry (and in language at large) the signifiers cloak and betray the "true" meanings of the signifieds. Hence, by means of the veil (itself a figure), both Poetry and Woman embody the problematic of language and signification. According to this gendered semiotics, the hermeneutic process involves striping off literature's literary devices in order to get to its "inner truth."

While my title may allude to a similar process of reading, my aim in *Unveiling Eve* was not to see Eve's "true" face as much as it was to view her very veils. It was the "literariness" of the texts which stood at the center of my interest rather than their "historicality" (or "authenticity"). My various chapters reflect on the ample ways in which those textual veils cover female faces and muffle female voices. My analyses attempted to map the positions and positioning of female figures and female voices within the patterns of male discourse and its procedures of signification: How were notions of presence/absence; speech/silence; subject/object thematized within the texts? How did the tools and devices of poetry and fiction (genres, conventions, imagery, rhetoric, irony, satire, allegory, and the like) enhance the presence of the female, or how were they employed to objectify, distance, and silence her? By listening to female voices arrested in male texts—though often muffled by male transmission, and serving the authors' androcentric ideologies—I attempted to show how these "illegitimate" utterances of the "other" threaten to undermine the dominant discourse within which they are situated. I suggest reading them as sites of embedded resistance and empowerment.

I see my work as participating in at least two larger projects. One is the feminist medievalist project, investigating gender and sexuality in Western literature and culture. The other is the now developing tendency in various disciplines in Jewish studies to explore such ancient and premodern Jewish discourses.

Being the first attempt of its kind in the field of medieval Hebrew literature, this book far from exhausts the potentialities of reading gender in medieval texts. There are more areas to be explored and approaches still waiting to be employed. I will briefly sketch here some of these. Homoerotic Hebrew poetry is a subject much debated (and generally puritanically denied) by previous critics. It certainly needs to be elucidated against its historical background and in light of recent trends in gay theory. The subject of masculinity was only slightly touched upon in this book. How is masculinity conceptualized and constructed in the Hebrew texts? What are its values? Who is the ideal Jewish male? The picture will not be complete until these questions are answered. Other areas and topics which remained out of the scope of this book and which need to be looked at in the future are: the gendered relationship between (male) God and (female) Israel in liturgical poetry; the problematic of the *kharja*s (foreign-language endings of Hebrew poems)—are they authentic "feminine" voices appropriated by male lyrics, or male-authored counterfeits? Additionally, huge narrative repositories of medieval Hebrew folktales (such as the book of *Zohar*, or the Ashkenazic *Sefer hasidim*) still await the feminist analytic eye.

Notes

Preface

1. Among many others, I will mention here Ilana Pardes, *Contradictions in the Bible: A Feminist Approach* (Cambridge, Mass.: Harvard University Press, 1992); Daniel Boyarin, *Carnal Israel: Reading Sex in Talmudic Culture* (Berkeley: University of California Press, 1993); Rachel Biale, *Women and Jewish Law: An Exploration of Women's Issues in Halakhic Sources* (New York: Schocken Books, 1984); Galit Hasan-Rokem, *Web of Life: Folklore and Midrash in Rabbinic Literature*, trans. Batya Stein (Stanford, Calif.: Stanford University Press, 2000), esp. chap. 6; Elliot R. Wolfson, *Circle in the Square: Studies in the Use of Gender in Kabbalistic Symbolism* (Albany: State University of New York Press, 1995); David Biale, *Eros and the Jews: From Biblical Israel to Contemporary America* (New York: Basic Books, 1992); Judith R. Baskin, ed., *Women of the Word: Jewish Women and Jewish Writing* (Detroit: Wayne State University Press, 1994); Lynn Davidman and Shelly Tenenbaum, eds., *Feminist Perspectives on Jewish Studies* (New Haven, Conn.: Yale University Press, 1995); Yael Azmon, ed., *A View into the Lives of Women in Jewish Societies: Collected Essays* (in Hebrew) (Jerusalem: Zalman Shazar Center for Jewish History, 1995).

2. For some recent discussions to this effect, see Judith Plaskow, *Standing Again at Sinai: Judaism from a Feminist Perspective* (New York: Harper and Row, 1990); T. M. Rudavsky, ed., *Gender and Judaism: The Transformation of Tradition* (New York: New York University Press, 1995); Maurie Sacks, ed., *Active Voices: Women in Jewish Culture* (Urbana: University of Illinois Press, 1995); Miriam Peskovitch and Laura Levitt, eds., *Judaism Since Gender* (New York: Routledge 1996).

3. For feminist criticism of modern Hebrew literature, see among others Naomi B. Sokoloff et al., eds., *Gender and Text in Modern Hebrew and Yiddish Literature* (New York: Jewish Theological Seminary, 1992); Lily Rattok, ed., afterword to *The Other Voice: Women's Fiction in Hebrew* (in Hebrew) (Tel Aviv: Hakibbutz Hameuchad, 1997); Yael S. Feldman, *No Room of Their Own: Gender and Nation in Israeli Women's Fiction* (New York: Columbia University Press, 1999); Hannah Naveh, "Miscellaneous, Marginal, Forgotten: Life Outside the Canon," in *Sex, Gender, Politics: Women in Israel* (in Hebrew), ed. Dafna N. Izraeli et al. (Tel Aviv: Hakibbutz Hameuchad, 2000), 49–106.

4. For women's situation in Israel, see Lesley Hazelton, *Israeli Women: The Reality Behind the Myth* (New York: Simon and Schuster, 1977); Dafna N.

Izraeli et al., eds., *The Double Bind: The Status of Women in Israel* (in Hebrew) (Tel Aviv: Hakibbutz Hameuchad, 1982); Yael Azmon and Dafna N. Izraeli, eds., *Women in Israel: A Sociological Anthology* (New Brunswick, N.J.: Transaction, 1993); Izraeli et al., *Sex, Gender, Politics*; Barbara Swirsky and Marilyn P. Safir, eds., *Calling the Equality Bluff: Women in Israel* (New York: Teachers' College Press, 1993).

5. See Rachel Eli'or, " 'Present/Absent,' 'Still Life' and 'A Pretty Maiden That Has No Eyes': Women as Present and Absent in the Holy Language, in Jewish Religion and in Israeli Life" (in Hebrew), *Alpayim* 20 (2000): 214–70.

6. Amalia Kahana-Carmon, "She Writes Rather Pleasingly, but on Things Marginal," *Yedi'ot Aharonot*, 24 February 1988. And see also Feldman, *No Room of Their Own*, 70 and notes.

7. Quoted from *Ha-'ir* (a local Tel Aviv paper), 15 October 1993. Dafna Izraeli wrote about it as early as 1989 but to no public consequence. And see also Dafna Izraeli, "They Have Eyes and See Not: Gender Politics in the Diaspora Museum," *Psychology of Women Quarterly* 17 (1994): 515–23.

8. Boyarin, *Carnal Israel*, 227.

9. Paul Zumthor, *Speaking of the Middle Ages*, trans. Sarah White (Lincoln: University of Nebraska Press, 1986), 33.

10. Boyarin, *Carnal Israel*, 229.

11. Quoted from Kalman P. Bland, "Medievals Are Not Us," in Peskowitz and Levitt, *Judaism Since Gender*, 143. Bland, a student of medieval Jewish philosophy, relates to his conversion to feminism as he realized that the philosophers he has studied were all "medieval Jewish men who were shaped by and reproduced medieval misogyny" (144).

12. Elaine Tuttle Hansen, *Chaucer and the Fictions of Gender* (Berkeley: University of California Press, 1992), 292.

13. Hans Robert Jauss, "Literary History as a Challenge to Literary Theory," in *New Directions in Literary History*, ed. Ralph Cohen (Baltimore: Johns Hopkins University Press, 1974), 27.

14. Elaine Tuttle Hansen, "The Feminization of Men in Chaucer's *Legend of Good Women*," in *Seeking the Woman in Late Medieval and Renaissance Writings: Essays in Feminist Contextual Criticism*, ed. Sheila Fisher and Janet E. Halley (Knoxville: The University of Tennessee Press, 1989), 52.

15. Translations throughout the book are mine (unless otherwise mentioned). The rhyme and meter so characteristic of medieval Hebrew poetry could not be reproduced in translation, nor could the rich web of biblical and other allusions.

Chapter 1. No-Woman's-Land

1. The poem was unearthed in the Cairo Geniza (a huge repository of medieval Jewish documents and literary manuscripts miraculously saved in Egypt and rediscovered at the end of the nineteenth century). It was Ezra Fleischer who first published it in "On Dunash Ben Labrat, His Wife, and His Son: New Light on the Beginnings of the Hebrew-Spanish School" (in Hebrew), *Jerusalem Studies in*

Hebrew Literature 5 (1984): 189–202. Relying on scribal testimony Fleischer attributes the poem with unrestricted certainty to Dunash's wife. That the poem was written by the wife herself, and not by Dunash in a female voice, is corroborated also by the husband's reply (also printed by Fleischer), where he addresses her as "a learned woman." (The poem's "she" and "he" should thus be understood as "I" and "you.") However, as Jane Burns and Roberta Krueger caution us, it should be kept in mind that "given the uncertainties of medieval manuscript-transmission, the female signature of a text does not guarantee identity with a historical woman author. It may invite us to read a female voice." See their editorial introduction to *Romance Notes* 25/3 (1985): 216. For a typology of women-voiced poems, see Alan Deyermond, "Sexual Initiation in the Woman's-Voice Court Lyric," *Courtly Literature, Culture and Context* 25 (1986): 125–58, esp. 127–28.

2. The translation is Peter Cole's, published in Shirley Kauffman, Galit Hasan-Rokem, and Tamar S. Hess, eds., *The Defiant Muse: Hebrew Feminist Poems from Antiquity to the Present: A Bilingual Anthology* (New York: Feminist Press of the City University of New York, 1999), 62–63. Translations throughout this book, if not otherwise specified, are mine.

3. For the emergence and nature of the Hebrew poetry of the Golden Age, see below. In adopting the Arabic metrical system, rhyme, poetic forms, and thematics, Dunash, a court poet of the Cordoban Jewish courtier Ḥasday Ibn Shaprut, lay the foundation for the new Hebrew poetic school.

4. Her poem is published in Kauffman, Hasan-Rokem, and Hess, *The Defiant Muse*, 64–65.

5. Katharina M. Wilson, *Medieval Women Writers* (Athens: University of Georgia, 1984), viii. See also, among others, Peter Dronke, *Women Writers in the Middle Ages* (Cambridge: Cambridge University Press, 1984); Meg Bogin, *The Women Troubadours* (New York: Norton, 1980); Francisco López Estrada, "Las mujeres escritoras en la Edad Media castellana," in *La condición de la mujer en la Edad Media*, ed. M. A. Ladero Quesada, D. Ozanam, and R. Pastor (Madrid: Universidad Complutense, 1986); Alan Deyermond, "Spain's First Women Writers," in *Women in Hispanic Literature: Icons and Fallen Idols*, ed. Beth Miller (Berkeley: University of California Press, 1983), 27–52.

6. About the position of the slave-girl singers and poets, see also the section "The Courtier-Rabbis as Love Poets" in Chapter 2 below. Lists and poems of Andalusian women poets appear in the histories of al-Suyūṭī (d. 1505) and al-Maqqarī (d. 1631). The Andalusian women's poetry was collected in Teresa Garulo, *Dīwān de las poetisas de al-Andalus* (Madrid: Hiperión, 1986). And see also J. M. Nichols, "Arabic Women Poets in Al-Andalus," *Maghrib Review* 4 (1979): 114–17; Celia del Moral, "Poesía de mujer, poesía de hombre: La differencia del género en la lírica andalusí," in *Árabes, judiás y cristianas: Mujeres en la Europa medieval*, ed. Celia del Moral (Granada: University of Granada, 1993), 173–93. Related is the most controversial issue whether the *kharja*s represent authentic Iberian oral women songs (see 8–9 and note 25 below).

7. Maria Viguera, "On the Social Status of Andalusi Women," in *The Legacy of Muslim Spain*, ed. Salma Khadra Jayyusi (Leiden: E. J. Brill, 1992), 709.

8. J. M. Nichols, "The Arabic Verses of Qasmūna bint Ismā'īl ibn Bagh-dāla," *International Journal of Middle East Studies* 13 (1981): 155–58; James A. Bel-lamy, "Qasmūna the Poetess: Who Was She?" *Journal of the American Oriental Society* 103 (1983): 423–24, identifies al-Suyūṭī's Ismā'īl Ibn Baghdāla with Samuel Ibn Naghrela.

9. Between Merecina and Rachel Morpurgo (Italy, nineteenth century), who is considered the first modern Hebrew woman poet, only three women-authored Hebrew poems have been preserved: one from sixteenth-century Kur-distan, one from eighteenth-century Central Europe and one from eighteenth-century Morocco. As pointed out in the most useful introduction to Kauffman, Hasan-Rokem, and Hess's *Defiant Muse* anthology, other women-authored po-ems might have been lost. Few Jewish women also wrote in Yiddish in the early modern period.

10. Elaine Showalter, "Feminist Criticism in the Wilderness," in *The New Feminist Criticism: Essays on Women, Literature and Theory* (London: Virago, 1986), 243–70.

11. Though illiteracy was the rule, exceptions can be numerated. See Co-lette Sirat, "Les femmes juives et l'écriture au Moyen Âge," *Les nouveaux cahiers* 101 (1990): 14–23; Renée Levine Melammed, "He Said, She Said: A Woman Teacher in Twelfth-Century Cairo," *AJS Review* 22 (1997): 19–35; Joseph Shatz-miller, "Women in the Medical Profession," in *Jews, Medicine and Medieval Soci-ety* (Berkeley: University of California Press, 1994), 108–12; David Nirenberg, "Female Rabbi in Fourteenth Century Zaragozza?" *Sefarad* 51 (1991): 179–82.

12. Quoted from the editors' introduction, Sheila Fisher and Janet E. Hal-ley, eds., *Seeking the Woman in Late Medieval and Renaissance Writings: Essays in Feminist Contextual Criticism* (Knoxville: University of Tennessee Press, 1989), 13.

13. Avraham Grossman, *Pious and Rebellious: Jewish Women in Europe in the Middle Ages* (in Hebrew) (Jerusalem: Zalman Shazar Center for Jewish His-tory, 2001), 18.

14. Shelomo Dov Goitein, *A Mediterranean Society: The Jewish Communi-ties of the Arab World as Portrayed in the Documents of the Cairo Geniza* (Berkeley: University of California Press), esp. vol. 3, *The Family* (1978); vol. 4: *Daily Life* (1983). The material from the Geniza (see note 1), contemporary with the literary works discussed in my book, includes rabbinical responsa, court hearings, com-munity registers, private letters, marriage and divorce contracts, trousseau and dowry lists, wills, and the like. And, as Goitein maintains, though the sources are mainly Jewish-Egyptian, they are reflective, by and large, of the lives of Jews (and Muslims) all over the Mediterranean. (And see, for instance, the use Leila Ahmed, *Women and Gender in Islam: Historical Roots of a Modern Debate* [New Haven, Conn.: Yale University Press, 1992], makes of Goitein's findings for the history of Islamic women.) Another comprehensive work reconstructing the lives of Jewish women in Europe is Grossman, *Pious and Rebellious.* More material pertinent to the lives of medieval Jewish women, family life, and sexuality can be found in S. D. Goitein, "The Sexual Mores of the Common People," in *Society and the Sexes in Medieval Islam,* ed. Afaf Lutfi Al-Sayyid-Marsot (Malibu, Calif.: Undena

Publications, 1979), 43–61; Judith R. Baskin, ed., *Jewish Women in Historical Perspective* (Detroit: Wayne State University Press, 1991), 94–103; L. M. Epstein, *Sex Laws and Customs in Judaism* (New York: Ktav Publishing House, 1948; second ed. 1967); Isadore Epstein, "The Jewish Woman in the Responsa 900 C.E.–1500 C.E," in *The Jewish Library 3: Woman*, ed. Leo Jung (London: Soncino, 1970), 41–62; Mordechai A. Friedman, "Halacha as Evidence for the Study of Sexual Mores among Jews in Medieval Islamic Countries: Face Coverings and Mutʿah Marriages" (in Hebrew), in Yael Azmon, *View into the Lives of Women in Jewish Societies* (Jerusalem: Zalman Shazar Center for Jewish History, 1995), 143–60; Mordechai A. Friedman, "The Ethics of Medieval Jewish Marriage," in *Religion in a Religious Age*, ed. S. D. Goitein (Cambridge, Mass.: Association for Jewish Studies, 1974), 83–101; Yom Tov Assis, "Sexual Behaviour in Medieval Hispano-Jewish Society," in *Jewish History: Essays in Honour of Chimen Abramsky*, ed. Ada Rapoport-Albert and Steven J. Zipperstein (London: P. Halban, 1988), 25–59; David Biale, *Eros and the Jews from Biblical Israel to Contemporary America* (New York: Basic Books, 1992); Jeremy Cohen, *"Be Fertile and Increase, Fill the Earth and Master it": The Ancient and Medieval Career of a Biblical Text* (Ithaca, N.Y.: Cornell University Press, 1989); Ron Barkaï, *Les infortunes de Dinah: Le livre de la génération: La gynécology juive au moyen âge* (Paris: Les édition du Cerf, 1991); Enrique Cantera Montenegro, "Actividades socio-profesionales de la mujer judía en los reinos hispanocristianos de la baja Edad Media," in *El trabajo de las mujeres en la Edad Media Hispana*, ed. Angela Muñoz Fernández and Cristina Segura Graiño (Madrid: Associación Cultural A-Mudayna, Institutio de la Mujer, Ministerio de Cultura, 1988), 143–60; Ladero Quesada, Ozanam, and Pastor, *La condición de la mujer*; Renée Levine Melammed, *Heretics or Daughters of Israel? The Crypto-Jewish Women of Castile* (New York: Oxford University Press, 1999). On Arabic Andalusi women, see Manuela Marin, *Mujeres en Al-Ándalus* (Madrid: Consejo Superior de investigaciones científicas), 2000; Maria J. Viguera, "On the Social Status of Andalusi Women," in Jayyusi, *The Legacy of Muslim Spain*, 709–24; Maria J. Viguera, ed., *La mujer en Al-Ándalus: Reflejos históricos de su actividad y categorías sociales* (Madrid: Ediciónes de la Universidad Autónoma de Madrid; Seville: Editoriales Andaluzas Unidas, 1989); Celia del Moral-Molina, "La mujer árabe en Andalucía durante la Edad Media," in *Las mujeres en la historia de Andalucía* (Cordoba: Publicaciónes de la consejeria de cultura y medio ambiente de la Junta de Andalucía, 1994), 35–40. Two most helpful bibliographies are José R. Ayaso, Maria José Cano, and Moisés Orfali, "Bibliografia sobre la mujer judía" in del Moral, ed., *Árabes, judías y cristianas*, 237–43; and Cheryl Tallan, "Medieval Jewish Women in History, Literature, Law, and Art: An Annotated Bibliography," *ORB: The Online Reference Book for Medieval Studies* at http://orb.rhodes.edu/encyclop/religion/Judaism/jew-wom.html>.

15. Joel L. Kraemer, "Women's Letters from the Cairo *Geniza*" (in Hebrew), in Azmon, *View into the Lives*, 161–82.

16. This pen/penis figure in modern writing is central to Sandra M. Gilbert and Susan Gubar, *The Madwoman in the Attic: The Woman Writer and the Nineteenth-Century Imagination* (New Haven, Conn.: Yale University Press,

1979). For the phallic pen/sword motif in Hebrew and Arabic laudatory poetry, see Israel Levin, "The Pen and the Rider" (in Hebrew), in *Shai le-Heyman: Papers on Medieval Hebrew Literature Presented to A. M. Habermann*, ed. Yonah David and Zvi Malachi (Jerusalem: Reuben Mass, 1977), 156–62.

17. For the history of medieval Hebrew literature, see Jefim Schirmann, *The History of Hebrew Poetry in Muslim Spain* (in Hebrew), edited, supplemented, and annotated by Ezra Fleischer (Jerusalem: Magnes, 1995); Jefim Schirmann, *The History of Hebrew Poetry in Christian Spain and Southern France* (in Hebrew), edited, supplemented, and annotated by Ezra Fleischer (Jerusalem: Magnes, 1997) (hereinafter cited as Schirmann-Fleischer, *Muslim Spain* and *Christian Spain*); Dan Pagis, *Change and Tradition in the Secular Poetry: Spain and Italy* (in Hebrew) (Jerusalem: Keter, 1976); Raymond P. Scheindlin, "Medieval Jewish Literature," in *From Mesopotamia to Modernity*, ed. Burton L. Visotzky and David E. Fishman (Boulder, Colo.: Westview Press, 1999), 127–66; Ross Brann, "The Fire of Love Poetry Has Kissed Me, How Can I Resist? The Hebrew Lyric in Perspective," in *Medieval Lyric: Genres in Historical Context*, ed. William D. Paden (Urbana: University of Illinois Press, 2000), 317–33; Ross Brann, *The Compunctious Poet: Cultural Ambiguity and Hebrew Poetry in Muslim Spain* (Baltimore: Johns Hopkins University Press, 1991), whose last chapters cover also Hebrew literature in Christian Spain, Italy and Provence, see 119–60. For Jewish culture in Christian Spain, see Bernard Septimus, *Hispano-Jewish Culture in Transition* (Harvard Judaic Monographs 4; Cambridge, Mass.: Harvard University Press, 1982).

18. See Joseph Weiss, "Courtly Culture and Courtly Poetry" (in Hebrew), *Sefer ha-Kinnus ha-ʿOlami le-Madʿe ha-Yahadut* 1 (Jerusalem, 1952): 396–403.

19. Brann, *The Compunctious Poet*, 119. And See also Pagis, *Change and Tradition*, 175–98.

20. For the demographic, social, and intellectual changes during the twelfth and thirteenth centuries, see the first three chapters in Yizhak Baer, *A History of the Jews in Christian Spain*, trans. L. Schoffman (Philadelphia: Jewish Publication Society, 1961), and Septimus, *Hispano-Jewish Culture in Transition*.

21. On the Arabic and Hebrew *maqāma*, see Rina Drory, "The *maqāma*," in *The Literature of Al-Andalus*, ed. María Rosa Menocal, Raymond P. Scheindlin and Michael Sells (Cambridge: Cambridge University Press, 2000), 190–210. On the Hebrew *maqāma* and its cognates, see Pagis, *Change and Tradition*, 199–244, Matti Huss discussed in length the terminological and generic problems concerning the relations between the *maqāma*-proper and other narrative genres; the differences between the Arabic and Hebrew genres as well as between the Eastern and the Andalusian patterns. See his doctoral thesis, *Critical Editions of "Minḥat Yehudah," "ʿEzrat Hanashim," and "ʿEin Mishpat" with Prefaces, Variants, Sources, and Annotations* (Jerusalem: Hebrew University, 1991), 1:17–29, and also his "It Never Happened nor Did It Ever Exist: The Status of Fiction in the Hebrew *Maqāma*" (in Hebrew), *Jerusalem Studies in Hebrew Literature*, 18 (2000): 57–104. For discussions of *maqāmāt*, see also Chapters 5–7 below.

22. Noteworthy among the anthologies and compilations of medieval Hebrew folktales (not discussed in this book) are the *Alpha-Beta of Ben-Sira, The*

Midrash of the Ten Commandments (both anonymous compilations of the Gaonic period, retold in many medieval variants), and *An Elegant Composition Concerning Relief after Adversity* by Rabbi Nissim of Qayrawān (which was most influential in its Hebrew translation after its eleventh-century Arabic original was lost). The Ashkenazic *Sefer Ḥasidim* whose main author is Rabbi Judah he-Ḥasid (twelfth century) includes hundreds of narrative exempla. The Zohar and other Kabbalistic works are also rich repositories of stories. Stories were treasured in historiographical compositions, the most significant of which is *The Scroll of Ahimaʿaz* (Italy, eleventh-century), which though unrelated to the *maqāma* is set in elegant rhymed prose. See Josef Dan, *The Hebrew Story in the Middle Ages* (in Hebrew) (Jerusalem: Keter, 1974); David Stern and Mark Jay Mirsky, eds., *Rabbinic Fantasies: Imaginative Narratives from Classical Hebrew Literature* (Philadelphia: Jewish Publication Society, 1990); and Eli Yassif, *The Hebrew Folktale: History, Genre, Meaning*, trans. Jacqueline S. Teitelbaum (Bloomington: Indiana University Press, 1999). Yassif's extensive chapter on the Middle Ages (245–351) is especially beneficial in pointing out contacts within the Hebrew narrative tradition, and between it and international folklore. It is also most relevant to our discussion in its emphasis on the representations of women.

23. For parallels between Indian, Persian, Arabic, Hebrew, and various European stories, see Haim Schwarzbaum, "International Folklore Motifs in Petrus Alphonsi's 'Disciplina Clericalis,' " in *Jewish Folklore: Between East and West: Collected Papers*, ed. Eli Yassif (Beer Sheva: Ben Gurion University of the Negev Press, 1989), 239–58.

24. Toril Moi, *Sexual/Textual Politics: Feminist Literary Theory* (London: Routledge), 42–49. Quotation is from p. 44. Representative of this approach in the early stage of feminist criticism were Mary Ellmann, *Thinking About Women* (New York: Harcourt Brace Jovanovitch, 1968), and Susan Koppelman Cornillon, ed., *Images of Women in Fiction: Feminist Perspectives* (Bowling Green, Ohio: Bowling Green University Popular Press, 1972). Several papers published in recent years listing "female images" or "feminine motifs" in medieval Hebrew literature acknowledge "Woman" as a topic for research, but are mostly descriptive, taxonomic, and uninformed by gender theories. See Yehudit Dishon, "Descriptions of the Ideal Woman in Secular Hebrew Poetry in the Middle Ages" (in Hebrew), *Yedaʿ ʿAm* 23 (1986): 3–15. Yehudit Dishon, "The Unfaithful Wife and Her Lover" (in Hebrew), *Bikoret u-Pharshanut* 30 (1994): 175–95; Judith Dishon, "Images of Women in Medieval Hebrew Literature," in *Women of the Word: Jewish Women and Jewish Writing*, ed. Judith R. Baskin (Detroit: Wayne State University Press, 1994), 35–50; Santiago Maspoch Bueno, "Retratos femeninos en poesía hebrea, árabe y castellana medieval," *Proyección histórica de España* 2 (1993): 461–73; Fernando Díaz Esteban, "Elogio y vituperio de la mujer: Una aportación de la literatura hispanohebrea," in *Proyección histórica de España* 3 (1993): 67–78; Carmen Caballero Navas, "Woman Images and Motifs in Hebrew Andalusian Poetry," *World Congress of Jewish Studies* 11, C3 (1994): 9–16; Maria José Cano, "El tratamiento de las mujeres en la literatura hispano-hebrea," in del Moral, *Árabes, judías y cristianas*, 161–72; Matti Huss, "Misogyny in the Andalusian School of Poetry" (in

Hebrew), in *Te'uda* 19, *Studies in Hebrew Literature of the Middle Ages and the Renaissance Presented to Professor Yonah David*, ed. Tova Rosen and Avner Holtzman, 27–53.

25. The *kharja*s are the concluding couplets, sung in vernacular Arabic or in Romance, of strophic Hebrew poems of the *muwashshaḥ* type. Whereas the body of the poems reiterates the courtly love style, many of the *kharja*s allow for the speech of women. For discussion of woman's voice in *kharja*s (not attended to in this book), see Tova Rosen, "On Tongues Being Bound and Let Loose: Women in Medieval Hebrew Literature," *Prooftexts* 8 (1988): 79–83 and note 53; and Tova Rosen, "The Muwashshaḥ" in Menocal, Scheindlin, and Sells, *The Literature of Al-Andalus*, 165–89. For a contestation of the hypothesized authenticity and femininity of the *kharja*s, see Mary Jane Kelly, "Virgins Misconceived: Poetic Voice in Mozarabic Kharjas," *La Coronica* 19 (1990–91): 1–23.

26. *Dîwân des Abu-l-Hasân Jehuda ha-Levi* (hereinafter, Judah ha-Levi, *Dîwān*), 4 vols., ed. Heinrich Brody (Berlin: Mekize Nirdamim, 1894–1930).

27. *Divan Shmuel Hanagid*, vol. 2, *Ben Mishle* (The son of Proverbs), ed. Dov Jarden (Jerusalem, 1982).

28. From Isaac, *Mishle 'Arav* ("Parables of the Arabs"), quoted from Dishon, "Descriptions of the Ideal Woman," 4.

29. On the theme of wicked wives in Hebrew literature, see Norman Roth, "The 'Wiles of Women' Motif in the Medieval Hebrew Literature of Spain," *Hebrew Annual Review* 2 (1978): 145–65; Haim Schwarzbaum, "Female Fickleness in Jewish Folklore," in *Jewish Folklore*, 173–96. Dishon, "The Unfaithful Wife and Her Lover." None of these applies feminist criticism.

30. This theme is treated in Chapter 5, "Domesticating the Enemy."

31. Translation is mine. For the Hebrew, see excerpts from *Sefer Sha'ashu'im* by Joseph Ibn Zabara in Jefim Schirmann, *Hebrew Poetry in Spain and Provence* (in Hebrew) (Jerusalem: Mosad Bialik; Tel Aviv: Dvir, 1960), 3:258. For an English translation of the entire work, see *The Book of Delight*, trans. Moses Hadas (New York: Columbia University Press, 1932).

32. This caution is also echoed in collection of proverbs by Moshe Nathan (Catalonia, fourteenth century): "If your wife acts wickedly, or rules over you— / reduce her to shoe-trodden mire. // Let her be a woman and be you the man. / Or else you'll be the wife and she—the husband!" Schirmann, *Hebrew Poetry in Spain and Provence*, 4:542.

33. For the beauty lists, see Chapter 2.

34. *Taḥkemoni*, ed. I. Toporowski (Tel Aviv: Maḥbarot Lesifrut, 1952). The translation of the prose section is Reichert's, and is cited from Roth, "The 'Wiles of Women,' " 155. The rest is my translation. This monstrous description is al-Ḥarizi's elaboration of a passage by Judah Ibn Shabbetai discussed in Chapter 5.

35. For Julia Kristeva's theory of the "abject" and discussion of the nexus between bodily wastes (excretions, menstruation) and the feminine maternal, see the chapter "Kristeva, Femininity, Abjection," in Barbara Creed, *The Monstrous Feminine: Film, Feminism, Psychoanalysis* (London: Routledge, 1993), 8–15.

36. Alluding to Leviticus 16:8, 22.

37. The sadistic compulsion invested in this limbs dissection can only match the physical brutality which the protagonist in this story committed. Right before he escaped from his bride, he muzzled her mouth and then beat her "until the blood of her heart came to her mouth. Then I tore her flesh off until her hymen blood ran over her body." Note that the analogy between the flow from her mouth and that from her vagina metaphorically identifies woman's speech with her menstruation.

38. For the theoretization of "the female grotesque," see Mary Russo, *The Female Grotesque: Risk, Excess, and Modernity* (New York: Routledge, 1995), esp. chap. 2 where Mikhail Bakhtin's theoretical contribution is expanded upon. For ridicule of women in Arabic literature, see Geert Jan Van Gelder, "Against Women and Other Pleasantries," *Journal of Arabic Literature* 16 (1985):61–72.

39. Other Hebrew appellations for Tevel are *eretz* and *adamah* (earth). This allegorical persona of Tevel entered Andalusian-Hebrew poetry following the theme in Arabic ascetic (*zuhd*) poetry. For the Arabic genre, see Andras Hamory, "Ascetic Poetry (Zuhdiyyāt)," in *Cambridge History of Arabic Literature: Abbasid Belles-Lettres*, ed. Julia Ashtiany et al. (New York: Cambridge University Press, 1990), 263–73. The term *tevel* (earth, universe) was chosen by the Hebrew poets as a feminine equivalent for the term *al-dunyā*, which denotes in Arabic spatial lowliness and moral inferiority. The grammatical feminine gender of both words enabled and encouraged the poets to introduce the purport of negative femaleness. For a most comprehensive comparison of al-*dunyā* and *tevel*, see Israel Levin, *The Embroidered Coat: The Genres of Hebrew Poetry in Spain* (in Hebrew) (Tel Aviv: Hakibbutz Hameuchad, 1995), 3:60–103. Huss insists on the affinity and interdependence between the image of the cruel and attractive lady in the love lyric and that of the demonic and tempting Tevel in ascetic poetry. See Matti Huss, "Misogyny in the Andalusian School of Poetry."

40. For the equation *corrupt world* = *whorish woman* in Islamic Sufi thinking, see Annemarie Schimmel, "Eros—Heavenly and Not So Heavenly—in Sufi Literature and Life," in Sayyid-Marsot, *Society and the Sexes*, 124.

41. Moses Ibn Ezra, *Secular Poems*, ed. Hayyim Brody (Berlin: Shocken, 1935).

42. Solomon Ibn Gabirol, *Secular Poems*, ed. Hayyim Brody and Hayyim Schirmann (Jerusalem: Schocken Institute, 1976).

43. As in Leviticus 20:12.

44. *Itzhak Ibn Khalfun: Poems*, ed. Aharon Mirsky (Jerusalem: Mosad Bialik, 1961).

45. The archetype of Mother Tevel in Hebrew poetry seems to lend itself to Freudian and Lacanian interpretations. Freud grounds male hostility and contempt toward women in the emergence of the oedipal recognition that the mother is a whore, that "long before his birth, the mother has already been unfaithful to him . . . [that] she has betrayed him by being desired by others." Furthermore, the infant's first encounters with the insecure world turn his frustration into "the fear

of the feminine." Men will thus continue to long for the phallic mother while rejecting female attraction. According to Lacan, "[The] process of social construction [of subjectivity and sexuality] is predicated on the necessary renunciation and
sacrifice of the child's access to the maternal body and the child's submission to
the Law of the Father. The paternal figure serves to separate the child from an
all-encompassing, engulfing, and potentially lethal relation with the mother. The
father intervenes in the imaginary dyad and represents the Law. The father embodies the power of the phallus." Elizabeth Grosz, *Jacques Lacan: A Feminist Introduction* (London: Routledge, 1990), 129, 142.

46. *Dīwān Shemuel Hanagid,* vol. 3, *Ben Qohelet (The son of Ecclesiastes),* ed.
Dov Jarden (Jerusalem, 1992).

47. The teeth in this context can also be interpreted as the *vagina dentata*
of the Terrible Mother. And see Erich Neumann, *The Great Mother: An Analysis of
the Archetype* (Princeton, N.J.: Princeton University Press, 1955), 168.

48. Tevel's invitation to this luxurious feast alludes to the temptations of the
gentile harlot in Proverbs 7.

49. Erich Neumann expounded on this collective archetype in *The Great
Mother* and in *The Fear of the Feminine and Other Essays on Feminine Psychology* (Princeton, N.J.: Princeton University Press, 1994). For Neumann the all-
pervasiveness of the equation of World/Earth and Woman is ahistorical and deep-
rooted in the collective subconscious. Mother Earth (the Great Goddess or Great
Mother) is both the Good and Terrible Mother: "She appears positively as the
child-bearing and protectively containing Mother, and negatively as the possessive, imprisoning, depriving, and devouring Mother. . . . her womb brings forth
all living things. . . . But . . . [she] . . . devours everything that is born, and swal-
lows it back pitilessly into herself. Her womb of death is a devouring maw of darkness, and as the grave, the flesh-devouring sarcophagus" (*The Great Mother,*
188–89).

50. Maimonides' interpretation of the story of Creation reveals this kind
of gendered ontology; and see also 79–80 and 137 below. According to the Kab-
balists, the demonic nature of woman and the feminine element of the cosmos
are linked. The demonic is an offspring of the feminine sphere. See Gershom
Scholem, *Major Trends in Jewish Mysticism* (New York: Schocken Books, 1961),
37–38; on Lilith, see Gershom Scholem, *Kabbala* (Jerusalem: Keter, 1974), chap. 13.

51. For this type of women's lamentations (not discussed in my book), see
Israel Levin, *The Lamentations over the Dead* (in Hebrew) (Tel Aviv: Hakibbutz
Hameuchad, 1973), 82–83, 216–25.

52. For this subject (not discussed in my book), see Raymond P. Scheindlin,
The Gazelle: Medieval Hebrew Poems on God, Israel, and the Soul (Philadelphia:
Jewish Publication Society, 1991).

53. Arthur Green discusses this question in his "Bride, Spouse, Daughter:
Images of the Feminine in Classical Jewish Sources," in *On Being a Jewish Femi-
nist: A Reader,* ed. Susannah Heschel (New York: Schocken Books, 1983), 249–61.
The opposition between female figures as symbols for sublime concepts of male

thought on the one hand and women's inferior reality on the other is a central paradox in Marina Warner's study on allegorical sculpture, *Monuments and Maidens: The Allegory of the Female Form* (London: Weidenfeld and Nicholson, 1985).

54. For the fruitful results of this intersection between "Medievalism and Feminism" in historical and literary scholarship, see Judith Bennet's article by that name in *Speculum* 68 (1993): 309–31.

55. Criticism of medieval Arabic literature suffers from similar belatedness with regard to feminist approaches. A two-volume book by ʿAli Ibrahīm Abu Zayd, *Surāt al-marʾah fī al-shiʿr al-ʿAbbasī* [The Image of Woman in Abbasid Poetry] (Cairo: Dar al-Maʿārif, 1983), for instance, is taxonomic and lacks any feminist insights. Noteworthy in recent years are the works of several feminists working in the field of Arabic culture (ancient as well as well as modern), including Fatima Mernissi, *Beyond the Veil: Male-Female Dynamics in Modern Muslim Society* (Cambridge, Mass.: Schenkman, 1975); Fatna A. Sabbah, *Woman in the Muslim Unconcious* (London: Pergamon Press, 1984); Fedwa Malti-Douglas, *Woman's Body, Woman's Word: Gender and Discourse in Arabo-Islamic Writing* (Princeton, N.J.: Princeton University Press, 1991), and Ahmed, *Women and Gender in Islam*.

56. *Prooftexts* 8 (1988): 67–87. While working on the present book I have published several other articles (see Acknowledgments).

57. Jefim Schirmann, "Problems in the Study of Post-Biblical Hebrew Poetry," *Israel Academy of Sciences and Humanities Proceedings* 2/12 (1967): 228–36.

58. See also Chapter 2, note 4.

59. See for instance Schirmann's discussion of one of al-Ḥarizi's most unequivocal misogynistic *maqāmāt* (sixth *maqāma*). Al-Ḥarizi's description of woman as monster appears under the heading "Humor" (Schirmann-Fleischer, *Christian Spain*, 211, 213), and a scene of a woman's most brutal abuse (from the same *maqāma*) is quoted under the heading of "A New Approach to Nature" (206).

60. Quoted from Judith Fetterley, *The Resisting Reader: A Feminist Approach to American Fiction* (Bloomington: Indiana University Press, 1978), xviii.

61. Judith Fetterley, *The Resisting Reader*, Introduction, xxiii.

62. Adrienne Rich, "When We Dead Awaken: Writing as Re-Vision," *College English* 34 (1972): 18.

63. The term *homotextual* is borrowed from Eve K. Sedgwick, *Between Men: English Literature and Male Homosocial Desire* (New York: Columbia University Press, 1985).

64. Daniel Boyarin, *Carnal Israel: Reading Sex in Talmudic Culture* (Berkeley: University of California Press, 1993), 229. The decontextualized quotation may not do full justice to Boyarin's far more complex approach. In dealing with a past culture which is our "Other," Boyarin proposed to adopt a "generous critique" ("anthropological ethics") and "to avoid assuming a position of cultural superiority from which to judge or blame the 'Other'." He sees it as imperative "to exculpate [the Talmud] from the charges of founding misogyny" (230). Com-

pared to the Talmud's unsystematic misogyny (as shown by Boyarin), the forma-
tions of medieval misogyny stem from a systematic ideology and, hence, are more
consistent and constitutive.

65. See Lewis's discussion of courtliness versus antifeminism in Andreas
Capellanus's *The Art of Courtly Love* in C. S. Lewis, *The Allegory of Love: A Study
in Medieval Tradition* (Oxford: Oxford University Press, 1965), 145. For a contestation of Lewis, see, for instance, E. Talbot Donaldson, "The Myth of Courtly
Love," in *Speaking of Chaucer* (London: Athlone Press, 1979), 158–63. For Donaldson, courtly love is a poetic myth, not historical fact, and the chaplain's book is
basically a clerical composition deriding adulterous carnal love. R. Howard Bloch,
Medieval Misogyny and the Invention of Western Romantic Love (Chicago: University of Chicago Press, 1991), sees Lewis's symmetry as "naturalizing" misogyny.
Endlessly discussed is the concurrence in medieval Europe of misogyny along with
the cult of the Virgin Mary and the admiration of the troubadours' lady. See, for
instance, Georges Duby *Women of the Twelfth Century*, trans. Jean Birrel, vol. 3,
Eve and the Church (Chicago: University of Chicago Press, 1998).

66. E. Jane Burns, "The Man behind the Lady in Troubadour Lyric," *Romance Notes* 25 (1985): 254–70.

67. Sabbah, *Woman in the Muslim Unconcious.* See also Chapter 2, 53. For
another view, see Vern L. Bullough, Brenda Shelton, and Sarah Slavin, who label
Islam "a sex-positive [religion] but with strong misogynistic tendencies." *The
Subordinated Sex: A History of Attitudes Toward Women* (Urbana: University of
Illinois Press, 1974), 113.

68. Bloch, *Medieval Misogyny*, 5. In his introduction, Bloch relates to the
controversy aroused by his definition of misogyny and to other critics who accused him of reproducing misogyny.

69. Ibid., 164. Bloch was also criticized for his ahistorical insistence that
misogyny was an "all-embracing" system throughout history. In referring to
Bloch here I distinctly relate to his statements on *medieval* misogyny.

70. Biale, *Eros and the Jews*, 86–89.

71. And see Toril Moi, *Sexual/Textual Politics: Feminist Literary Theory*
(London and New York: Routledge), 42–49.

72. Moi, *Sexual/Textual Politics*, 46.

73. Boyarin, *Carnal Israel*, 12.

74. Robert Hodge cited by Boyarin, *Carnal Israel*, 11.

75. Fisher and Halley, *Seeking the Woman*, 13.

76. Roberta L. Krueger, "Double Jeopardy: The Appropriation of Woman
in Four Old French Romances of the 'Cycle de la Gageure,' " in Fisher and Halley, *Seeking the Woman*, 45.

77. E. Jane Burns, *Bodytalk: When Women Speak in Old French Literature*
(Philadelphia: University of Pennsylvania Press, 1993).

78. Roberta L. Krueger, "Misogyny, Manipulation, and the Female Reader
in Hue de Rotelande's *Ipomedon*," *Courtly Literature, Culture and Context* 25
(1990): 395–409.

Chapter 2. Gazing at the Gazelle

1. Extant discussions of Hebrew (and, similarly, though to a lesser extent, also of Arabic) love lyric, tend to treat hetero- and homosexual love poems indiscriminately, accentuating the shared motifs and avoiding the gender difference. See Israel Levin's extensive chapter on love poetry in *The Embroidered Coat: The Genres of Hebrew Poetry in Spain* (in Hebrew) (Tel Aviv: Hakibbutz Hameuchad, 1995), 2:287–434. In Dan Pagis's anthology *The Scarlet Thread: Hebrew Love Poems from Spain, Italy, Turkey, and the Yemen* (in Hebrew) (Tel Aviv: Hakibbutz Hameuchad, 1979), poems to women and to boys appear under the same headings. In Raymond P. Scheindlin's translated anthology *Wine, Women, and Death: Medieval Hebrew Poems on the Good Life* (Philadelphia: Jewish Publication Society, 1986), poems to males fall under the section "Women." The homoerotic poetry was produced in the climate of the Andalusian courts where homosexuality was—against the injunctions of Islam—practiced and tolerated. Homosexual alliances usually involved mature men and young boys, mostly slaves. Whether or not the homoerotic Hebrew poems can be taken as evidence that Jews took part in homosexual affairs had been an issue hotly debated. While, admittedly, both varieties show great affinity (in depiction of male and female beauty, in imagery and forms of address), I am of the opinion that, for reasons embedded in cultural circumstances, as well as for reasons related to gender criticism, they have to be treated separately. However, despite my original intention, a chapter on homosexual poetry will regretfully be missing from this book, a lack which I hope to tend to in a future project. The first to write openly about Hebrew homosexual poetry was Jefim Schirmann, whose "The Ephebe in Medieval Hebrew Poetry," *Sefarad* 15 (1955): 55–68, raised great objection among orthodox scholars. Norman Roth has written extensively and unreservedly about the subject. See his " 'Deal Gently with the Young Man': Love of Boys in Medieval Hebrew Poetry of Spain," *Speculum* 57 (1982): 20–51; " 'Fawns of My Delight': Boy-Love in Arabic and Hebrew Verse," in *Poetics of Love in the Middle Ages*, ed. Moshe Lazar and Norris J. Lacy (Fairfax, Va.: George Mason University Press, 1989), 96–118. The affinity between descriptions of the female beloved in heterosexual love poems and the male beloved in homoerotic ones (the male gazelle is effeminate, similar in beauty and cruelty to the female gazelle, and he too is portrayed as domineering in the relationship) is often raised in attempts to refute feminist interpretations. To this I will shortly and tentatively answer here that since the male beloved was often a teenage slave, inferior by social class and age, his was the "female" position in the relationship.

2. This chapter's main concern is gender issues. It does not intend to serve as a historical survey, nor to exhaust all other aspects of the genre. Related modes (like wedding song, the *muwashshah* and its *kharja*) are briefly mentioned in Chapter 1. The widest survey of love themes in Hebrew poetry (and its Arabic models) is Israel Levin, *The Embroidered Coat*, 2:287–434. On Andalusian love poetry, see Michael Sells's essay "Love" in *The Literature of Al-Andalus*, ed. María

Rosa Menocal, Raymond P. Scheindlin, and Michael Sells (Cambridge: Cambridge University Press, 2000), 126–58. Arie Schippers, *Spanish Hebrew Poetry and the Arabic Literary Tradition: Arabic Themes in Hebrew Andalusian Poetry* (Leiden: E. J. Brill, 1994), 145–80, is a comparative taxonomy of motifs; Dan Pagis, "Convention and Experience: Hebrew Love Poetry in Spain and Italy," in *Hebrew Poetry of the Middle Ages and the Renaissance* (Berkeley: University of California Press, 1991), 45–71, is an overview of thematic and evolution; Scheindlin, *Wine, Women, and Death*, 77–134, is a translated anthology of love poems with close readings and an illustrative introduction. For Arabic, see Andras Hamori, "Love Poetry (*ghazal*)," in *Cambridge History of Arabic Literature: ʿAbbasid Belles-Lettres*, ed. Julia Ashtiany et al. (Cambridge: Cambridge University Press, 1990), 202–18; Henri Pérès, *La poésie andalouse en arabe classique au XIᵉ siècle* (Paris: Librarie d'Amerique et d'Orient, Adrien-Maisonneuve, 1953), 397–431.

3. Jonathan Culler, *On Deconstruction: Theory and Criticism after Structuralism* (Ithaca, N.Y.: Cornell University Press, 1982), 42.

4. On the belated entry of feminist criticism to the field of medieval Hebrew literature, and on the ideological biases impeding it, see Chapter 1 ("No-Woman's-Land"), 18–20. In the early phase of medievalist scholarship, the passionate utterances of the love lyric, coming from the pens of medieval revered rabbis and philosophers, were readily harnessed to the modern ideas of Jewish revival in these "hedonistic" antecedents. During the second half of the twentieth century critical discussions focused on the thematic and figurative language of the love lyrics, as well as on its affinity to Arabic literature. See Dan Pagis, *Secular Poetry and Poetic Theory: Moses Ibn Ezra and His Contemporaries* (in Hebrew) (Jerusalem: Mosad Bialik, 1970), 267–280; Pagis, *Hebrew Poetry*; Levin, *The Embroidered Coat*; Schippers, *Spanish Hebrew Poetry*; Yehuda Ratzaby, "Love in the Poetry of Samuel Ha-Nagid" (in Hebrew), *Tarbiz* 39 (1970): 137–69. Love lyrics were found especially suitable for close readings (in the "new critical" fashion), endeavoring to uncover their "beauty" and "unity" and to expose, through them, the school's aesthetic principles. See Eddie Zemach, *Like Tree's Roots: New Readings of Eleven Secular Poems by Solomon Ibn Gabirol* (in Hebrew) (Jerusalem: Achshav, 1962); Tova Rosen-Moked and Eddie Zemach, *A Sophisticated Work* (readings in the poems of Samuel ha-Nagid; in Hebrew) (Jerusalem: Keter, 1983); Scheindlin, *Wine, Women, and Death*. Noteworthy is Dan Pagis's contribution to structuralist analysis of love poems in *Secular Poetry and Poetic Theory*. Except for a brief remark in Nechama Aschkenasy, *Eve's Journey: Feminine Images in Hebraic Literary Tradition* (Philadelphia: University of Pennsylvania Press, 1986), 17, the first sortie in feminist reading of medieval Hebrew love poetry (and as far as I know also hitherto the last) is included in Tova Rosen, "On Tongues Being Bound and Let Loose: Women in Medieval Hebrew Literature," *Prooftexts* 8 (1988): 67–68. And see also Tova Rosen, " 'Like a Woman': Gender and Genre in a Love Poem by Isaac Ibn Khalfun," *Prooftexts* 16 (1996): 5–13. The extent to which feminist criticism is still an anathema for critics of medieval Hebrew literature can be proved by Tsur's attack on my latter article, using it as a vantage point for an unbased wholesale discreditation of feminist (and postcolonial) theory and

criticism. Reuven Tsur, "Ibn Khalphun's 'When Desire Awakens Me': On Relativism, Absolutism and Perspectivism in the Study of Mediaeval Hebrew Poetry," *Jewish Studies Quarterly* 6 (1999): 113–39.

5. For the contribution of the feminist perspective to medieval studies see Judith M. Bennett, "Medievalism and Feminism," *Speculum* 68 (1993): 309–31.

6. Roberta L. Krueger, "Double Jeopardy: The Appropriation of Woman in Four Old French Romances of the 'Cycle de la Gageure,'" in *Seeking the Woman in Late Medieval and Renaissance Writings: Essays in Feminist Contextual Criticism*, ed. Sheila Fisher and Janet E. Halley (Knoxville: University of Tennessee Press, 1989), 45.

7. Nancy Miller, "Rereading as a Woman: The Body as Practice," in *The Female Body in Western Culture: Contemporary Perspectives*, ed. Susan Suleiman (Cambridge, Mass.: Harvard University Press, 1986), 355. Is feminist reading confined only to "reading *as* a woman"? Can a man read *like* a woman? On essentialism versus political position in feminist reading theories, see "Reading Like a Feminist," in Diana Fuss, *Essentially Speaking: Feminism, Nature, and Difference* (London: Routledge, 1989), 23–37.

8. About the unique and conscious way in which the Andalusian courtier-rabbis synthesized their own religious heritage with the dominant Arabic Islamic culture, see Scheindlin, *Wine, Women, and Death*, 3–11; Ross Brann, *The Compunctious Poet: Cultural Ambiguity and Hebrew Poetry in Muslim Spain* (Baltimore: Johns Hopkins University Press, 1991), 6–8. When, in the mid tenth century, Andalusian Jews began to write secular poetry in the Hebrew language, love poetry in Arabic was already full-fledged and cast in a variety of modes. The *nasīb* was an erotic-sentimental introduction to the lengthy ode (the *qaṣīda*, of a Bedouin origin). The *ghazal* was a short, ornamented courtly poem (addressed to, or describing, female or male beloveds). At precisely that time an innovative, strophic, quintessentially Andalusian genre, the *muwashshaḥ* was in its formative stage. This genre too revolves largely around the theme of love. (See Chapter 1, note 25.) Already in the beginning of the eleventh century all these forms were being adopted by the Hebrew poets.

9. Rhymed narratives, in which love was one of the central themes, were introduced to Hebrew literature in the second half of the twelfth century. Several such love stories are discussed in Chapters 6 and 7 below.

10. About sexual mores and concepts in medieval Islamic culture, see Abdelwahab Bouhdiba, *Sexuality in Islam*, trans. Alan Sheridan (London: Routledge and Kegan Paul, 1985); Fatna A. Sabbah, *Woman in the Muslim Unconcious* (London: Pergamon Press, 1984); Leila Ahmed, *Women and Gender in Islam* (New Haven, Conn.: Yale University Press, 1992). Based on nonliterary everyday Jewish documents coming from the Cairo Geniza, S. D. Goitein reconstructed "The Sexual Mores of the Common People"; see his article by that title in *Society and the Sexes in Medieval Islam*, ed. Afaf Lutfi Sayyid-Marsot (Malibu,Calif.: Undena Publications, 1979), 43–61. In his opinion the mores of Egyptian Jews (regarding family norms, as well as extramarital affairs, homosexuality, and pedophilia) did not differ much from those of their Muslim neighbors and from those of Jews

in other Mediterranean communities, including Muslim Spain. And see also Mordechai A. Friedman, "The Ethics of Medieval Jewish Marriage," in *Religion in a Religious Age*, ed. S.D. Goitein (Cambridge, Mass.: Association for Jewish Studies, 1974), 83–101.

11. Moses Ibn Ezra, *Secular Poems*, ed. Heinrich Brody (Berlin: Shocken, 1935). Translated by Scheindlin, *Wine, Women, and Death*, 91.

12. Cited from J. C. Bürgel, "Love, Lust and Longing: Eroticism in Early Islam as Reflected in Literary Sources," in Sayyid-Marsot, *Society and the Sexes*, 83.

13. Bürgel, "Love, Lust, and Longing," 82.

14. The earliest Hebrew love poem known to have been written in al-Andalus (cited and discussed below in this chapter) was dubiously interpreted as autobiographical. See Aharon Mirsky, ed., *Itzhak Ibn Khalfun: Poems* (Jerusalem: Mosad Bialik, 1961), 19. Unique among the Spanish Hebrew poets was Todros Abulafia, the thirteenth-century Toledan courtier of Alphonso X. Being the editor of his own *dīwān* (*Dīwān of Don Tadros Son of Yehuda Abu-l-afia*, also known as *Gan ha-meshalim ve-ha-ḥidoth* [*The Garden of Proverbs and Riddles*] 2 vol., 3 parts, ed. David Yellin [Jerusalem: Dfus ha-Sefer, 1932–37], hereinafter: *Dīwān*), he accompanied the poems with his own inscriptions, specifying the circumstances of the writing of the poems. Some of these inscriptions disclose a intriguing variety of romantic experiences. Among these are flirtations and gambling with Christian noblewomen (*Dīwān*, vol. 1, p. 120, lines 82–86); an alleged sexual relationship with his Muslim maid (vol. 2, part 1, pp. 50–51, lines 7–13); possible involvements with Muslim courtesans, whom he prefers to Christian prostitutes (vol. 2, part 1, p. 130, first poem), and an exchange of love letters with a noble lady whom he worships spiritually, in the way of the troubadours (vol. 1, p. 189, lines 70–72).

15. Scheindlin, *Wine, Women, and Death*, 78.

16. Ibid., 86–87.

17. *Divan Shmuel Hanagid, Ben Tehilim* (*The son of Psalms*) (hereinafter: Samuel ha-Nagid, *Dīwān*), ed. Dov Jarden (Jerusalem: Hebrew Union College Press, 1966).

18. James M. Nichols, "The Concept of Woman in Medieval Arabic Poetry," *Maghreb Review* 6 (1981): 87. For the *qiyān*, see also Celia del Moral Molina, "La imagen de la mujer a través de los poetas árabes Ándaluces," in *La mujer en Andalucía: Primer encuentro interdisciplinar de estudios de la mujer*, ed. Pilar Ballarín and Teresa Ortiz (Granada: Universidad de Granada, 1990), 717–19, and Levin, *The Embroidered Coat*, 2:374.

19. The treatise is by the famous Arabic writer al-Jaḥiẓ, quoted in Bürgel, "Love, Lust, and Longing," 103–4.

20. *Dîwân des Abu-l-Hasân Jehuda ha-Levi* (hereinafter, Judah ha-Levi, *Dīwān*), 4 vols., ed. Heinrich Brody (Berlin: Mekize Nirdamim, 1894–1930), 7–10.

21. This is specifically typical of the courtly male love lyric, where the lady never returns love or speaks. Other genres, though similarly androcentric, allow for the speech of amorous women. For wedding songs and for *kharja*s see Chapter 1, 8–9 and n. 25. In certain *maqāmāt* women are represented as speakers, active

lovers, and even as writers of love poetry. See Chapter 5, p. 112; Chapter 6, p. 133.

22. E. Jane Burns, "The Man behind the Lady in Troubadour Lyric," *Romance Notes* 25 (1985): 264.

23. Elizabeth Grosz, *Jacques Lacan: A Feminist Introduction* (London: Routledge, 1990), 138. And see also "The Fiction of Loverhood" section in this chapter and notes.

24. A Persian parallel (similarly following Arabic poetry) reads: "Should you think there is no punishment for you from God . . . for the blood of lovers such as I?—There is!" (Quoted in Julie Scott Meisami, *Medieval Persian Court Poetry* (Princeton, N.J.: Princeton University Press, 1987), 260. Typical of the Hebrew adaptation is the exoploitation of biblical idiom: The slave threatens his lady by legalistically alluding to the biblical law regarding a physical injury (or death) inflicted by master to slave: "When a man strikes his slave . . . and the slave dies on the spot, he must be punished" (Exodus 21:20–21).

25. Solomon Ibn Gabirol, *Secular Poems*, ed. Hayyim Brody and Hayyim Schirmann (Jerusalem: Schocken Institute, 1976).

26. The theme of the belligerent lady is popular also in Arabic storytelling. As argued by Remke Kruk, in "Warrior Women in Arabic Popular Romance," *Journal of Arabic Literature* 24 (1993): 213–30, legendary figures of gallant female warriors show traces of the "classical Amazon myth" (226). And see also Chapter 7 below, the section "From Martial to Marital."

27. J. C. Bürgel, "The Lady Gazelle and Her Murderous Glances," *Journal of Arabic Literature* 20 (1989): 1–11, traces the poetic oxymoron of the "hunting gazelle" back to the early Bedouin lore, where tales are told about demonic gazelles who, after being trapped and then freed, kill their hunters. Attempting a "psychological" explanation, Bürgel concludes that "the gazelle metaphor expresses the strange mixture of fear and fascination evoked by the irritating fusion of weakness and power in woman" (9). In an Arabic eighth-century line quoted by Bürgel, a lover likens himself to "a lion chased by a graceful gazelle! Never before you [hunted me] did a gazelle hunt a lion" (5). And compare to Judah ha-Levi: "Have you ever seen [in one] a lion's heart and gazelle's eyelids?" (*Dīwān*, 2:6, 13); "You are a gazelle—Why do you devour like a lion?" (2:17, 11). For the motif of the wounding eyes in Hebrew and Arabic poetry, see Schippers, *Spanish Hebrew Poetry*, 173–78.

28. The second line evokes simultaneously two biblical images: Joseph's robe, dipped in goat's blood, sent by his brothers to their father Jacob (Genesis 37:23, 31–32), and the smell of Esau's hunting outfit (Genesis 27:27). The image of Joseph's bloodstained robe is further amplified by the blood of gazelles smeared on the huntress's face (line 4) and by the "pit" (line 1, alluding to Genesis 37:24). While these are not proper allusions (as they do not participate in the production of meaning in the poem), they are still part of the reader's response. The competent reader is supposed to identify the biblical references and, at the same time, realize their irrelevance to the poem's situation. This play of association and dissociation, of "detect and reject," is part of the aesthetic process.

29. The poem's last verse alludes to Canticles 4:9: "You have attracted [or empowered; Hebrew: *libabhtini*] my heart with one of your eyes, with one bead of your necklace." This meaning aids the first interpretation. The second, more macabre interpretation suggested above, is supported by the grammarian Jonah Ibn Janah, Samuel ha-Nagid's contemporary and compatriot. In his dictionary *Sefer ha-shorashim* (ed. B. Z. Bacher, Berlin, 1896), he writes: "And the meaning of *libabhtini* is you wounded my heart with the arrow of your eyes" (238).

30. This is Raymond Scheindlin's brilliant translation, *Wine, Women, and Death*, 119.

31. For the theme of "woman's deceiving beauty," see Chapter 3, "Veils and Wiles."

32. Bouhdiba, *Sexuality in Islam*, 39.

33. In Ibn Ḥazm's famous treatise on the phenomenology of love, *The Ring of the Dove*, trans. A. J. Arberry (London: Luzac and Company, 1953), 68–70. And see Lois Anita Giffen, "Ibn Hazm and the *Tauq al-ḥamāma*," in *The Legacy of Muslim Spain*, ed. Salma Khadra Jayyusi (Leiden: Brill, 1992), 421–41. Ibn Ḥazm's ideas about love are traceable in his contemporary Samuel ha-Nagid, as well as in other Hebrew poets, and see Levin, *The Emroidered Coat*, 2:378–409. See also A. C. Spearing, *The Medieval Poet as Voyeur: Looking and Listening in Medieval Love-Narratives* (Cambridge: Cambridge University Press, 1993). Spearing (p. 9) repeats the suggestion that theories of looking in European medieval literature may have originated in Arabic erotic literature.

34. About the gaze as transgression, see Bouhdiba, *Sexuality in Islam*, 36: "There is a psycho-sociology of the look here, but one that apprehends it as the beginning of 'transgressing' the limits laid down by God."

35. From Laura Mulvey's pioneering essay on feminist reading of cinema, "Visual Pleasure and Narrative Cinema," in *Visual and Other Pleasures* (Bloomington: Indiana University Press, 1989), 14–25, quote on p. 20. Basing her observations on Freud's definition of "scopophilia" (the pleasure taken in subjecting others to a controlling and objectifying gaze), Mulvey argues that the fascination of film is reinforced by preexisting patterns of scopophilic fascination, and that these unconscious patterns of patriarchal perception have structured film form and the enjoyment of it.

36. This reversal and simultaneous presence of the life-giving and the death-dealing elements is the basis for Erich Neumann's archetype of the Great Mother. See Chapter 1 at note 49.

37. "The Medusa's Head," *The Standard Edition of the Complete Psychological Works of Sigmund Freud*, trans. James Strachey (London: Hogarth Press, 1960; London: Vintage, 2001), 18:273–74.

38. Mulvey, *Visual Pleasure*, 21.

39. Sarah Kofman, *The Enigma of Woman: Woman in Freud's Writing*, trans. Catherine Porter (Ithaca, N.Y.: Cornell University Press, 1987), 86.

40. Grosz, *Jacques Lacan: A Feminist Introduction*, 132–33. For a feminist disavowal of the phallus as *the* signifier in Lacan, see Hélène Cixous, "The Laugh of the Medusa," *Signs* 1–4 (1976): 875–93.

41. For the difference between *scopophilia* in Freud, the *look* in Sartre and the *gaze* in Lacan, often conflated by feminists, see Elizabeth Grosz, "Voyeurism/Exhibitionism/the Gaze," in *Feminism and Psychoanalysis: A Critical Dictionary*, ed. Elizabeth Wright et al. (Oxford: Blackwell, 1992), 447–49.

42. Bouhdiba, *Sexuality in Islam*, 37.

43. This is the first part of a self-referential, self-ironic longer poem. The poem dismisses the art of poetry as such on the basis of its "lies." (For poetry as deception, see also Chapter 3, "Veils and Wiles").

44. This is in his book of poetics, *Kitāb al-muḥāḍara wa-al-mudhākara* (The Book of Discussions and Conversations), ed. and trans. A. S. Halkin (Jerusalem: Mekize Nirdamim, 1976), 276–77.

45. Scheindlin, in *Wine, Women, and Death*, writes: "Hebrew love poetry is conventional in content and stylized in form. Its themes and rhetorical figures are drawn from the common fund of literary material that the Jewish literati first acquired through their education in Arabic poetry, then used and recycled" (77). This is also the view in Pagis, *Secular Poetry and Poetic Theory*, 267–71. However, in "Convention and Experience" (in his *Hebrew Poetry*) Pagis trics to trace expressions of personal love experiences.

46. My application of insights from medievalist and medievalist-feminist critics (like Goldin and Burns, see below) to Hebrew poetry leans on the apparent resemblances and parallels between European, and especially troubadour, poetry and the Hebrew/Arabic tradition. For a similar adoption of Western criticism to medieval Persian court poetry, see Meisami, *Medieval Persian Court Poetry*. I have consciously avoided the thorny field of influence theories. For an extensive survey of the long debated issue of Arabic influence on troubadour poetry, see María Rosa Menocal, *The Arabic Role in Medieval Literary History* (Philadelphia: University of Pennsylvania Press, 1990). Menocal is an avowed partisan of the theory of continuous literary contacts between Europe and the Arabs. For this issue, see in Jayyusi, *Legacy of Muslim Spain*, James T. Monroe, "Hispano-Arabic Poetry and the Romance Tradition," 398–419, and Roger Boase, "Arab Influences on European Love Poetry," 457–82.

47. Burns, *The Man behind the Lady*, 255–56

48. Meisami, *Medieval Persian Court Poetry*, 251.

49. Frederick Goldin, "Array of Perspectives in the Early Courtly Love Lyric," in *In Pursuit of Perfection: Courtly Love in Medieval Literature*, ed. Joan M. Ferrante and George D. Economou (Port Washington, N.Y.: Kennikat Press, 1975), 52–53.

50. The inversion of gender power relations is made even more acute against the background of social realities. While in medieval Judaism and Islam women were barred from access to power, within the family and outside it, poets depict them as powerful tyrants, hunters, and fighters. Similarly astonishing is the presence of powerful women figures in Greek drama and in the medieval poetry of courtly love, as opposed to women's inferior status in real life. And see also below about the "feminized lover."

51. A century after Judah ha-Levi, the great Arabic Sufi poet, Ibn al-ʿArabi,

writes about the "gazelle religion": "I follow the religion of Love; wherever Love's camels turn, there Love is my religion and my faith" (quoted from Bürgel, "The Lady Gazelle and Her Murderous Glances", 10).

52. Arabic treatises on "the religion of love" are treated in Lois Anita Giffen, *Theory of Profane Love among the Arabs: The Development of the Genre* (New York: New York University Press, 1971).

53. The King of Love (or The Commander of the Troops of Love) is a character in an allegorical *maqāma* discussed in the section "The Melodrama of the Soul," Chapter 4 below.

54. In Arabic courtly tradition plenty of stories exist about princes and kings falling madly in love with slave girls (or boys). Ibn Ḥazm furnishes many such stories.

55. Tova Rosen, "Literary Mannerism as an Aspect of Cultural Archaism: A Cultural Portrait of Todros Abulafia" (in Hebrew), in *Sadan: Studies in Hebrew Literature*, ed. Dan Laor, 1 (1994): 49–74, esp. 63–67.

56. Jefim Schirmann, *Hebrew Poetry in Spain and Provence* (in Hebrew) (Jerusalem: Mosad Bialik, Tel Aviv: Dvir, 1960), 4: 417.

57. Meisami, *Medieval Persian Court Poetry*, 245.

58. Scheindlin, *Wine Women and Death*, 85.

59. For Freud, romantic love replicates pre-oedipal modes of attachment. By investing his narcissistic energy onto the (m)other, the infant is actually in love with himself. For a summary on Freud's views of romantic love, see Grosz, *Jacques Lacan*, 126–31.

60. In Lacanian terms the "Other" is God, the obstacle between the lover and the unattainable "other" whom he desires. "The Other is always beyond the other." The demand for "the other" in love, as for God in religious faith, is an impossibility. "This Other is the condition of . . . love, but also dooms any project that seeks the One through love." For men, courtly or romantic love is a kind of self-deception, a result of their refusal to recognize the rupture between "the Other" and "the other." The frigid lady is the counterpart of the courtly lover. By being frigid she saves herself for the Other. "It is thus the condition of courtly love, that both partners direct themselves towards the third partner, the Other." Grosz, "Lacan and Romantic Love," in *Jacques Lacan*, 132–40.

61. Frederick Goldin, *The Mirror of Narcissus in the Courtly Love Lyric* (Ithaca, N.Y.: Cornell University Press, 1967).

62. Goldin, "Array of Perspectives," 54–55.

63. Burns, "The Man behind the Lady," 265–266.

64. Sabbah, *Woman in the Muslim Unconcious*, 24.

65. Ibid., 25, 26, 27. According to Nichols, "The concept of Women in Medieval Arabic Poetry," 86–87, the Arabic canon of female beauty includes white visage, black curly locks, dark curving eyebrows, antelope eyes, rounded pink cheeks, pearl-like teeth, lips thin like a crimson thread, ivory neck and bosom, plump arms, delicate hands, firm breasts, slender waist, heavy hips and buttocks, plump legs and small feet. Nichols traces such lists back to a traditional Arabic tribal custom to send older women to spy on prospective brides and to return

with detailed descriptions. (For Hebrew examples for brides' descriptions made by old female matchmakers, see Judah al-Ḥarizi's sixth *maqāma*, and Judah Ibn Shabbetai's *Minḥat Yehuda*, discussed in Chapter 5). While right in his assertion that women, collaborating with this ideal may have contributed to handing down this tradition, Nichols ignores that such lists, constituting the male ideal of "woman," derive from male imagination and tend to male's needs and demands. For comparative lists in Arabic and Hebrew, see Levin, *The Embroidered Coat*, 2:292–93, 318–22, Schippers, *Spanish Hebrew Poetry*, 157–8.

66. This epigram is in fact the last in a series of fifteen, all having as their subject of description an apple cast in gold, a perfect artifact. In all other epigrams the inedible golden apple is superior to the real fruit. The last epigram transforms the equation: the wife is as perfect as an artificial apple and yet is ready for consumption.

67. For text and English translation, see T. Carmi, ed. and trans., *The Penguin Book of Hebrew Verse* (New York: Penguin Books, 1981), 360–61. I replaced Carmi's "hips" with "waist" (line 13).

68. Relating to the effect of face and body close-ups in narrative cinema, Laura Mulvey argues that they destroy the illusion of depth and result in "flatness, the quality of a cut-out or icon." ("Visual Pleasure and Narrative Cinema," 20)

69. By Joseph ha-Kohen (sixteenth century, Italy). For poem and translation, see Carmi's *Penguin* anthology, 456–57. I use this poem, despite its lateness, since, as shown by Yehuda Ratzabi its genealogy can be detected back to two earlier medieval Arabic models (which, on their part, group the female attributes not in threes but in fours). See his "Arabic Influences on Spanish [Hebrew] Literature," *Bar-Ilan Yearbook* 6 (1968): 326–28. However, unlike Ratzabi, I am not sure whether ha-Kohen did necessarily rely directly upon Arabic models. A fifteenth-century English exploitation of this same technique (see below) suggests that the Arabic topos already migrated (via Italy?) to England. Hence, Joseph ha-Kohen could be acquainted with it through its possible Italian adaptations.

70. This is Sheila Delany's observation concerning an anonymous fifteenth-century English poem similar in technique to the Hebrew poem in point. See her *Impolitic Bodies: Poetry, Saints and Society in Fifteenth Century England: The Work of Osbern Bokenham* (Oxford: Oxford University Press, 1998), 112.

71. Carmi's translation skips the word *tzofe* (beholder). I also changed Carmi's "hips" to "waist" since elsewhere in the poem the poet specifies (and so translated Carmi) that hips should be *wide*. The comparison with the English poem (Delany, *Impolitic Bodies*, 112) is striking. Not only does this poem "break down the lady's body . . . to a set of fifteen beauties, listed in series of threes," but it also lists, among three round things, the vagina: "and anothir *thing* which I speke not of at all." Unaware of its Arabic antecedents, Delany sees this fragmenting technique as "extension of a rhetorical habit . . . implicit in the blazon." Delany also argues that the anatomical dissection and methodical classification exploited in the English poem might well betray the English author's medical profession. As for Joseph ha-Kohen, it is known that he practiced medicine in Italy.

72. Naomi Wolf, *The Beauty Myth: How Images of Beauty Are Used against Women* (New York: William Morrow, 1991), 12. The following longer quotation is from pp. 12–13.

73. Scheindlin, *Wine, Women, and Death*, 85. Troubadour poetry too is "essentially formal, a highly stylized system of registers [and] *topoi*, shows similar traits" (Burns, *The Man behind the Lady*, 255).

74. Scheindlin, *Wine, Women, and Death*, 85.

75. See Chapter 6, "Among Men: Homotextuality in the *Maqāma*."

76. Schirmann, *Hebrew Poetry in Spain and Provence*, 1:52 explained *shaʿaru* as "acknowledged" (i.e., "all lovers have acknowledged your beauty"). Relying on the practice of the poets to use Hebrew roots in their Arabic designations, I translated *shaʿaru* as deriving from the parallel Arabic root from which the word for poetry (*shiʿr*) derives.

77. Grosz, *Lacan*, 129–30.

78. Roland Barthes, *A Lover's Discourse: Fragments*, trans. Richard Howard (London: Jonathan Cape, 1979), 13–14.

79. Elaine Tuttle Hansen, "The Feminization of Men in Chaucer's *Legend of Good Women*," in *Seeking the Woman*, ed. Fisher and Halley, 58–61.

80. *Itzhak Ibn Khalfun: Poems*, 19. See also note 14 above. For another English version and commentary, see Scheindlin, *Wine, Women and Death*, 114–17. For a detailed reading of the poem, see Rosen, " 'Like a Woman.' "

81. The girl's designation (in the second line) *kevudah* (literally, "honorable"; here translated as "cloistered") elliptically alludes to Psalm 45:14, a verse which has long been interpreted by rabbinical commentaries as defining the woman's place within the inner recesses of the house. Woman is perceived as both the sign and the locus of the family's honor, hence her place must be secluded.

82. Hansen, "Feminization of Men," 61. The idea of feminization was extended from the lover's psychology also to the sociohistorical realm. Some scholars suggested that the admiration of women in the literature of courtly love answered the unconscious needs of male society itself, thus promoting the feminization of feudal civilization and heralding a pre-Renaissance "feminism." R. Howard Bloch's *Medieval Misogyny and the Invention of Western Romantic Love* (Chicago: University of Chicago Press, 1991) is a critique of woman's idealization (and see esp. 194–97). Another hypothesis suggests that the cultivation of courtly love was itself a kind of male protest against the institution of arranged marriages, and even against the sexual moral code of the Church. See J. F. Benton, "Clio and Venus: An Historical View of Medieval Love," in *The Meaning of Courtly Love*, ed. F. X. Newman (Albany: State University of New York Press, 1968), 19–42.

83. Judith Fetterley, "Introduction: The Politics of Literature," *The Resisting Reader: A Feminist Approach to American Fiction* (Bloomington: Indiana University Press, 1978), xi–xxvi.

84. Roberta L. Krueger, "Misogyny, Manipulation, and the Female Reader in Hue de Rotelande's *Ipomedon*," *Courtly Literature, Culture, and Context* 25 (1990): 406.

85. This is the forty-fifth *maqāma* in Judah al-Ḥarizi, *Taḥkemoni*, ed. I. Toporowski (Tel Aviv: Maḥbarot Lesifrut, 1952).

86. Krueger, "Misogyny," 406.

87. Patrocinio P. Schweickart, "Reading Ourselves: Towards a Feminist Theory of Reading," in *Gender and Reading: Essays on Readers, Texts, and Contexts*, ed. Elizabeth A. Flynn and Patrocinio P. Schweickart (Baltimore: Johns Hopkins University Press, 1986), p. 42

88. Ibid., 43–44.

89. As an art historian Dovev is interested in the woman-viewer's response to the magnificent nudes painted by the greatest masters. Only in those most excellent works, where beauty is encoded with morality, says Dovev, following Adorno, "beauty becomes a promise for happiness." See Lea Dovev, "The Eye and the Body: Malaise in the Feminist Aesthetics," *Zmanim: A Historical Quarterly* (Tel Aviv University) 12 (1993): 88–105.

Chapter 3. Veils and Wiles

1. For feminine/feminist skepticism as a condition of discourse and philosophy, and for the relevant discussion of Nietzsche and Derrida, see "The Violence of Rhetoric" in Teresa de Lauretis, *Technologies of Gender: Essays on Theory, Film and Fiction* (Bloomington: Indiana University Press, 1987), 31–50. Quotation from Gayatri Spivak is from p. 47.

2. The Aristotelian shift among Jewish thinkers (resulting in, among other things, negative views regarding both poetry and women) coincided more or less with the watershed of the Berber Almohad invasion of al-Andalus (1140) and the ending of the first Reconquista War (1150), after which most Jewish population and cultural centers shifted from Muslim to Christian territories. These cataclysmic events in Iberian history resulted in the consequent decades in major transformations in Jewish society, its culture and literature. For a general overview of Jewish history and culture during the twelfth and thirteenth centuries, see the first three chapters in Yizhak Baer, *A History of the Jews in Christian Spain*, trans. L. Schoffman (Philadelphia: Jewish Publication Society, 1961), and Bernard Septimus, *Hispano-Jewish Culture in Transition* (Harvard Judaic Monographs 4; Cambridge, Mass.: Harvard University Press, 1982). For the literary shifts in Hebrew literature at that period, see Dan Pagis, *Change and Tradition in the Secular Poetry: Spain and Italy* (in Hebrew) (Jerusalem: Keter, 1976), 173–96.

3. Moses Ibn Ezra, *Kitāb al-muḥāḍara wa-al-mudhākara* (The book of discussion and conversation) (bilingual Arabic-Hebrew edition), ed. and trans. A. S. Halkin (Jerusalem: Mekize Nirdamim, 1976), 137, and see also 225.

4. For a profound discussion of Moses Ibn Ezra's view on poetic language see Dan Pagis's chapter "The Poem as an Ornamented Garment" in *Secular Poetry and Poetic Theory: Moses Ibn Ezra and His Contemporaries* (in Hebrew) (Jerusalem: Mosad Bialik, 1970), 35–54.

5. Ibn Ezra, *Kitāb al-muḥāḍara*, 225.

6. Ibid., 223–24.

7. The grammatical disposition of the Hebrew word for poetry—*shira*—may partly explain its feminine metaphorization. Bride or virgin as metaphor for an elegant or original poem seems to be rarer in Arabic. For two examples, see Suzanne Pinckney Stetkevych, "The Qaṣīda and the Poetics of Ceremony: Three ʿId Panegyrics to the Cordoban Caliphate," in *Languages of Power in Islamic Spain*, ed. Ross Brann (Bethseda, Md.: CDL Press, 1977), 46–47.

8. This poem by Joseph Ibn Ḥasday is known by the name *shira yetoma* (a female orphan poem). A bilingual homonym is exploited here, referring also to *yatīma* in the Arabic sense, namely, outstanding, one of a kind. The poem was preserved in the *Dīwān* of ha-Nagid; see Dov Jarden, ed., *Divan Shmuel Hanagid: Ben Tehilim* (hereinafter: Samuel ha-Nagid, *Dīwān*) (Jerusalem: Hebrew Union College Press, 1966), 163, lines 41–43. Numbers here and hereafter refer to page and line.

9. The use of ornaments is forbidden for Muslim men in order to preserve a visible difference between the sexes. See Abdelwahab Bouhdiba, *Sexuality in Islam*, trans. Alan Sheridan (London: Routledge and Kegan Paul, 1985), 33.

10. See Judah al-Ḥarizi, *Taḥkemoni*, ed. I. Toporowski (Tel Aviv: Maḥbarot Lesifrut, 1952), sixth *maqāma*, 19. For Judah Ibn Shabbetai's *The Misogynist*, see Chapter 5 ("Domesticating the Enemy"). In both *maqāmāt* a beautiful bride was swapped by old shrewd female matchmakers for an ugly one.

11. In Ibn Ṣaqbel, and in al-Ḥarizi's twentieth *maqāma;* see Chapter 7 ("Clothes Reading").

12. Elizabeth Grosz, *Jacques Lacan: A Feminist Introduction* (London: Routledge, 1990), 121, 132.

13. Sarah Kofman, *The Enigma of Woman: Woman in Freud's Writings*, trans. Catharine Porter (Ithaca, N.Y.: Cornell University Press, 1985), 48. The relevant passage from Freud's "Femininity" is cited in Chapter 8, note 28.

14. Kofman, *Enigma of Woman*, 49.

15. *Divan Shmuel Hanagid,* vol 2, *Ben Mishle* (The son of Proverbs), ed. Dov Jarden (Jerusalem, 1982).

16. *The Canterbury Tales*, in *Riverside Chaucer*, ed. Larry D. Benson (Boston: Houghton Mifflin, 1987), 109, lines 337–56.

17. Abraham Ibn Ḥasday, *The Prince and the Monk*, ed. A. M. Habermann (Tel-Aviv: Maḥbarot Lesifrut, 1950), 195.

18. In Judah Ibn Shabbetai's *The Misogynist*, and see the section "The Wife Speaks," Chapter 5 ("Domesticating the Enemy").

19. This figure, called *al-dunyā* in Arabic, *Tevel* in Hebrew, appears in ascetic poems and in moralistic literature. See Chapter 1 above.

20. Moses Ibn Ezra, *Secular Poems*, ed. Hayyim Brody (Berlin: Schocken, 1935), 1:151. For the full text, see Chapter 1 above.

21. *Genesis Raba* 3:7, ed. Jehuda Theodor and Chanoch Albeck (Jerusalem: Wahrmann, 1965), 175.

22. Quoted in R. Howard Bloch, "Medieval Misogyny," *Representations* 20 (1987): 14. Reprinted in *Misogyny, Misandry, and Misanthropy*, ed., R. Howard Bloch and Frances Ferguson (Berkeley: University of California Press, 1989), 14. Bloch discusses Christian attitudes toward femininity, beginning with the Fathers of the Church until the latter part of the Middle Ages, and examines the link between the idea that woman is secondary—mere ornament—and the ambiguity of rhetorical/poetic language in the medieval European literary tradition.

23. Roland Barthes, *Système de la mode* (Paris: Editions du Seuil, 1967), is his investigation of the semiology of fashion and the treatment of clothing as a language, having syntax, grammar, and signification.

24. And compare "fabric" and "fabrication"; "yarn" and "spin a yarn."

25. Joseph ben Meir Zabara, *The Book of Delight*, trans. Moses Hadas, with an introduction by Merriam Sherwood (New York: Columbia University Press, 1932), 66. The topos is repeated in *Maḥberot Immanuel ha-Romi*, ed. Dov Jarden (Jerusalem: Mosad Bialik, 1957), 113, 117.

26. Moses Ibn Ezra's definition of poetry appears in his essay *Maqālat al-ḥadīqa* (The book of the garden), investigating the figurative language in biblical utterances about God. In Arabic *bāṭin* relates to the allegorical meaning of the Qurān. Quoted from the manuscript by Dan Pagis in *Secular Poetry*, 41.

27. Moses Ibn Ezra, *Kitāb al-Muḥāḍara*, 83–87, 15, 117–19. Ibn Ezra claims that in "the best of the poem—its lie" he is citing Aristotle, but he follows, in fact, the Arab author al-Farābī.

28. For a brilliant investigation of this issue, see Raymond Scheindlin, "Rabbi Moses Ibn Ezra on the Legitimacy of Poetry," *Medievalia et Humanistica* n.s.7 (1976): 101–15. For Ibn Ezra, see also Ross Brann, *The Compunctious Poet: Cultural Ambiguity and Hebrew Poetry in Muslim Spain* (Baltimore: Johns Hopkins University Press, 1991), 71–83. The topos of the "lying poet" was extensively and insightfully treated in Brann (though he does not consider the link between poetry and the female); and see esp. his pp. 124–57 on Shem Tov Falaqera and Todros Abulafia. Concepts of truth and lie in Arabic poetics are discussed in detail in Matti Huss, "It Never Happened nor Did It Ever Exist: The Status of Fiction in the Hebrew Maqāma," *Jerusalem Studies in Hebrew Literature* 18 (2000): 83–104.

29. In Jefim Schirmann, *Hebrew Poetry in Spain and Provence* (in Hebrew) (Jerusalem: Mosad Bialik, Tel Aviv: Dvir, 1960), 2:565. Translation is by Raymond Scheindlin, in *Rabbinic Fantasies: Imaginative Narratives from Classical Hebrew Literature*, ed. David Stern and Mark Jay Mirsky (Philadelphia: Jewish Publication Society, 1990), 264.

30. Schirmann, *Hebrew Poetry in Spain and Provence*, 3:303.

31. Todros Abulafia, *Gan ha-meshalim ve-ha-ḥidoth* (The garden of proverbs and riddles; hereafter: *Dīwān*), 2 vols. 3 parts, ed. David Yellin (Jerusalem: Dfus ha-Sefer, 1932–37). This poem is also discussed in the section "The Fiction of Loverhood" in Chapter 2.

32. Following Ecclesiastes 12:4, "And the daughters of poetry will be humbled."

33. *Dīwān Shlomo da-Piera,* ed. Shimon Bernstein (New York: Alim, 1942).

34. Published from the ms. in Tirza Vardi's doctoral dissertation *The Group of Poets in Zaragoza* (in Hebrew) (Jerusalem: Hebrew University, 1996), vol. 1, 98.

35. Hyperboles escalate as Pinḥas boasts with his son's "peg," while Abulafia brags that *his* potent sons thrust their "peg" every day into Pinḥas's good-for-nothing son. Angel Sáenz-Badillos relates these obscenities to the influence of a similar vein in contemporary Provençal-Catalonian and Galician bards, familiar at the time in Toledo. See his "Hebrew Invective Poetry: The Debate between Todros Abulafia and Phinehas Halevi," *Prooftexts* 16 (1996): 49–73. The series appears in Abulafia's *Dīwān,* vol. 2, book 1, 25–26.

36. Printed by Shimon Bernstein, "The Poems of Don Vidal Joseph Ben Lavi" (in Hebrew), *Tarbiz* 8 (1937): 365, poem 3.

37. Published from the ms. in Vardi's *Group of Poets,* 1:97.

38. Qalonymos ben Qalonymos, *Even boḥan,* ed. A. M Habermann (Tel Aviv: Maḥbarot Lesifrut, 1956). For excerpts see Schirmann, *Hebrew Poetry in Spain and Provence,* 4:514–17.

39. Feminine poetry is emblematically represented here by both the hollowness and the "holes" of the flute. The root *n.k.v.* in Hebrew denotes (1) hole; and (2) the female and her "cavity." A third designation refers to all other body orifices (as in the Jewish morning prayer "neqavim-neqavim ḥalulim-ḥalulim"), thus associating poetry with the body's excretions. This crude implication conforms with a story told by Immanuel of Rome (a contemporary and a friend of Qalonymos) about an inferior poet who ingested a laxative, and while waiting for the medicine to take effect, he composed a poem full of errors ("base and foul, reeking and scum"). And Immanuel explains: "for what he had to excrete through the bottom hole, he excreted through the top hole." *Maḥberoth Immanuel ha-Romi,* 2:416. On Qalonymos and femininity, see also Chapter 8.

40. Excerpts from Falaqera's *Sefer ha-mevaqqesh* appeared in Schirmann, *Hebrew Poetry in Spain and Provence,* 3:331–42. For the full Hebrew text, see *Sefer ha-mevaqqesh,* ed. M. Tama (The Hague–Amsterdam; L. Zusmensch, 1779). The edition I quoted from (Warsaw: Traqlin; no mention of editor or date) is in all likelihood a reprinting of the Amsterdam edition. Its first part was translated into English by M. Herschel Levine as *Falaqera's Book of the Seeker* (New York: Yeshiva University Press, 1976).

41. The translation is cited from Brann, *Compunctious Poet,* 125–26. Falaqera is a paradigmatic case of the "compunctious poet" trope. See Brann's attentive analysis of Falaqera's complex and ambiguous stance on poetry, 125–37. Citations below, slightly altered, are based on Levine's and Brann's translations.

42. See Brann, ibid, 128–29, 134. A similar retreat from poetry to prose takes place in Qalonymos's *Even boḥan.* Schirmann (*Hebrew Poetry in Spain and Provence,* 4:501) relates this stylistic change to "fatigue" rather than viewing it as a deliberate rejection of poetry.

43. The social types he meets (a rich man, a warrior, an artisan, a pious man) parallel, in general lines, the estates of medieval society. Subsequently, he meets masters of the sciences and arts (a grammarian, a poet, a mathematician, an as-

tronomer, a musician, a rhetorician, and a philosopher). The latter figures parallel, in a somewhat different order, the *trivium* and *quadrivium*, or the seven subjects of classical education.

44. Falaqera is influenced by similar Arabic works which outline the study course (*paideia*) of the young man: humanist education begins with the study of religion, ethics, arithmetic, and geometry, and reaches its climax with philosophy. The ultimate end is spiritual redemption. On the other hand, "negative education," the path which leads to sin, includes the study of music and poetry. See Joel L. Kraemer, *Humanism in the Renaissance of Islam* (Leiden: E. J. Brill, 1986), 231. This Arabic tradition of rejecting poetry and poets relies on Al-Farābī's and Ibn Rushd's interpretations of Plato's *Republic* (ibid., note 64).

45. Falaqera's metaphor of the poet as a hunter of souls is in line with his following straightforward misogynist utterance: "I made a covenant with my soul not to have a wife since a wife is a fatal illness. As said the sage: 'Women are a trap in which only the fools fall' . . . And they said: 'A wise man avoids being hunted by women, since he who falls in their traps will have his wing plucked, and his feathers will never grow again," *Iggeret ha-Musar* (Epistle on Ethics), published by A. M. Habermann, *Qovetz ʿal Yad* (n.s.) 1 (1936): 75–76. And compare also to the smooth rhetoric of an old female matchmaker ("Her palate is sleeker than oil, nectar on her tongue, poison in her throat") in al-Ḥarizi's sixth *maqāma*.

46. The translation is partly based on Brann, *Compunctious Poet*, 129–30; Omissions, additions, and italics are mine.

47. Translation is Brann's. *Compunctious Poet*, 130. Omissions, additions, and italics are mine.

48. Matheolus, *Lamentations*, quoted from Bloch, "Medieval Misogyny," 17.

49. Bloch, "Medieval Misogyny," 5, 17, 19.

50. Fleischer's note 15 in Schirmann, *The History of Hebrew Poetry in Christian Spain and Southern France* (in Hebrew), edited, supplemented, and annotated by Ezra Fleischer (Jerusalem: Magnes, 1997), 282 (herinafter: Schirmann-Fleischer, *Christian Spain*).

51. Falaqera is also known for his detailed commentary on Maimonides's *Guide of the Perplexed*, frequently published together with the *Guide*.

52. Maimonides, *Maqāla fi sināʿat al-mantiq*, parts 8 and 9. For the Arabic original and Hebrew translations, see *Maimonides' Treatise on Logic*, ed. Israel Efros (New York: American Academy for Jewish Research, 1938). For al-Farābī as Maimonides's inspiration, see Brann, *Compunctious Poet*, 73.

53. "And this faculty of imagination is surely a corporeal faculty." Maimonides, *The Guide of the Perplexed*, trans. Shlomo Pines (Chicago: University of Chicago Press, 1963), 2:36. "The imagination is also [an aspect of the] evil instinct . . . since any deficiency in speech or morals is the work of the imagination" (2:12).

54. In his biblical exegesis he explained the creation of Adam as an allegory for the creation of the intellectual soul in man, and that of Eve as allegorical of the animal soul. See Sara Klein-Braslavy, *Maimonides' Interpretation of the Adam*

Stories in Genesis (in Hebrew) (Jerusalem: Reuven Mass, 1986), particularly pp. 200–205.

55. In several instances (e.g., *The Guide*, 1:33), Maimonides (following Aristotle) compares the limited intellect of women to that of the uneducated masses, or to the intellect of slaves and infants. Abraham Melamed suggests that Maimonides' overt misogyny be viewed as a cover for a covert and radical egalitarian stance. See his "Maimonides on Women: Formless Matter or Potential Prophet?" in *Perspectives on Jewish Thought and Mysticism*, ed. A. L. Ivry et al. (Amsterdam: Harwood Academic publishers, 1998). I am grateful to Abraham Melamed for letting me read his article before publication and for furnishing me with several references to Maimonides. Although I greatly benefited from Dr. Melamed's article, I am solely responsible for the conclusions stated here. On women's intellectual potential in Maimonides, see Chapter 6, note 49.

56. Hayyim Schirmann remarks on this briefly in his paper, "Maimonides and Hebrew Poetry," *Moznayim* 3 (1935): 433–36 (in Hebrew), and more broadly in Schirmann-Fleischer, *Christian Spain*, 279–86; notes 6–8 on pp. 280–81 list poems dubiously ascribed to Maimonides, panegyrics addressed to him, and poems involved in the controversies around Maimonides writings, which do not, on the whole, reverse my argument. Also see Norman Roth, *Maimonides: Essays and Texts, 850th Anniversary* (Madison, Wis.: Hispanic Seminary of Medieval Studies, 1985), 109–22. Roth is fairly apologetic regarding Maimonides and concludes that Maimonides' objection to poetry was not complete—a conclusion which I do not share.

57. Maimonides' preface to "Perek Ḥelek," in *Maimonides' Prefaces to the Mishna* (in Hebrew), ed. Itzhaq Shilat (Jerusalem: Maʿaliyot, 1982), 140.

58. And, in particular, a certain type of songs (*muwashshaḥāt*) that were played to music in feasts and weddings. *Tractate Avot with Maimonides' Commentary*, ed. Itzhaq Shilat (in Hebrew) (Jerusalem: Maʿaliyot, 1994) 21.

59. *Maimonides' Epistles* (in Hebrew), ed. Itzhaq Shilat (Jerusalem: Maʿaliyot, 1987), 426–29. Italics are mine.

60. See Schirmann-Fleischer, *Christian Spain*, 281–82, and note 10.

61. *Shemona perakim* (Eight Chapters), ed. Joseph I. Gorfinkle (New York: AMS Press reprint 1966 [1912]), 5:31.

62. Abraham Ibn Ḥasday, *The Prince and the Monk*, 131. Judah ha-Levi, himself an erotic poet, precedes Maimonides in this matter. In his *Kitāb ar-radd* (known as *Sefer ha-Kuzari*, 2:60), he cautions the student of science and the praying man, that "whoever wishes to purify his soul . . . will find . . . excessive eating and drinking harmful, and similarly will find harm in . . . women, . . . in jesters, and in . . . erotic and facetious poetry." (This translation is Brann's, *Compunctious Poet*, 95.)

63. For instance, in *The Guide*, 3:48.

64. See Klein-Braslavy, *Maimonides' Interpretation*, 193–208 in particular.

65. "I looked through the window and suddenly I saw . . . a boy innocent of heart . . . and then a woman came into his path, a hard-hearted woman, a harlot, loud and stubborn . . . praying at every corner. She held him and kissed him,

pertinently told him: . . . 'Let's go and make love all night, for my husband is gone on a distant trip' " (Proverbs 7:6–19).

66. For the definite Platonic-Aristotelian identification in Maimonides of inferior matter with the female, see *The Guide*, 1:17. Aristotle says: "It is matter [which craves to form] like female to male and like the ugly to the beautiful" (*Physics*, 1:9).

67. This issue also appears at the end of the introduction to the first part of *The Guide*, where Maimonides uses this fable as a paradigm for a certain type of prophetic allegory (in which only the central analogy is to be considered, while other details carry no signification).

68. *The Guide*, 3:8, Pines's translation, quoted and commented upon in Daniel Boyarin, *Carnal Israel: Reading Sex in Talmudic Culture* (Berkeley: University of California Press, 1993), 58–59. This passage is also referred to at the end of the section "Her Body Is the Prize" in Chapter 6 ("Among Men") below.

69. Boyarin, *Carnal Israel*, 58–59. While joining Boyarin's view, I refer the reader to Abraham Melamed's opposed view about implications of egalitarian attitudes on gender in Maimonides, discussed in the section "When the Object Speaks," Chapter 6 ("Among Men") below.

70. On the literary aspect of the story of the Garden of Eden in Maimonides, see Klein-Braslavy, *Maimonides' Interpretation*, 181–92. The identification of the "fable" as "female" and the "moral" as "male" is my own and is not inferred by Klein-Braslavy.

71. Maimonides's tolerance of allegory (as opposed to his rejection of poetry and metaphor) is evident from his reception of " 'Ne'um Tuviah ben Tzidqiyah': Yosef ben Shime'on's Maqāma Dedicated to Maimonides" (as is the title of Yosef Yahalom's article in *Tarbiz* 66 (1997): 543–77). This story of Philosophy marrying the Torah is summarized in note 60 of Chapter 4. Maimonides referred favorably to this *maqāma* when he dedicated later his *Guide of the Perplexed* to Ben Shime'on. Yahalom (p. 560), including allegory under the category of figurative poetry, and wondering how Maimonides was not disturbed by Yosef ben Shime'on's erotic imagery, concludes that Maimonides was probably aware of the contradiction between his theoretical rejection of poetry and his practical acceptance of it. In my view, and as this case proves, Maimonides's opposition to poetry did not include allegory, even erotic, of which he was all in favor.

Chapter 4. Poor Soul, Pure Soul

1. Genevieve Lloyd, *The Man of Reason, 'Male' and 'Female' in Western Philosophy* (London: Methuen, 1984), ix-x; Elizabeth Grosz, *Volatile Bodies: Toward a Corporeal Feminism* (Bloomington: Indiana University Press, 1994), 4.

2. As shown by Daniel Boyarin, talmudic psychology afforded an alternative to the Greek dichotomy of Body and Soul, embedding the human ethical dimension in the body itself. *Carnal Israel: Reading Sex in Talmudic Culture* (Berkeley: University of California Press, 1993), esp. chap. 2. This perception is

totally alien to the psychology of the Andalusian *piyyut*. (For *piyyut*, see note 5 below.)

3. Grosz, *Volatile Bodies*, 3.

4. Joan M. Ferrante, *Woman as Image in Medieval Literature from the Twelfth Century to Dante* (New York: Columbia University Press, 1975), 5–6. Ferrante associates this tendency with the Neoplatonic belief in the realism of ideas as well as in the reality of metaphor (39–40). For the differentiation in Latin between the masculine, intellectual *animus*, and the feminine, vital *anima*, see p. 38.

5. *Piyyut* is the tradition of synagogal liturgy which began in Byzantine Palestine, spread to the Orient and Europe, and reached its highest peak in eleventh- and twelfth-century al-Andalus, where all major poets contributed to it. For *piyyut* in general, see Ezra Fleischer, *Hebrew Liturgical Poetry in the Middle Ages* (in Hebrew) (Jerusalem: Keter, 1975). For Andalusian *piyyut*, see Raymond P. Scheindlin, *The Gazelle: Medieval Hebrew Poems on God, Israel, and the Soul* (Philadelphia: Jewish Publication Society, 1991), and Adena V. Tanenbaum's doctoral thesis, "Poetry and Philosophy: The Idea of the Soul in Andalusian *Piyyut*" (Harvard University, Cambridge, Mass., 1993). Neither Scheindlin nor Tanenbaum focuses particularly on the feminine bearings of the soul.

6. See, for instance, Psalms 42:2–3, 63:2, 84:3, 103:1, 2, 22, 104:1, 35.

7. This pertains to the individual soul as well as to the cosmic soul (*anima mundi*). The latter, identical with "Nature," emanates from the divine cosmic intellect and descends to formless matter to shape and enliven it. Plotinus's philosophy was familiar among Muslim and Jewish thinkers through a composition known as *The Theology of Aristotle*. See Paul B. Fenton, "The Arabic and Hebrew Versions of *The Theology of Aristotle*," in *Pseudo-Aristotle in the Middle Ages: The Theology and Other Texts*, ed. Jill Kraye et al. (London: Warburg Institute, 1986), 239–64. On its influence on Ibn Gabirol's Neoplatonism, and on his concept of the soul, see Jacques Schlanger, *La Philosophie de Salomon ibn Gabirol: Etude d'un néoplatonisme* (Leiden: E. J. Brill, 1968), chap. 4.

8. See also Lloyd, *Man of Reason*, 6–7.

9. See Annemarie Schimmel, "Women in Mystical Islam," *Women's Studies International Forum* 5 (1982): 146. Schimmel also alludes to the tendency in Islam to equate all evil in the world with the female, which resulted in representing the world as a hideous ghastly hag, who seduces men and then devours them. For this theme in Hebrew poetry, see my Chapter 1 ("No-Woman's-Land"). Schimmel, however, adds that the Islamic mystics, "despite all their theoretical aversion to the *nafs*—woman in general—rarely used such crude expressions about women as are found in Christian medieval monastic literature."

10. Ferrante, *Woman as Image*, 4–5, relates to such examples of fusion (and confusion) of male and female characteristics in symbolical personifications (including that of the Neoplatonic *anima mundi*) in Christian literature and art.

11. *The Liturgical Poems of Abraham ibn Ezra*, ed. Israel Levin (Jerusalem: Israel Academy of Sciences and Humanities, 1975–80), 2 vols.

12. The apostrophe to the soul in the imperative mode is characteristic of

the *tokheḥa* (literally, reproach), a common penitential subgenre in Spanish liturgy. On this and other penitential genres, see Fleischer, *Hebrew Liturgical Poetry*, 402–10; Scheindlin, *The Gazelle*, 157–59.

13. *Enneads*, ed. and trans. by A. H. Armstrong, 7 vols. (Cambridge, Mass.: Harvard University Press, 1966–88).

14. *The Liturgical Poetry of Rabbi Solomon Ibn Gabirol*, ed. Dov Jarden (Jerusalem, 1979), 2 vols.

15. The combination of women, dance, and drums appears in Miriam's song (Exodus 15:20); the dancing of Jefthah's daughter (Judges 11:34), and the daughters of Israel (1 Samuel 18:6).

16. For a detailed discussion of this theme, see Tanenbaum, *Poetry and Philosophy*, 126–27, 147–62.

17. *Moses ibn Ezra: The Collected Liturgical Poetry*, ed. Shimon Bernstein (Tel Aviv: Massadah, 1957).

18. The allusion to a priest's widowed or divorced daughter who "comes back to her father's house as in her youth" (Leviticus 22:13) conflates the images of wife and daughter and introduces an incestuous overtone present also in the midrash. In *Shir ha-Sirim Raba* 3, for instance, God is compared to a king who, out of his love for his daughter Israel, calls her "my sister," "my wife," and "my mother."

19. *The Liturgical Poetry of Rabbi Yehuda Halevi*, ed. Dov Jarden, 4 vols. (Jerusalem, 1978–85).

20. The first Jewish exegetes to suggest that the Canticles be read as an allegory of love between God and the Soul come from the Maimonidean age. According to Arthur Green, the first known Canticles' commentary in this vein is Joseph Ibn 'Aqnin's Aristotelian *allegoresis*. See Green, "Shekhinah, the Virgin Mary, and the Song of Songs," *AJS Review* 26/1 (2002): 12–13. (Green's article, published after the completion of my chapter, expounds on the parallel evolution of Canticle exegesis in Judaism—midrash, poetry, philosophy, Kabbalah—and Christianity. He lays special emphasis on the female/erotic element in the various interpretations.) According to Tanenbaum, *Poetry and Philosophy*, 126–27, Maimonides himself alludes in *Mishneh Torah* to the identification of the Canticles' beloved with the Soul. An even earlier evidence to a deviation from the midrashic allegory of the love between God and Israel comes from Abraham Ibn Ezra. In the introduction to his exegesis of Canticles he acknowledges the existence of an innovative allegorical reading of the book as love *between body and soul*, but rejects it completely in favor of the traditional national allegory.

21. This *piyyut* belongs to the liturgical subgenre of *reshut le-nishmat*, typically elaborating on the theme of the soul. For the liturgical function of this type, see Scheindlin, *The Gazelle*, 144–48. For his translation and interpretation of this poem, see ibid., 160–63.

22. In Arabic as well as in Hebrew poetry the notion of moral awakening is tied to the motif of the growing of gray (white) hair (line 4). The topos of black versus white hair enhances the opposition between the indulgence of the immature

soul in the concerns of the lowly, ephemeral world (represented here by Time), and the preoccupation of the mature soul with her moral and intellectual goals.

23. The passage from the *Epistles of the ikhwan al-ṣāfaʾ* (Brethren of purity), no. 27, is quoted here from Tanenbaum, *Poetry and Philosophy*, 46. I changed the pronoun "it" (in Tanenbaum's translation) to "she" in keeping with the Arabic original.

24. Lloyd, *The Man of Reason*, 2.

25. The bird metaphor is central in the *Birds Epistle* by the Andalusian philosopher Ibn Sina (d. 1037). There the soul is a fallen fledgling who, when suf-ficiently matured, shakes the dust off its wings and ascends to the top of a moun-tain where she beholds "that which sleeping eyes cannot see." Quoted from Tanenbaum, *Poetry and Philosophy*, 49. For a Hebrew elaboration of Ibn Sina, see Israel Levin, "The Gazelle and the Birds" (in Hebrew), *Jerusalem Studies in He-brew Literature* 10–11 (1988), part 2, 577–612.

26. Some of the contrasts in this poem (one/many, male/female, rest/motion, light/dark, good/bad, determinate/indeterminate) conform to the Pythagorean table of ten opposites (see Lloyd, *Man of Reason*, 3). In Greek thought maleness was aligned with active, precise, determinate form; femaleness with passive, vague, indeterminate matter.

27. *The Poems of Joseph Ibn Zaddik*, ed. Yonah David (New York: American Academy for Jewish Research, 1982), 55–56. Quoted here are two (out of four) strophes. Liturgically, this poem functions as a *reshut le-nishmat* intended for the Sabbath morning. For Scheindlin's different translation and his comments, see *The Gazelle*, 143–48.

28. Compare to Ibn Gabirol's use of "hidden" in the meaning of "abstract" in his address to the soul: "For you, like God, have everlasting life / and he is *hid-den* just as you are *hid*" (Scheindlin, *The Gazelle*, 203). The alliteration in *ʿalma naʿalama* enhances also the meaning of the Arabic root *ʿalama* as denoting knowledge, science, teaching, and learning. Hence *ʿalma naʿalama* could also connote "the knowledgeable / rational soul" who is capable of learning, or the soul as the object of philosophical speculation.

29. It is not unlikely that *ʿalma* functions here as a trilingual homonym. Be-sides the Hebrew/Arabic pun alluded to in the preceding note, a Hebrew/Span-ish homonym is possible too. In Hebrew *ʿalma* is synonymous with a young woman, a virgin, while in the Spanish *alma* means "soul." Both meanings serve the two levels—the overt and the covert—of the allegory. That Ibn Zaddiq and his audience were familiar with the Romance vernacular is evident from two such endings (*kharja*s) to his secular strophic poems (of the *muwashshah* type). See David's edition, *Poems*, 33, 46.

30. Compare to Ibn Gabirol's address to God (in "Keter Malkhut," par. 3, lines 1–2): " 'How,' 'Why' and 'Where' are inapplicable to Thee" (*The Liturgical Poetry of Rabbi Solomon Ibn Gabirol*, 40; Ibn Gabirol, *The Kingly Crown*, , trans. Bernard Lewis [London: Vallentine, Mitchell, 1961]). These queries follow Ibn Gabirol's use of Aristotelian ontological categories in his purely philosophical work *Fons Vitae* (The Fount of Life), 5:24: "I maintain that there are four distinct

stages in the universe, discernible according to the following questions: 'Does it exist?' 'What is it?' 'Why is it?' 'What is it for?' " Written originally in Arabic, Christians attributed this work to "Avencebrolis" whom they thought to be an Andalusi Christian (or Muslim). The book was translated into Latin in the Middle Ages by Johannes Hispanus and Dominicus Gundusalvi (*Fons Vitae*, ed. Clemens Baeumker [Münster: Aschendorff, 1895]). Only as late as the nineteen century was the author's identity uncovered. I relied on the Hebrew translation, *Meqor Hayyim*, trans. Yaacov Bluvstein (Tel Aviv, 1950).

31. Ibn Gabirol (*The Kingly Crown*, par. 29) employs the very same metaphor to describe the mission of the female soul to the body: She was sent to the body by God "to toil and to guard it" (alluding to Adam's task, Genesis 2:15).

32. "Phaedo," in *The Dialogues of Plato*, trans. Benjamin Jowett (New York: Random House, 1937), 1:441–504. See also its discussion in Lloyd, *Man of Reason*, 6. The soul/"daimon" in this myth is not necessarily or specifically feminine. It is in "Timaeus" (par. 50d) that Plato compared form to the father and matter to the mother, thus "reinforcing the long-standing association between maleness and form, femaleness and matter" (Lloyd, 4–5).

33. And see also Lloyd, *Man of Reason*, 6. For the parallel paragraph in Plotinus, see his *Enneads*, 4:3.24. Isaac Israeli, the first Jewish Neoplatonist, has his version on this theme: "If the sinful soul is not . . . cleansed from the defilement of this world . . . it is then worthy of remaining in exile from the world of intellect . . . instead it must revolve . . . perplexed and full of desire, hungering and thirsting to . . . go home." Israeli might have inspired Ibn Gabirol's passage below. (For all parallels, see Tanenbaum, *Poetry and Philosophy*, 94–96.)

34. Ibn Gabirol, *The Kingly Crown*, par. 30, slightly altered from Lewis's translation. The last sentence cites Leviticus 12:4, regarding the woman's postnatal bleeding, her purification and isolation.

35. Grosz, *Volatile Bodies*, 3–4. The animality of the body is referred to in the *piyyut*, e.g., "like a horse, a brainless mule, a slumbering drunkard, a perplexed man" (Ibn Paqūda, in Jefim Schirmann, *Hebrew Poetry in Spain and Provence* (in Hebrew) (Jerusalem: Mosad Bialik; Tel Aviv: Dvir, 1960), 2:345.

36. Sara Klein-Braslavy, *Maimonides' Interpretation of the Adam Stories in Genesis* (in Hebrew) (Jerusalem: Reuven Mass, 1986), esp. 205–8. And see also the section "Ontological Whoredom," Chapter 3 ("Veils and Wiles") above.

37. Klein-Braslavi notes that a Neoplatonic allegorical exegesis of Creation by Ibn Gabirol (referred to in Abraham Ibn Ezra's exegesis on Genesis and now lost) did in all likelihood influence Maimonides' interpretation (*Maimonides' Interpretation*, 206 n.17).

38. I am aware of the fact that the *conceptual* femaleness of the body does not correspond to its masculine grammatical gender.

39. See Grosz, *Volatile Bodies*, 196–97.

40. In Schirmann, *Hebrew Poetry in Spain and Provence*, 2:346.

41. Quoted from Grosz's comment on Mary Douglas, in Grosz, *Volatile Bodies*, 196. The views of Douglas, Kristeva, and Irigaray quoted below are taken from Grosz's profound survey on the signification of body fluids, ibid., 193–210.

For the symbolism of body fluids, male and female, see chap. 8 ("Gender Opposition in Rabbinic Judaism: Free-flowing Blood in a Culture of Control") in Lawrence A. Hoffman, *Covenant of Blood: Circumcision and Gender in Rabbinic Judaism* (Chicago: University of Chicago Press, 1996), esp. 143–54.

42. It is the first of ten *maqāmāt* in his collection "Sefer ha-meshalim" (The book of parables), published by Yonah David as *The Love Stories of Jacob Ben Eleazar* (in Hebrew) (Tel Aviv: Ramot, 1992–93). About Jacob Ben Eleazar, see Jefim Schirmann, *The History of Hebrew Poetry in Christian Spain and Southern France* (in Hebrew), ed., Ezra Fleischer (Jerusalem: Magnes, 1997), 222–55, and esp. 251–52 (hereinafter, Schirmann-Fleischer, *Christian Spain*).

43. Quoted from his chapter on the *Roman de la Rose* in C. S. Lewis, *The Allegory of Love: A Study in Medieval Tradition* (Oxford: Oxford University Press, 1965), 113.

44. The similarities (and possible relation) between the two works merit a further investigation, which I intend to follow in the future.

45. On Prudentius's classical model and its influence on medieval allegories, see James J. Paxson, *The Poetics of Personification* (Cambridge: Cambridge University Press, 1994), 63–81.

46. As in all his other stories, the narrator assumes here the generic name of Lemu'el ben Ithi'el. Lemu'el is a name of an ancient sage (Proverbs 31:1) and Ithi'el (Proverbs 30:1) is an appellation of King Solomon to whom the book of Proverbs is ascribed. The choice of this name probably connotes the author's gnomic purpose. In choosing to call his narrator son of Ithi'el, Ben Eleazar also alludes to the title of al-Ḥarizi's translations (*Maḥberot Ithi'el*) of al-Ḥarīrī's Arabic *maqāmāt*, whereby associating himself with the tradition of the classical *maqāma*. However, right in his introduction, Ben Eleazar identifies the fictive Lemu'el with the biographical author: "Following the Arabic convention to veil the authors' names, I have not mentioned my own name in my stories . . . but I will disclose it now: it is Jacob ben Eleazar." Furthermore, in several instances in the story (lines 77, 156), the narrator assumes the author's name, Jacob.

47. "Tziv'ot ha-ḥesheq." The author puns here on the double designation of *tzeva'oth* as meaning in Hebrew both "armies" and "gazelles" (lovers). For the allegorical persona of Love as a powerful ruler of souls, see section 'The Fiction of Loverhood" in Chapter 2 above.

48. The scene invokes two biblical allusions. One is that of the kings Ahab and Jehoshaphat sitting on their chairs, as in a show, watching the prophets prophesying before them (1 Kings 22:10); the other is Jeremiah's (1:15) prophecy about the kings of the north who will sit on their chairs while besieging Jerusalem.

49. By citing Genesis 28:16 "And Jacob awakened from his dream" (line 77), the author not only inserts his name, but furthermore, he alludes to the symbolism of Jacob's ladder "which rested on the ground with its top reaching the heaven" (Genesis 28:13). The ladder stands here for the uninterrupted Neoplatonic "chain of being," which will be mentioned later on in the text (in the soul's philosophical rhymed lecture, line 195): "And know that all of them [the parts of

Creation] are linked to each other and hung upon each other." The ladder stretching from earth to heaven may also prefigure the itinerary of the soul upward. In another vain, the ladder could also be self-referential to the allegorist's task—climbing from material figuration to abstract ideas.

50. Ben Eleazar's dispute between body and soul leans on a long rhetorical tradition going back to Sanhedrin 91 (and other sources). The ancient examples recount a parable about a king who hired a blind man and a lame man (representing body and soul) to guard his orchard. When caught stealing the fruit, they started disputing and blaming each other. The king judged them and decreed that both were responsible. This dialogue became a model for penitential *piyyutim* of the *tohekha* type. For its circulation in ancient *piyyut*, see Yosef Yahalom, *Poetry and Society in Jewish Galilee of Late Antiquity* (in Hebrew) (Tel Aviv: Hakibbutz Hameuchad, 1999), 24–34; and in Spain, see Masha Itzhaki, *Man the Vine, Death the Reaper* (in Hebrew) (Lod: Habermann Institute, 1987), 9–25. (Ibn Gabirol's poem *Liturgical Poetry*, 1:32–33, quoted above, partakes in this subgenre.) The debate between body and soul in all the above sources takes place in the celestial court on the Day of Judgment and revolves around the question of moral responsibility. Each party blames the burden of sin on the other. The body dismisses itself by reducing itself to dust and ashes, inert matter, unable to act without the animating soul. The soul acquits herself by claiming that it is her bodily dwelling that incited her to sin. The debate always concludes in God's (or the poet's) injunction that both are liable and that it is the individual, not his disjoined parts, who has to take responsibility for his deeds. Another tradition present here is that of the dialogue between intellect and soul in moralistic literature. An early example is found in Baḥya Ibn Paqūda's famous composition known in Hebrew as *Sefer Ḥovot ha-Levavot*, Gate 3. For the English translation done from the original Arabic, see *The Book of Direction to the Duties of the Heart*, trans. Menahem Mansoor (London: Routledge and Kegan Paul, 1973). Baḥya's example was followed also in Ben Eleazar's "The Book of the Garden of Learning" (unpublished), a moralistic composition consisting of conversations between the rational soul and the intellect (see Schirmann-Fleischer, *Christian Spain*, 223). Similarly to Ben Eleazar, Judah al-Ḥarizi, his contemporary and compatriot, fused these two dialogic traditions and cast them into the *maqāma* form in his thirteenth *maqāma* (titled "The Soul's Debate with Body and Intellect, as to Who of the Three Is the Scoundrel," *Taḥkemoni*, ed. I. Toporowski [Tel Aviv: Maḥbarot Lesifrut, 1952, 138–48]). Compared to al-Ḥarizi's straightforward rhetorical dispute, Ben Eleazar's *maqāma* is far more innovative in its narrative sophistication and dramatic imagination. However, in al-Ḥarizi, too, the "biography" of the soul, cast in a lengthy monologue, is unfolded as a failed love story: "Yesterday, I was still a merry maiden, sitting in my Rock's lap, clinging to Him. Then, as virgin, I was betrothed to a man, a defiled body, who impregnated me with his bastard offspring. Even so, I went on longing for my first pure lover, weeping for him day and night. . . . Why did he desert me, as if I fornicated—and I did not!"

51. On the stereotypical identification of women's voices and bodies, and on reading "bodytalk" as a voice of resistance and dissent in French fabliaux, see

E. Jane Burns, *Bodytalk: When Women Speak in Old French Literature* (Philadelphia: University of Pennsylvania Press, 1993).

52. The use of personal and possessive pronouns in lines 124–25 is quite confusing. As David's edition has it, it seems that it is Jacob who urges the soul to go on the voyage. But this is contradicted by Jacob's reluctance in lines 128–30. Hence, my reading does not agree with the grammar of the passage but with the logic of the dialogue.

53. In her speech in Proverbs 8 the female *Ḥokhma* presents herself as God's darling daughter, his playmate, and his first creation. Raphael Patai, *The Hebrew Goddess* (NewYork: Avon, 1978), 100–102, assumes that she represents an authentic goddess of ancient Hebrew mythology. Erotic involvement with Ḥokhma occurs in Ibn Gabirol's poetry: "If you say that Wisdom is closed . . . let me open her closets! How should I leave her after being betrothed to her by God? How could she leave me—she is like mother to me and I to her like baby?" *Secular Poems*, ed. Hayyim Brody and Hayyim Schirmann (Jerusalem: Schocken, 1974), 72. For *Ḥokhma* and its relation to male reason, see B. L. Mack, *Logos und Sophia* (Göttingen: Vandenhoeck and Ruprect, 1977), 34–62, 153–58. And see also Elliot R. Wolfson, "Female Imaging of the Torah: From Literary Metaphor to Religious Symbol," in *From Ancient Israel to Modern Judaism: Essays in Honor of Marvin Fox,* vol. 2, ed. Jacob Neusner et al. (Atlanta, Ga.: Scholars Press, 1989), 271–307 and his bibliographical note (no. 1).

54. "Symposium," *The Dialogues*, 328.

55. *Enneads*, 3:5. A most famous interpretation of this Platonic allegory is Judah Avrabanel (Leone Ebreo), *Dialoghi Amore* (translated into English by F. Friedberg et al. as *The Philosophy of Love* [London: Soncino Press, 1937]), where the male Philo and the female Sophia converse.

56. *The Dialogues*, 250–52.

57. Lloyd, *Man of Reason*, 21.

58. Ibid., 20–21.

59. On reading instructions in the allegorical mode, see C. Clifford, *The Transformation of Allegory* (London: Routledge and Kegan Paul, 1974), 36.

60. The relevance to Maimonides might also be hinted in the text itself. On their way to the garden the soul tells Jacob about a "prophet, a man of spirit" who knows the way to the garden, and "whose name I will not pronounce lest jealous foes hear it" (lines 161,165–66). Schirmann (in Schirmann-Fleischer, *Christian Spain*, 252) conjectures that this alludes to Maimonides, and that this enigmatic hint is to be explained away by the circumstances—the *maqāma* was probably written during the fierce controversy about Maimonides' writings. Notwithstanding Maimonides' own critique of poetic creativity, the figure of Maimonides appears explicitly (and ironically enough) in several other contemporary allegorical-erotic *maqāmāt* (and see Fleischer's supplement in Schirmann, *Christian Spain*, 273–78). Maimonides' tolerance of allegory (as opposed to his rejection of poetry and metaphor) is evident from his reception of a *maqāma* dedicated to him by an admirer. See Yosef Yahalom, " 'Ne'um Tuviah ben Tzidqiyah': Yosef ben Shimeon's *maqāma* dedicated to Maimonides," *Tarbiz* 66

(1997): 543–77. This erotic narrative features the marriage of Philosophy and the Torah. The story's protagonist, Maskil (literally, an intellectual, a philosopher) is in desperate love with Yemimah (here representing the Torah). She will become his, she explains, only if her adopting father, who in the past saved her from captivity, will approve. Her father, who is none other than "the leader Moses" (Maimonides), does approve, and the marriage takes place. Thanks to this *maqāma*, sent and dedicated to Maimonides during the 1180s, the author, Yosef ben Shimeon, became the great teacher's disciple. Moreover, it is to him that Maimonides dedicated later his *Guide of the Perplexed*, referring nostalgically in its preface to this *maqāma* which marked the beginning of their relationship. For Maimonides' views on allegory, see end of Chapter 3 (and note 71 there).

Chapter 5. Domesticating the Enemy

1. The literary route of this anecdote is symptomatic of medieval intercultural contacts. Its earliest occurrence is in the third-century Greek work of Diogenes Laertius, *Lives of the Eminent Philosophers*, ed. R. D. Hicks (London: D. Heinemann, 1925), 2:53. This and other anecdotes were recycled in Arabic, Hebrew, and European texts. For an Arabic version, see Fedwa Malti-Douglas, *Woman's Body, Woman's Word: Gender and Discourse in Arabo-Islamic Writing* (Princeton, N.J.: Princeton University Press, 1991), 40. Joseph Ibn Zabara, a Hebrew author from Barcelona, late twelfth century, adopted from the Arabic several such anecdotes in his novella *The Book of Delight*, trans. Moses Hadas, with an introduction by Merriam Sherwood (New York: Columbia University Press, 1932), 67.

2. For aspects of gender in Islamic asceticism, see Annemarie Schimmel, "Eros—Heavenly and Not So Heavenly—in Sufi Literature and Life," in *Society and the Sexes in Medieval Islam*, ed. Afaf Lutfi al-Sayyid-Marsot (Malibu, Calif.: Undena Publications, 1979), 119–41.

3. Printed in M. Y. Bin Gorion, *Mimekor Yisrael* (Tel Aviv, 1966). Parts were edited and printed in Jefim Schirmann, *Hebrew Poetry in Spain and Provence* (Jerusalem: Mosad Bialik; Tel Aviv: Dvir, 1960), 3:70–86. I relied on, and greatly benefited from, the texts, apparatuses, and discussions in Matti Huss's excellent doctoral thesis, *Critical Editions of "Minḥat Yehudah," "'Ezrat Hanashim," and "'Ein Mishpat" with Prefaces, Variants, Sources, and Annotations*, 2 vols. (Jerusalem: Hebrew University, 1991). Huss printed the two versions of *Minḥat Yehuda* (one from 1208, the other probably from 1228). My references follow the first version. For problems of dating, see Huss, 1:207–21. Parts of the work were translated (and introduced) by R. P. Scheindlin in *Rabbinic Fantasies: Imaginative Narratives from Classical Hebrew Literature*, ed. David Stern and Mark J. Mirsky (New Haven, Conn.: Yale University Press, 1990), 269–94. Translations, unless otherwise stated, are his. About Ibn Shabbetai, see Schirmann, *Hebrew Poetry in Spain and Provence*, 3:67–70 and Huss, *Critical Editions*, 1:183–88.

4. Huss, *Critical Editions*, 1:190.

5. Also published by Huss, ibid.

6. *Maqāmāt* were intended mainly as entertainment; however, they range widely in style and purpose—from the rhetorical, allegorical, gnomic, didactic, to the humoristic, narrative and even lyrical. The insertion of poems within the prose is one of the genre's characteristics. In my use of the term *maqāma* here and elsewhere in this book, I follow the broad definition offered by Schirmann and Huss. On the scholarly disagreement about the generic definition of *Minḥat Yehuda*, and of the different subgenres included under *maqāma*, see Dan Pagis, "Variety in Medieval Rhymed Narratives," *Jerusalem Studies in Hebrew Literature* 27 (1978): 79–97, and Matti Huss's comprehensive discussion in *Critical Editions*, 1:17–40. See also H. Nemah, "Andalusian *Maqāmāt*," *Journal of Arabic Literature* 5 (1974): 83–92. The *maqāma* and its literary cognates shared themes and topoi with contemporary folkloristic stories—Jewish and non-Jewish. On the Jewish folkloristic novellas, their relation to international folklore, and especially on their misogynistic leanings, see Eli Yassif, *The Hebrew Folktale: History, Genre, Meaning*, trans. Jacqueline S. Teitlebaum (Bloomington: Indiana University Press, 1999), 343–51. And also Haim Schwarzbaum, "Female Fickleness in Jewish Folklore," in *Jewish Folklore between East and West: Collected Papers*, ed. Eli Yassif (Beer Sheva: Ben Gurion University of the Negev Press), 173–96.

7. There are some differences, though, between the Latin models and our work (in the Latin the philosopher is usually celibate; the address is in epistolary form; the addressee is a specific friend facing an imminent marriage, not mankind in general), however, the affinity cannot be denied. The relation to the Latin model is widely discussed by Huss, *Critical Editions*, 1:55–59. The medieval examples follow a tradition rooted in antiquity. Famous examples are Juvenal's *Sixth Satire* to His Friend Postumus; St Jerome's treatise *Against Jovinian* (quoting the *Liber Aureolus de Nuptis* attributed to a certain pagan named Theophrastus); Walter Map's *Epistola Valerii* written by Valerius to his friend Rufinus and many others. Even Héloïse's dissuasions from marriage written to Abelard can be considered as part of this male tradition. For more examples and for further bibliography, see Katharina M. Wilson and Elizabeth M. Makowski, *Wykked Wyves and the Woes of Marriage: Misogamous Literature from Juvenal to Chaucer* (Albany: State University of New York Press, 1990).

8. This biblical name (2 Samuel 23:8) deriving from the root *h.k.m.* (wise, wisdom), denotes age-old patriarchal wisdom.

9. The theme of angelic warning, typical of apocalypse, might come from the Jewish biblical or postbiblical apocalyptic tradition. But association between an angelic agency and antimarriage propaganda (and of marriage as cause for doomsday) probably draws on a Christian theme. In an anonymous poem, *De conjuge non ducenda* (dated around 1222–50), three angels warn the poet against marriage. See Wilson and Makowski, *Wykked Wyves*, 124–32. Though the *De conjuge* is later than *Minḥat Yehuda*, it may reflect earlier traditions with which Ibn Shabbetai could also have been familiar. Other textual similarities between the two works corroborate this conjecture.

10. Lines 122–24; translation mine.

11. This is the first occurrence of such a list in Hebrew literature. Lists of wicked women from the Bible and from antiquity are commonplace in the Latin tradition since St. Jerome's famous list in *Against Jovinian* "exercised a quasi-hypnotic influence on medieval anti-feminism" (Jill Mann, *Geoffrey Chaucer* [Atlantic Highlands, N.J.: Humanities Press International, 1991], 49). The first appearance of this theme in Arabic literature occurs only much later. See also Malti-Douglas, *Woman'n Body*, 55. The next Hebrew poet to employ a list of bad wives was Immanuel of Rome. See *Mahberot Immanuel ha-Romi*, ed. Dov Jarden (Jerusalem: Mosad Bialik, 1957), lines 494–595 in the first *mahberet*.

12. As far as I could trace, the striking analogy between Tahkemoni's speech and the "Testament of Reuben," included in the pseudepigraphic "Testaments of the Twelve Patriarchs," went hitherto unnoticed. Dying Reuben gathers his offspring lecturing to them: "Do not devote your attention to the beauty of women, my children, nor occupy your minds with their activities. . . . For women are evil, my sons . . . they scheme treacherously . . . by means of their looks" and so forth. Moreover, Reuben, like Tahkemoni, relates his wisdom to a divine visitation: "The Angel of the Lord told me and instructed me that women are more easily overcome by the spirit of promiscuity than men." James H. Charlesworth, *The Old Testament Pseudepigrapha*, vol. 1, *Apocalyptic Literature and Testaments* (Garden City, N.Y.: Doubleday, 1983), 783–74. The "Testaments" literature, written probably by Hellenized Jews and preserved in the Christian realm, was translated into Hebrew from the Latin by medieval Jews. See Yassif, *The Hebrew Folktale*, 39, 80.

13. For the biblical and rabbinic sources for Tahkemoni's speech, see Huss, *Critical Editions*, 2:192–95. This citational discourse is admittedly not exclusive to misogynist writings as such. Known as *shibbutz*, this technique is, in fact, one of the most characteristic stylistic features of both medieval Hebrew poetry and rhymed prose. For Arabic misogynist literature, see Malti-Douglas's chapter "Sacred History as Misogyny," in *Woman's Body*, 54–66.

14. Mann, *Chaucer*, 50. R. Howard Bloch says about this tradition: "The ritual denunciation of women . . . constitutes something of a cultural constant. Reaching back to the Old Testament as well as to ancient Greece [it extends] through classical Hellenic, Judaic, and Roman traditions all the way to the fifteenth century. . . . The discourse of misogyny runs like a vein throughout medieval literature." *Medieval Misogyny and the Invention of Western Romantic Love* (Chicago: University of Chicago Press, 1991), 7.

15. "Bet is," quod he, "thyn habitacioun
　　Be with a leon or a foul dragoun'
　　Than with a womman usynge for to chyde.
　　Bet is," quod he, "hye in the roof abyde,
　　Than with an angry wyf doun in the hous."

Geoffrey Chaucer, *Canterbury Tales* 3:775–79, *Riverside Chaucer*, 3rd ed., ed. Larry Benson (Boston: Houghton Mifflin, 1987).

16. Malti-Douglas, *Woman's Body*, 85. Chapter 4 of her book treats the

problem of gender in Ibn Tufayl's (twelfth-century) masterpiece about an abandoned infant who grows up on an uninhabited womanless island. He is nurtured
by a gazelle, rejects the opportunity of returning to "normal" society, and eventually chooses to lead a life of meditation on his own island. In her chapter 5 she discusses the mythical island of al-Waq-Waq, devoid of women and inhabited by
woman-trees, that is, by "trees [which] bore women like fruit."

17. It appears in a poem added by the author in the second version; see
Huss, *Critical Editions*, 1:72, lines 341–43)

18. For the Andalusian garden, see James Dickie, "The Hispano-Arab Garden, Its Philosophy and Function," *Bulletin of the School of Oriental Studies* 31
(1968). For gardens in Hebrew poetry, see Raymond P. Scheindlin, *Wine, Women
and Death: Medieval Hebrew Poems on the Good Life* (Philadelphia: Jewish Publishing Society, 1986), 1–11.

19. This is in his compelling chapter on Bertha Pappenheim (Freud's pa-
tient "Anna O"), the hysteric who became feminist. Daniel Boyarin, *Unheroic
Conduct: The Rise of Heterosexuality and the Invention of the Jewish Man* (Berkeley: University of California Press, 1997), 316. And see also there Boyarin's argument with Hélène Cixous's model of hysteria, 314–316.

20. As in the famous talmudic saying "Woman's voice is nudity" (Berakhot
24.1). For a contemporary contention around the issue of the woman's sexual sat-
isfaction (*'onah*), see below.

21. Lines 288–95. This assembly of women, "young and old, widows and
virgins, trembling with anger," brings to mind a possible analogy with Aristopha-
nes' comedy *Lysistrata*. But unlike the Athenean women who refuse sex in protest
against men's belligerent politics, our women are devastated at the menace of
men's abstinence. In both works women's power is related to their alleged trickery, which they openly admit. Compare the women's words in our piece ("Where
have all deceivers gone? . . . Where are women's ruse and their wiles and tricks and
schemes and deceit and cunning?" lines 297–300) to Lysistrata's words in the
Greek play, "Because the men account us all to be sly, shifty rogues," and to
Calonice's reply, "And so, by Zeus, we are." *Lysistrata*, trans. B. B. Rogers (New
York: Putnam's, 1924), lines 10–12.

22. *K.z.b.* and *sh.k.r.* are Hebrew roots for deceit and lie; *y.r.sh.* denotes in-
heritance or heritage. Thus, the woman's name is literally "heir of falsehood."
The relevant biblical allusions add further negativity to her name. Kozbi bat Tsur
(Numbers 25:15), a Midianite woman with whom an Israelite man fornicated in
Baal Peor, was slain together with the man by Phinehas the priest. "The sin of
Peor" and Kozbi became symbols for adultery, both sexual and religious. For the
negative figure of the female matchmaker in Hebrew, Arabic, and Spanish literature, see Michelle M. Hamilton, "Celestina and the Daughters of Lilith," *Bulletin
of Hispanic Studies* 75 (1998): 153–72).

23. Lines 445–48, translation mine.

24. R. Howard Bloch, "Medieval Misogyny," *Representations* 20 (1987): 15.
Reprinted in *Misogyny, Misandry, and Misanthropy*, ed. R. Howard Bloch and
Frances Ferguson (Berkeley: University of California Press, 1989), 15.

25. The role of the bride as a Hebrew poetess, skilled in the art of male love lyric, is, of course, unrepresentative of women's real absence from Hebrew poetry. Famous exchanges of male and female poets in Andalusian-Arabic courtly poetry are those of Ibn Zaidūn and Wallāda, and Abu Gaʿfar and Ḥafṣa. See A. R. Nykl, *Hispano-Arabic Poetry and its Relations with the Old Provençal Troubadours* (Baltimore: J. H. Furst, 1946), 317–23.

26. Translations are mine.

27. The theme of a "topsy-turvy world" is of significance in carnivalesque contexts. Talya Fishman argues convincingly that the work was designed to be read at the home of Ibn Shabbetai's patron on Purim eve, the only day on the Jewish calendar when the reading of comical texts was licensed. *Minḥat Yehuda* is indeed full of allusions to the scroll of Esther which is read on Purim in celebration of Esther's victory over the Jews' enemies. See Talya Fishman, "A Medieval Parody of Misogyny," *Prooftexts* 8 (1988): 101–2. See also note 58 below.

28. The first part of the quotation is in Scheindlin's translation. The latter part (from Ibn Shabbetai's second edition, lines 740–43) is my translation. Judah al-Ḥarizi's sixth *maqāma* in *Sefer Taḥkemoni* imitates and even surpasses the description of the wife's appalling portraiture. See the section "The Good, the Bad, and the Ugly" in Chapter 1 ("No-Woman's-Land"). Compare also to the wife's physique in the *Lamentations* of the thirteenth-century Matheolus: "Alas! Now my heart is very sad, for she is now so mangy, stooped, humpbacked and pot-bellied, disfigured and undone that she seems to be a deformed person. Rachel has become Leah, all gray . . . rough, senile, and deaf . . . her chest is hard and her breasts . . . are wrinkled . . . like wet-bags" (quoted in Bloch, "Medieval Misogyny," 24 n. 45).

29. The topos of the bride's replacement goes back to the biblical story of Jacob's wives in which Leah replaced Rachel (Genesis 29:25).

30. Ibn Zabara, *Book of Delight*, 66. And see also my treatment of this anecdote in the section "Turn It Inside Out," Chapter 3 ("Veils and Wiles").

31. The list is another topos Ibn Shabbetai culled from European misogamous sources. It appears in St. Jerome's *Against Jovinian* and reappears in Deschamps's late-fourteenth-century *Miroir de Mariage* ("clothes, jewels, luxurious furnishings, household goods, spices and cooking materials"), see Mann, *Chaucer*, 74; Wilson and Makowski, *Wykked Wyves*, 151.

32. For woman's speech as resistance, see also the section "When the Object Speaks" in Chapter 6 ("Among Men") below.

33. This is added in the second edition of *Minḥat Yehuda*, Huss, *Critical Editions*, 2:76, lines 442–43. My translation.

34. Scheindlin's translation slightly revised.

35. Compare to *De conjuge non ducenda* where "the husband always serves; the wife always commands . . . in order to fill their bellies, the husband is reduced to cheating and crime." Wilson and Makowski, *Wykked Wyves*, 127–28. See also note 9 above.

36. For more data see Huss, *Critical Editions*, 1:263–73.

37. See Huss's interpretation, ibid., 1:96.

38. Norman Roth, " 'The Wiles of Women' Motif in the Medieval Hebrew Literature of Spain," *Hebrew Annual Review* 2 (1978): 150.

39. Israel Davidson, *Parody in Jewish Literature* (New York: Columbia University Press, 1907), 10.

40. Schirmann, *Hebrew Poetry in Spain and Provence*, 3:68.

41. Dan Pagis, *Change and Tradition in the Secular Poetry: Spain and Italy* (in Hebrew) (Jerusalem: Keter, 1976), 192.

42. Scheindlin, in Stern and Mirsky, *Rabbinic Fantasies*, 271.

43. Fishman, "Parody," 94.

44. The same device is employed also in '*Ezrat ha-nashim*, a profeminist response to *Minhat Yehuda* discussed below. See also the ending of Ibn Ṣaqbel's *maqāma* (Schirmann, *Hebrew Poetry in Spain and Provence*, 2:565, and in R. P. Scheindlin's translation in Stern and Mirsky, *Rabbinic Fantasies*, 264). Judah al-Ḥarizi (the master of Hebrew *maqāma* and Ibn Shabbetai's contemporary) ends many of his fifty *maqāmāt* with the discovery by the first-person narrator that he has fallen victim to the fabrication of his fictitious protagonist. And see Matti Huss, "It Never Happened nor Did It Ever Exist: The Status of Fiction in the Hebrew Maqāma," *Jerusalem Studies in Hebrew Literature* 18 (2000): 57–104.

45. As in Fishman, "Parody," 93: " 'The Misogynist' draws upon an established and vibrant eastern tradition of misogynist writing . . . consciously . . . distancing himself from [this] literary tradition." Or in Schirmann, *Hebrew Poetry in Spain and Provence*, 3:67: "The subject was in fact favored by medieval Moslem and Christian authors more than by Jewish ones."

46. Huss, *Critical Editions*, 1:100.

47. Ibid., 102.

48. Sigmund Freud, "Jokes and Their Relation to the Unconscious," in *The Standard Edition of the Complete Psychological Works of Sigmund Freud*, trans. J. Strachey (London: Hogarth Press, 1978), 4:96–100.

49. Shoshana Felman, *What Does a Woman Want? Reading and Sexual Difference* (Baltimore: Johns Hopkins University Press, 1993), 95–96.

50. For the text, see Huss, *Critical Editions*, 2:100–112; Schirmann, *Hebrew Poetry in Spain and Provence*, 3:87–96. For discussion, see Huss, *Critical Editions*, 1:10–14, 154–73. He also attacks Ibn Shabbetai ad hominem, blaming him for hating all women on account of "the black woman" that he married.

51. Here is the tale in brief: A dying father, Absalom, instructs his son Hovav to marry a virtuous pious virgin. He adjures him never to betray her and adds a list of biblical precedents in favor of marriage and procreation. Hovav marries his beloved Rachel against the will of her avaricious relatives who conspire to kill him. On their escape the young couple encounter a series of dangers. It is only thanks to Rachel's resourceful trickery (which here is considered virtue, not vice) that they are saved once and again from death. It is also thanks to her that they find a treasure, which enables them to return to town and be welcomed by her relatives. This happy ending is followed by an epilogue where the angel reappears. It turns out now that the angel is no other than Todros ha-Levi ha-Nasi, Isaac's

patron, who is very pleased with the tale, and claims that Rachel resembles his own wife. Upon declaring the fictitiousness of the tale, the author dedicates it to the patron's wife and gets his full reward. On the "good woman" as the heroine of medieval Jewish folkloristic tales, see Yassif, *The Hebrew Folktale*, 349–50.

52. *Ein mishpat* (Huss, *Critical Editions*, text, 2:113–21; discussion, 1:14–17) unfolds the allegorical-apocalyptic fiction of *Minḥat Yehuda* and takes place in a similar biblical ambience. In the assembly of the King of Demons and his allies (including the biblical foes of Israel, Ibn Shabbetai, and other enemies of wedlock), a pact was signed to invalidate the *ketuba* (marriage contract), to humiliate women, and, furthermore, to eradicate them. Loyal husbands are lynched, and the one who escaped warns the Israelite king Malkitzedek (literally, King of Justice). In the heat of the battle the two camps exchange hostile retorts for and against women and wedlock, giving examples of women, good and bad. A referee, probably Isaac's patron, is chosen who decrees that "when women are good they are very good, but when they are bad they are horrid."

53. *Ohev nashim* was published by Adolf Neubauer in *Jubelschrift zum neunzigsten Geburtstag des Dr. L. Zunz* (Berlin: L. Gerschel, 1884), 1–19, 138–40. Here too an allegorical battle is fought between Wisdom and Folly. The fools wish to annihilate marriage, and the women fight them. The women, saved by a virtuous heroine, celebrate their victory together with the narrator. Ibn Shabbetai descends from Paradise, indignant and armored, to defend his work. After a debate both authors go for a literary trial. The judges, respectful of both authors, refrain from a literary verdict; however, they decree that marriage should be sanctioned, whereby Ibn Shabbetai, who lost his case, returns to Paradise.

54. Alcuin Blamires, The *Case for Women in Medieval Culture* (Oxford: Clarendon Press, 1997), 12.

55. Bloch, *Medieval Misogyny*, 5.

56. Daniel Boyarin, *Carnal Israel: Reading Sex in Talmudic Culture* (Berkeley: University of California Press, 1993), 46.

57. Dates are not unimportant here: *Minḥat Yehuda* was first written in 1208 and *'Ezrat ha-nashim* in 1210. At about that time (in the reign of Pope Innocent III, 1198–1216), the struggle against clerical marriages reached its climax. It was also in the first decade of the century that several delegations of vagabond monks (including also a Spanish order) were sent to southern France to preach to the Cathars. Zeraḥ's vagabond "order" seems to be cast in the mold of these mendicant preachers. However, in spreading his ascetic doctrines to all, he resembles more the Cathars who preached celibacy to laity and clergy alike.

58. David Biale, *Eros and the Jews: From Biblical Israel to Contemporary America* (New York: Basic Books, 1992), 97–98.

59. Ibid., 99–100.

60. The supposition the story was intended to be read in Purim (see note 26) may support the assumption that our story was a Purim satire on Christianity. Satires on Christian custom and rituals were read in Jewish communities during the holiday of Purim. Recording violent anti-Christian practices throughout the

ages, Elliott Horowitz goes back to a fifth-century Palestinian *piyyut* (published in Joseph Yahalom and Michael Sokoloff, *Jewish Palestinian Aramaic Poetry* [in Hebrew] [Jerusalem: Israel Academy of Sciences and Humanities, 1994]) in which Christ on the Cross addresses Haman on the tree. See "The Rite to be Reckless: On the Perpetration and Interpretation of Purim Violence," *Poetics Today* 15 (1994): 9–54. Textual evidence, though, comes from a much later period. See Davidson, *Parody*, 40–41, esp. 29.

61. Biale, *Eros*, 89.

62. For a comprehensive discussion on the value of and attitudes toward procreation in Jewish tradition, see Jeremy Cohen, *"Be Fertile and Increase, Fill the Earth and Master It": The Ancient and Medieval Career of a Biblical Text* (Ithaca, N.Y.: Cornell University Press, 1989).

63. Boyarin, *Carnal Israel*, 47.

64. Daniel Boyarin, "Internal Opposition in Talmudic Literature: The Case of the Married Monk," *Representations* (1991): 87–113, esp. 87–88.

65. In Saadia's *Book of Beliefs and Opinions*, trans. Samuel Rosenblatt (New Haven, Conn.: Yale University Press, 1948), chapters on abstinence, 366; intercourse, 371; children, 381–83. Saadia was the first Jewish philosopher to be influenced by Islamic thought, and one of the most revered rabbinic authorities of all times.

66. The poem quoted is from his collection of ascetic poems, *Dīwān Shemuel Hanagid*, vol. 3, *Ben Qohelet (The Son of Ecclesiastes)*, ed. Dov Jarden (Jerusalem, 1992), 10, poem 19.

67. Solomon Ibn Gabirol, *Secular Poems*, ed. Hayyim Brody and Hayyim Schirmann (Jerusalem: Schocken Institute, 1976), 41.

68. Ibn Paqūda was the author of an extremely popular moralistic treatise, *The Duties of the Heart*. For his ascetic views, see Joseph Dan, *Hebrew Ethical and Homiletical Literature* (in Hebrew) (Jerusalem: Keter, 1975), 52–53.

69. Biale, *Eros*, 92.

70. Ibid., 91–93.

71. Ibid., 95. Jeremy Cohen analyzes RaABaD's views against the intellectual climate within which he lived, and especially against the background of ongoing patristic and medieval Christian discussions of conjugal sex. See his "Rationales for Conjugal Sex in RaABaD's *Baalei ha-nefesh*," *Jewish History* 6 (1992): 65–78.

72. Underlying this statement is the assumption that man's desire is more controllable by "intention" than the woman's. As shown by Cohen, the question of the legitimacy of sexual pleasure was widely and simultaneously discussed among Christian theologians.

73. In real life, as shown by Yom Tov Assis (based on court records and responsa), it was bigamy or the husband's business trips which were most often the causes for the neglect of women's needs. However, there were many cases in which "the woman's lack of enthusiasm about her conjugal life" caused a husband's complaint. See "Sexual Behaviour in Medieval Hispano-Jewish Society," in *Jewish History: Essays in Honour of Chimen Abramsky*, ed. A. Rapoport-Albert and Steven J. Zipperstein (London: P. Halban, 1988), esp. 31–33.

Chapter 6. Among Men

1. *Tractate Avot with Maimonides' Commentary*, ed. Itzhaq Shilat (in Hebrew) (Jerusalem: Maaliyot, 1994), 7.

2. Shelomo Dov Goitein, *A Mediterranean Society: The Jewish Communities of the Arab World as Portrayed in the Documents of the Cairo Geniza* (Berkeley: University of California Press), esp. vol. 3, *The Family* (1978), 313. And see also my notes 1 and 14 in Chapter 1.

3. S. D. Goitein, "The Sexual Mores of the Common People," in *Society and the Sexes in Medieval Islam*, ed. Afaf Lutfi al-Sayyid-Marsot (Malibu, Calif.: Undena Publications, 1979), 43.

4. As a literary form (introduced by al-Hamadhānī, Persia, 967–1008, and further developed by al-Ḥarīrī, Iraq, 1054–1122), the *maqāma* became a receptacle for mixed materials (moral proverbs, stories, anecdotes and rhetorical contests). Basically written in rhymed prose, it also incorporates metered poems.

5. Judah al-Ḥarizi, *Taḥkemoni*, ed. I. Toporowski (Tel Aviv: Maḥbarot Lesifrut, 1952). The reader is referred to two English translations of the *Taḥkemoni*. One is Victor Emannuel Reichert's (2 vols.; Jerusalem: Raphael Haim Cohen, 1973), of which I have not made use due to its rarity; the other is David Simha Segal's (London: Littman Library of Jewish Civilization, 2001), with which I became acquainted only after the completion of this book.

6. Male discourse proves to be a generic structure also in other varieties of rhymed prose which are not strictly speaking *maqāmāt*. In the prologue to Judah Ibn Shabbetai's *The Misogynist*, for instance, the author's comrades urge him to tell his life story in order to edify all malekind in matters of marriage (see Chapter 5). In Abraham Ibn Ḥasday's *The Prince and the Monk* the conversations between the two male characters constitute the skeleton of the story.

7. For an even more elaborate example of an after-dinner lecture by Ḥever, see al-Ḥarizi's third *maqāma*. Disguised as an old beggar, lacking in table manners and garrulous, Ḥever surprises the guest with a lecture on the history of Hebrew poetry in Spain with which he buys his meal this time.

8. Sheila Fisher and Janet E. Halley, "The Lady Vanishes: The Problem of Women's Absence in Late Medieval and Renaissance Texts," in *Seeking the Woman in Late Medieval and Renaissance Writings: Essays in Feminist Contextual Criticism*, ed. Sheila Fisher and Janet E. Halley (Knoxville: University of Tennessee Press, 1989), 4. On this subject, see also Eve Kosofsky Sedgwick in *Between Men: English Literature and Male Homosocial Desire* (New York: Columbia University Press, 1985).

9. Immanuel of Rome (born mid-thirteen century, died before 1336). See also Dov Jarden's introduction to his edition of *Maḥberot Immanuel ha-Romi*, 2 vols. (Jerusalem: Mosad Bialik, 1957). About Italian influence on Immanuel, see Dan Pagis, *Change and Tradition in the Secular Poetry* (Jerusalem: Keter, 1976), 261–62, and note 17 below.

10. The reason I relate here to Shakespeare's *Lucrece* and not to his models

(Ovid and Livy) is because in his version Tarquin fatally falls in love with Lucrece's verbal description, even before seeing her, whereas in his classical precedents it is the sight of her beauty which ignites him. The story of Lucrece in all its versions (it was retold, among others, also by Augustine and Chaucer) begins in a light-hearted after-dinner bragging contest. A group of Roman officers competes over women's description, each praising the virtues of his own wife. This rhetorical beauty contest (Whose description is superior?) turns soon into a moral contest (Whose wife is the most virtuous?). Returning to Rome to check on their wives, the men found the wives all reveling—except for loyal Lucrece who stays home. Tarquin, inflamed with Lucrece's description by her own husband, went back to her suite and defiled her, after which she took her life with her own hands. Her husband won the contest but lost her.

11. Nancy J. Vickers, "This Heraldry in Lucrece's Face," in *The Female Body in Western Culture: Contemporary Perspectives*, ed. Susan Suleiman (Cambridge, Mass.: Harvard University Press, 1986), 209–10, 214, 219.

12. The poetic game of "Praising the Beautiful and Defaming the Ugly" in Immanuel's second *maqāma* (*Maḥberot Immanuel*, 35–43), furnishes the occasion for the nun's story in his third *maqāma* (pp. 45–70). Quotations refer to line numbers in this edition.

13. Immanuel does, however, contribute some original hyperboles: If the angels knew Tamar, they would snatch her to heaven; and if she were in heaven, the pagans would worship her and not the sun and the moon. If the sun knew her, it would not have chosen the moon as its partner. And if she lived in Moses and Aaron's days, they would marry her.

14. Roberta L. Krueger, "Double Jeopardy: The Appropriation of Woman in Four Old French Romances of the 'Cycle de la Gageure,' " in Fisher and Halley, *Seeking the Woman*, 21–43.

15. In her *Ravishing Maidens: Writing Rape in Medieval French Literature* (Philadelphia: University of Pennsylvania Press, 1991), 5.

16. Quoted in Vickers, "This Heraldry," 210.

17. See my discussions on feminist reading in Chapters 1 ("No-Woman's-Land") and 2 ("Gazing at the Gazelle").

18. The mystery of Immanuel's "nun" has not been satisfyingly settled. Could this half-sister of the patron be a Christian nun? (According to her own testimony, she had lived in a monastery for twenty years.) Or does the appellation *nezirah* connote the extreme religiosity and ascetic way of life of a Jewish female? (For "The Educational and Religious Activities of Jewish Women in Italy," see Howard Adelman's article in *Shlomo Simonsohn Jubilee Volume*, ed. Aharon Oppenheimer et al. [Tel Aviv: Tel Aviv University, 1993], 9–23.) Does the story have a biographical core to it, or is it sheer fiction? Although these questions are marginal to my main line of argument, I propose that answers should not be sought in the realm of biography but in the field of Immanuel's literary models. In his introduction to *Maḥberot Immanuel* (p. 31), Jarden states, without naming any specific model, that "the story about the passionate lover and the nun . . . is a typical

Italian *novella*." Moshe David Cassuto in *Dante ve-Immanuel ha-Romi* (Jerusalem: Mosad Bialik, 1966), 36–46, had convincingly shown influences of the contemporary Italian *dolce still nuovo* on Immanuel, and especially pointed at parallels between Immanuel's lofty beloved and Dante's Beatrice. However, in stressing the aspect of spiritual love (which in our story turns up only after the nun's death), Cassuto ignores the more prominent topos of the carnal temptation of a nun. That the latter topos was fashionable in the Italian storytelling of the time can be attested to by Immanuel's younger contemporary Boccacio. (See, for instance, *Decameron*, the first story of the third day.) Yet, this does not explain Immanuel's epistolary device. Given that the letters of Abelard and Héloïse were familiar in Italy one generation after Immanuel, we may conjecture that they might have been known in Immanuel's time as well. We know Immanuel's younger contemporaries, Boccacio and Petrarch, to be readers of this famous correspondence. Petrarch, in fact, owned (and annotated) a copy of the letters (considered now the earliest extant manuscript, dating to the mid-thirteenth century). See Peter Dronke, "Abelard and Héloïse in Medieval Testimonies," in his *Intellectuals and Poets in Medieval Europe* (Rome: Edizioni di storia e letteratura, 1992), 290–94.

19. Jarden, *Maḥberot Immanuel*, 2:275–86, 287–307.

20. Immanuel recites to the patron two sonnets that the wife (that is, actually, he himself, Immanuel) composed. Immanuel, Petrarch's contemporary is, in fact, one of the earliest sonnet writers in Italy. His Hebrew sonnets are the first sonnets ever to be written in a language other than Italian. In allowing the wife to compose sonnets, not just women's folksongs, Immanuel creates her as an educated and well-versed woman and makes her, as it were, a pioneer of the Hebrew sonnet.

21. According to Jarden's introducton to *Maḥberot Immanuel*, 31, the wife's lament in the sixteenth maqāma is inspired by similar contemporary poems written by Italian poets such as Compagnetto da Prato or the poetess Compiuta Donzella, in which the speakers are abandoned wives or, like in our text, young women forced to marry against their will.

22. Similar is Immanuel's narrative poem where a virgin unabashedly offers a man to have half of her body: from the belt up or from the belt down. Embarrassed he chooses the upper part, upon which she lets her belt fall to the ground and allows him to have her from the belt up (ibid., 1:77–80).

23. For Immanuel as a devoted reader of Maimonides, see his own testimony in his *Maḥberot Immanuel*, 11:163–173.

24. "I looked through the window and suddenly I saw . . . a boy innocent of heart . . . and then a woman came into his path, a hard-hearted woman, a harlot, loud and stubborn . . . praying at every corner. She held him and kissed him, pertinently told him: . . . 'Let's go and make love all night, for my husband is gone on a distant trip (Proverbs 7:6–19).' "

25. Translation is from Shlomo Pines, *The Guide of the Perplexed* (Chicago: University of Chicago Press, 1963), 431. Daniel Boyarin, *Carnal Israel: Reading Sex in Talmudic Culture* (Berkeley, Los Angeles, Oxford: University of California Press, 1993), 58–59, discusses Maimonides' misogynistic metaphysics, calling it

"ontologial whoredom." And see also the Chapter 3 ("Veils and Wiles"), 79–81 and notes.

26. *The Guide*, ibid., 43. It is most probable that Maimonides referred here to the explicit equation of Woman = Matter in Aristotle, and not to Plato's myth in *Timaeus*.

27. In her *Speculum of the Other Woman*, trans. Gillian C. Gill (Ithaca, N.Y.,: Cornell University Press, 1985), 135, Luce Irigaray analyzes the "economy of discourse . . . whereby the silent allegiance of the one guarantees the auto-sufficiency, the auto-nomy, of the other as long as no questioning of this mutism as a symptom—of historical repression—is required. But what if the object started to speak?"

28. E. Jane Burns, *Bodytalk: When Women Speak in Old French Literature* (Philadelphia: University of Pennsylvania Press, 1993), 2.

29. On Christine de Pisan and her response to the *Roman de la Rose*, see Helen Solterer, *The Master and Minerva: Disputing Women in French Medieval Culture* (Berkeley: University of California Press, 1995), 151–75. Solterer studied the phenomena of literate women who challenged the male clerical world of learning. On the Wife of Bath, see Elaine Tuttle Hansen, *Chaucer and the Fictions of Gender* (Berkeley: University of California Press, 1992), 26–57. Susan Schibanoff makes a comparison between the literate Christine and the illiterate Wife in their undermining the monopoly of male writing; and see her "Taking the Gold out of Egypt: The Art of Reading as a Woman," in *Gender and Reading: Essays on Readers, Texts, and Contexts*, ed. Elizabeth A. Flynn and Patrocinio P. Schweickart (Baltimore: The Johns Hopkins University Press, 1986), 83–106.

30. Schibanoff, "Taking the Gold," 87–88.

31. The famous "women polemics" in Hebrew literature took place between male defamers and defenders of women in a series of four rhymed stories written in Spain and Provence during the thirteenth century. Some of these works were dedicated to the wives of the poets' patrons. (For this polemic, see my Chapter 5, and the reference to Matti Huss's doctoral thesis there). Another debate pro and con women, cast in various poetic forms, occurred in Italy during the whole of the sixteenth century. Though, again, the authors were exclusively male, this time Jewish women did participate as active readers and patrons of the poets. See Dan Pagis, "The Controversy Concerning the Female Image in Hebrew Poetry in Italy" (in Hebrew), *Jerusalem Studies in Hebrew Literature* 9 (1986): 259–300.

32. From "The Story of the Pious Man's Wife from Ashdod," in Isaac Ibn Sahula, *Meshal ha-Qadmoni*, ed. Israel Zemora (Tel Aviv, Maḥbarot Lesifrut, 1953), 79–80.

33. In Ibn Shabbetai's *The Mysogynist*. The passage is discussed in the section "the Wife Speaks" in Chapter 5 ("Domesticating the Enemy").

34. R. Howard Bloch, *Medieval Misogyny and the Invention of Western Romantic Love* (Chicago: University of Chicago Press, 1991), 2.

35. Fisher and Halley, "The Lady Vanishes," 1–17.

36. Burns, *Bodytalk*, xvi, 47.

37. Judah al-Ḥarizi, *Taḥkemoni*, 317–25.

38. Norman Roth, " 'The Wiles of Women' Motif in the Medieval Hebrew Literature of Spain," *Hebrew Annual Review* 2 (1978): 155.

39. Jefim Schirmann, *History of Hebrew Poetry in Christian Spain and Southern France* (in Hebrew), edited, supplemented and annotated by Ezra Fleischer (Jerusalem: Magnes, 1997), 211. (Hereinafter Schirmann-Fleischer, *Christian Spain*.)

40. In the Arabic story (*The Assemblies of al-Ḥarīrī*, trans. Thomas Chenery [London: Williams and Norgate, 1867–98], vol 2, no. 40) a couple goes to the qadi to settle a marital conflict. The man complains that his wife is a bitch and a liar, frigid, ugly, and dirty. She complains, in turn, that her husband is stinking, stupid, and good for nothing. Thanks to her familiarity with Islamic law, the wife succeeds in convincing the judge of her husband's inability to satisfy her sexually and to provide for her, which precipitates the judge's threatening her husband with divorce. The couple is ultimately appeased through the judge's dispensation of charity, at which point the reader is allowed to discover that the whole episode was merely the wife's ruse to extort money from the judge.

41. This type of poetic debate is common among al-Ḥarizi's *maqāmāt*, where two or more poets improvise verses concerning the pros and cons of a certain topic. At times it is one poet who sophistically speaks from both sides of his mouth.

42. Hence capitalization is used here for the Man and the Woman as the disputing figures. Lowercased "man" and "woman" are used for mankind and womankind.

43. Our piece is found in a cluster of debating *maqāmāt* (no. 39, Night and Day; 40, Pen and Sword; 41, Man and Woman; 42, Miserliness and Generosity; 43, Sea and Land). On the debate genre in medieval Hebrew literature, see Schirmann-Fleischer, *Christian Spain*, 42–46 (and notes), 210–11, 252–53.

44. Until his belated exposure, see note 64 below.

45. The *maqāma* ends with the Man's rhymed tirade. By granting the Man the only poetic part in this *maqāma* (the Woman speaks only prose) the author might have implied that, after all, man's supremacy in poetry remains unrivaled.

46. For the significance of *mum*, see my Chapter 8, notes 18 and 19. Synonymous with *mum* is *pegimah* ("defect" as well as "notch"), used for the woman's organ in Ibn Sahula's story (see note 32 above).

47. Burns, *Bodytalk*, 57, 58.

48. In Numbers 12:2 they ask: "Is Moses the only one with whom the Lord has spoken? Has He not spoken with us as well?" Both siblings alike are silenced by God Himself who sanctifies Moses' authority. However, the punishment of leprosy (and subsequent quarantine) is dealt to Miriam alone, not to Aaron, as if to prove that woman's subversiveness is considered more dangerous than man's.

49. For Maimonides' identification of woman with matter, see toward the end of Chapter 3. Quoted there is Daniel Boyarin's statement that this view renders Maimonides as a "virulent misogynist." Abraham Melamed hotly debates Boyarin and other "non-experts" on Maimonides who classify him as bluntly misogynist. See Abraham Melamed, "Maimonides on Women: Formless Matter

or Potential Prophet?" in *Perspectives on Jewish Thought and Mysticism*, ed. A. L. Ivry et al. (Amsterdam: Harwood Academic Publishers, 1998), 99–134. According to Melamed, it is possible to discern in Maimonides, notwithstanding his more known antifeminist utterances, a radical, egalitarian view on women as having the same potential as man for moral and intellectual improvement. Miriam's high status as a prophetess plays a key-role in Melamed's line of argumentation. He argues that Maimonides made his favorable point by his very choice of a positive midrash on Miriam (who, according to the sages, died, like her brothers, "by a kiss" of the Lord)." Melamed adds other utterances made by Maimonides in favor of woman's intellectual potential. Melamed also mentions another follower of Maimonides, the late-thirteenth-century Provençal scholar Isaac ben Yeda'aya, who was also preoccupied with women's prophecy. Isaac interprets "Miriam's Well" as spouting the water of philosophy. Miriam spread the learning of metaphysics among women who then spread it among their husbands and children. However, Isaac insists that Miriam was a singular example. It might well be that these two tendencies in Maimonides' thought reflect, or correspond with, similar tendencies in Islamic thought. In her *Women and Gender in Islam* (New Haven, Conn.: Yale University Press, 1992), 64–65, 72–75, Leila Ahmed distinguishes between the Islamic dominant androcentric view and a silenced egalitarian view. According to her analysis, ancient Arabian Islam saw women as equal to men in their spiritual potential. In the Qurān (Sura 33:35), God addressed equally men and women. Muhammad is known to have listened to women's views on various spiritual issues. Additionally, women are mentioned as authoritative transmitters of the prophet's word in the *ḥadith* (Islamic oral tradition). On the other hand, orthodox Islam (as it crystallized in the Abbassid period) has silenced the egalitarian approach in favor of an androcentric social order, relegating women to familial, social, and spiritual inferiority.

50. The midrash tends to downgrade and ridicule women's prophecy. In the midrashim Miriam is often described as a gossipy, quarrelsome shrew. In Deborah's generation, so say the sages, a prophetess was chosen since there were no males fit for prophecy. Ḥuldah and Miriam are said to be prophets for women only. The sages also related to name etymologies, deriving Miriam from the same root as rebellion and bitterness, and pointing out that Ḥuldah and Deborah were named after biting animals. See D. Steinmetz, "A Portrait of Miriam in Rabbinic Midrash," *Prooftexts* 8 (1988): 35–65. And see also Melamed, *Maimonides on Women*, 104–5 and note 15.

51. The Old Man has it wrong. The Jewish male is indeed endowed with 613 precepts, but there are three that the Jewish woman has to keep too. For a discussion of the women's *mitzvoth*, see Chapter 8, 181–83.

52. Quotation is from Fatima Mernissi, "Virginity and Patriarchy," *Women's Studies International Forum* 5 (1982): 183.

53. Genesis 2:23: "This shall be called woman for from man was this taken." The derivation of *isha* from *ish* is of course wrong etymology. See Ernest Klein, *A Comprehensive Etymological Dictionary of the Hebrew Language* (New York: Macmillan, 1987), 57.

54. Elizabeth Grosz, *Volatile Bodies: Toward a Corporeal Feminism* (Bloomington: Indiana University Press, 1994), 13.

55. Elizabeth Grosz, *Jacques Lacan: A Feminist Introduction* (London: Routledge, 1990), 176.

56. Grosz, *Volatile Bodies*, 3. Though chronologically much later than al-Ḥarizi's text, I choose to illustrate this view with a zoological example from Joseph Albo's *Sefer ha-ʿiqqarim*, 1:2 (finished in 1425), where he compares the human female to the animal female. He claims that the simultaneous creation of male and female in the animal world proves that they were equally biologically designed for the end of continuing the species. In humans the female was created after the male and is thus inferior to him. The male was created to fulfill the end of his spiritual existence, while the woman was made to be his material helper.

57. Grosz, *Volatile Bodies*, 22.

58. Ibid.

59. This idea appears in a medical composition by al-Ḥarizi's Syrian contemporary, Ibn Abī Uṣaibiʿa: "Deal with them like you do with carcasses. Eat of them only if you are compelled to do so and as much as keeps you alive. But if you eat more than needed, they will cause your sickness and death" (*ʿUyūn al-anbā*, ed. A. Müller [Königsberg, 1884], 1:49). And compare also to Shem Tov Falaqera (thirteenth century, Spain): "If you cannot do without women—consider [having sex with] them the same as eating rotten carcasses. Do not do it unless you are forced to." "Iggeret ha-musar" (Epistle on Ethics), ed. A. M. Habermann, in *Qovetz ʿal Yad* (n.s.) 1 (1936): 75. This goes a bit further than the comparison of woman's body to (kosher) meat in the Talmud: "A man is allowed to do with his wife whatever he desires, the same as with the meat he brings from the slaughterhouse. If he so wishes he eats it salty, or roasted, or cooked, or boiled" (Nedarim, 20:2). For Boyarin's comment on this passage, see *Carnal Israel*, 113–16.

60. Notice that there is only one word in Hebrew for "flesh" and "meat."

61. Grosz, *Volatile Bodies*, 13.

62. These are Gabrielle M. Spiegel's words from a book review cited on the back cover of Solterer's book *The Master and Minerva*.

63. Al-Ḥarizi supported Maimonides in several polemical poems. He also translated Maimonides' commentary on the Mishna and his *Guide of the Perplexed*. His translations were not as accurate and as successful as those of his contemporary and competitor Samuel Ibn Tibbon. See Schirmann-Fleischer, *Christian Spain*, 147–50.

64. Only when the *maqāma* reaches its end does the narrator, Heman (the author's surrogate), recognize the protagonist as his old pal Ḥever, the charming imposter, "Father of great tricks and master of all wiles." Unlike their merry reunion at the ending of other pieces, here Heman turns his back on Ḥever. Does it mean that Ḥever's misogyny is rejected by the author? Is it an indication for the reader to reverse the antifeminist animus of the Old Man?

65. See the introduction to Judith Fetterley, *The Resisting Reader: A Feminist Approach to American Fiction* (Bloomington: Indiana University press, 1978).

Chapter 7. Clothes Reading

1. On this topic, see Yehudit Dishon, "On the Motif of Disguise in the Hebrew *Maqāma* in Spain" (in Hebrew), *Yedaʿ ʿAm* 22 (1984): 41–53.

2. Marjorie Garber, *Vested Interests: Cross-Dressing and Cultural Anxiety* (New York: Routledge, 1992), 390.

3. The *ghulāmiyāt* were women (usually slave girls) dressed as men, who served in wine parties in Islamic courts. Conversely, there were in these circles also young boys dressed as girls, colored in henna, and taught to speak in soft effeminate voices. These phenomena are not altogether identical with hermaphroditism and pederasty. See Adam Mez, *Renaissance of Islam*, trans. Sallahudin Khuda Bukhs and D. S. Margoliouth (Beirut: United Publishers, 1973), 357; Abdelwahab Bouhdiba, *Sexuality in Islam*, trans. Alan Sheridan (London: Routledge and Kegan Paul, 1985), 40. For poetic examples of the effeminate young boy, see Norman Roth " 'Deal Gently with the Young Man': Love of Boys in Medieval Hebrew Poetry of Spain," *Speculum* 57 (1982): 20–51; " 'Fawns of My Delight': Boy-Love in Arabic and Hebrew Verse," in *Poetics of Love in the Middle Ages*, ed. Moshe Lazar and Norris J. Lacy (Fairfax, Va.: George Mason University Press, 1989), 96–118, and Arie Schippers, *Spanish Arabic Poetry and the Arabic Literary Tradition: Arabic Themes in Hebrew Andalusian Poetry* (Leiden: E. J. Brill, 1994), 147. For medieval Europe, see Vern L. Bullough, "Transvestites in the Middle Ages," *American Journal of Sociology* 79 (1974): 1381–94; Vern L. Bullough and Bonnie Bullough, *Cross-Dressing, Sex and Gender* (Philadelphia: University of Pennsylvania Press, 1993), 45–73.

4. The four *maqāmāt* treated here are all either close elaborations of Arabic models, or include distinct applications of Arabic themes. However, only one of them (al-Ḥarizi's "Bandit") is a close elaboration of an Arabic model (by al-Hamadhānī). No distinct Arabic source could be found for the other three. For the general question of the literary models of the Hebrew *maqāma*, see Matti Huss, *Critical Editions of "Minḥat Yehuda," ʿEzrat Hanashim," and ʿEin Mishpat" with Prefaces, Variants, Sources and Annotations* (in Hebrew), 2 vol. doctoral thesis (Jerusalem: Hebrew University, 1991), 23–38. For Ben Eleazar's possible sources, see below.

5. Abdelwahab Bouhdiba, *Sexuality in Islam*, 30–35.

6. S. D. Goitein, *A Mediterranean Society: The Jewish Communities of the Arab World as Portrayed in the Documents of the Cairo Geniza*, vol. 4, *Daily Life* (Berkeley: University of California Press, 1983), 153–55.

7. Out of the four *maqāmāt*, only one (Ibn Ṣaqbel's), the first Hebrew example of the genre, is known to have been written in Muslim Spain. The two pieces by al-Ḥarizi, a native of Christian Toledo, were written during his voyage to the Muslim East. That by Ben Eleazar, al-Ḥarizi's follower and compatriot, was written in Toledo and seems to draw on, besides Arabic sources, also European models.

8. The source is believed to be a yet unknown Arabic model. It has also been suggested that this piece was part of a collection of *maqāmāt* by Ibn Ṣaqbel.

Published in Jefim Schirmann, *Hebrew Poetry in Spain and Provence* (in Hebrew) (Jerusalem: Mosad Bialik; Tel Aviv: Dvir, 1960), 2:556–65. Translations here are Raymond Scheindlin's, published in David Stern and Mark Jay Mirsky, eds., *Rabbinic Fantasies: Imaginative Narratives from Classical Hebrew Literature* (Philadelphia: Jewish Publication Society, 1990), 257–67. For discussions of the story, see Scheindlin's introduction (ibid., 253–56); Raymond Scheindlin, "Fawns of the Palace and Fawns of the Field," *Prooftexts* 6 (1986): 189–203, and Jefim Schirmann, *The History of Hebrew Poetry in Christian Spain and Southern France* (in Hebrew), ed. by Ezra Fleischer (Jerusalem: Magnes, 1997), 100–109 and notes (hereinafter: Schirmann-Fleischer, *Christian Spain*).

9. The theme of a man who penetrated into a harem in a woman's disguise is popular in Arabic stories. In a Hebrew version the infiltrator "played" with the king's wives and was executed. See Joseph Ibn Zabara, *The Book of Delight*, trans. Moses Hadas with an introduction by Merriam Sherwood (New York: Columbia University Press 1932), 71–76.

10. For the veil in Islam as *the* signifier of woman's modesty, and of the separation of sexes, see Bouhdiba, *Sexuality in Islam*, 35–37. For an anthropological approach to the veil and its double codes, see Leila Abu Lughod, *Veiled Sentiments: Honor and Poetry in Bedouin Society* (Berkeley: University of California Press, 1988).

11. From the eleventh-century on, North African (Muslim, non-Arab) Berbers ruled parts of Muslim Spain. The custom of veiling for Berber males still exists among the ferocious Tuareg, "a tribe of veiled men . . . shrouding themselves so completely that only their eyes show" (Garber, *Vested Interests*, 335, in her discussion of Paul Bowles's novel *The Sheltering Sky*, set among the twentieth-century Tuareg).

12. For the veil as an upper-class custom in Islam, see Leila Ahmed, *Women and Gender in Islam* (New Haven, Conn.: Yale University Press, 1992), 55–56.

13. Bouhdiba, *Sexuality in Islam*, 34–35. For the beard in Judaism, see Elimelech Horowitz, "On the Signification of the Beard in Jewish Communities in the East and in Europe in the Middle Ages and in Early Modern Period" (in Hebrew) *Pe'amim*, 59 (1994): 124–46.

14. This interpretation of the story as an embryonic bildungsroman is inspired, in its general lines, by Raymond Scheindlin's reading in "Fawns of the Palace." However, in Scheindlin's interpretation the emphasis is put on the protagonist's training in the rules of courtly love. The Adullamite is Asher's master in the art of love, tutoring him its rules. But "Asher foolishly reverses the roles of men and women by coyly refusing to respond to the love message. To teach him a lesson, he is humiliated by a woman dressed like a man, and a man dressed like a woman, until he is completely bewildered by the sexual identity of everyone around him. The rule of courtly love . . . is that everyone must play his traditional part" ("Fawns," 200). In my reading the hero's construction of socially acceptable gender identity is pivotal, whereas in Scheindlin's it is only a means toward his instruction in courtliness.

15. Judah al-Ḥarizi, *Taḥkemoni*, ed. I. Toporowski (Tel Aviv: Maḥbarot Lesifrut, 1952), 202–7. Translations are mine.

16. The story might be an abridged (add to that, dull and schematic) adaptation of Ibn Ṣaqbel's *Neum Asher ben Yehuda*. (For a comparison of the two, see Scheindlin, "Fawns.") An astounding parallel is the account of Ulrich von Lichtenstein, a knight from Styria (now Austria) and a contemporary of al-Ḥarizi, who journeyed through Europe in 1227, "disguised as the Goddess Venus, dressed in dazzling white raiment, and accompanied by a splendidly attired [female] retinue of twenty." Some suspected that he was not a woman, like the countess who came to kiss him and found that he kept his beard underneath his veil. See Bullough and Bullough, *Cross-Dressing*, 62–63.

17. Mikhail Bakhtin, *The Dialogic Imagination*, ed. Michael Holquist, trans. Caryl Emerson and Michael Holquist (Austin: University of Texas Press, 1981), 159.

18. Garber, *Vested Interests*, 29. She also reminds us that historically "the stage was a privileged site of [transvestite] transgression" (35), and that "transvestite theater is the *norm*, not the abberation" (39) of theatrical performance.

19. Divon and Heshbon are names of biblical towns in Moab.

20. My symbolical equation of eye = water-spring = vagina might be supported by Hebrew and Arabic etymologies. To the Hebrew homonym *'ayin* (for "eye" and "spring"), we may perhaps add in this context the Arabic symbolical affinity between eye and genitalia (especially the vagina). Bouhdiba, *Sexuality in Islam*, 37–39, points out that the Arabic word *'aura* designates "genitalia" as well as "blindness" resulting from the unlawful gaze at the genitals of the other sex.

21. Why did al-Ḥarizi add a transvestite theme that is missing in the Arabic model? Why is this theme on the whole more common in the Hebrew *maqāma* than in the Arabic? An answer to these questions is attempted toward the end of this chapter.

22. Yehudit Dishon, " 'The Bandit *Maqāma*,' Its Sources and Design" (in Hebrew), *Biqoret u-Pharshanut* 16–17 (1981–82): 71–83, quote on 81.

23. Yonah David, *The Love Stories of Jacob ben Eleazar* (in Hebrew) (Tel Aviv: Ramot, 1992–93), 56–71.

24. This exaggerated depiction echoes the description of a ferocious Negro (*kushi*) warrior in Ben Eleazar's sixth *maqāma* (ibid.).

25. Emphasis added. An almost identical account of a male duel appears also in Ben Eleazar's sixth *maqāma*.

26. Helen Solterer, "Figures of Female Militancy in Medieval France," *Signs: Journal of Women in Culture and Society* 16 (1991): 522–49.

27. For the sexual exposure of women warriors, see parallels below in the Arabic stories surveyed by Remke Kruk, and see also notes 30, 31 below.

28. The story's ending is the symmetrical reverse of its beginning. It opens with Yoshfe's exile following social disorder in his homeland and closes with the restoration of order and Yoshfe's repatriation. Analogously, the order of marriage reverses the emotional turmoil of the protagonists; bigamy replaces the duel; sharing replaces theft. Male activism is restituted. Marriage also recovers both the social hierarchy (noble Yoshfe regains power over his slavewives) and gender superiority (the man is on top of not only one woman, but of two!).

29. Relating to this and other themes Raymond Scheindlin strongly suggests that students of Ben Eleazar should look for his sources in Romance literature. See "The Love Stories of Jacob Ben Eleazar: Between Arabic and Romance Literatures" (in Hebrew), *The Proceedings of the Eleventh World Congress for Jewish Studies*, vol. 3 (Jerusalem, 1994), 16–20. For Ben Eleazar's possible sources, see also Schirmann-Fleischer, *Christian Spain*, 233–40.

30. Remke Kruk, "Warrior Women in Arabic Popular Romance," *Journal of Arabic Literature* 24 (1993): 213–30. According to Kruk, some of these stories may be traced back to the classical Amazon myth (226).

31. Kruk furnishes abundant examples of what she calls "the Brunhilde-motif," Christian female warriors, in Arabic lore. Only few would suffice here. Qattālat ash-Shujʿān was a beautiful princess who fought in male costume and was finally disclosed by her soft female voice. She falls in love with the Arab warrior who won her in battle and is abducted by another. Princess Alūf, who detested marriage and had "an inclination for the ladies," was engaged in a series of wrestling contests with the Muslim warrior Maslama. Confused by the intimate contact with her body, he fell in love with her. Later, she not only consented to marry him and convert to Islam, but also joined the Muslim army to fight the Christians in Byzantium. Similar is the story of Nūrā, who, disguised as a knight, defeated many Muslim heroes. When the warriors approached her, mistaking her for a man, she would smile seductively and expose her "pomegranate breasts." Nūrā too married a Muslim warrior whom she joined against the Franks. The theme of a single combat between two women is also found in this collection. Karna, a Christian princess, defeated a whole army of Muslims in a series of single duels. She is finally captured by the Bedouin heroine Dhāt al-Himma, she too in disguise. The theme is also found in several stories in the *Arabian Nights*. In one of them the Christian princess Abrīza defeated her would-be lover Sharkān in combat, as well as in chess games.

32. Quoted in Solterer, *Figures of Female Militancy*," 540.

33. Ibid., 524.

34. Ibid., 542. By 1210 the papacy had granted women the legal right to join the Crusades (ibid., 536).

35. Asher confesses in the prologue that in his youth he did not observe the Sabbath. In the Bible "the Adullamite" is a Canaanite friend of Judah (Genesis 38:1, 20). The Adullamite in our story is labeled also as "Philistine," a Hebrew denomination used by Spanish Jews for the North African Berbers.

36. Maimonides in Egypt reluctantly consented to concubinage with gentile women, while rabbis in Christian Spain during the thirteenth century preached against it. On concubinage in medieval Judaism see Avraham Grossman, *Pious and Rebellious: Jewish Women in Europe in the Middle Ages* (in Hebrew) (Jerusalem: Zalman Shazar Center for Jewish History, 2001), 233–39.

37. Garber, *Vested Interests*, 16, 17, 36–37.

38. For a wide survey of the period, its transitions and literary innovations, see Dan Pagis, *Change and Tradition in the Secular Poetry* (in Hebrew) (Jerusalem: Keter, 1976), 175–89, 199–201.

39. Rina Drory, "Literary Contacts and Where to Find Them: On Arabic Literary Models in Medieval Literature," in *Models and Contacts: Arabic Literature and Its Impact on Medieval Jewish Culture* (Leiden: Brill, 2000), 215–32.

40. For more on the introduction of the *maqāma* and other rhymed prose forms into Hebrew, see Schirmann-Fleischer, *Christian Spain*, 93–144, esp. 93–97.

41. Their introductions are quoted and discussed by Drory, "Literary Contacts." In her fine analysis she shows how different authors reacted differently to the changing circumstances, depending on their various provenances, surroundings, and audiences.

42. Quoted in Drory, ibid., 221–22.

43. Ibid., 229.

44. See Dan Pagis, "Variety in Hebrew Rhymed Narratives," *Jerusalem Studies in Hebrew Literature* 27 (1978): 79–98, and Huss, *Critical Editions*, 17–38.

Chapter 8. Circumcised Cinderella

1. *Even boḥan*, ed. A. M. Habermann (Tel Aviv: Maḥbarot Lesifrut, 1956). The passage discussed here appears on pp. 17–21. It was also partly printed in Jefim Schirmann's anthology *Hebrew Poetry in Spain and Provence* (in Hebrew) (Jerusalem: Mosad Bialik; Tel Aviv: Dvir, 1960), 4:503–4. Translation is mine. Qalonymos was born in 1286 in Arles, Provence, and died after 1328. *Even boḥan* was completed in 1322, during his stay in Catalonia. For his life and work, see Jefim Schirmann, *History of Hebrew Poetry in Chritian Spain and Southern France* (in Hebrew), ed. Ezra Fleischer (Jerusalem: Magnes, 1997), 514–41 (hereinafter, Schirmann-Fleischer, *Christian Spain*).

2. "Military service" here is not necessarily in the literal sense, but in the sense of having to fulfill arduous manly duties. The "service" of the Jewish male is expounded elsewhere in the text as religious duties and intellectual discipline.

3. Quoted from Joshua Levinson, "Cultural Androgyny in Rabbinic Literature," *From Athenes to Jerusalem: Medicine in Hellenized Jewish Lore and in Early Christian Literature*, ed. Samuel Kottek et al. (Rotterdam: Erasmus Publishing, 2000), 130.

4. Christine de Pizan, *The Book of the City of Ladies*, trans. Earl Jeffrey Richards, revised ed. (New York: Persea Books, 1998), 5 (par 1.1.2). On Christine, see, for instance, Sheila Delany, *Writing Woman: Women Writers and Women in Literature Medieval to Modern* (New York: Schocken Books: 1983), the chapter "A City, a Room," 197–81, and Helen Solterer, *The Master and Minerva: Disputing Women in French Medieval Culture* (Berkeley: University of California Press, 1995), 151–75.

5. In the miracle to Abraham the text alludes to Bereshit Raba 38, where Nimrod almost threw Abraham to the furnace. For God's miracles to Moses, see Exodus 4:3, 4:6–7, 14:16, and Psalms 66:6, 114:8.

6. In Berakhot 60a and Tanḥuma 19:5 Leah offered to God to change her fetus to female, and as reward asked that her barren sister Rachel be able to give

birth to a son. Another transsexual miracle, related in BT Shabbat 53b, occurred to a widower who grew women's breasts so that he could feed his suckling orphan.

7. Midrash Tanḥuma 7:5 indicates that she was a prostitute.

8. The earliest sources for the Jewish blessings are Tosefta Berakhot 6:16, PT Berakhot 9:1, 63b, and BT Menahot 43a–44b. Similar formulations existed in other cultures in antiquity. Diogenes Laertius (3:11) quotes Socrates as being "grateful to Fortune for being born a human and not animal; a man and not a woman; a Greek and not a barbarian." For Christian parallels, see Galatians 3:28 and Colossians 3:11.

9. Mishna Berakhot 9:3.

10. Jacob ben Asher, *Arbaʿat ha-turim* (Jerusalem: Makhon Yerushalayyim, 1993), vol. 1, *Oraḥ ḥayyim*, 208. His younger contemporary David Abudarham, in his commentary on prayer (written in Seville circa 1340), repeats this report. He reiterates the common explanation for the male blessing, that is, that women are not obligated to bless God since they were not given the mitzvot. Sometimes, he adds, she is "not able to fulfill even those mitzvot that she was commanded to because of fear of her husband." In his view, a woman is entitled to be rewarded for mitzvot even though she is not expected to fulfill them. *Abudarham ha-shalem* (Jerusalem: Even Israel, 1985), 49. I am grateful to Haym Soloveitchik for referring me to relevant sources. My thanks to Joseph Tabory, who permitted me to quote his article "The Benedictions of Self-Identity and the Changing Status of Women and of Orthodoxy" from the manuscript, now published in *Kenishta* 1 (2001): 107–38. As shown by Tabory, the fourteenth and fifteenth centuries were a period of great innovations concerning the prayer customs of women. Manuscript evidence shows that *siddurim* copied for women in various Romance languages (in Hebrew letters) employ the formula "according to His will." Some manuscripts introduce changes in gender: "female-slave" and "gentile woman" instead of "slave" and "Gentile." A fifteenth-century Judeo-Provençal translation has the unusual version "Blessed art Thou . . . who hast made me a woman." A fifteenth-century Hebrew-Italian *siddur* (MS Jewish Theological Seminary 8255, fol. 5b) reads: "who made me woman and not man." Tabory follows the fate(s) of the woman's blessing in various Jewish traditions to our day. (It is perhaps ironic that despite the Spanish origin of the blessing, the highest Sephardi halakhic authority in present Israel, Rav Ovadia Yosef, issued a responsum stating that women should not recite the blessing in its full liturgical formula, since this is a mention of God's name in vain. Information is based on Bar-Ilan University computerized Responsa project.)

11. Jeremiah 15:10, with the exchanging of "a man of strife" for "a male child."

12. Mishna Ketubot 13:3. He protests against the ruling that in the case of a small estate, the daughters receive their maintenance first, and if nothing is left, the sons must go begging. The Gemara (Ketubot 108b) discusses the question whether it is just that the male loses because he is engaged in Torah study.

13. Kidushin 82b. See also note 29 below.

14. The root *l.q.h.* bears these two meanings. Additionally, it means to be defective, lacking, and deficient.

15. In Sanhedrin 38a, God coined all human beings "in the coin of the First Adam." Note that *matbeʿa* (coin) and *tebhaʿ* (a Hebrew neologism for "nature" coined, as it were, by medieval translators) derive from a common root. Thus, the "male coin" is synonymous with "male nature." Qalonymos (who knew Latin) could have also intended here a wordplay on the Latin word *natura* in the sense of "genitalia" (see Oxford Latin Dictionary).

16. The Hebrew is *mum kavuʿa*, a talmudic legal term (Sanhedrin 5b) for an irremediable, irreversible physical injury or defect.

17. Aristotle, *Generation of Animals*, Loeb Classical Library (Cambridge, Mass.: Harvard University Press, 1958), 765b. Qalonymos was familiar with Aristotle's writings through Ibn Rushd, the Islamic Aristotelian philosopher, ten of whose compositions he translated from Arabic into Hebrew. For a list of Qalonymos's translations, see M. Steinschneider, *Die hebraeischen Überstetzungen des Mittelalters und die Juden als Dolmetscher* (Berlin, 1893). On the influence of Greek and Arabic thinkers on medieval Jewish medical writings, see Ron Barkaï, *Les infortunes de Dinah: Le livre de la génération, ou la gynécology juive âu moyen âge* (Paris: Les édition du Cerf, 1991).

18. The Hebrew word *mum* signifies both a defect and a lack. Solomon Mandelkern in his *Concordance to the Bible* (Jerusalem: Schocken, 1972), 656, 661, relates *mum* (defect) to *me'um* (nothing, nil). In Judah al-Ḥarizi's forty-first *maqāma*, "Debate between the Man and the Woman," *mum* stands for the female organ (see Chapter 6, the section "When the Object Speaks").

19. A commonplace in feminist thought is the attack on the patriarchal identification of the female organ, and femaleness, with lack and absence. "Patriarchy requires that female sexual organs be regarded as the absence or lack (or castration) of male organs . . . [but, in fact] the condition under which patriarchy is psychically produced is the constitution of women's bodies as lacking. If women do not lack in any ontological sense . . . men cannot be said to have. In this sense, patriarchy requires that female bodies and sexualities be socially produced as a lack." Elizabeth Grosz, *Volatile Bodies: Toward a Corporeal Feminism* (Bloomington: Indiana University Press, 1994), 57–59; quotation from p. 59. For Jacques Lacan, the process of the penis becoming phallus is the very condition of signification and the paradigm of language itself. The penis/phallus constitutes sexual binarization: the male is defined as having the phallus, the female as lacking it and thus desiring it. For a critical survey of the status of penis and phallus in Freud and Lacan, and on the identification of the phallus with signification, see Elizabeth Grosz, *Jacques Lacan: A Feminist Introduction* (London: Routledge, 1990), 115–26. Thomas Laqueur contests the universality of the conceptualization of femaleness as lack, and views it as the product of the modern discourse of the body, that discourse which "invented" sex difference as biological fact. He argues that up to the eighteenth century the prevailing medical model was that of the one-sex body, in which male's (external) sex organs were conceived as homologous to the female's (internal) ones. Woman was not perceived as lacking of penis

and testes, but as having them inverted and introverted. See Thomas Laqueur, *Making Sex: Body and Gender from the Greeks to Freud* (Cambridge, Mass.: Harvard University Press, 1990).

20. Grosz, *Volatile Bodies*, 140–41.

21. Although in the talmudic era oil candles were of a vaginal rather than phallic shape, the erect wax candles used in medieval times can certainly carry the symbolism suggested here.

22. The medieval educational curriculum included the *trivium* (grammar, logic, and rhetoric) and the *quadrivium* (arithmetic, music, geometry, and astronomy). Like other Jewish Provençal scholars, Qalonymos inherited this model from Andalusian culture. For the parallel course of learning in Islam, see Joel L. Kraemer, *Humanism in the Renaissance of Islam* (Leiden: Brill, 1986), 9, 231, and notes.

23. In Schirmann-Fleischer, *Christian Spain*, 514.

24. A translation cannot convey the subtle play on words in the last sentence of the last quotation: the Hebrew for "custom" is here *mishpat* (law, from *sh.f.t.*) and for "hearth" *shefathayim* (from *sh.f.th*). It is patriarchal *mishpat* that assigns woman her proper place, near the cooking fire. Another possible wordplay is between *shefathayim*, the woman's locus, and the homonymous *sefathayim*, labia, the woman's organ.

25. Erich Neumann, *The Great Mother: An Analysis of the Archetype* (Princeton, N.J.: Princeton University Press, 1955), 132, 284–85. Similarly, in her study of Greek cultural history, Page DuBois writes: "The analogy between the female body or, more particularly, the uterus, and the oven is a commonplace of Greek thought." Page DuBois, *Sowing the Body: Psychoanalysis and Ancient Representations of Woman* (Chicago: University of Chicago Press, 1988), 110 ff.

26. Miriam B. Peskowitz, *Spinning Fantasies: Rabbis, Gender, and History* (Berkeley: University of California Press, 1997), 130–39. Her analysis shows that the scene of women spinning thread beneath the moonlight is not at all idyllic. Nor is Qalonymos's allusion to it innocent. In the Mishna (Sotah 6:1), the gossip of the women spinners is used by men as incriminating testimony against their wives in divorce cases.

27. Helen Solterer, "At the Bottom of Mirage," in *Feminist Approaches to the Body in Medieval Literature*, ed. Linda Lomperis and Sarah Stanbury (Philadelphia: University of Pennsylvania Press, 1993), 221. And see Rozsika Parker, *The Subversive Stitch: Embroidery and the Making of the Feminine* (London: Woman's Press, 1996), 10–11.

28. "It seems that women have made few contributions to . . . civilization; there is, however, one technique which they may have invented—that of plaiting and weaving. If that is so, we should be tempted to guess the unconscious motive of the achievement. Nature herself would seem to have given the model which this achievement imitates by causing the growth at maturity of the pubic hair that conceals the genitals." Sigmund Freud, "Femininity," in *The Standard Edition of the Complete Psychological Works of Sigmund Freud*, trans. James Strachey (London: Vintage, 2001 [first published: London: Hogarth Press, 1960]), 22:132. See

also Luce Irigaray's retort to Freud, in *Speculum of the Other Woman*, trans. Gillian C. Gill (Ithaca, N.Y.: Cornell University Press, 1985), 115–17.

29. The rare expression "furrow-like stitches" refers in Kidushin 82b to a list of fortunate and less fortunate occupations. It seems that Qalonymos intended also to allude here to Rabbi's interpolation amidst this list: "Lucky is he whose children are males, and woe to him whose children are females."

30. An interim type of speech between direct and indirect speech, usually merging two voices, that of the narrator and that of a character. See, for instance, Ann Banfield, "The Formal Coherence of the Represented Speech and Thought," *Poetics and Theory of Literature* 3 (1978): 289–314.

31. There is, though, a slight ungrammaticality in the transitory sentence, which can be easily straightened out. The man, who speaks now as woman, switches from first person ("I might") to third ("her hands") and back to first person ("I and my"). This can be explained by the *shibbutz* from Exodus 35:25 (describing women's contribution to the art of the Tabernacle): "And each skilled woman *spun with her own hands*, and brought what they had spun, in blue, purple, and crimson yarns, and in fine linen." Yet the grammatical instability might indicate that the male speaker finds it still awkward to refer to himself in the first person feminine.

32. Ketubot 5:5 lists the "labors that the wife does for her husband: grinding, baking, laundering, cooking, nursing children, tending the beds, and working in wool." She is exempt and "may sit upon a chair of leisure" only if she brought with her no fewer than four slaves. Rabbi Eliezer insists that the husband forces her working in wool "because leisure brings about sexual temptations." And the Gemara adds that "even when she sits upon a chair of leisure," she has to pour his wine and tend his bed and wash his hands and feet" (Ketubot 61a).

33. See discussion below.

34. Sigmund Freud, "Jokes and Their Relationship to the Unconscious," *Standard Edition*, 8:96–100; Shoshana Felman, *What Does a Woman Want? Reading and Sexual Difference* (Baltimore: Johns Hopkins University Press, 1993), 95–96. For a wider discussion see the section "Misogyny Remains Intact" in Chapter 5 above.

35. Genesis Raba 17, Jehuda Theodor and Chanoch Albeck edition (Jerusalem: Wahrmann, 1965), 158–59.

36. Daniel Boyarin, *Carnal Israel, Reading Sex in Talmudic Culture* (Berkeley: University of California Press, 1993), 90.

37. These are views cited by Lawrence A. Hoffman, *Covenant of Blood: Circumcision and Gender in Rabbinic Judaism* (Chicago: University of Chicago Press, 1996), 147 (and see also his notes 37 and 38). His own interpretation in his chapter 8 ("Gender Opposition in Rabbinic Judaism: Free-flowing Blood in a Culture of Control") is different.

38. For discussions about the exclusion of mothers from circumcision ceremonies, see Hoffman's chapter 11, "Medieval Rabbinism and the Ritual Marginalization of Women," ibid., 190–207.

39. Habermann, *Even bohan*, 177. Pagis labeled it "a facetious grumbling

against being born male and not female," Dan Pagis, *Change and Tradition in the Secular Poetry: Spain and Italy* (in Hebrew) (Jerusalem: Keter, 1976), 232.

40. Fleischer's note 81 (in Schirmann-Fleischer, *Christian Spain*, 535) is the most detailed treatment of the passage. In his opinion, "although a true feat of humor, the passage is a failure in terms of its satirical effect."

41. I allude here to Judith Butler's inseminating book *Gender Trouble: Feminism and the Subversion of Identity* (New York: Routledge, 1990).

42. Sarah Kofman, *The Enigma of Woman: Woman in Freud's Writings*, trans. Catherine Porter (Ithaca, N.Y.: Cornell University Press, 1985), 82.

43. The different course of socialization of sons and daughters as effected by the attitude to the feminine/maternal and the constitution of maleness through differentiation from the mother are the main themes of Nancy Chodorow's feminist classic *The Reproduction of Mothering: Psychoanalysis and the Sociology of Gender* (Berkeley: University of California Press, 1978).

44. For the problematics of medieval masculinity, and about the dialectics of men's studies as an offshoot of feminist criticism, see Clare A. Lees, ed., *Medieval Masculinities: Regarding Men in the Middle Ages* (Minneapolis: University of Minnesota Press, 1994).

45. Habermann, in *Even boḥan*, 177.

46. Schirmann, in Schirmann-Fleischer, *Christian Spain*, 501.

47. Pagis, *Change and Tradition*, 232.

48. Schirmann, in Schirmann-Fleischer, *Christian Spain*, 532.

49. Ibid., 535, and Fleischer's note 81.

50. Here is the book's content: (a) introduction: the author's lament over the tribulations of Jews in his time and his apology for choosing a preacher's position; (b) exhortations against the temptations of the flesh; confessions of being tempted by attire, passion, and riches; (c) *the wish to become a female*; an exhortation to parents who prefer male to female babies; (d) satirical pictures of Jewish festivals as celebrated in contemporary communities in Provence; a series of caricatures on professions (the grammarian, the physician, the scholar, the rich man, the poet). The second, unrhymed, part of the book consists of praises to God, prayers, and confessions.

51. See his discussion of the *manipea* genre in Mikhail Bakhtin, *Problems of Dostoyevsky's Poetics*, ed. and trans. Caryl Emerson (Minneapolis: University of Minnesota Press, 1984), 114–18.

52. In Rome, Qalonymos also wrote *Tractate Purim*, a description of the Jewish carnival as celebrated by the Jews of Rome, as a parody on a talmudic tractate. For more, see Schirmann-Fleischer, *Christian Spain*, 524.

53. In a passage prior to ours (*Even boḥan*, 13), the speaker confesses, among his other weaknesses, an uncontrollable passion for elegant clothes. The fetishistic list includes official attire and leisure apparel, nightgowns and embroidered bedcovers, linens, silks, laces, gauzes, crimsons, purples, turquoises, and so on. This vestmentary catalog not only betrays a "feminine" (or effeminate) obsession with elegant clothes, but it also includes a reference to women's clothes in particular (and perhaps also an anxiety about transvestism): "O my heart, you

seduced me [to desire . . .] precious attire . . . and . . . fine linen of the kind that virgin princesses wear."

54. Froma Zeitlin's terms "intersexuality" and "intertextuality" were modified here to suit my context. She uses them for the analogy between transvestism and mimetic parody of texts. See Froma I. Zeitlin, *Playing the Other: Gender and Society in Classical Greek Literature* (Chicago: University of Chicago Press, 1996), 377.

Index

absence of women, 27, 140; as authors, xiii, 1–2; as critics, 18; discourse of, 59; female anatomy as, 142, 248n. 19; as historical subjects, x–xi, 3; in love lyric, 30–37, 54, 57, 59, 80, 108, 187–88

Abudarham, David, 247n. 10

Abulafia, Todros, 41, 42, 46–50, 57, 61, 73, 74, 206n. 14, 215n. 28; and the feudal metaphor, 49–50

Against Jovinian (St. Jerome), 228n. 7, 229n. 11, 231n. 31

Albo, Joseph, 241n. 56

allegory, 26, 71, 201n. 53, 215n. 26, 224n. 45, 225n. 49, 233nn. 52–53; of Canticles, 89, 221n. 20; on Form and Matter in Maimonides, 78, 80–82, 94, 101, 137–38, 217n. 54, 219nn. 67, 71, 221n. 20, 226n. 60; of *Kneset Israel*, 17, 221n. 10; of the soul, 49, 95–102; of *Tevel*, 14, 199n. 39

Almohad, 6, 165–66, 213n. 2

Alphonsi, Petrus, 7

ambiguity: and allegory, 101; ambiguous geography, 108, 156, 164; poetry as embodiment of, 65, 215n. 22, 217n. 45; as structure in *Minhat Yehuda*, 104, 115; transvestite as embodiment of, 151; and the veil, 69, 156; woman as embodiment of, 65, 77; and woman's modesty, 69, 152–53

ambivalence: to beauty, 68; of clothing and veil, 70, 71, 153; to marriage, xiv, 15, 104, 119–23; of poetic language, 215n. 22; to women and the erotic, 20, 25, 29, 119–23, 215n. 22

al-Andalus, 6, 153, 212n. 2; and courtier-rabbis, 5, 31–35, 56–57, 205n. 8; Jewish culture in, 5–6, 25, 249n. 22; Muslim courts in, 51; and women poets, 2–3. *See also* Andalusian-Hebrew poetry; Arabic literature; Berbers; garden, Andalusian

Andalusian-Hebrew poetry, xiii, 32, 40–41, 50, 60, 206n. 14, 209n. 45; and ars-

poeticas, 64–67, 71–72; and biblical idiom, 1, 6, 40, 84, 207nn. 24, 28, 229n. 13; homoerotic, 189, 203n. 1; its ascetic/hedonistic dual face, 5–6, 25; liturgical, 83–95; and love lyric, 31–35; and women poets, 1–2. *See also* Arabic literature; Hebrew literature

androcentrism, xiii, 4, 19, 28, 29, 31, 56, 62, 133, 184, 189, 206n. 21, 240n. 49

androgyny, 29, 86

antifeminism, 23, 24–25, 107, 117. *See also* misogyny

Aphrodite, 100, 169

Arabic literature, 5–6, 18, 150, 162–63, 165–66, 207n. 26, 210n. 54, 215n. 28, 229n. 13; ascetic, 221n. 22; concept of female in, 24, 53–55; 210n. 65; erotic, 31, 208n. 33; and love poetry, 31–33, 205n. 8; misogynistic, 107; neoplatonic, 90, 221nn. 22–24; and women writers, 2–3. *See also ghazal; maqāma; muwashshah; nasīb; qasīda*

Aristotelian philosophy, 66, 78, 80, 82, 94, 146, 213n. 2, 218n. 55, 219n. 66, 222n. 30, 238n. 26, 248n. 17; and woman as distorted male, 173. *See also* Maimonides

asceticism, 16, 23, 25, 69–70, 85–86, 92, 94, 103, 108–9, 121–22, 132, 134, 199n. 39, 227n. 2, 234n. 68. See also *zuhd*

Assis, Yom Tov, 234n. 73

"Averroistic," 6

Bakhtin, Mikhail, 155, 186

Barthes, Roland, 59, 70, 215n. 23

beard, 111, 153–54, 155, 243n. 13

beauty, 23, 30; as artifice, 68–69; beauty lists, 53–56, 210n. 65; beauty myth, 56; of boys, 203n. 1; courtly devotion to, 51–52, 57–58; description of, 126–27; and female sexuality, 53–55, 68–69; feminist attitude to, 62–63; of ideal woman, 35, 39–43, 56, 110–11; Jewish attitude to, 20; and the male gaze, 46–47; and male rhetoric,

Acknowledgments

FRIENDS, COLLEAGUES, EDITORS, AND STUDENTS helped me bring this book to its final shape, whether in conversations, in classes, in remarks at public lectures, or in comments on earlier drafts of chapters included here. Maureen Bassan, Ron Barkaï, Ross Brann, Deborah Bregmann, Jeremy Cohen, Sheila Delany, Rina Drory, Nili Gold, Michael Gluzman, Roni Halpern, Andras Hamori, Avner Holtzman, Matti Huss, Shulamith Shahar, Ray Scheindlin, Haim Soloveitchik, David Stern, Ofra Yaglin, and Eli Yassif read portions of my work. Each of them contributed his or her perspective. To all of them I am indebted and wish to pay my gratitude for invaluable comments and genial encouragement. I am especially obliged to Daniel Boyarin; he accompanied this book from its inception and was a constant source of support and good advice.

I owe a great debt to the Center for Advanced Judaic Studies at the University of Pennsylvania, and to its director, David Ruderman, for a generous grant and a fruitful half-year stay in 1999, during which the significant breakthrough in writing occurred. This stay was also a rare opportunity to meet and exchange ideas with the fine group of specialists on medieval Hebrew literature that was gathered there that year. I owe warm thanks to Esther Lassman of the Center for her vital assistance. I wish also to extend special thanks to my students and devoted research assistants at Tel Aviv University, Adi Sorek and Ilana Sobel, who helped, each in her turn, to bring this book to completion.

I wish to express my thanks to Jerome E. Singerman, Humanities Editor at the University of Pennsylvania Press, whose expertise and kindness made the production of this book an enjoyable experience. I also benefited from the competence and responsiveness of Associate Managing Editor Erica Ginsburg and Jennifer Shenk, my copyeditor.

The research for this book was made possible by a generous grant given to me for three years (1994–97) by the Israel Science Foundation (established by the Israel Academy of Sciences and Humanities). I am also grateful for the financial support during the first stages of my research by the Fund for Basic Research at Tel Aviv University and the Memorial Foundation for Jewish Culture.

Somewhat different versions of portions of this book were printed as articles. A previous version of Chapter 5 appeared as "Sexual Politics in a Medieval Hebrew Marriage Debate," *Exemplaria* 12 (2000): 157–84. Chapter 2 was published in Hebrew under the title *"Tzed ha-tzevia: Qeri'ah hatranit be-shire ahavah ivriyim mi-yme ha-benayim"* ["Gazelle Hunting: Feminist Critique of Medieval Hebrew Love Poems"], *Mikan: A Journal for the Study of Hebrew Literature* (Ben Gurion University) 2 (2001): 95–124. A previous version of Chapter 8 appeared as "Circumcised Cinderella: The Fantasies of a Fourteenth Century Jewish Author," *Prooftexts* 20 (2000): 87–111.